Introduction to Design of Experiments
with JMP® Examples
Third Edition

Jacques Goupy

Lee Creighton

The correct bibliographic citation for this manual is as follows: Goupy, Jacques, and Lee Creighton. 2007. *Introduction to Design of Experiments with JMP® Examples, Third Edition.* Cary, NC: SAS Institute Inc.

Introduction to Design of Experiments with JMP® Examples, Third Edition

Copyright © 2007, SAS Institute Inc., Cary, NC, USA

ISBN 978-1-59994-422-7

All rights reserved. Produced in the United States of America.

For a hard-copy book: No part of this publication may be reproduced, stored in a retrieval system, or transmitted, in any form or by any means, electronic, mechanical, photocopying, or otherwise, without the prior written permission of the publisher, SAS Institute Inc.

For a Web download or e-book: Your use of this publication shall be governed by the terms established by the vendor at the time you acquire this publication.

U.S. Government Restricted Rights Notice: Use, duplication, or disclosure of this software and related documentation by the U.S. government is subject to the Agreement with SAS Institute and the restrictions set forth in FAR 52.227-19, Commercial Computer Software-Restricted Rights (June 1987).

SAS Institute Inc., SAS Campus Drive, Cary, North Carolina 27513.

1st printing, October 2007

SAS® Publishing provides a complete selection of books and electronic products to help customers use SAS software to its fullest potential. For more information about our e-books, e-learning products, CDs, and hard-copy books, visit the SAS Publishing Web site at **support.sas.com/pubs** or call 1-800-727-3228.

SAS® and all other SAS Institute Inc. product or service names are registered trademarks or trademarks of SAS Institute Inc. in the USA and other countries. ® indicates USA registration.

Other brand and product names are registered trademarks or trademarks of their respective companies.

Contents

Preface xiii

Chapter 1 Gaining Knowledge with Design of Experiments 1

1.1 Introduction 2
1.2 The Process of Knowledge Acquisition 2
    1.2.1 Choosing the Experimental Method 5
    1.2.2 Analyzing the Results 5
    1.2.3 Progressively Acquiring Knowledge 5
1.3 Studying a Phenomenon 5
1.4 Terminology 6
    1.4.1 Factor Types 6
    1.4.2 Experimental Space 7
    1.4.3 Factor Domain 8
    1.4.4 Study Domain 9
1.5 Centered and Scaled Variables 11
1.6 Experimental Points 13
1.7 Design of Experiments 14
    1.7.1 Methodology of Designs without Constraints 14
    1.7.2 Methodology of Designs with Constraints 15
    1.7.3 The Response Surface 17
    1.7.4 The a priori Mathematical Model of the Response 18

Chapter 2 Your First Designed Experiment 21

2.1 Introduction 21
2.2 Example 1: Control Your Car's Gas Consumption 22
    2.2.1 Preparing the Designed Experiment 22
    2.2.2 Choosing the Design 24

2.2.3 Running the Experiment 27
2.2.4 Interpreting the Coefficients 28
2.2.5 Interpreting the Results 40

Chapter 3 A Three-Factor Designed Experiment 45

3.1 Introduction 45
3.2 Example 2: Gold Jewelry 46
    3.2.1 Preparing the Designed Experiment 46
    3.2.2 Choosing the Design 51
    3.2.3 Running the Experiment 53
    3.2.4 Interpreting the Results 54
    3.2.5 Study Conclusion 67

Chapter 4 Four-Factor Full-Factorial Experiments 69

4.1 Introduction 69
4.2 Example 3: The Galette des Rois 70
    4.2.1 Preparing the Designed Experiment 70
    4.2.2 Choosing the Design 73
    4.2.3 Running the Experiment 74
    4.2.4 Interpreting the Results 76
    4.2.5 Desirability Functions 83
    4.2.6 Study Conclusion 91

Chapter 5 Statistical Concepts for Designed Experiments 93

5.1 Introduction 94
5.2 Example 4: Lifespan of Disposable Cutting Tools 95
    5.2.1 Preparing the Designed Experiment 95
    5.2.2 Experimentation 97
    5.2.3 Interpeting the Results of the Calculations 98
    5.2.4 Statistical Concepts Used in DOE 99
    5.2.5 Factors and Influential Interactions 113

5.2.6 Analysis of Variance (ANOVA)   115
5.2.7 Application   119
5.2.8 Residual Analysis   125
5.2.9 Study Conclusion   126

Chapter 6 Fractional Factorial and Screening Designs   131

6.1 Introduction   132
6.2 Example 5: Measuring Tellurium Concentration   133
    6.2.1 Preparing the Designed Experiment   133
    6.2.2 Running the Experiment   135
    6.2.3 Interpreting the Results   136
6.3 Alias Theory   137
    6.3.1 Definition of Contrasts   138
    6.3.2 New Interpretation Hypotheses   140
6.4 Box Calculations   141
    6.4.1 Box Notation   141
    6.4.2 Operations on the Column of Signs   142
    6.4.3 Rules to Remember   144
6.5 Equivalence Relation   144
    6.5.1 Basic Design   144
    6.5.2 Equivalence Relation   146
6.6 Alias Generating Functions   147
    6.6.1 Alias Generating Function of the Upper Half Design   147
    6.6.2 Alias Generating Function of the Lower Half Design   148
    6.6.3 Reading Aliases in Software   149
6.7 Practical Construction of a Fractional Factorial Design   149
    6.7.1 2^3 Full Factorial Design   151
    6.7.2 2^{4-1} Fractional Factorial   152
    6.7.3 2^{5-2} Fractional Factorial   154
    6.7.4 2^{7-4} Fractional Factorial   156
6.8 Maximum Number of Factors from a Base Design   157

6.9 Aliasing Theory with the Tellurium Example 157
    6.9.1 Confounding in the Tellurium Example 158
    6.9.2 Application of the Interpretation Assumption to the Tellurium Example 158
    6.9.3 Study Conclusion 159

Chapter 7 Examples of Fractional Factorial Designs 161

7.1 Introduction 162
7.2 Example 6: Sulfonation 163
    7.2.1 Preparing the Designed Experiment 163
    7.2.2 Carrying Out the Experiment 165
    7.2.3 Interpreting the Results 166
    7.2.4 Study Conclusion 173
7.3 Example 7: Spectrofluorimetry 174
    7.3.1 Preparing the Designed Experiment 174
    7.3.2 Carrying Out the Experiment 180
    7.3.3 Interpreting the Results 180
    7.3.4 Building the Complementary Design 190
    7.3.5 Study Conclusion 196
7.4 Example 8: Potato Chips 198
    7.4.1 Preparing the Designed Experiment 198
    7.4.2 Carrying Out the Experiment 201
    7.4.3 Interpreting the Results 201
    7.4.4 Study Conclusion 204

Chapter 8 Trial Order and Blocking 205

8.1 Introduction 206
8.2 The Nature of Errors 207
    8.2.1 Blocking 208
    8.2.2 Anti-Drift Designs 209
    8.2.3 Random Variation 210
    8.2.4 Small Systematic Variations 211

8.3 Example 9: Penicillium Chrysogenum (Blocking Example) 212
    8.3.1 Preparing the Designed Experiment 212
    8.3.2 Constructing the Plan and Checking the Blocking Advantage 214
    8.3.3 Carrying Out the Trials 217
    8.3.4 Interpreting the Results 218
    8.3.5 Study Conclusion 224
8.4 Example 10: Yates's Beans 225
    8.4.1 Preparing the Designed Experiment 225
    8.4.2 Running the Experiment 228
    8.4.3 Interpreting the Results 230
    8.4.4 Study Conclusion 232
8.5 Example 11: "The Crusher" (Example of an Anti-Drift Design) 233
    8.5.1 Introduction 233
    8.5.2 Preparing the Designed Experiment 236
    8.5.3 Carrying Out the Trials 237
    8.5.4 Interpreting the Results 238
    8.5.5 Study Conclusion 241
8.6 Advantages and Dangers of Randomization 242

Chapter 9 Response Surface Designs 245

9.1 Introduction 247
9.2 Composite Designs 247
9.3 Box-Behnken Designs 249
9.4 Doehlert Designs 250
9.5 Example 12: The Foreman's Rectification (Example of a Composite Design) 255
    9.5.1 Preparing the Designed Experiment 255
    9.5.2 Responses and Objectives of the Study 256
    9.5.3 Factors 257
    9.5.4 Study Domain 257
    9.5.5 Choosing the Design 257
9.6 Experimentation (Factorial Design) 258
9.7 Interpreting the Factorial Design Results 258

- 9.7.1 Verification of the Linear Model   259
- 9.7.2 Positions of Star Points   260
- 9.8 Second-Degree Complementary Design   262
- 9.9 Interpreting the Results   263
  - 9.9.1 Modeling   263
  - 9.9.2 Graphical Representation of the Results   264
  - 9.9.3 Confirming the Results   268
- 9.10 Study Conclusion   268
- 9.11 Example 13: Soft Yogurt (Box-Behnken Design Example)   269
  - 9.11.1 Preparing the Design Experiment   269
  - 9.11.2 Factors   270
  - 9.11.3 Study Domain   271
  - 9.11.4 Responses   271
  - 9.11.5 Choosing the Design   271
- 9.12 Experimentation   271
- 9.13 Interpreting the Design   272
  - 9.13.1 Model   272
  - 9.13.2 Interpreting the Results   274
- 9.14 Study Conclusions   276
- 9.15 Example 14: Insecticide (Example of a Doehlert Design)   277
  - 9.15.1 Preparing the Designed Experiment   277
  - 9.15.2 Factors and Study Domain   277
  - 9.15.3 Responses   278
  - 9.15.4 The Designed Experiment   278
- 9.16 Experimentation   278
- 9.17 Interpreting the Results   279
  - 9.17.1 Calculating the Coefficients   279
  - 9.17.2 Modeling   281
  - 9.17.3 Residual Analysis   282
  - 9.17.4 Graphical Representation of the Results   282
- 9.18 Study Conclusion   286

Chapter 10 Mixture Designs 287

    10.1 Introduction 288
    10.2 Fundamental Constraint of Mixtures 289
    10.3 Geometric Representation of a Mixture 289
        10.3.1 Two-Component Mixtures 289
        10.3.2 Reading a Binary Mixture Plot 291
        10.3.3 Reading a Ternary Mixture Plot 293
        10.3.4 Four-Component Mixture 294
    10.4 Classical Mixture Designs 295
        10.4.1 Simplex-Lattice Designs 295
        10.4.2 Simplex-Centroid Designs 297
        10.4.3 Augmented Simplex-Centroid Designs 298
    10.5 Mixture Design Mathematical Models 299
        10.5.1 First-Degree Models 299
        10.5.2 Second-Degree Models 300
        10.5.3 Third-Degree Models 301
    10.6 Example 15: Three Polymers 302
        10.6.1 Preparing the Designed Experiment 302
        10.6.2 Running the Experiment 303
        10.6.3 Interpreting the Results 304
        10.6.4 Study Conclusion 306

Chapter 11 The Concept of Optimal Designs 307

    11.1 Introduction 308
    11.2 Hotelling's Example 308
    11.3 Weighing and Experimental Design 311
        11.3.1 Standard Method 312
        11.3.2 Hotelling's Method 313
    11.4 Optimality 314
        11.4.1 Maximum Determinant (D-Optimal) Criterion 315
        11.4.2 Computing Optimal Designs 315
    11.5 Optimal Designs with a Linear Model 319
    11.6 When to Use Optimal Designs 322
    11.7 Adaptability of Optimal Designs 323

11.8 Example 16: Developing a Fissure Detector 326
    11.8.1 Preparing the Designed Experiment 326
    11.8.2 Using a 2^3 Factorial with Center Points 327
    11.8.3 Using a D-Optimal Design with Repetitions 330
11.9 Example 17: Pharmaceutical Tablets 333
    11.9.1 Preparing the Designed Experiment 333
    11.9.2 The Design 335
    11.9.3 Running the Experiment 336
    11.9.4 Analysis of the 28-Run Design 337
    11.9.5 Study Conclusion 340
11.10 Example 18: Self-Tanning Cream (Rescuing a Bad Design) 343
    11.10.1 Why a Design Can Be Bad 343
    11.10.2 Preparing the Designed Experiment 344
    11.10.3 Running the Experiment 345
    11.10.4 Interpreting the Results 345
    11.10.5 Study Conclusion 349

Chapter 12 Latin Squares and Similar Designs 351

12.1 Introduction 352
12.2 Example 19: Salaries and One Categorical Factor 353
    12.2.1 Mathematical Model 353
    12.2.2 Global Effect of a Factor 355
12.3 Example 19: Salaries and Two Categorical Factors 356
    12.3.1 Preparing the Designed Experiment 356
    12.3.2 Mathematical Model 357
    12.3.3 Effect of the Factors 359
    12.3.4 Analysis of Sums of Squares 361
    12.3.5 Analysis of Variance 365
12.4 Latin Squares 365
12.5 Greco-Latin Squares 367
12.6 Youden Squares 368

12.7　Example 20: Penetrometry Study　370
　　　12.7.1　Preparing the Designed Experiment　370
　　　12.7.2　Running the Experiment　370
　　　12.7.3　Interpreting the Results　371
12.7　Study Conclusion　373

Chapter 13　Summary and Advice　375

13.1　Introduction　376
13.2　Choosing the Experimental Method　376
　　　13.2.1　Posing the Problem Well　376
　　　13.2.2　Preliminary Questions　378
　　　13.2.3　Choosing a Design　381
13.3　Running the Experiment　382
13.4　Interpreting the Results　382
　　　13.4.1　Critical Examination　382
　　　13.4.2　What to Do Next　384
13.5　Progressively Acquiring Knowledge　385
13.6　Recommendations　386
13.7　What Experiments Cannot Do　386

Chapter 14　Using JMP to Design Experiments　389

14.1　Introduction　390
14.2　Designing an Experiment　390
　　　14.2.1　Screening Designer (Classical Designs Only)　391
　　　14.2.2　Custom Designer (Classical and Other Optimal Designs)　393
14.3　The JMP Data Table　396
14.4　Choosing and Fitting a Model　398
　　　14.4.1　The Screening Designer　401
14.5　Examining and Analyzing Results　402
14.6　Principal Graphics and Analysis Reports　404
14.7　Transferring and Saving Analysis Results　406

Appendix A Example Data Sources 409

Appendix B Comparing Two Independent Means 413

Appendix C Introduction to Matrix Calculations 415

Bibliography 431

Index 439

Preface

This book first appeared in 1988. Since then, the use of designed experiments (DOE) has developed considerably in the industrial and academic worlds. Many software packages dedicated to designed experiments have appeared, and these have simplified design construction, removed difficulties in calculation, and allowed rapid visualization of graphs that give unique insights into experimental results.

These developments compelled us to update the original *Introduction aux Plans d'Expériences* in order to take these rapid changes into account. We also saw an opportunity to share the concepts with an even broader audience. This is why SAS Press in the USA and Dunod in France decided to offer a third edition in both English and French. The first and second editions deal only with full- and fractional-factorial designs. The third edition adds chapters on response surface designs, mixture designs, *D*-optimal designs, and designs for discrete variables. This diversity would have not been possible without modern software, which easily constructs all of these designs (and more), and which carries out the most complex calculations easily and swiftly.

The examples and illustrations in this edition are carried out using JMP (pronounced "jump") software from SAS Institute Inc. Data tables are available for download from the SAS Press companion Web site for this book (support.sas.com/goupycreighton). Additionally, a blog to accompany the French-language version of this text is found at www.plansdexperiences.com and www.chimiometrie.org, where you can find additional explanations on our examples in English and French as well as a short French introduction to JMP. You can contact us using any of these sites. Up-to-date documentation is also available from www.jmp.com.

Publishing a book is always a group process, and this one is no different. We would like to thank Michel Genetay, Rémi Longeray, Lalatiana Rakotozafy, and Jacques Vaillé, who read the original French manuscript and who offered many helpful suggestions and sage advice. Thanks also to Ann Lehman, Brad Jones, and Marissa Langford, who read early versions of the English text, and whose comments undoubtedly made this a better book. Thanks also to Ronite Tubiana and Martine Lemonnier from Dunod and to Stephenie Joyner, Mary Beth Steinbach, Caroline Brickley, and Candy Farrell from SAS who helped us in the editing process and who ensured that our manuscript would eventually become a book.

We advise all of you who want to deepen your understanding of DOE to augment your reading by working out the examples with JMP itself. Using JMP deepens understanding of the analyses and encourages proper interpretation of results. We have tried to furnish all the tools necessary so that these methods are immediately applicable to your work. All that remains is for us to wish you "Happy Experimenting!"

Jacques Goupy, Paris (France)
Lee Creighton, Cary (North Carolina, USA)

Chapter 1

Gaining Knowledge with Design of Experiments

1.1 Introduction   2
1.2 The Process of Knowledge Acquisition   2
    1.2.1 Choosing the Experimental Method   5
    1.2.2 Analyzing the Results   5
    1.2.3 Progressively Acquiring Knowledge   5
1.3 Studying a Phenomenon   5
1.4 Terminology   6
    1.4.1 Factor Types   6
    1.4.2 Experimental Space   7
    1.4.3 Factor Domain   8
    1.4.4 Study Domain   9
1.5 Centered and Scaled Variables   11
1.6 Experimental Points   13
1.7 Design of Experiments   14

> **1.7.1 Methodology of Designs without Constraints** 14
> **1.7.2 Methodology of Designs with Constraints** 15
> **1.7.3 The Response Surface** 17
> **1.7.4 The a priori Mathematical Model of the Response** 18

1.1 Introduction

If you are reading this book, you probably do experiments that you would like to organize well. Ideally, you want to conduct only those experiments whose results yield the best possible information and insights.

This book is written to help you. It describes methods and tools that allow you to consistently design useful experiments, ensuring that you extract the maximum amount of information from each one. You will be able to efficiently solve problems and make decisions while gaining experience using JMP software.

We initially look at how experimental design is integrated into the process of knowledge acquisition. Then, we examine some basic concepts that make it possible to properly define a study, and how to interpret a study's results.

1.2 The Process of Knowledge Acquisition

The process of acquiring knowledge can be thought of as answering carefully posed questions. For example, if a farmer wants to know how a fertilizer influences corn yield, the following (and certainly more) questions are reasonable to ask:

- Can the field produce ten more bushels of corn per acre if I increase the quantity of fertilizer?
- How does the amount of rain affect the effectiveness of fertilizer?
- Will the quality of corn remain good if I use a certain fertilizer?
- How much fertilizer should I apply to get the biggest harvest (the most bushels of corn per acre)?

These questions frame both the problem and the solution. They also specify what work should be carried out. It is therefore important to ask questions that are truly representative of the problem.

Of course, before doing any experiments, it is good practice to verify that the question hasn't already been answered. To this end, you can review current literature from a bibliography, consult subject-matter experts, conduct some theoretical calculations, simulations, or do anything else that may answer your questions without experimentation. If, after conducting this research, you find that the question is answered, then there is no need to conduct experiments. More typically, however, these investigations cause you to modify your questions or generate new ones. This is the point when experiments—well-designed ones—are necessary to completely solve the problem. Unquestionably, this preliminary work is part of the experimenter's job. However, we do not focus on these preliminaries in this book.

For questions that don't have readily available answers, it is necessary to carry out experiments. How can the experiments be designed so that they accomplish the following goals?

- Quickly arrive at the best possible results
- Omit unnecessary trials
- Give results with the best possible precision
- Progress without failure
- Establish a model for the studied phenomenon
- Discover the optimal solution

The three essential aspects of the knowledge acquisition process are shown in Figure 1.1:

- The choice of the experimental method
- The analysis of the results
- The progressive acquisition of knowledge

Figure 1.1 Design of experiments optimizes the three highlighted parts of the knowledge acquisition process.

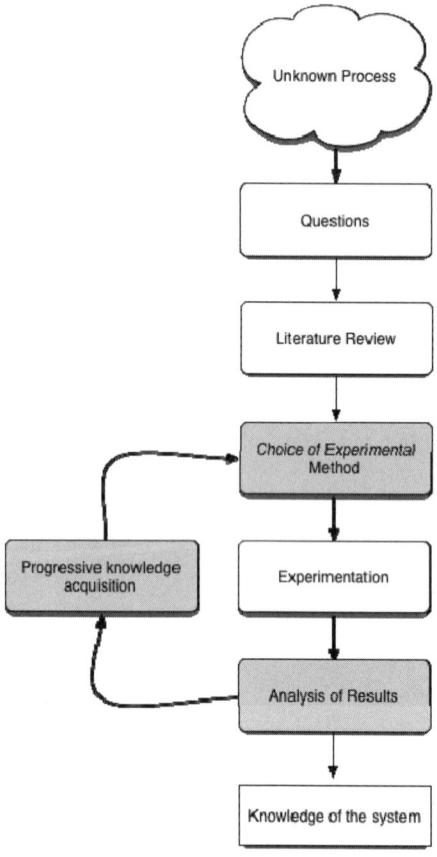

Let's look at these three aspects in detail, remembering that experiments are organized to facilitate the analysis of the results and to allow the progressive acquisition of knowledge.

1.2.1 Choosing the Experimental Method

The experimental method must facilitate the interpretation of the results. However, it should also minimize the number of runs without sacrificing quality. Using designed experiments ensures the conditions that give the best possible precision with the smallest number of runs. Designed experiments give maximum efficiency using the smallest number of trials, and therefore the minimum cost.

1.2.2 Analyzing the Results

Analyzing the results of experiments is linked to the initial design choice. If the experiments are well-prepared, the results are easy to interpret, and they are also rich in information.

Thanks to computers and software, the construction of experimental designs and the necessary analysis calculations have become simple. These tools also support graphical representations that illustrate the results spectacularly and increase understanding of the phenomenon.

1.2.3 Progressively Acquiring Knowledge

An experimenter who undertakes a study obviously does not know at the outset the final results or what they reveal. Therefore, it is wise to advance gradually, to be able to adjust the experimental runs based on initial results. Using an initial outline, for example, makes it possible to direct the tests towards only the interesting aspects of the study and to avoid dead ends.

An initial batch of experiments leads to preliminary, tentative conclusions. Using these initial conclusions, the experimenter can carry out a new series of improved tests. Both series of experiments are used to obtain precise results. In this way, the experimenter accumulates only the results that are needed, and has the flexibility to stop when the results are satisfactory.

1.3 Studying a Phenomenon

Studying a phenomenon is often thought of as focusing on a particular measurement: a car's gasoline consumption, the wholesale price of a chemical, or the corn yield per acre. This measurement (consumption, price, or yield) depends on a great number of variables.

For example, gas consumption is related to the speed of the vehicle, the engine horsepower, driving style, the direction and force of the wind, the inflation of the tires, the presence (or not) of a luggage rack, the number of people in the car, the make of car, and so on. The price of a chemical depends on the quality of the raw materials, the yield of each manufacturing unit, external specifications, conditions of manufacture, and many other quantities. Corn yield, too, depends on the quality of the soil, the quantity of incorporated fertilizer, sun exposure, climate, corn variety, and so on.

Mathematically, we can write the measurement of interest as y, (which we will call the *response*) as a function of several variables x_i (which we will call *factors*) as

$$y = f(x_1, x_2, x_3, \cdots, x_k)$$

The study of a phenomenon boils down to determining the function f that relates the response to the factors $x_1, x_2, \ldots, x_k$.

To look at this approach in more detail, it is necessary to introduce a few special ideas and also some terminology specific to designed experiments.

1.4 Terminology

This section describes terms related to factors and their representation.

1.4.1 Factor Types

The construction of designs and the interpretation of their results depend largely on the types of factors involved in the study. Statisticians distinguish among several types of factors. We discuss four types:

Continuous Factors

Pressure is an example of a continuous factor. For a given interval, any value in the interval can be chosen. Other examples are wavelength, concentration, or temperature. Values taken by continuous factors are therefore represented by continuous numbers.

Discrete Factors

On the other hand, discrete factors can take only particular values. These values are not necessarily numeric. The color of a product (say, blue, red, or yellow) is an example of a discrete factor. A discrete factor can take values that are names, letters, properties, or numbers. In the latter case, the number is really just a numeric label, and does not represent a numeric quantity. It is merely a name or a reference.

Ordinal Factors

Ordinal factors are discrete factors that can be placed in a logical order. For example, size may be represented as large, medium, or small. Ranks, also, are ordinal: first, second, third, and fourth.

Boolean Factors

Boolean factors are discrete factors which can take only two levels: high and low, open or closed, black and white, −1 and 1, and so on.

The border is sometimes fuzzy among these various types of factors. Color (orange, red, blue, etc.), apparently a discrete factor, can be transformed into an ordinal measurement, and even a continuous measurement if the concept of wavelength is introduced. A continuous factor, like speed, can be transformed into an ordinal or discrete factor: rapid and slow, or speed A and speed B. This possibility is not a disadvantage—it is an additional flexibility that the experimenter can use when interpreting results. In fact, the choice sometimes makes it easier to highlight certain aspects of the study.

Changing the variable type is also a means of adapting the answer to the aim of the study. For example, consider the age of the members of a population. If the study looks at average age, the variable "age" is regarded as continuous. If, however, the study examines the number of people reaching a certain age, the variable "age" is an ordinal variable, since there are several age categories: young people, teenagers, adults, and seniors. Finally, if we were studying only the proportion of young people younger than 18, the variable "age" is Boolean: younger than 18 and older than 18.

1.4.2 Experimental Space

Understanding experimental design also requires grasping the essential concept of *experimental space* of the variables in the study. We now examine this fundamental concept in detail using continuous factors, since they are the most frequently used.

To graphically illustrate an experimental space, we use a two-dimensional area. This representation allows an easy extension to multidimensional spaces.

One continuous factor can be represented by a directed and graduated axis. If there is a second continuous factor, it is represented by a similar axis. This second axis is drawn orthogonally to the first (i.e., they form a 90° angle). Mathematically, this gives a Cartesian plane that defines a Euclidean space in two dimensions. This area is called the

8 Introduction to Design of Experiments with JMP Examples

experimental space (Figure 1.2). The experimental space is composed of all the points of the plane factor 1 × factor 2 where each point represents an experimental trial.

Figure 1.2 Each factor is represented by a graduated and oriented axis. The factor axes are orthogonal to each other. The space thus defined is the *experimental space.*

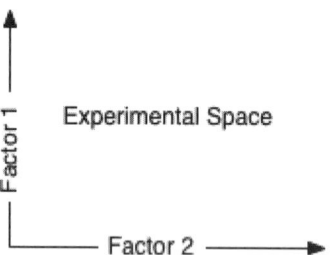

If there is a third factor, it too is represented by a directed and graduated axis, positioned perpendicularly to the first two. With four factors or more, the same construction applies, but it is not possible to represent the space geometrically. A purely mathematical representation (a hypercube of four dimensions) of the experimental space is necessary.

1.4.3 Factor Domain

The value given to a factor while running an experimental trial is called a *level*.

Figure 1.3 The domain of variation for speed contains all the speeds between 45 mph and 80 mph. The low level of the factor is written as −1 and the high level as +1.

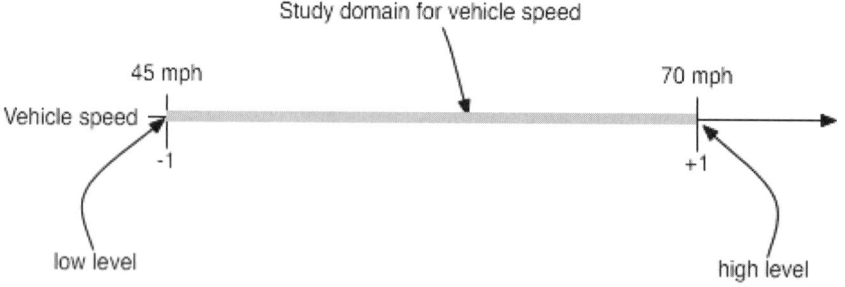

When we study the effect of a factor, in general, we restrict its variation to be between two limits. The experimenter defines these two levels according to specifics of the study. The lower limit is the *low level*. The upper limit is the *high level*. For example, to study the effect of a vehicle's speed on its gas usage, its speed is allowed to vary between 45 and 70 miles per hour. The speed of 45 mph is the low level and the speed of 70 mph is the high level. The set containing all the values between the low and the high level that the factor can take is called the factor's *domain of variation* or, more simply, the factor's *domain*.

If there are more factors, each has its own domain. Since the different factors may have different units of measurement, it useful to have a common representation for all of them. In design of experiments (DOE), it is common to denote the low levels by –1 and the high levels by +1. Here we designate the speed of 45 mph as the –1 level and 70 mph as the +1 level.

The interior of a factor's domain contains all the values that it can theoretically take. Two, three, or more levels can therefore be chosen according to the needs of the study. For example, if the study uses a second-degree (quadratic) model, three or four levels should be chosen. That is, we should choose three or four different speeds.

1.4.4 Study Domain

In practice, the experimenter chooses a portion of the experimental space to carry out the study. This special zone of the experimental space is the *study domain* (Figure 1.4). This domain is defined by the high and low levels of all the factors and possibly by constraints among the factors. Let's suppose that the second factor is a vehicle's additional weight, defined as any additional mass aside from that of the vehicle and the driver. The lower level of this additional weight is 0 lbs; the high level may be, say, 550 lbs. If there are no constraints, the study domain is represented by all the points where additional weight lies between 0 and 600 lbs and whose speeds lie between 45 and 70 mph.

Figure 1.4 The study domain is defined by the union of the domains from the different factors. Here, there are no constraints.

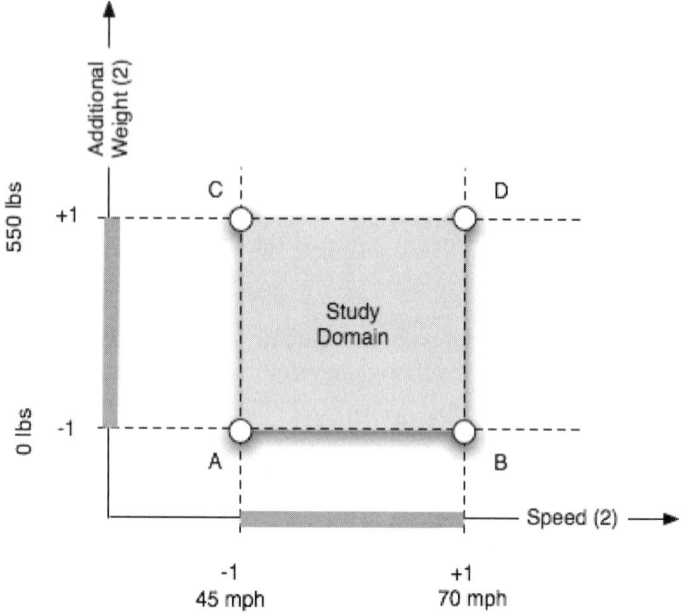

There may be constraints on the study domain. For example, it might be impossible to attain a speed of 70 mph with a lot of additional weight. Figure 1.5 illustrates this possible reduction of the initial study domain.

Figure 1.5 The study domain with constraints is represented by the shaded area.

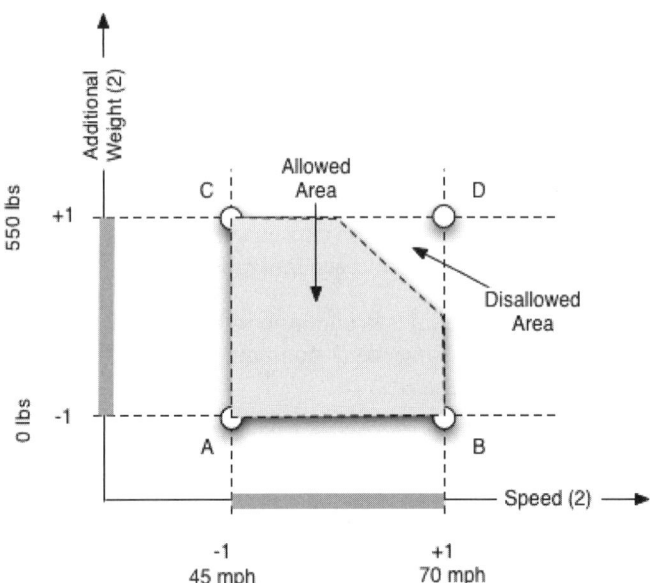

1.5 Centered and Scaled Variables

When the lower level of a factor is represented by −1 and the upper level is represented by +1, two important changes occur:

- The center of the measurements moves.
  In our example, the middle of the interval [−1, 1] is zero and corresponds to the value 57.5 mph. The numerical value of the new zero origin, therefore, differs from the origin when expressed in the original experimental units (sometimes called *engineering units*).

- The measurement units change.
  In our example, the lower level of the speed factor is 45 mph and the high level is 70 mph, so there are 25 mph between these two values, i.e., 25 times the speed unit. Between −1 and 1 there are two new units: the newly defined unit corresponds to 25 mph, and is given the name of *step*.

These two changes involve the introduction of new variables called *centered and scaled variables* (*csv*). Centering refers to the change of origin, and scaling refers to the change of units. These new variables are also commonly called *coded variables* or *coded units*.

The conversion of the original variables A to the coded variables X (and vice versa) is given by the following formula, where A_0 is the central value in engineering units.

$$x = \frac{A - A_0}{\text{Step}} \tag{1.1}$$

The advantage to using coded units lies in their power to present designed experiments in the same way, regardless of the chosen study domains and regardless of the factors. Seen this way, DOE theory is quite generalizable.

The use of coded variables is common in DOE software. For example, finding the best experimental points using the *D*-optimality criterion (see Chapter 11) is possible only when using coded variables.

Coded variables result from the ratio of two same-sized physical units, so they have no dimension. The absence of natural units is due to the fact that all the factors have the same domain of variation (two coded units), allowing direct comparison of the effects of the factors among themselves.

Example 1

An experimenter chooses for the speed factor to be 45 mph at the low level and 70 mph at the high level. In coded units, what is the corresponding speed for 55 mph?

Let's calculate the step for the speed factor. It's equal to half the difference between the high and low levels, so

$$\text{Step} = \frac{A_{+1} - A_{-1}}{2} = \frac{70 - 45}{2} = 12.5$$

A_0 is the center value between the high and low levels; that is, it is half of the sum of the high and low levels:

$$A_0 = \frac{A_{+1} + A_{-1}}{2} = \frac{70 + 45}{2} = 57.5$$

Applying equation (1.1):

$$x = \frac{A - A_0}{\text{Step}} = \frac{50 - 57.5}{12.5} = -0.6$$

A speed of 55 mph is therefore, for this example, equal to −0.6 in coded values.

Example 2
We may also want the value in original units, knowing the coded value. In engineering units, what is the value of the speed factor corresponding to +0.5 in coded units? Write equation (1.1):

$$+0.5 = \frac{A - 57.5}{12.5}$$

So

$$A = 57.5 + 0.5 \times 12.5 = 63.75$$

The coded speed 0.5 corresponds to a speed of 63.75 mph.

1.6 Experimental Points

In a two-dimensional space, level i of factor 1, written as $x_{1,i}$, and level j of factor 2, written as $x_{2,j}$, can be considered as the coordinates of a point of the experimental space or of the study domain (Figure 1.6). For example, if the speed level is 55 mph and the additional weight is 250 lbs, the coordinates of the experimental point are

$x_{1,i} = 55$ mph

$x_{2,j} = 250$ lbs

One run of the experiment can be represented by a single point in this axis system. This is the reason that a run is often designated by the expression *experimental point*, *experiment point* or, even just *point*. A designed experiment is therefore represented by a collection of experimental points situated in an experimental space. In our current example, the experiment is conducted on a vehicle that is moving at 55 mph with an additional weight of 250 lbs.

Figure 1.6 In the experimental space, the factor levels are specified by experimental points.

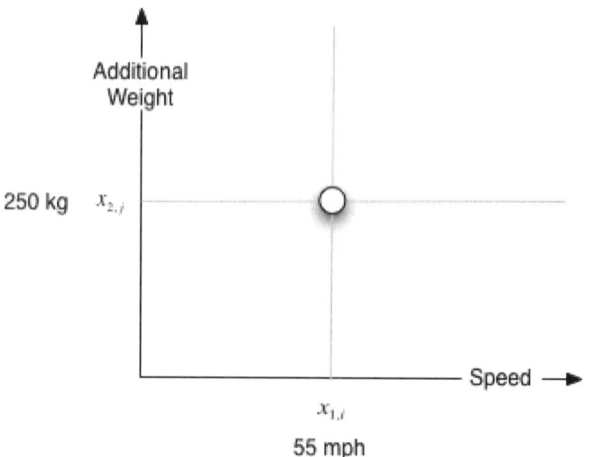

With up to three factors, it is possible to physically draw the study domain. With more than three factors, we use a tabular representation, called a *matrix*, which is more general because it allows representation of the experimental points in a multidimensional space with any number of dimensions.

1.7 Design of Experiments

1.7.1 Methodology of Designs without Constraints

The choice of the number and the placement of experimental points is the fundamental problem of designed experiments. Ideally, we want to carry out the minimum number of trials while reducing the influence of the experimental error on the models that will be used to make decisions. This goal is achieved by considering the mathematical and statistical properties that relate the response to the factors. When there are no constraints on the study domain, there are classical designs that have excellent statistical qualities and which allow the modeling of responses under the best conditions (Figure 1.7). If there are constraints on the design, we must construct custom designs by finding point positions which lead, in the same way, to quality statistics and good response modeling.

Figure 1.7 Example of the arrangement of the experimental points in a domain without constraints

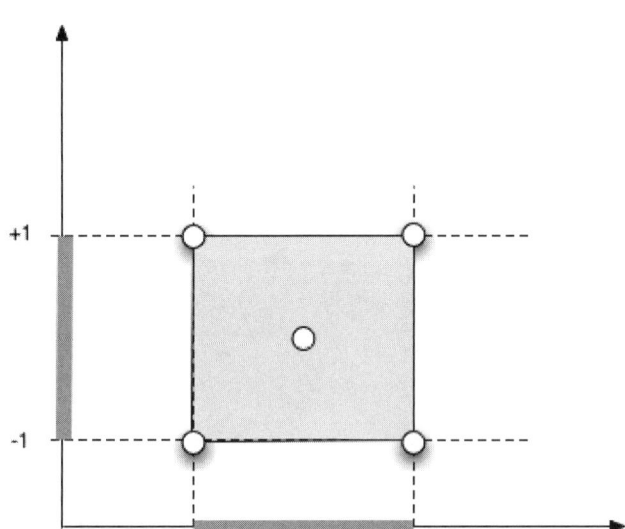

1.7.2 Methodology of Designs with Constraints

The construction procedure of designs where the domain is constrained is as follows:

1. Define the domain of each factor (low level and high level).

2. Define any constraints that restrict the factors. These constraints are expressed as inequalities among the factors, and they define allowed areas (where trials can be carried out), and disallowed areas (where trials cannot be carried out).

3. Define any other factor levels that may be interesting for the study (other than the high and low levels, which are already defined). When used, between two and five additional levels for each factor are specified.

4. Construct a grid by taking into account all the combinations of factor levels. This grid should contain only realistic experimental points; that is, it should contain points in the allowed experimental areas. These points form the *candidate set* (Figure 1.8).

Figure 1.8 The grid of candidate points is made up of possible trials in the study domain.

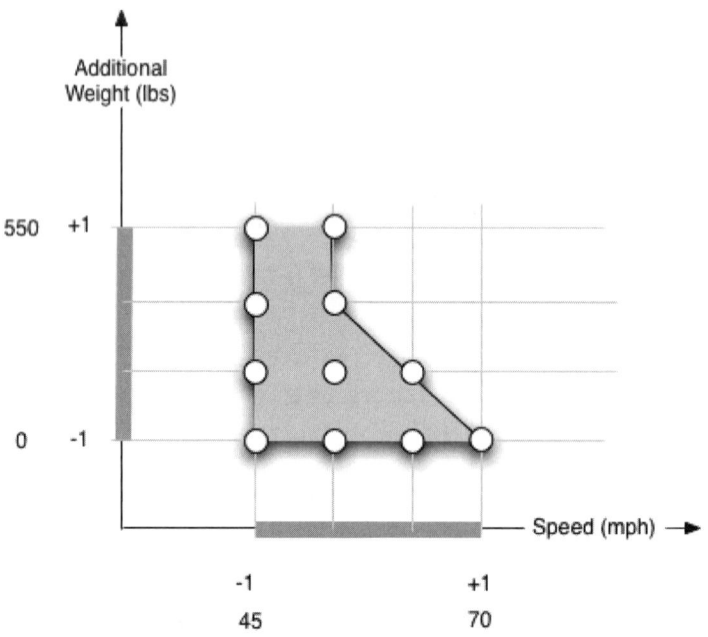

5. Choose a function a priori that relates the response to the factors.

6. Select, according to the chosen optimality criterion, the number and placement of experimental points most useful for modeling the phenomenon (Figure 1.9). This selection requires many long and tedious calculations, and selection is not possible without the aid of DOE software.

Figure 1.9 Optimal points as selected by software

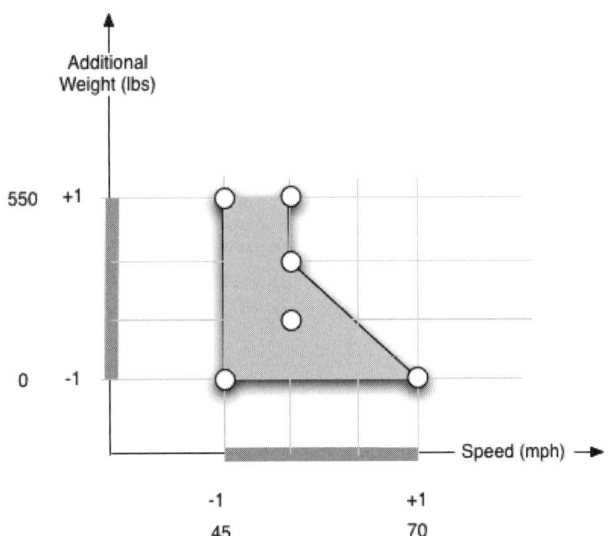

1.7.3 The Response Surface

Each point in the study domain corresponds to a response. Together, all the points in the study domain correspond to a collection of responses located on a surface. We call this the *response surface* (Figure 1.10).

Figure 1.10 The collection of responses that correspond to all the points in the study domain forms the response surface.

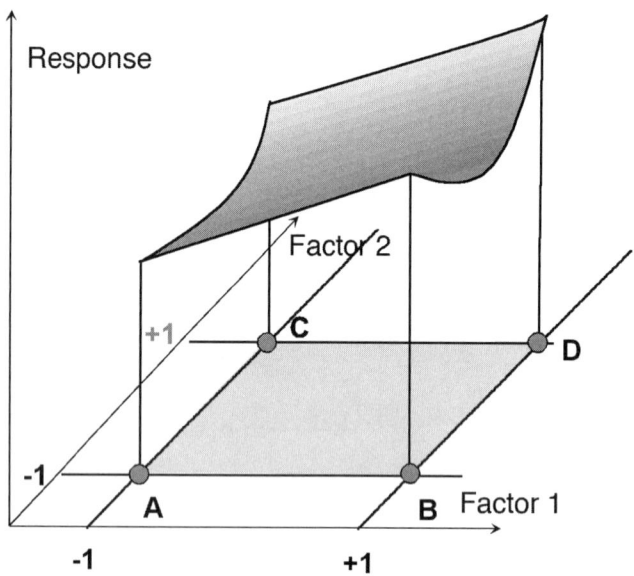

In general, only a few responses are known: those that correspond to the experimental points chosen by the experimenter. To obtain the response surface, it is necessary to interpolate using a mathematical model.

Those points chosen using DOE theory ensure the best possible precision of the form and position of the response surface.

1.7.4 The a priori Mathematical Model of the Response

Mathematical modeling
We use a first-order linear model to approximate the response.

$$y = a_0 + \sum a_i x_i + \sum a_{ij} x_i x_j + \sum a_{ii} x_i^2 + \cdots \tag{1.2}$$

where

- y is the response or measurement of interest to the experimenter.
- x_i represents a level of factor i.

- x_j represents a level of factor j.
- a_0, a_i, a_{ij}, a_{ii} are the coefficients of the polynomial.

This model is called the *a priori* model, or the *postulated* model.

The predetermined models are valid prediction models inside the study domain, which must always be precisely established. These are not theoretical models based on physiochemical or mechanical laws.

Experimental modeling

Two concepts must be added to the purely mathematical model described above.

The first is the *lack of fit*. This term expresses the fact that the model chosen by the experimenter before the trials is probably a little different from the true model of the studied phenomenon. There is a difference between these two models. This difference is the lack of fit, denoted by the Greek letter delta (Δ).

The second concept is the random nature of the response. In reality, measuring the same response several times at the same experimental point does not give exactly the same result. There is a dispersion of the results. Dispersions like these are called *random error* or *pure error* and are denoted by the Greek letter epsilon (ε).

The general equation (1.2) must be modified as follows:

$$y = f(x_1, x_2, x_3 \cdots, x_n) + \Delta + \varepsilon \tag{1.3}$$

This equation is used in Chapter 5 where we show how to estimate the lack of fit Δ, and the pure error ε.

System of equations

Each experimental point corresponds to a response value. However, this response is modeled by a polynomial whose coefficients are unknowns that must be determined. An experimental design results in a system of n equations (for n trials) in p unknowns (for the p coefficients in the *a priori* model). This system can be written in a simple way using matrix notation.

$$y = X\ a + e \tag{1.4}$$

where

y is the *response vector*.

X is the *model matrix* or the *design matrix* which depends on the experimental points used in the design and on the postulated model.

a is the *coefficient matrix*.

e is the *error matrix*.

This system of equations cannot be, in general, solved simply because there are fewer equations than there are unknowns. There are n equations and $p + n$ unknowns. To find the solution, we must use special matrix methods generally based on the criterion of least squares. The results are estimations of the coefficients, denoted as **â**.

The algebraic result of the least-squares calculations is

$$\hat{a} = (X' X)^{-1} X' y \qquad (1.5)$$

where X' is the transpose of X (for details, see Appendix C, "Introduction to Matrix Calculations"). A number of software packages exist (like JMP and SAS/STAT) that will carry out these calculations and that directly give the coefficient values.

Two matrices appear frequently in the theory of experimental design:

- The *information matrix* $X' X$.

- The *dispersion matrix* $(X' X)^{-1}$.

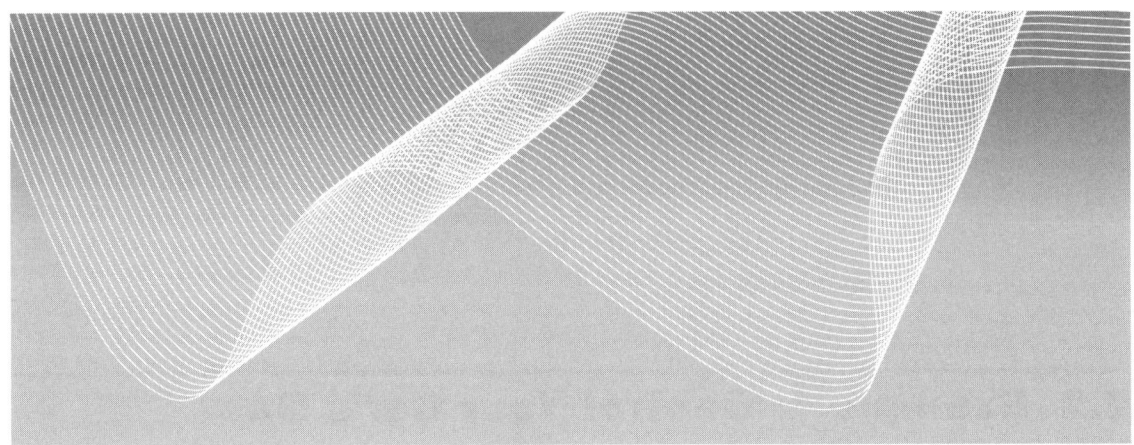

Chapter 2

Your First Designed Experiment

2.1 Introduction 21
2.2 Example 1: Control Your Car's Gas Consumption 22
    2.2.1 Preparing the Designed Experiment 22
    2.2.2 Choosing the Design 24
    2.2.3 Running the Experiment 27
    2.2.4 Interpreting the Coefficients 28
    2.2.5 Interpreting the Results 40

2.1 Introduction

If you read the previous chapter, you know enough to tackle your first designed experiment. We follow an approach whose principal stages are:

- Preparation of the study

- Choice of experimental design
- Experimentation
- Interpretation of the results
- Decision to stop or continue the study

We examine each of these steps using our first example.

2.2 Example 1: Control Your Car's Gas Consumption

2.2.1 Preparing the Designed Experiment

This stage breaks into several steps, the most important of which are described in the following paragraphs.

2.2.1.1 Defining the Study Objective
This study is straightforward to set up and its subject is easy to relate to. The objective is to know the gas consumption of a car when you drive with or without extra weight, while driving fast or slow.

2.2.1.2 Describing the Experimental Subjects
The experimental trials of the study were performed using one of the author's cars. The car, with only one occupant, was driven on an interstate highway. If it were possible, we would carry out the trials on a race track, where it is easy to maintain all the conditions imposed on the experiment. It is always much easier to carry out experimental trials on a track, in a laboratory, a pilot workshop, or any place specially built for the experiment's activity.

2.2.1.3 Choosing the Appropriate Response
The response is the consumption of gas in miles per gallon (mpg).

2.2.1.4 Researching the Factors That May Influence the Response

What are the factors that may influence a car's gas consumption?

There are, of course, the two factors that we are going to study (additional weight and speed of the car). However, there are other factors, too. For example, the brand and inflation pressure of the tires, the presence or absence of a luggage rack, the direction of the wind or rain, the tuning of the motor, the number of starts and stops, and the quality of the road. It is a good idea to write down all the possible factors. To complete the list, we visit an expert—our mechanic—to ask him if he can think of any other factors that may affect gas mileage. Always be interested in covering the complete problem. We are not forced to study every suggested factor, but we are interested in which factors may be influential. Any of the factors that are not studied in the experimental design are, in general, fixed at a constant level throughout the experiment.

2.2.1.5 Defining the Factor Levels

We now choose the high and low levels of each factor.

The speed should not be too slow nor too fast, and since we are on an interstate highway, it cannot exceed speeds required by law. In our example (using a North Carolina interstate), the low speed is 45 mph and the high speed is 70 mph.

The empty weight of the car is defined by the weight of the car and driver without luggage. The additional weight is defined by any weight exceeding the empty weight. If there are three additional people, and each carries 25 lbs of luggage, the additional weight is approximately 3×150 = 450 lbs for the passengers and 4×25=100 lbs for the luggage of the three passengers and the driver. Therefore, there are about 550 lbs of additional weight. Rather than bother our neighbors to sit in the car for these tests, we instead used 550 lbs of cast iron weights on the seats and in the trunk.

The low level of the additional weight factor is the driver and car alone, without weights.

The high level of the additional weight factor is the car, driver, and the additional load of 550 lbs, distributed evenly in the car.

It's a good idea to summarize this information in a table (Table 2.1).

Table 2.1 Factors and study domain

Factor	Low Level (−)	High Level (+)
Speed (1)	45 mph	70 mph
Additional weight (2)	0	550 lbs

This table is important because the conclusions of the study are valid only inside the study domain. If we were to load the car with 600 lbs and drive at 100 mph, we would not be able to use the results of this study to predict gas mileage.

2.2.1.6 Examining the Constraints

While you are driving, the amount of gas in the tank decreases. The weight of the vehicle therefore changes during the experiment. So, it is necessary to begin each experimental run with a full tank so that this nuisance factor does not drastically influence the results. This forces us to begin the test at a service station near the interstate.

It's also necessary that the weather (temperature, wind, rain) remain constant for all the tests. So, we try to do the tests all in the same day—preferably one without wind and rain. Weather changes also affect the driving distance.

We choose the same course and same direction for each test, so that the influence of coasting down and climbing hills balances out.

In addition, before each test, we check the tire pressure to ensure that it is the same.

In essence, we're making a list of precautions that must be taken to control the experiment and ensure that the experiment gives as accurate results as possible.

2.2.2 Choosing the Design

There are two factors to study. The low and high levels of each factor have been defined. The factors that must remain constant throughout the experiment are the driving distance (that is, the number of miles), the driving direction, the starting point, the stopping point, and the tire pressure.

Having two factors, each taking two levels, the simplest design to choose is a 2^2 full factorial. The notation 2^2 has the following significance: the 2 in the exponent shows the number of factors, while the 2 in the base shows the number of levels each factor takes. This design is well suited to our problem because it corresponds exactly to our two chosen factors, both of which have two levels. The experimental points have coordinates that are the high and low levels of the factors.

There are many equally good choices for representing this design. For example, we can first draw the domain of study in the experimental space, and then add the experimental points by using their levels as coordinates (Figure 2.1).

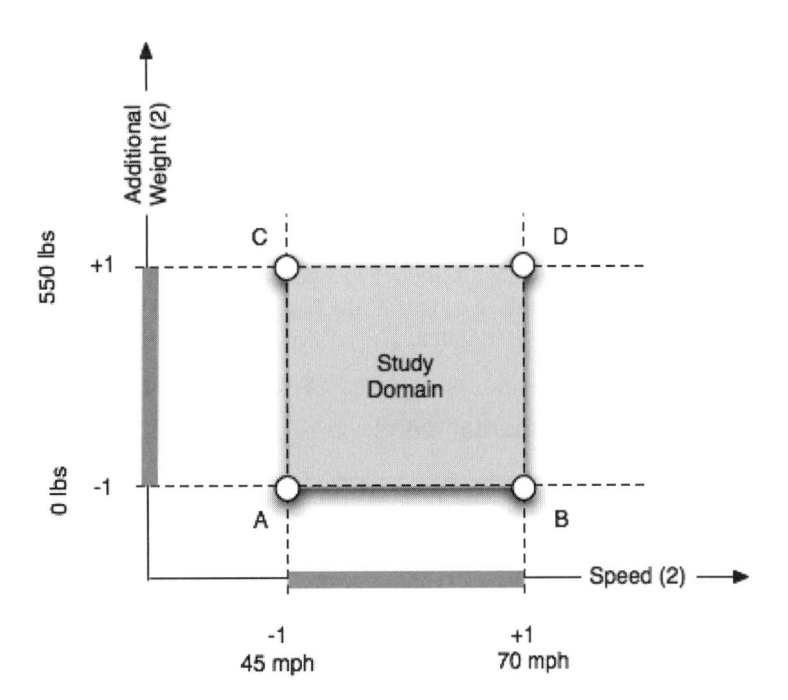

Figure 2.1 Representation of the experimental design

The experimental runs can be arranged in tabular form, using either the engineering measurements (mph and lbs) or the coded measurements (−1 and +1). With engineering measurements, the table is called the *experimental table worksheet*. With coded measurements, the table is called the *experimental design* or the *experimental matrix*.

The first column of the experimental table worksheet is used to designate the trials (Table 2.2). These can simply be numbered, or given names. The second column holds the first factor, with its designated levels listed in order. The third column holds the second factor, and also lists the experimental runs in order. The first trial, trial 1 or trial A, is executed with a speed of 45 mph and without any additional weight. The second trial, trial 2 or trial B, is executed with a speed of 70 mph and no additional weight. The third trial, trial 3 or trial C, is executed with a speed of 45 mph and an additional weight of 550 lbs. Finally, the fourth trial, trial 4 or trial D, is executed with a speed of 70 mph and an additional weight of 550 lbs. The table is quite useful while running the experiment.

Table 2.2 Experimental table worksheet

Trial	Speed	Additional Weight
	Factor 1	*Factor 2*
1 (A)	45 mph	0 lbs
2 (B)	70 mph	0 lbs
3 (C)	45 mph	550 lbs
4 (D)	70 mph	550 lbs

The first column of the experimental matrix (Table 2.3) is used to show the names of the factors. The second column holds the first factor, and we list there its experimental levels in coded form, i.e., with 1's and −1's. The third column has the coded levels of the second factor. Note the two lines at the bottom of the table that show the meaning of the −1 and +1 levels of each factor. This table is used during the construction of the design.

Table 2.3 Experimental matrix

Trial	Speed	Additional Weight
	Factor 1	*Factor 2*
1 (A)	−1	−1
2 (B)	+1	−1
3 (C)	−1	+1
4 (D)	+1	+1
−1 Level	45 mph	0 lbs
+1 Level	70 mph	550 lbs

To interpret the results of the trials, you can use either the experimental table worksheet or the experimental matrix, depending on which facts you are interested in.

2.2.3 Running the Experiment

This is the most technical part of the study. The experimental trials must be carried out carefully, and it is necessary to be sure of the results' quality. In this example, the order of the tests is not really important. However, this is not always the case. In Chapter 8, we illustrate principles that govern the ordering of trials. For our current example, we arrange them randomly.

The course was chosen to be 70 miles long, i.e., approximately 5 hours and 6 minutes of driving. The down time needed to add gas, to measure gas consumption, to check the tire pressure, and to load the car is estimated to take approximately 2 hours. So, we should be able to complete all four experimental runs in a single day.

After carrying out the first trial (45 mph, no additional weight), we write down the amount of gas consumed. After 70 miles, 2.33 gallons were used (that is to say, 30 mpg). The second trial (70 mph, no additional weight) used 2.8 gallons (25 mpg). The two other tests (trials 3 and 4) used 2.59 (27 mpg) and 3.33 gallons (21 mpg). The results are written in the fourth column of the experimental matrix (Table 2.4).

Table 2.4 Experimental matrix with results

Trial	Speed	Additional Weight	Consumption
	Factor 1	*Factor 2*	mpg
1 (A)	−1	−1	30
2 (B)	+1	−1	25
3 (C)	−1	+1	27
4 (D)	+1	+1	21
−1 Level	45 mph	0 lbs	
+1 Level	70 mph	550 lbs	

We can show these results on the study domain (Figure 2.2).

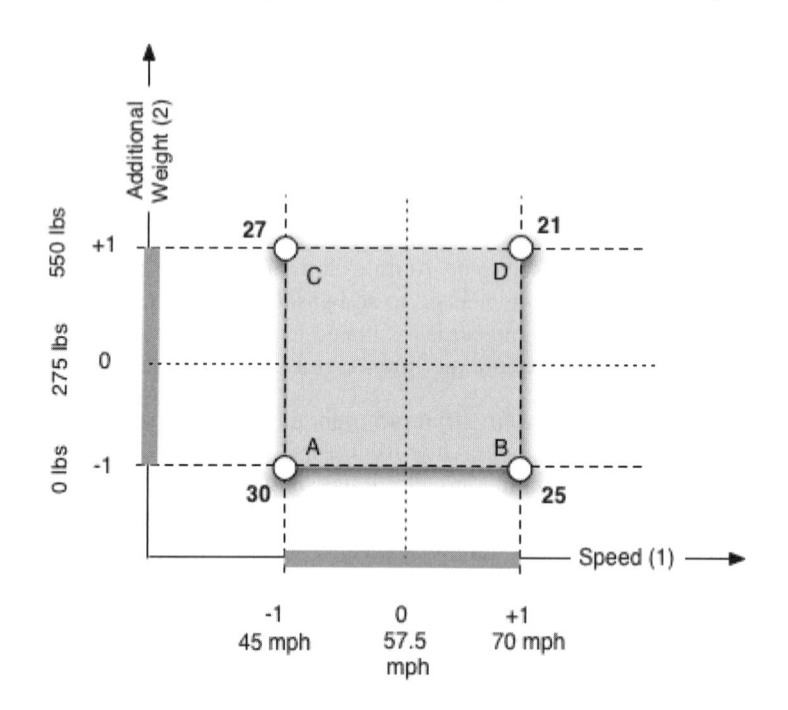

Figure 2.2 Value of the response for various points in the study domain

[Figure 2.2: A square study domain plotted with Speed (1) on the x-axis and Additional Weight (2) on the y-axis. The x-axis shows -1 = 45 mph, 0 = 57.5 mph, +1 = 70 mph. The y-axis shows -1 = 0 lbs, 0 = 275 lbs, +1 = 550 lbs. Four corner points: A (-1, -1) = 30; B (+1, -1) = 25; C (-1, +1) = 27; D (+1, +1) = 21.]

2.2.4 Interpreting the Coefficients

No simple interpretation springs to mind when looking at the table of measured consumptions. We would like to answer questions like: "What is the mileage of my car when I load it with 100 lbs and then drive at 55 mph?" or "What is the change in mileage when I drive at 70 mph instead of 55 mph?" Answers to these questions certainly exist. These answers are, in effect, "hidden" in the results we gathered, but for the moment we can't see them. We have to transform our raw data into interpretable results to gain clear and precise answers. This is the essence of the interpretation phase. The importance of design of experiments (DOE) software now becomes clear, since it is the tool that helps us to make all the transformations, calculations, and illustrations that allow us to truly see the results.

For a 2^2 full factorial, the postulated model is

$$y = a_0 + a_1 x_1 + a_2 x_2 + a_{12} x_1 x_2 \qquad (2.1)$$

where

- y is the response, gas consumption in this example.
- x_1 represents the level of the speed factor (factor 1), 45 mph (–1) or 70 mph (+1) for our experiment.
- x_2 represents the level of the additional weight factor (factor 2), 0 lbs (–1) or 550 lbs (+1) for our experiments.
- $x_1 x_2$ is the product of the levels of the speed and additional weight factors (i.e. factor 1 × factor 2). In this example, using coded units, this product is equal to –1 ($x_1 x_2 = -1 \times +1 = +1 \times -1 = -1$) or +1 ($x_1 x_2 = -1 \times -1 = +1 \times +1 = +1$).
- a_0 is the *intercept* of the model (also called the *constant term*).
- a_1 is the coefficient of the speed factor (factor 1).
- a_2 is the coefficient of the additional weight factor (factor 2).
- a_{12} is the coefficient of the $x_1 x_2$ (the *interaction*) term.

This model is called the *first-degree model with interaction*, and we now examine the meaning of each coefficient.

2.2.4.1 Interpreting the Intercept

To find the meaning of the intercept, a_0, simply assign the value 0 (in coded units) as the level of both factors. This representative experimental point then corresponds to the center of the study domain (Figure 2.3) and the response at this point has a value, denoted y_0.

Figure 2.3 The response value at the intercept is at the center of the domain.

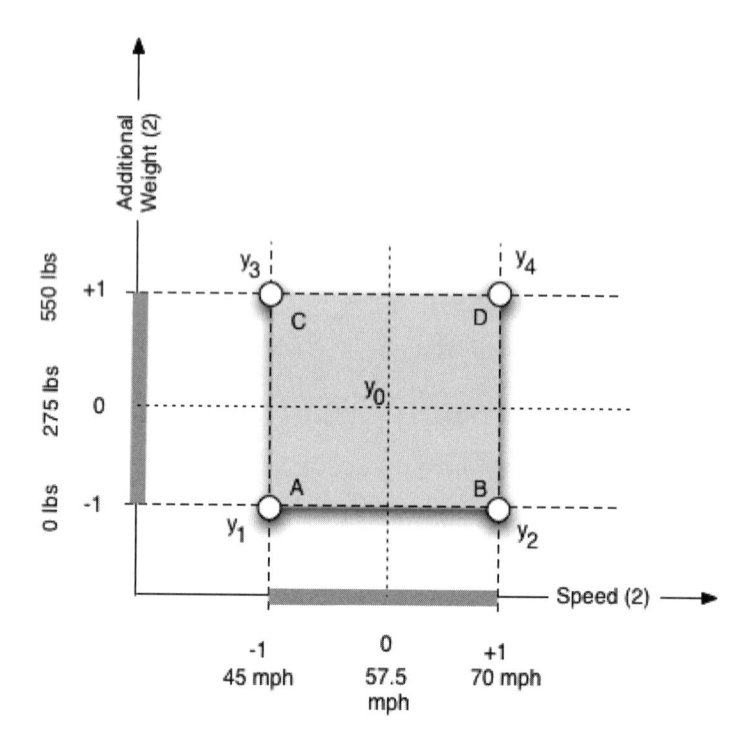

Equation (2.1) becomes

$$y_0 = a_0 + a_1 \times 0 + a_2 \times 0 + a_{12} \times 0 \times 0$$

$$y_0 = a_0$$

The value of the intercept a_0 is equal to the predicted response at the center of the study domain.

2.2.4.2 Interpreting the Coefficient of Speed (Factor 1)

Let's consider both points, B and D, which are located at the high level of factor 1 (speed), shown in Figure 2.3. The coordinates of these points are, in coded units:

$$B \begin{vmatrix} x_1 = +1 \\ x_2 = -1 \end{vmatrix} \quad D \begin{vmatrix} x_1 = +1 \\ x_2 = +1 \end{vmatrix}$$

We can obtain the response at B, denoted y_2, by using corresponding factor levels in their coded units:

$$y_2 = a_0 + a_1 \times (+1) + a_2 \times (-1) + a_{12} \times (+1) \times (-1) = a_0 + a_1 - a_2 - a_{12}$$

Similarly, we can obtain the response at D, denoted by y_4, by using corresponding factor levels as coded units:

$$y_4 = a_0 + a_1 \times (+1) + a_2 \times (+1) + a_{12} \times (+1) \times (+1) = a_0 + a_1 + a_2 + a_{12}$$

Finally, add the two responses y_2 and y_4:

$$y_2 + y_4 = 2(a_0 + a_1)$$

Next, repeat the same calculation for points A and C, the lower levels of the speed factor where the responses are denoted y_1 and y_3 respectively. This gives

$$y_1 + y_3 = 2(+a_0 - a_1)$$

Subtracting the second equation from the first gives

$$4a_1 = -y_1 + y_2 - y_3 + y_4$$

which can be written as

$$a_1 = \frac{1}{2}\left[\frac{y_2 + y_4}{2} - \frac{y_1 + y_3}{2}\right]$$

Now note that $\frac{y_2 + y_4}{2}$ is the mean of the responses at the high level of the speed factor. Call this mean $\bar{y}_+$. The expression $\frac{y_1 + y_3}{2}$ is the mean of the responses at the low level of the speed factor, so call it $\bar{y}_-$. Since speed is factor 1, this lets us write

$$a_1 = \frac{1}{2}[\bar{y}_+ - \bar{y}_-]$$

The coefficient a_1 is therefore half the difference between the mean of the responses at the high level of the speed factor and the mean of the responses at the low level of the speed factor.

Changing from the low level to the high level, the response varies, on average, like the difference $[\bar{y}_+ - \bar{y}_-]$. If this difference is large, the response varies a lot. If this difference is small, the response does not vary much. This, therefore, gives us a way to know how the response varies due to speed (factor 1). This is the reason why the coefficient of a_1 is called the speed *effect*, or the *effect of* speed.

Application
We know the four responses, so we can easily calculate the coefficient

$$a_1 = \frac{1}{4}\left[-y_1 + y_2 - y_3 + y_4\right]$$

$$a_1 = \frac{1}{4}\left[-30 + 25 - 27 + 21\right] = -2.75$$

The speed effect (the effect of factor 1) is –2.75 mpg. This means that if the speed goes from 57.5 mph to 70 mph, the mileage decreases by 2.75 miles. If the speed goes from 45 mph to 70 mph, the mileage decreases by 5.5 miles.

2.2.4.3 Representing the Speed Coefficient

The mean of the responses at the high level of speed, $\bar{y}_+$, lies on the response surface and is plumb with the point M_+, the midpoint of segment BD (Figure 2.4). It therefore has coordinates:

$$M_+ \begin{vmatrix} x_1 = +1 \\ x_2 = 0 \end{vmatrix}$$

The mean of the responses at the low level of the speed factor lies on the response surface, and is plumb with the point M_-, the midpoint of segment AC. Therefore, it has coordinates:

$$M_- \begin{vmatrix} x_1 = -1 \\ x_2 = 0 \end{vmatrix}$$

Figure 2.4 The coefficient of the speed factor is the slope of the line that connects the two responses $\bar{y}_+$ and $\bar{y}_-$.

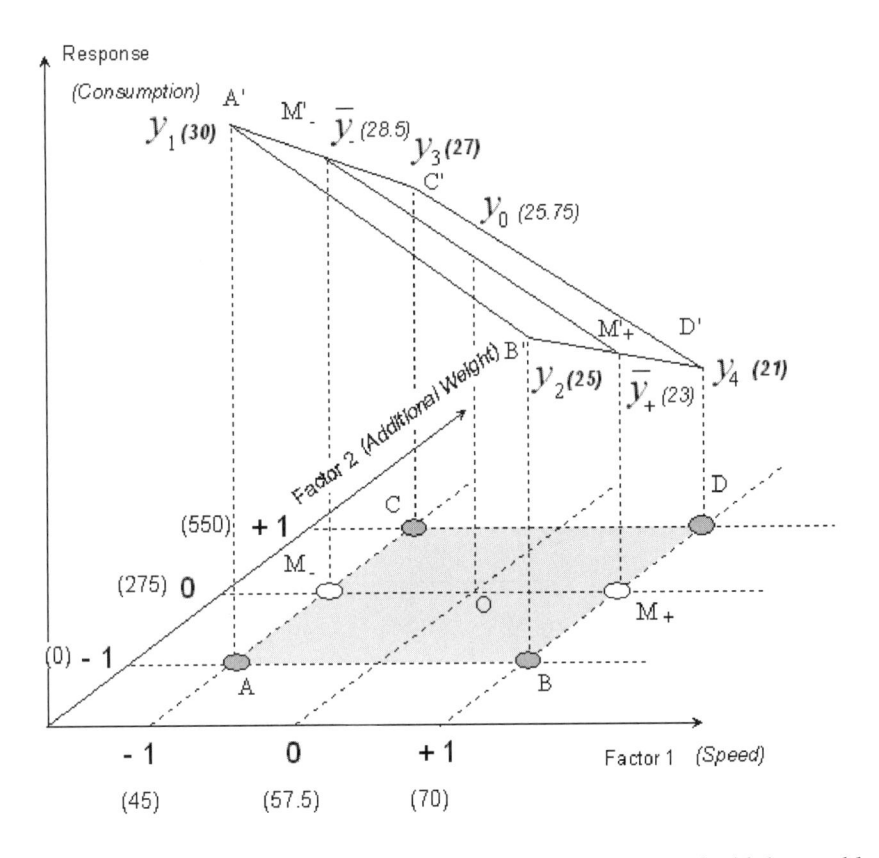

The variation of the response between the mean of the responses at the high speed level, $\bar{y}_+$, and the mean of the responses at the low speed level, $\bar{y}_-$, is $\bar{y}_+ - \bar{y}_-$, i.e., twice the coefficient a_1.

The coefficient a_1 is therefore equal to the variation of the response between y_0, the response at the center of the domain, and $\bar{y}_+$, the mean of the responses at the high level of the speed factor. Equally, the coefficient a_1 can be seen as the slope of the line $M'_- M'_+$.

One can also say that the coefficient a_1 is equal to the average variation of the response when speed goes from zero to the high level. It thus represents the influence of speed in the field of study.

2.2.4.4 Illustration of the Speed Effect

In order to clearly see the line $M_-' M_+'$ and illustrate the effect of speed, extract the plane $M_+ M_- M_-' M_+'$ from Figure 2.4. This gives Figure 2.5, which is much easier to read and interpret.

Figure 2.5 Illustration of the speed effect

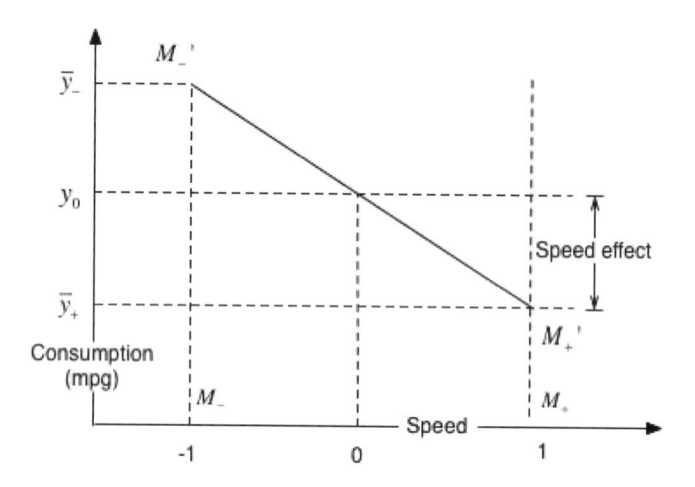

The effect of factor 1 can be positive or negative, the same as the sign of the coefficient.

Application

The mean consumption at the high level of speed (factor 1) is

$$\bar{y}_+ = \frac{y_2 + y_4}{2} = \frac{25 + 21}{2} = 23$$

The mean consumption at the low level of speed is

$$\bar{y}_- = \frac{y_1 + y_3}{2} = \frac{30 + 27}{2} = 28.5$$

Mileage changes, on average, from 28.5 mpg to 23 mpg when the speed increases from 45 mph to 70 mph. Mileage at the center is half the two means, that is, 25.75 mpg.

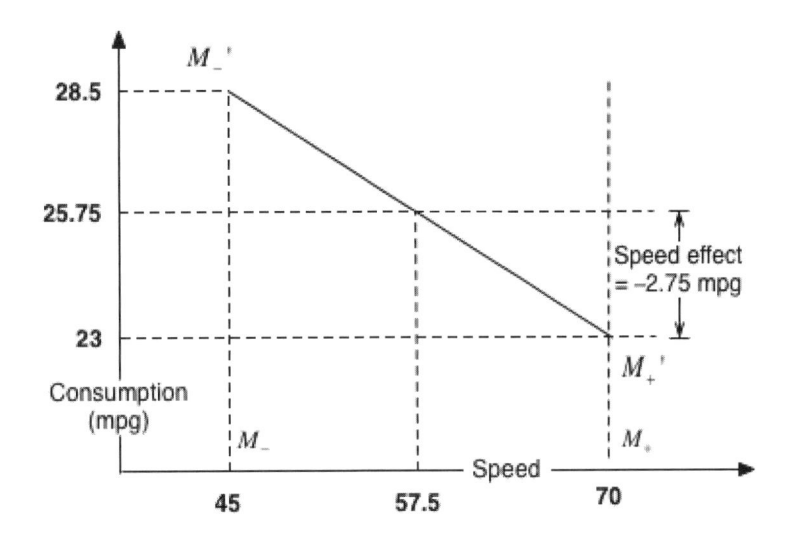

Figure 2.6 Evaluation of the speed effect

2.2.4.5 Meaning of the Coefficient of Additional Weight (Factor 2)

Using the same reasoning, the coefficient a_2 is equal to the average variation of the response when factor 2 passes from level zero to the high level. It represents the influence of factor 2 in the study domain. This is called "the effect of factor 2."

Generally, when the selected model is a polynomial, the coefficients of the first-degree terms are the effects of the factors.

Application
Knowing the four responses, it is straightforward to calculate the coefficient of a_2:

$$a_2 = \frac{1}{4}\left[-y_1 - y_2 + y_3 + y_4\right]$$

$$a_2 = \frac{1}{4}\left[-30 - 25 + 27 + 21\right] = -1.75$$

The effect of the additional weight (factor 2) is −1.75 mpg. This means that if the additional weight goes from 0 to 275 lbs, the gas consumption increases. The mileage decreases, on average, by 1.75 mpg if the additional weight goes from 0 to 275 lbs or from 275 lbs to 550 lbs.

The mean gas consumption for the high level of additional weight (factor 2) is

$$\overline{y}_+ = \frac{y_3 + y_4}{2} = \frac{27 + 21}{2} = 24$$

The mean gas consumption of the low level of additional weight (factor 2) is

$$\overline{y}_- = \frac{y_1 + y_2}{2} = \frac{30 + 25}{2} = 27.5$$

Figure 2.7 Illustration of the additional weight effect

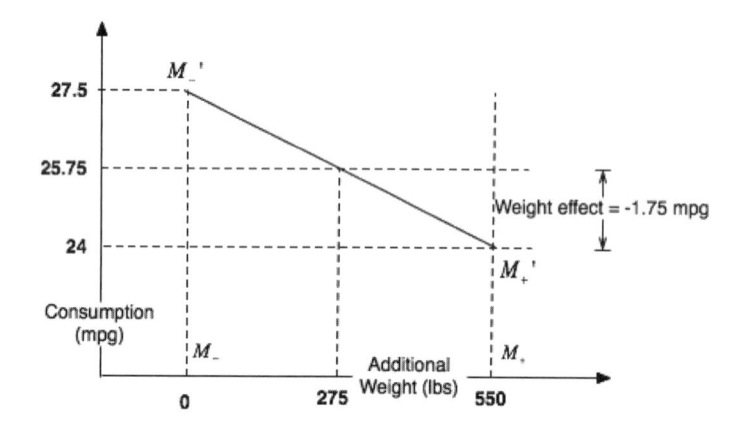

Mileage decreases, on average, from 27.5 to 24 mpg when the additional weight goes from 0 lbs to 550 lbs. Gas consumption in the center is half of the two averages, 25.75 mpg.

Mileage decreases, on average, from 25.75 to 24 mpg when the additional weight goes from 275 lbs to 550 lbs. This decrease of 1.75 mpg is the effect of the additional weight factor (Figure 2.7).

2.2.4.6 Meaning of the Coefficient a_{12}

We calculate the coefficient a_{12} by an analogous method to the one that was used for the coefficients a_1 and a_2. The coefficient a_{12} is found to be equal to

$$a_{12} = \frac{1}{2}\left[\frac{y_4 - y_3}{2} - \frac{y_2 - y_1}{2}\right]$$

However, $\frac{y_4 - y_3}{2}$ is the effect of factor 1 when factor 2 is at its high level. It is half of the variation of the response between y_4 and y_3. This effect is illustrated by the slope of the line C'D' (Figures 2.4 and 2.8).

The expression $\frac{y_2 - y_1}{2}$ is the effect of factor 1 when factor 2 is at its low level. It is half of the variation of the response between y_2 and y_1. This effect is illustrated by the slope of the line A'B' (Figure 2.8).

The coefficient a_{12} is half of the difference between the two effects.

The coefficient a_{12} therefore measures the variation of factor 1 when the level of factor 2 is changed. It can also be shown that the same coefficient (a_{12}) equally measures the variation of the effect of factor 2 when the level of factor 1 is modified in the same way.

The coefficient a_{12} is called the *interaction between the factors 1 and 2*.

The interaction between two factors can be illustrated by extracting the planes ABA'B' (low level of factor 2) and CDC'D' (high level of factor 2) from Figure 2.4 and by projecting these planes onto the same plane (Figure 2.8).

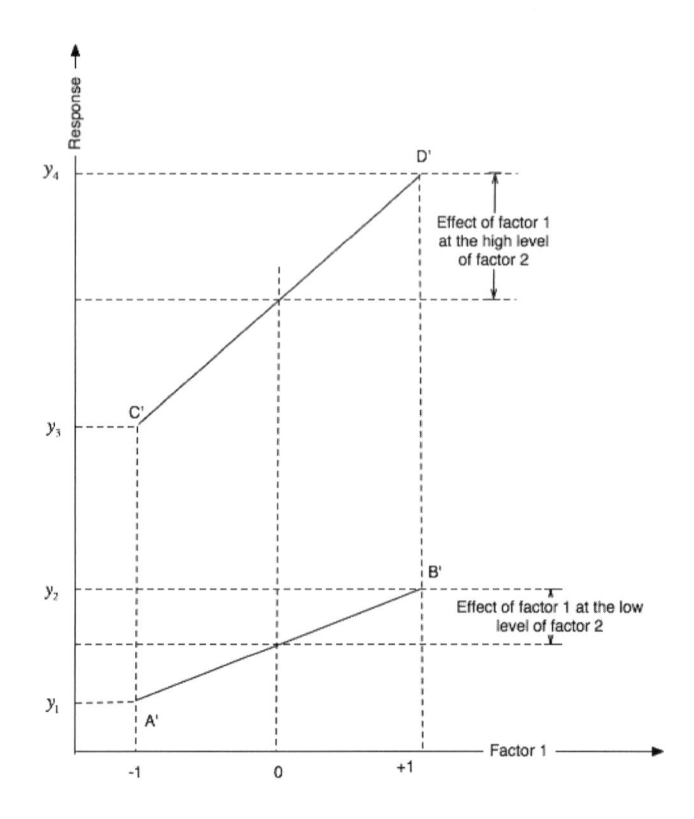

Figure 2.8 Illustration of the interaction effect

If there is no interaction between the two factors, the slopes of the lines A'B' and C'D' are the same. That is, the lines are parallel.

If there is an interaction between the two factors, the slopes of the two preceding lines are not the same. The more different the slopes, the stronger the interaction.

Application
We can therefore calculate the interaction as

$$a_{12} = \frac{1}{4}\left[+y_1 - y_2 - y_3 + y_4\right]$$

$$a_{12} = \frac{1}{4}\left[+30 - 27 - 25 + 21\right] = -0.25$$

The interaction between factors 1 and 2 is –0.25 mile per gallon. This means that the effect of speed is a little higher when the car is loaded. When speed is 45 mph, the effect of the additional weight is –1.5 mpg. When speed is 70 mph, the effect of the additional weight is –2 mpg.

That also means that the effect of the additional weight is more important when driving faster. When driving with no extra load, the effect of speed is –2.5 mpg. When the additional weight is 550 lbs, the effect of speed is –3 mpg (Figure 2.9).

The interaction is half the difference between the effect at high level and the effect at low level, that is to say $\frac{-2-(-1.5)}{2} = -0.25$ or $\frac{-3-(-2.5)}{2} = -0.25$ mpg.

Figure 2.9 Illustration of the interaction between speed and additional weight. This interaction is weak, so the two slopes are almost the same.

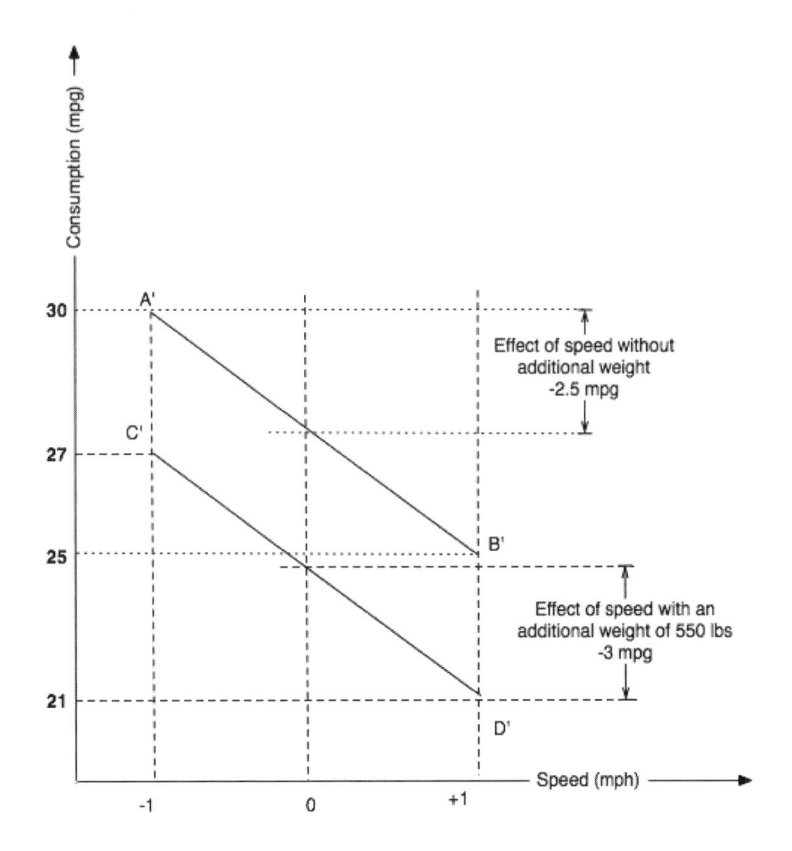

2.2.5 Interpreting the Results

We now know the following values:

- The intercept, $a_0 = 25.75$
- The coefficient of factor 1 (speed), $a_1 = -2.75$
- The coefficient of factor 2 (additional weight), $a_2 = -1.75$
- The interaction a_{12} between the speed and the additional weight, $a_{12} = -0.25$

We can use these values in equation (2.1)

$$y = 25.75 - 2.75x_1 - 1.75x_2 - 0.25x_1x_2 \tag{2.2}$$

It is understood that with this model, we can calculate all the responses in the study domain. It is enough to assign values to the levels x_1 and x_2 to immediately obtain the estimated gas consumption. Since the model is in coded units, we must do the calculations in these units and then transform the obtained results into the natural (engineering) units. To use the natural units directly, we need to transform the model in equation (2.2) itself. In this case, we need only to apply equation (1.1):

$$x = \frac{A - A_0}{\text{step}}$$

Factor 1 (Speed)

$$x_1 = \frac{A_1 - A_{0,1}}{\text{Step}_1} = \frac{A_1 - 57.5}{12.5}$$

Factor 2 (Additional weight)

$$x_2 = \frac{A_2 - A_{0,2}}{\text{Step}_2} = \frac{A_2 - 275}{275}$$

$$y = 25.75 - 2.75\left(\frac{A_1}{12.5} - \frac{57.5}{12.5}\right) - 1.75\left(\frac{A_2}{275} - \frac{275}{275}\right) - 0.25\left(\frac{A_1}{12.5} - \frac{57.5}{12.5}\right)\left(\frac{A_2}{275} - \frac{275}{275}\right)$$

$$y = 25.75 - \frac{2.75 A_1}{12.5} + \frac{2.75 \times 57.5}{12.5} - \frac{1.75 A_2}{275} + 1.75 - 0,25\left(\frac{A_1 A_2}{12.5 \times 275} - \frac{A_1}{12.5} - \frac{57.5 A_2}{12.5 \times 275} + \frac{57.5}{12.5}\right)$$

$$y = 25.75 + \frac{2.75 \times 57.5}{12.5} + 1.75 - \frac{0.25 \times 57.5}{12.5} + \left[-\frac{2.75}{12.5} + \frac{0.25}{12.5} \right] A_1 + \left[-\frac{1.75}{275} + \frac{0.25 \times 57.5}{12.5 \times 275} \right] A_2 - \left[\frac{0.25 A_1}{12.5} \frac{A_2}{275} \right]$$

From this we obtain the model in natural units.

$$y = 39 - 0.2 \; A_1 - 0.0021818 \; A_2 - 0.00007272 A_1 A_2 \qquad (2.3)$$

We can therefore easily answer the questions at the beginning of section 2.2.4 by using either equation (2.2) or equation (2.3).

Application

We asked "What is the consumption of our car when we add 100 lbs and drive at 55 mph?" Apply equation (2.3):

$$y = 39 - 0.2 \times 55 - 0.0021818 \times 100 - 0.00007272 \times 55 \times 100$$

$$y = 39 - 11 - 0.218 - 0.399 = 27.38$$

The answer is that if we drive at 55 mph with a load of 100 lbs, our estimated mileage is 27.38 mpg, or (stated equivalently), we use approximately 0.0365 gallons per mile.

Application

We asked "What is the extra consumption when we drive at 70 mph instead of 55 mph with a weight of 275 lbs?" Start by transforming the natural units into coded units:

55 mph = –0.2 in coded units
70 mph = 1 in coded units
275 lbs = 0 in coded units

Now apply equation (2.2) to calculate the consumption for the two speeds.

$$y = 25.75 - 2.75 \times (-0.2) - 1.75 \times (0) - 0.25 \times (-0.2) \times (0)$$

$$y = 26.30 \text{ mpg}$$

When we drive at level –0.2 (55 mph) with a load of level 0 (275 lbs), the estimated mileage is 26.3 mpg.

$$y = 25.75 - 2.75 \times (1) - 1.75 \times (0) - 0,25 \times (1) \times (0)$$

y = 23 mpg

When we drive at level 1 (70 mph) with a load at level 0 (275 lbs), the estimated mileage is 23 mpg.

The answer is therefore: with a load of 275 lbs, the mileage is decreased by $y = 26.3 - 23 = 3.3$ mpg when the driving speed increases from 55 mph to 70 mph.

In this way, it is possible to answer questions like these and many others involving speed and load. However, these calculations are repetitive, trivial, and tiresome, and they do not teach us much about the process. Our efforts could be used in much more productive tasks than simple calculations. This is why we advise you to use software such as JMP for designed experiments. All the calculations that you have seen (and many others) are carried out easily and rapidly. Computers also draw graphs that emphasize and clarify the characteristic principles of the study. They multiply the experimenter's power of reasoning and carry out calculations that are impossible by hand. In fact, as soon as the number of factors increases by just a small number, the calculations become inordinately complicated and the use of software makes the experimenter's task easier.

As an example, the two following diagrams show the power of software. Both were generated by JMP. The first diagram (Figure 2.10) shows the effect of the two factors (speed and additional weight), as well as the corresponding value of the response. This plot is interactive; you can choose any desired levels within the study domain. The response value is shown for each pair of letters. We can therefore easily answer the first question without being obliged to make detailed calculations. This same diagram also makes it possible to answer the second question.

Figure 2.10 Value of the response for a speed of 55 mph and an additional weight of 275 lbs

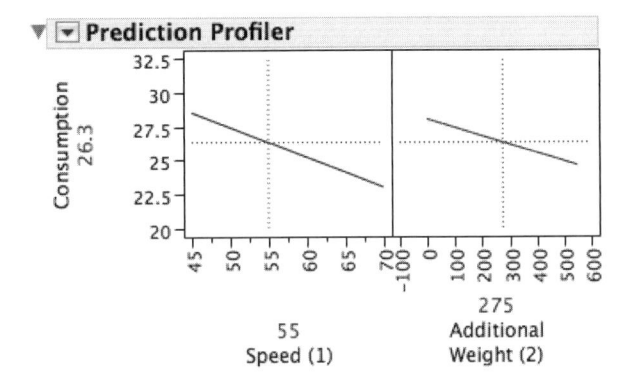

The second diagram (Figure 2.11) shows contour curves in the study domain using the Contour Plot facility in JMP. The curve labeled 25 shows all the combinations of speed and of additional weight that generate a mileage of 25 mpg. If I want to attain 27 mpg, the graph shows the necessary changes in speed due to the additional weight: for example, if the additional weight is 300 lbs, the speed never needs to exceed 51 mph.

Figure 2.11 With an additional weight of 300 lbs, speed will be limited to 51 mph in order to drive 27 miles with one gallon.

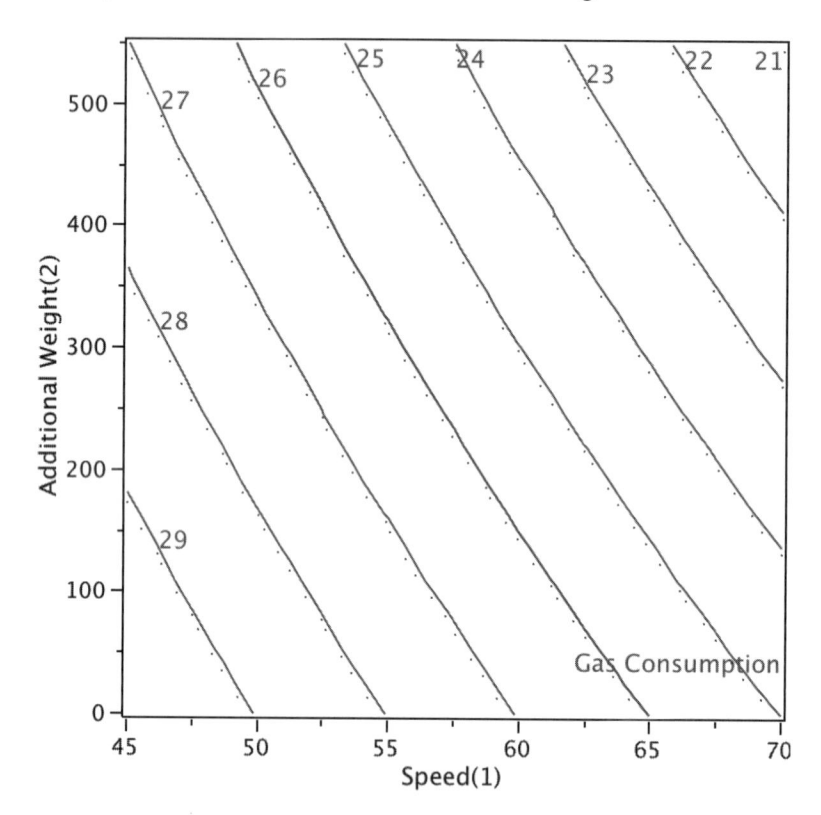

To carry out these calculations and produce these plots yourself, see Chapter 14 and the book's companion Web site at support.sas.com/goupycreighton. There you can find detailed explanations that demonstrate these techniques. The example data tables from this book are also found at this site.

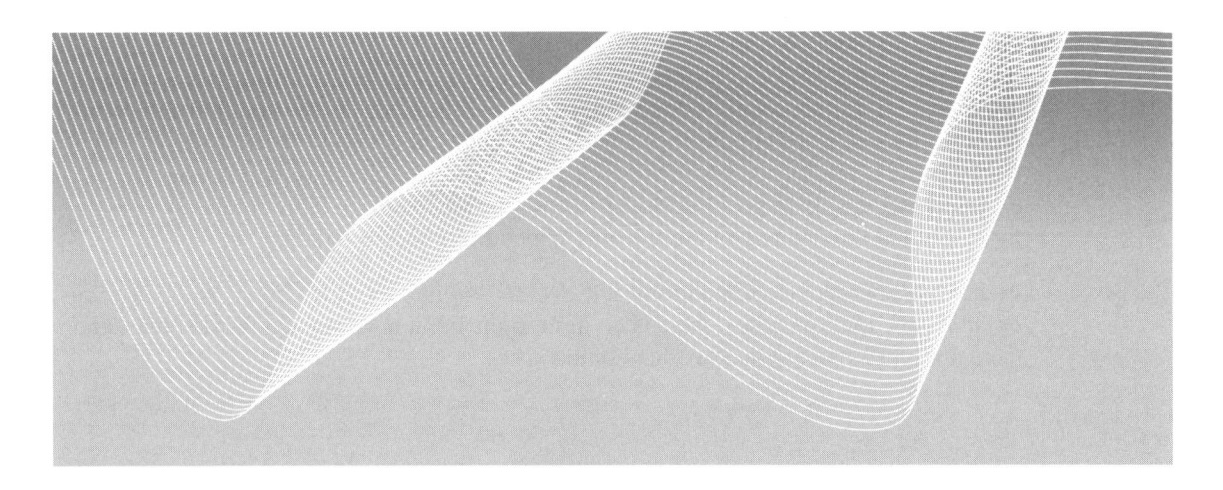

Chapter 3

A Three-Factor Designed Experiment

3.1 Introduction 45
3.2 Example 2: Gold Jewelry 46
    3.2.1 Preparing the Designed Experiment 46
    3.2.2 Choosing the Design 51
    3.2.3 Running the Experiment 53
    3.2.4 Interpreting the Results 54
    3.2.5 Study Conclusion 67

3.1 Introduction

Chapter 2 shows how to glean a lot of information with a simple two-factor, four-point design. If so much information can be extracted with a two-factor study, it's easy to see that a multi-factor study can be even more fruitful. We therefore describe a multi-factor study in this chapter. We start with three factors and work our way up to a study using seven factors. The principles are the same, regardless of the number of factors, so it is possible to explore even more factors than we do here. In fact, it's easy to find published articles or conference proceedings involving designs of more than 10 factors. At that point, the difficulties arise not from the theory, but from the implementation and control of the factor levels during the experiment. Take an example of 11 factors, where 110 levels must be carefully controlled for each trial, and imagine the effort needed to examine each result. With 12 trials, 132 levels are involved. In large studies such as these, a small error in any of these levels can compromise the study.

In the case of computer simulations, it's easy to program the calculations and be certain of the levels. In these cases, there is no limit to the number of studied factors, but rather there are limits that are due to other complexities.

3.2 Example 2: Gold Jewelry

3.2.1 Preparing the Designed Experiment

Gold is prized because it never tarnishes, always keeping its brilliant polish. However, it is quite expensive, so many objects are merely covered in a thin gold film, giving them a solid gold appearance and protection without the high cost. Gold-plated jewelry is covered with a thin layer of gold that must look identical to solid gold, and also have mechanical resistance to ensure a long life.

In the plating process, the deposits are laid down using electrolysis. The metal to be covered in gold is connected to a battery cathode and submerged in a solution containing a gold salt (Figure 3.1). These deposits must mimic gold's mechanical ability to withstand the various abuses that jewelry encounters every day. To increase the quality of the deposition, manufacturers add other metals and additives to form alloys as by-products. The most useful alloys are generally based in nickel or cobalt. In this example, we examine alloys of gold and cobalt. To do this, we make a solution of electrolytes containing the cyanides of both metals.

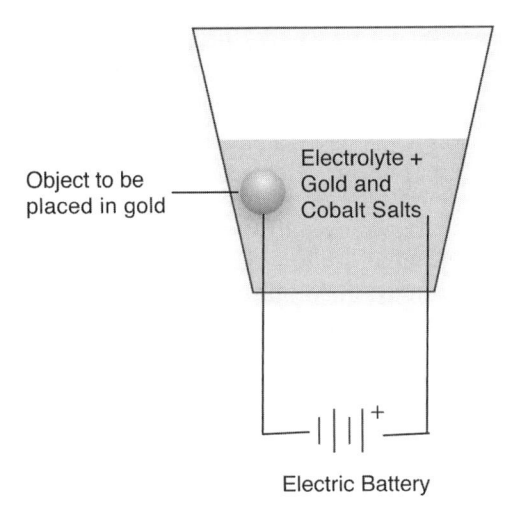

Figure 3.1 General diagram of gold deposits using electrolysis

Object to be placed in gold

Electrolyte + Gold and Cobalt Salts

Electric Battery

3.2.1.1 Defining the Study Objective
The study objectives are:

- Carry out the deposition as quickly as possible while maintaining quality.
- Obtain an alloy cobalt concentration ranging from 3500 to 4500 parts per million (ppm).

A successful study gives factor settings that achieve both of these goals.

3.2.1.2 Choosing the Responses to Reach the Goal
The first response corresponds to the first objective. Therefore, we choose the deposition speed and measure it in milligrams per minute (mg/min). To ensure the profitability of the process, the deposition speed must be no less than 80 mg/min.

The second response corresponds to the second objective. Therefore, we choose the cobalt content of the alloy, measured in ppm. To ensure the quality of the deposit, the cobalt content of the alloy must be between 3500 and 4500 ppm.

3.2.1.3 Search for Factors That May Influence the Responses

What are factors that might change the deposition speed and the cobalt content of the alloy? It's necessary to think about any factor that could alter the response. Frequently, a fishbone diagram (also known as an Ishikawa diagram) is used. See Figure 3.2. These diagrams are commonly associated with parts of the Six-Sigma DMAIC (Design, Measure, Analyze, Improve, Control) methodology.

In designing a study, we need to choose factors that might have influence on the responses. For example, we first ask ourselves if the raw materials may have an influence. In this study, the origin and the purity of the gold salt can change the results, as could the type or brand of salt. The same goes for the cobalt, any additives, the water, and even the electric current.

After examining the raw materials, we turn to the manufacturing methods, i.e., the operating conditions: amperage and voltage of the electric current, continuous electrolysis vs. sequential electrolysis, and so on. This systematic search of the factors makes it possible to examine the problem from all sides and keeps us from forgetting a factor that may have a large influence.

Figure 3.2 Simplified example of an Ishikawa diagram

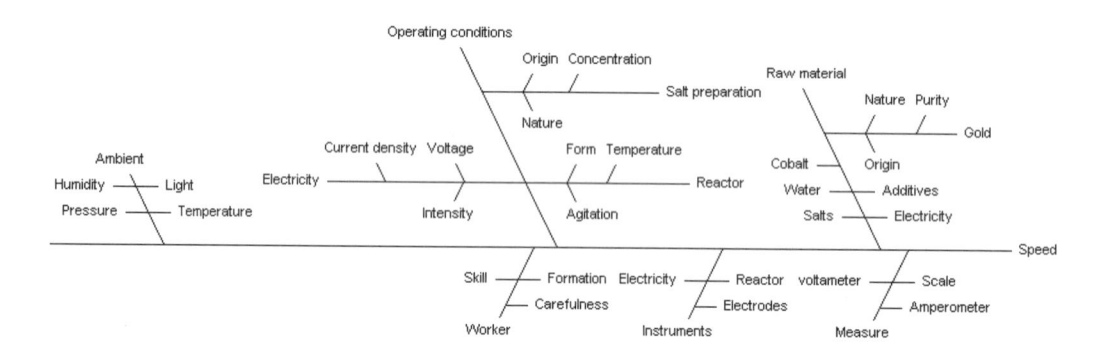

Let's build an Ishikawa diagram showing some factors that may be influential. We've already started a list of these factors above. The actual researchers who carried out this study made a much more comprehensive list.

- The temperature of the electrolytic solution
- The pH of the electrolytic solution
- The gold concentration of the electrolyte

- The kind and the concentration of the additives added to the electrolyte
- The cobalt concentration of the electrolyte
- The kind of mount
- The surface of the mount
- The movement of the mount
- The position of the electrodes
- The form of the reactor
- The agitation of the solution
- The form of the electrodes
- The amperage, voltage, and density of the electric current

Starting with this list, we choose the factors that are thought to be influential and divide them into two categories: the factors to be studied using a designed experiment, and those that are not studied during the experiment, but whose levels are fixed at a constant value. In this study, three factors are used to construct the designed experiment:

- The gold concentration of the electrolytic solution
- The cobalt concentration of the electrolytic solution
- The current density

Other selected factors that may change the responses are fixed at a constant level throughout the trials. For example, in this experiment, the following are fixed:

- The pH at 4.5
- The kind and origin of the salts
- The kind and origin of the additives
- The reactor and the electrodes
- The electric conditions of the electrolysis
- The temperature of the electrolytic bath

The factors that remain fixed during the experiment and the factors used in the design are the *controlled factors*. All other factors are *uncontrolled factors*. If the uncontrolled factors have a small influence or if they stay at the same level during all the trials, they cause only small variations in the response. These uncontrolled factors are the source of the *experimental error*. If, by random chance, an influential factor is not taken into account and changes level during the experiment, the experimental error would grow considerably, and the study might be compromised. Therefore, it is necessary to be vigilant when establishing the list of factors to be used in trials, making sure not to forget any important ones. One advantage of designed experiments, compared to one-factor-at-a-time methods, is that the experimenter is forced to think about the problem and to specifically avoid the omission of important factors.

3.2.1.4 Defining the Factor Levels

Defining factor levels boils down to choosing the high and low levels of the three (in this example) factors selected:

- Gold concentration in the electrolytic solution (in grams per liter, g/L)
- Current density (in amperes per square decimeter, A/dm^2)
- Cobalt concentration in the electrolytic solution (in grams per liter, g/L)

It's a good idea to summarize these levels in a table (Table 3.1).

Table 3.1 Factors and study domain

Factor	Low Level (-)	High Level (+)
Gold concentration (1)	2 g/L	15 g/L
Density of the current (2)	5 A/dm^2	25 A/dm^2
Cobalt concentration (3)	0.5 g/L	1.5 g/L

The importance of precisely specifying the endpoints of the study domain cannot be overemphasized. It is crucial to know their specific values when using computer software. The conclusions of the study are valid only in the interior of this study domain. Outside, it is possible to guess at the results, but these results should never be regarded as true predictions, and should not be used to draw conclusions without holding additional verification trials.

3.2.2 Choosing the Design

Since we have three factors each taking two levels, and since we think that a linear model is sufficient to explain the phenomena, a 2^3 factorial design is used.

$$y = a_0 + a_1 x_1 + a_2 x_2 + a_3 x_3 + a_{12} x_1 x_2 + a_{13} x_1 x_3 + a_{23} x_2 x_3 + a_{123} x_1 x_2 x_3 \qquad (3.1)$$

We will see that if a quadratic (i.e., second-degree) model is suspected, a different design would be chosen.

The notation 2^3 has the following significance. The 3 in the exponent represents the number of factors, and the 2 in the base represents the number of levels of each factor.

The design can be represented in an illustration (Figure 3.3) by specifying the study domain and the experimental points. The coordinates of the experimental points are the high and low levels of the factors. This is equivalent to representing the plan with a matrix, the experimental matrix (in engineering units) or the design matrix (in coded units).

Figure 3.3 Illustration of the designed experiment

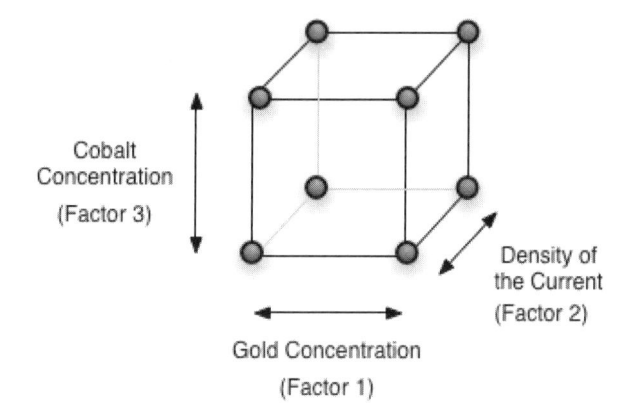

The experimental matrix (Table 3.2) contains six columns: the trial numbers, the three factors, and the two responses.

Table 3.2 Experimental matrix

Trial	Gold Concentration (g/L)	Density of the Current (A/dm^2)	Cobalt Concentration (g/L)	Speed (mg/min)	Cobalt Content (ppm)
	Factor 1	*Factor 2*	*Factor 3*		
1	2	5	0.5		
2	15	5	0.5		
3	2	25	0.5		
4	15	25	0.5		
5	2	5	1.5		
6	15	5	1.5		
7	2	25	1.5		
8	15	25	1.5		

The design matrix (Table 3.3) also contains six columns, but two lines have been added to specify the meaning of −1 and +1.

Table 3.3 Design matrix

Trial	Gold Concentration (g/L)	Density of the Current (A/dm^2)	Cobalt Concentration (g/L)	Speed (mg/min)	Cobalt Content (ppm)
	Factor 1	*Factor 2*	*Factor 3*		
1	−1	−1	−1		
2	+1	−1	−1		
3	−1	+1	−1		
4	+1	+1	−1		
5	−1	−1	+1		
6	+1	−1	+1		
7	−1	+1	+1		
8	+1	+1	+1		
−1 Level	2 g/L	5 A/dm^2	0.5 g/L		
+1 Level	15 g/L	25 A/dm^2	1.5 g/L		

For the interpretation of the test results, use either the experimental matrix or the design matrix according to characteristics that you are interested in.

3.2.3 Running the Experiment

After the tests are carried out in accordance with the experimental design, the results are recorded in the design matrix (Table 3.4).

Table 3.4 Design matrix and results

Trial	Gold Concentration (g/L)	Density of the Current (A/dm²)	Cobalt Concentration (g/L)	Speed (mg/min)	Cobalt Content (ppm)
	Factor 1	Factor 2	Factor 3		
1	−1	−1	−1	53	4100
2	+1	−1	−1	122	3510
3	−1	+1	−1	20	3950
4	+1	+1	−1	125	1270
5	−1	−1	+1	48	4870
6	+1	−1	+1	70	2810
7	−1	+1	+1	68	7750
8	+1	+1	+1	134	3580
−1 Level	2 g/L	5 A/dm²	0.5 g/L		
+1 Level	15 g/L	25 A/dm²	1.5 g/L		

3.2.4 Interpreting the Results

The model we assumed above, for a 2^3 factorial, is shown again here:

$$y = a_0 + a_1 x_1 + a_2 x_2 + a_3 x_3 + a_{12} x_1 x_2 + a_{13} x_1 x_3 + a_{23} x_2 x_3 + a_{123} x_1 x_2 x_3 \quad (3.1)$$

In this model,

y is one of the responses.

x_i represents the levels of the factors that take only one of two possible values.

a_i are the effects of the factors.

a_{ij} are the second-order interactions.

a_{123} is the third-order interaction.

Initially, we examine each factor separately.

3.2.4.1 Deposition Speed

We report the results of deposition speed inside the study domain (Figure 3.4). According to engineers, the speed of 80 mg/min is easily obtained and it is even possible to increase this speed. The maximum speed is around 134 mg/min. Note that high speeds tend to be associated with high gold concentrations.

Figure 3.4 Value of the deposition speed at the corners of the study domain

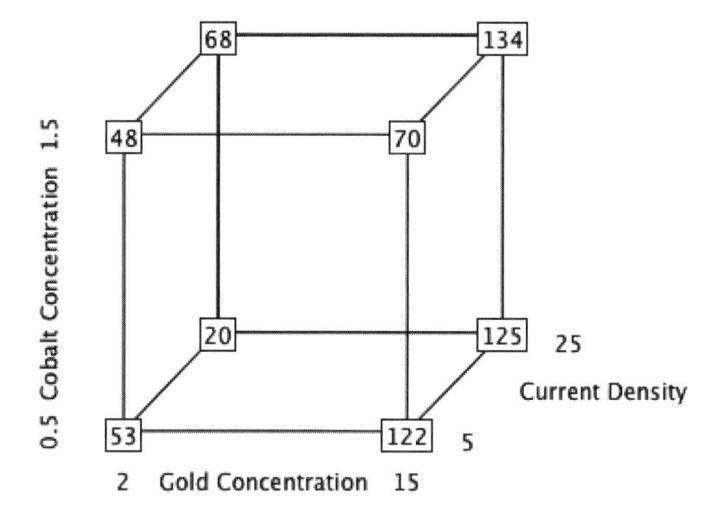

To further interpret and understand the results, the phenomena must be statistically modeled, and therefore we must calculate the various quantities (like the coefficients) of the linear model. We start by calculating the effects of the factors and their interactions (Table 3.5).

Table 3.5 Effects and interactions of the factors (coded units)
Response: Deposition speed

Effect	Value
Intercept	80
Gold concentration (1)	32.75
Current density (2)	6.75
Cobalt concentration (3)	0
1×2 Interaction	10
1×3 Interaction	−10.75
2×3 Interaction	14.25
1×2×3 Interaction	1

Factor 1, gold concentration, is the most influential. Factors 2 and 3 are not directly influential, but they are influential via their second-order interactions. The three second-order interaction terms are close to one another except for the difference in sign. The third-order interaction is small by comparison. These results allow us to write the model giving deposition speed according to the levels of the three factors (in coded units):

$$y_{speed} = 80 + 32.75 x_1 + 6.75 x_2 + 10 x_1 x_2 - 10.75 x_1 x_3 + 14.25 x_2 x_3 + x_1 x_2 x_3 \quad (3.2)$$

We use this equation to make calculations and to draw graphs.

Figure 3.5 shows a bar chart that allows us to quickly see the relative importance of the factors. In addition, it shows an equivalent chart from a JMP analysis report.

Figure 3.5 Illustrations of Table 3.5

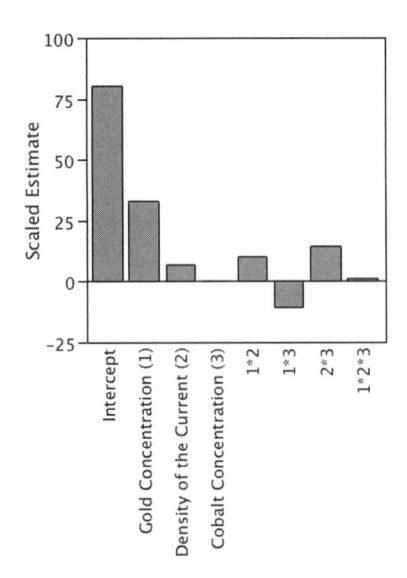

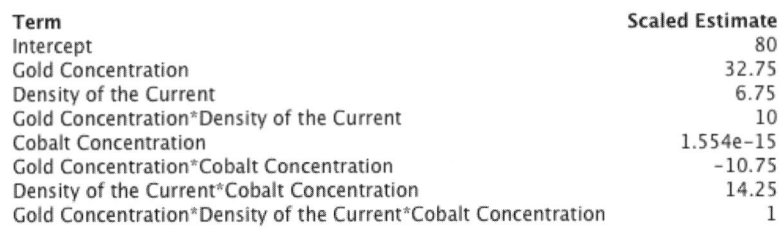

Term	Scaled Estimate
Intercept	80
Gold Concentration	32.75
Density of the Current	6.75
Gold Concentration*Density of the Current	10
Cobalt Concentration	1.554e-15
Gold Concentration*Cobalt Concentration	-10.75
Density of the Current*Cobalt Concentration	14.25
Gold Concentration*Density of the Current*Cobalt Concentration	1

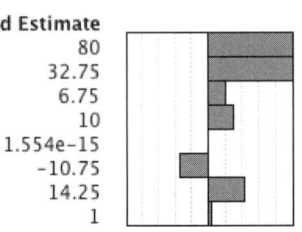

Two other diagrams are useful for a deeper understanding of the influence of the factors: the *effect diagram* (called the *prediction profiler* in JMP), which indicates the principal effects of the factors, and the *interaction diagram* (called the *interaction profiler* in JMP), which shows the second-order interactions among the factors.

Effect Diagram (Prediction Profiler)

The prediction profiler shows the principal effects of the factors, i.e., the coefficients of the first-degree terms of the mathematical model. The diagram can be constructed with coded units or with engineering units (Figure 3.6), since the appearance is the same. When presenting results, it is much easier to use the engineering units, which give immediate values for comparison.

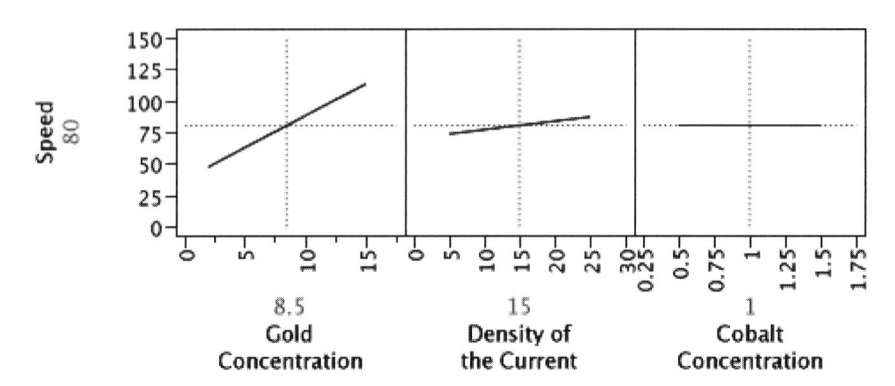

Figure 3.6 Effect of the factors on the response

[Graph showing Speed (y-axis, 0-150) vs three factors: Gold Concentration (centered at 8.5), Density of the Current (centered at 15), and Cobalt Concentration (centered at 1). The gold concentration line rises steeply, the current density line rises slightly, and the cobalt concentration line is flat.]

The deposition rate grows larger as the solution contains more gold and as the current density is slightly raised. The cobalt concentration of the electrolytic solution does not seem to play any part in the reaction. But, to have a complete interpretation of the results, we have to take the interactions into account, and we have seen that they are not negligible.

Interaction Diagram (Interaction Profiler)

An interaction diagram shows the effects of a factor at low and high levels on another factor. The diagram in Figure 3.7 can be interpreted as follows.

The response is shown on the *y*-axis and the scales of the factors are on the *x*-axis. In the upper right square, the effect of the current density factor is shown for low (2) and high (15) levels of gold concentration. In the lower left square, the gold concentration factor is shown for low (5) and high (25) levels of the current density factor.

If the lines are not parallel, there is a significant interaction. This is the case for two factors where the slopes of the effects are different, and the lines cross each other.

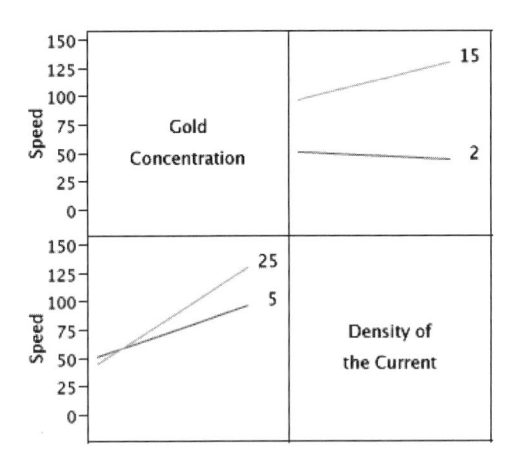

Figure 3.7 Interaction profile illustrating the importance of the interactions

We could also present the interaction plot by taking the interactions two at a time and drawing them in a single table as in Figure 3.8.

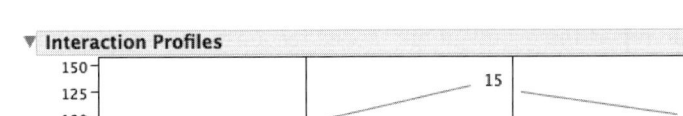

Figure 3.8 Interaction profiles regrouped into a single table

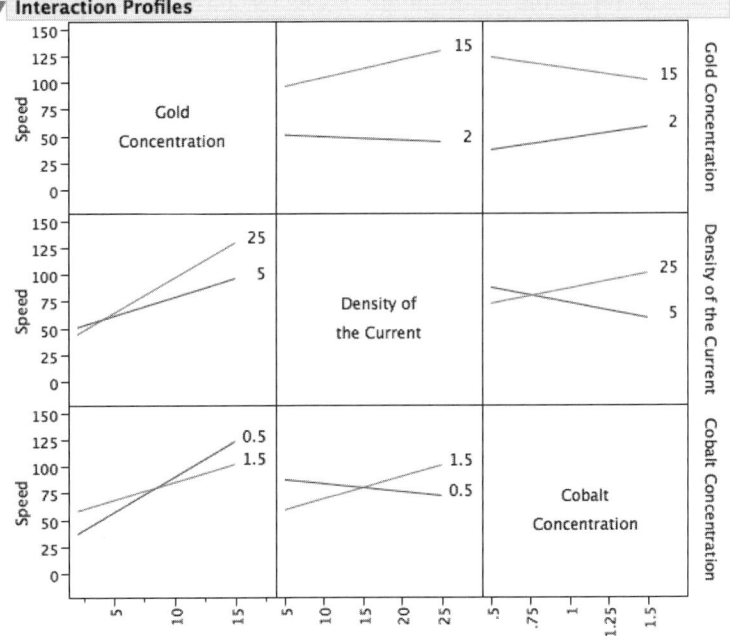

The interaction plot clearly shows that the interactions are not negligible and that they must be taken into account during the interpretation of the results.

The maximum deposition speed is attained when the three factors are at their high levels: 15 g/L of gold, 1.5 g/L of cobalt in the electrolytic solution, and a current density of 25 A/dm^2 (Figure 3.9), which gives a deposition speed of 134.

Figure 3.9 The highest deposition speed is attained when the three factors are at their high levels.

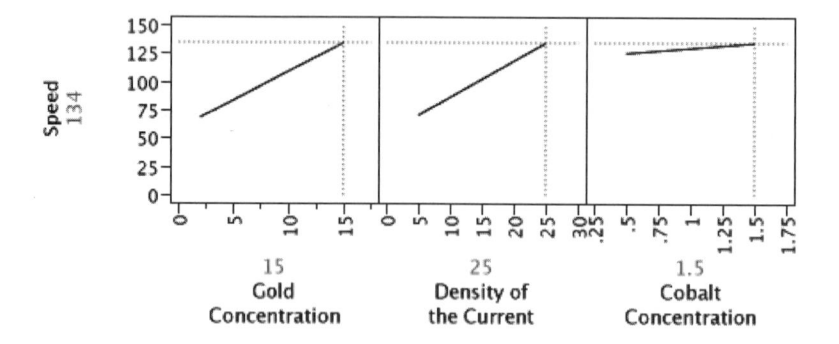

3.2.4.2 Alloy Cobalt Content

We can report the results of the second response, the alloy cobalt content (Figure 3.10), in the same way.

Strong alloy cobalt contents are obtained when the gold concentration is weak in the electrolytic solution. Note also that the cobalt content in the electrolyte increases with both the current density and the cobalt concentration.

Figure 3.10 Value of the alloy cobalt content response at the corners of the study domain

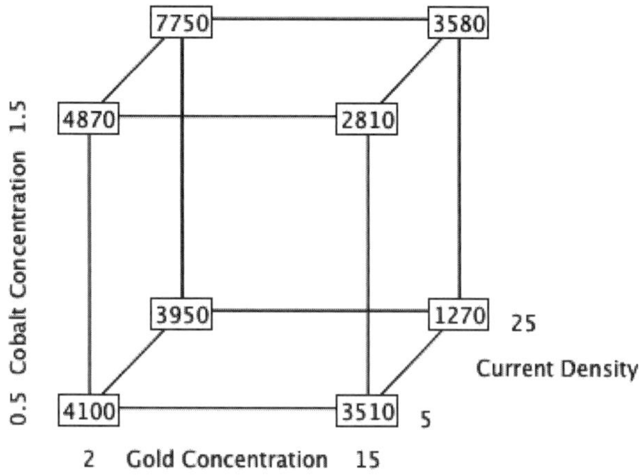

```
                    7750─────────3580
                   ╱│            ╱│
              4870─────────2810  │
               │  │          │   │
   1.5         │  │          │   │
Cobalt         │  │          │   │
Concentration  │  3950───────│──1270   25
               │ ╱           │ ╱    Current Density
   0.5        4100──────────3510    5
              2    Gold Concentration   15
```

Now examine the effects of the factors and their interactions (Table 3.6).

Table 3.6 Effects and interactions (in coded units) for the alloy cobalt content response

Effect	Value
Intercept	3980
Gold concentration (1)	−1187.5
Current density (2)	157.5
Cobalt concentration	772.5
1×2 Interaction	−525
1×3 Interaction	−370
2×3 Interaction	755
1×2×3 Interaction	−2.5

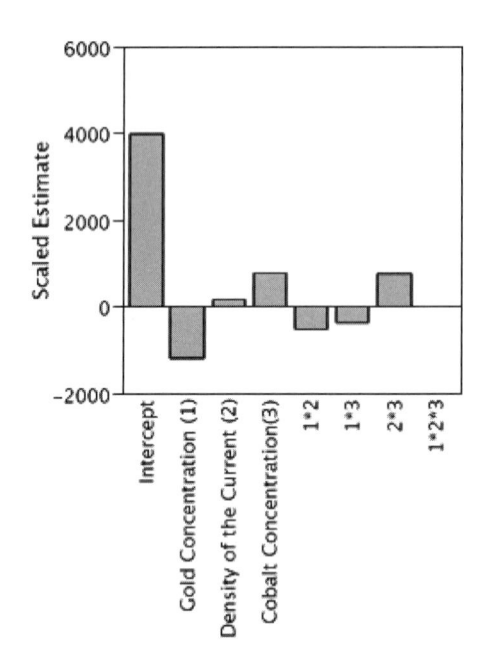

Figure 3.11 Illustration of Table 3.6

Gold concentration (factor 1) and cobalt concentration (factor 3) are the most influential (Figure 3.11). However, they have opposite signs. The effect of gold concentration is negative, which means that the response decreases as this factor changes from its low level to its high level. The effect of factor 3 is positive, which means that the response increases when this factor moves from its low level to its high level. Second-order interactions are important (Figure 3.12), but the third-order interaction is not.

With these results, we can write the model relating alloy cobalt concentration as a function of the levels of the three factors (coded units):

$$y_{cobalt} = 3980 - 1187.5x_1 + 157.5x_2 + 772.5x_1 - 525x_1x_2 - 370x_1x_3 + 755x_2x_3 - 2.5x_1x_2x_3 \quad (3.3)$$

This equation is used by software like JMP to carry out calculations and draw graphs.

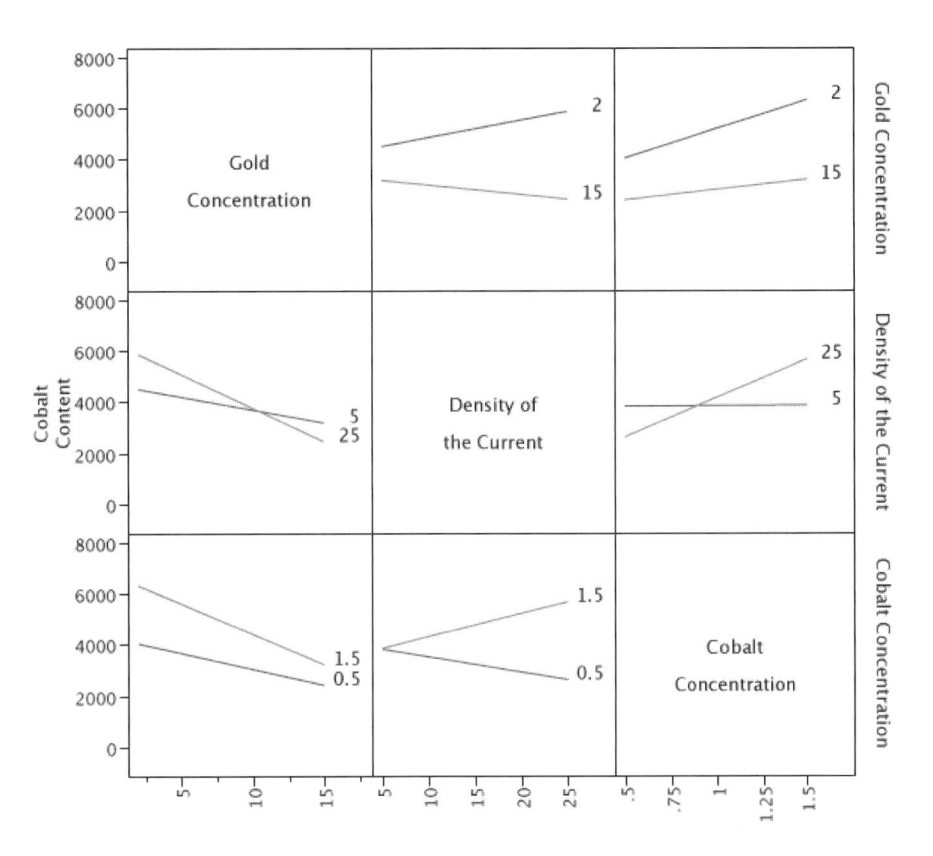

Figure 3.12 Interaction profiles for the alloy cobalt content response

The alloy cobalt concentration must lie between 3500 and 4500 ppm. These two values can be reached since the response varies from 1270 to 7750 ppm in the interior of the study domain. To get a bird's eye view of the response, we must draw the isoresponse curves of the response surface corresponding to the two most influential factors: gold concentration and cobalt concentration (see Figure 3.13). The 4000 ppm curve is drawn and the limits of 3500 and 4500 ppm are also shown.

The shaded zones are outside the objective and the non-shaded zones represent all the combinations of concentrations that allow the objective to be attained. The diagram is drawn for three levels of current density: 5, 15, and 25 A/dm^2. In general, higher current densities narrow the zone of appropriate responses.

These diagrams can be constructed with statistical software such as JMP.

Figure 3.13 The objective of alloy cobalt content is not obtained in the shaded areas.

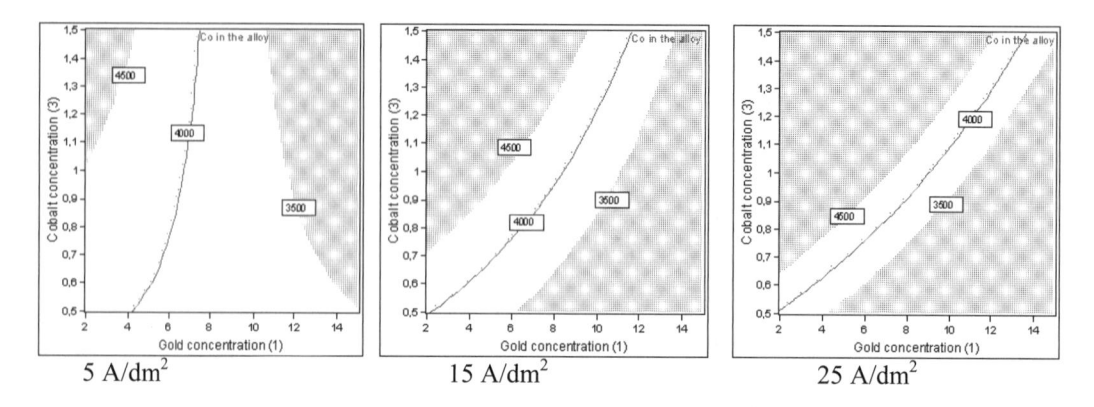

$5 \text{ A/dm}^2 \qquad 15 \text{ A/dm}^2 \qquad 25 \text{ A/dm}^2$

3.2.4.3 Finding Operating Conditions for Both Objectives

Since there are two objectives, a deposition speed of at least 80 mg/min and an alloy cobalt content between 3500 ppm and 4500 ppm, we are going to superimpose the results of the deposition speed onto the results of the alloy cobalt content (5 A/dm^2 15 A/dm^2 25 A/dm^2). We're also going to rule out speeds less than 80 mg/min.

For weak current densities, note that weak gold concentrations are removed. Therefore, there is only one useful area on the contour graph of strong gold concentrations and weak cobalt concentrations.

For average current densities, also note that the zone of weak gold concentrations is removed. Therefore, there is only one zone where both objectives are respected: the zone with strong gold concentrations and weak cobalt concentrations.

For strong current densities, the zone of weak gold concentrations is removed. There is therefore only one zone that appears in the average current densities.

The zones that appear in the non-shaded zones, taken together, allow us to respond to the two objectives of the study. The experimenter, then, has a broad range of solutions and can choose the solution that answers any additional constraint, like a solution that gives a better surface appearance, or one that is more economical.

Figure 3.14 The objectives are attained in the non-shaded areas

5 A/dm²   15 A/dm²   25 A/dm²

3.2.4.4 Can We Do Better?

We could ask ourselves, "Under what conditions could we work faster, say, at 100 mg/min?" The answer: simply replace the 80 mg/min speed with 100 mg/min. This results in contours similar to those shown in Figure 3.15.

Figure 3.15 With a deposition speed of 100 mg/min, the objectives are achieved only in the two non-shaded areas.

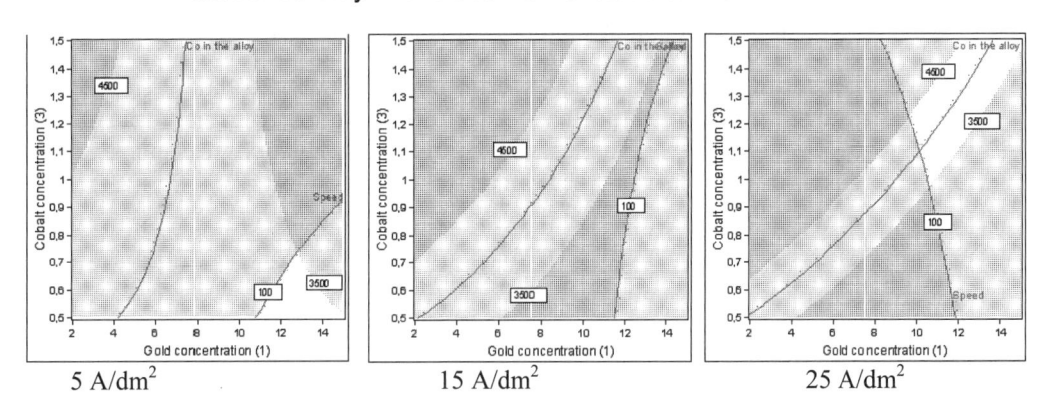

5 A/dm²   15 A/dm²   25 A/dm²

To work at 100 mg/min, the current density must be either weak or strong. There are no settings if the density is in the middle.

For weak current densities, a strong gold concentration and a weak cobalt concentration are chosen.

For strong current densities, both a strong gold concentration and a strong cobalt concentration are needed.

The experimenter can use JMP to use the previously established model to make predictions for these operating conditions. For example, solutions using strong current densities can be chosen, which allow the use of cobalt concentrations of 4000 ppm. Low current densities don't allow this option. We cannot make this conclusion, however, without running verification trials. One or more control experiments must be made (Figure 3.16). Constant factors are set at their levels, and experimental variables follow the following design:

- Gold concentration in the electrolytic solution is maintained at 12 g/L.
- Cobalt concentration in the electrolytic solution is maintained at 1.3 g/L.
- Current density is set at 24 A/dm^2.

With our previously established model, the experimenter can calculate the corresponding speed to be 115 mg/min and the alloy cobalt content to be 4011 ppm.

For verification, two control experiments under these conditions are carried out. They result in a deposition speed of 110 and 105 mg/min and an alloy cobalt concentration of 3950 and 3920 ppm. These results confirm the predictions. Recommendations can therefore be made using these increased-speed results.

Figure 3.16 Predictions of the responses indicate that the objectives can be obtained if the gold concentration in the electrolyte is 12 m/L and the concentration of the cobalt is 1.3 mg/L for a current density of 25 A/dm^2.

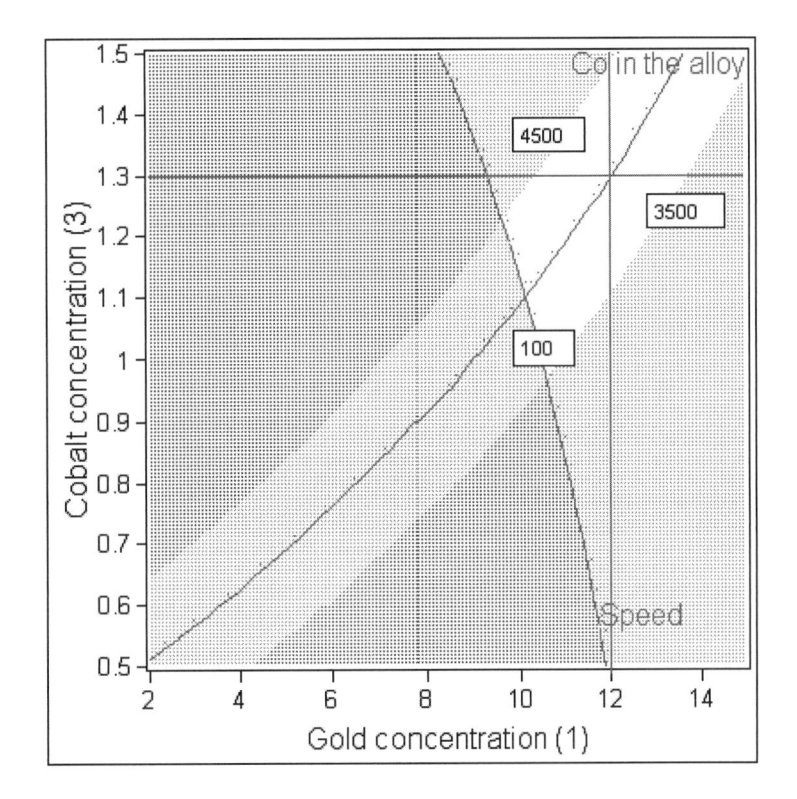

3.2.5 Study Conclusion

We specified the operating conditions allowing gold deposition at the quality requirements defined at the beginning of the study. We stated the material, the nature, origin and property of the raw materials, the implementation of the raw materials, and the levels of the factors that were fixed during the experimentation. Finally, we stated the settings of the four principal factors:

- The pH of the electrolytic solution is set at 4.5.
- The gold concentration of the electrolytic solution is set at 12 g/L.

- The cobalt concentration of the electrolytic solution is set at 1.3 g/L.
- The current density is set at 25 A/dm^2.

Under these conditions, we should get a deposition speed greater than 100 mg/min and an alloy cobalt content around 3900 ppm. The objectives of the study were not only met, but even surpassed.

Chapter 4

Four-Factor Full-Factorial Experiments

    4.1 Introduction 69
    4.2 Example 3: The Galette des Rois 70
        4.2.1 Preparing the Designed Experiment 70
        4.2.2 Choosing the Design 73
        4.2.3 Running the Experiment 74
        4.2.4 Interpreting the Results 76
        4.2.5 Desirability Functions 83
        4.2.6 Study Conclusion 91

4.1 Introduction

Previous chapters highlighted a complete factorial design with both two and three factors. In these two designs, the factors had only two levels: low and high. The first design was a 2^2 factorial (two factors each taking two levels). The second design was a 2^3 factorial (three factors each taking two levels). We now explore a design utilizing four factors, each taking two levels, i.e., a 2^4 design. The number of trials is therefore 16, which is still reasonable. As the number of factors increases in factorial designs, the number of trials increases exponentially with the number of factors. For five factors, a full factorial contains 32 trials, and for six factors, 64 trials. It is thus rare to carry out a full-factorial design having more than five or six factors. We will see that it is possible, making certain assumptions, to reduce the number of trials without decreasing the number of factors. Fractional-factorial designs (Chapters 6 and 7) were invented to solve this problem.

In this chapter, our example is a straightforward and uncomplicated design. However, its interpretation is neither typical nor rote, and the experimenter should use subject-area knowledge and common sense to make a good recommendation. The experimenter will present different alternatives to the decision makers so that the company can make the best choice.

France has a holiday tradition that involves a pastry called *la galette des rois*, which is sold by retailers from the end of December throughout January. This cake has one exceptional difference from most: during preparation, a small bean is mixed into the pastry. Family and friends come together to eat the cake, and the father or mother of the house divides the cake among the people in attendance. The youngest child faces away from the cake, and the cake cutter asks, "Who gets this piece?" after each cut. The child then says, for example, "my sister." The piece of cake is given to the sister. This continues until the entire cake is gone, and the person who has the bean in his or her cake is pronounced the king or queen of the evening, receiving applause and congratulations. Children, of course, adore the galette des rois and really hope to be named king or queen (although, secretly, adults like it too). During this process, children are told to make a completely random choice, so the galette des rois is a good initiation into statistical science.

This example will allow us to present a useful method of optimization for several criteria: the *desirability function*.

4.2 Example 3: The Galette des Rois

4.2.1 Preparing the Designed Experiment

4.2.1.1 Study Description
The galette des rois is prepared from a special puff pastry that is spread onto a sheet pan until it is about half an inch thick. It is then cut into circles. These pastry circles are

called *layers*. To make a galette, two layers are needed. On the first, lower layer, the baker spreads a good dose of almond paste and places the bean so that it is perfectly hidden. The baker then covers this with the second layer, which is then *docked*, that is, pierced repeatedly so that steam can escape through the numerous small holes. The galette is placed in an evenly heated, constant-temperature oven to bake for 30 minutes.

This study is concerned only with industrially produced galettes, which, once baked, are frozen and distributed to retail stores. As they are removed from the oven, each galette is examined. Only those that don't show defects are frozen. They are then conditioned and distributed to sellers, always maintaining the freezing temperature. Galettes are usually purchased within three weeks of manufacture, but these have a four-week shelf life.

Some galettes unfortunately have separated layers or slits in the layers, resulting in dissatisfied clients who return them to get a replacement cake. The principal complaint is that the galettes reveal the bean; therefore, the magic of the cake is completely ruined.

Before facing such a travesty, the manufacturer immediately reacts by convening a panel of its best technicians. They analyze the situation and decide to conduct a study without delay to find the origin of these two faults. Galettes should not show any defects for four weeks after they leave the bakery. The two defects of concern are the separation and the slits, which in bakery jargon are called *pipes*.

4.2.1.2 Study Objective
The objective of the study is to find fabrication conditions that allow the reduction or, if possible, the elimination of the separations and pipes in frozen galettes having a four-week shelf life.

4.2.1.3 Responses
Choosing a response that allows precise measurement of the magnitude of interest and assigning it a grade is quite often difficult to do. Here, the measure of separation has several difficulties. The separation is irregular, and often there are several areas of separation of differing sizes in the same cake. Some areas adhere completely, others half adhere, and some are completely separated. Attempts at measuring separation via length, depth, and thickness are often unsuccessful. Similar problems arise when measuring pipes. Some are broader than others, some deeper than others, and some straighter than others. Rather than using a numerical response, we establish a scale with defect tests, which makes it possible to rate each galette involved in the study.

Separation is estimated on a scale between 0 and 3, where 3 is most desirable, and is the absence of any separation. A rating of 0 is the worst possible separation seen.

Piping is also measured on a scale between 0 to 3, where 3 is most desirable, representing an absence of piping. A rating of 0 is a galette possessing a large number of pipes.

The objective, therefore, is a 3 rating for both separation and piping.

4.2.1.4 Factors and Study Domain

The manufacturer and his team drew up the list of all the factors that may influence the appearance of defects. Then they selected those that they thought likely to cause the two defects.

Factor 1: Ratio of weight of the layers. That is, the ratio $\dfrac{\text{weight of the upper layer}}{\text{weight of the lower layer}}$

    Low level: 0.9

    High level: 1.1

Factor 2: Number of holes in the upper layer

    Low level: Few

    High level: Many

Factor 3: Heat profile of the baking oven

    Low level: High at the start

    High level: High at the end

Factor 4: Baking time

    Low level: 29 minutes

    High level: 31 minutes

The factors and their levels are shown in Table 4.1.

Table 4.1 Factors and study domain

Factor	Low Level	Middle Level	High Level
Layer weight ratio (1)	0.9	1	1.1
Number of holes (2)	Few	Normal	Many
Heat profile (3)	High at start	Homogeneous	High at end
Baking time (4)	29 min	30 min	31 min

The middle level corresponds to the manufacturing conditions used before the current design.

4.2.2 Choosing the Design

The principal investigator decided to study the four factors with a 2^4 full factorial design because he expects several interactions among the factors. The plan has $2^4=16$ trials (Table 4.2).

Table 4.2 Designed experiment for studying the galette des rois

Trial	Layer Weight Ratio	Number of Holes	Heat Profile	Baking Time
	(1)	(2)	(3)	(4)
1	−	−	−	−
2	+	−	−	−
3	−	+	−	−
4	+	+	−	−
5	−	−	+	−
6	+	−	+	−
7	−	+	+	−
8	+	+	+	−
9	−	−	−	+
10	+	−	−	+
11	−	+	−	+
12	+	+	−	+
13	−	−	+	+
14	+	−	+	+
15	−	+	+	+
16	+	+	+	+
− 1	0.9	Few	High at start	29 min
+ 1	1.1	Many	High at end	30 min

The design presentation follows a classic trial order, known as *Yates order*. The levels of the first column are alternated and start with −1. The levels of the second column are alternated two at a time: two negative signs, two positive signs, and so on. The levels of the third column are alternated four at a time: four negative signs, four positive signs, and so on. The levels of the fourth column are alternated every eight rows: eight negatives followed by eight positives. This order will be used for all designed experiments in this book as well as all computer files.

Note that the actual run order of the design in practice is not necessarily the same as what is presented in this book's tables. Run order is an important question that we study in detail in Chapter 8.

4.2.3 Running the Experiment

The galettes are baked in an industrial conveyor oven. At the entrance of the oven, cakes are deposited on a conveyor belt and placed one after the other in several lines. They progress regularly through the oven and bake gradually, remaining in the oven for a prescribed amount of time. After exiting the oven, they are cooled, then evaluated for defects before freezing. We select a random sample of 100 galettes prepared under identical conditions. They are packed, labeled, and stored for four weeks. At the end of four weeks, an expert examines each galette by hand and rates both the piping and the separation. A second expert verifies the rating of the first, and in cases of disagreement, both experts work together to get the most precise possible rating. Each trial progresses in this manner.

A design like this requires excellent organization if it is to succeed. Organization is important because the cost of this research is considerable. Fortunately, in this case, all the trials and all the measurements could be carried out. Rather than give the results of all 100 trials, we give the averages for each of the two responses. The results are shown in Table 4.3.

Table 4.3 Results of the Galette des Rois experiment

Trial	Layer Weight Ratio (1)	Number of Holes (2)	Heat Profile (3)	Baking Time (4)	Separation	Piping
1	−	−	−	−	2.8	2.2
2	+	−	−	−	3	2.8
3	−	+	−	−	2.2	1.2
4	+	+	−	−	3	2.6
5	−	−	+	−	3	1.4
6	+	−	+	−	2.6	2
7	−	+	+	−	3	1.4
8	+	+	+	−	2.4	2.2
9	−	−	−	+	1.4	2.4
10	+	−	−	+	2.8	3
11	−	+	−	+	0.8	1.2
12	+	+	−	+	1.6	3
13	−	−	+	+	1.4	1.4
14	+	−	+	+	2.6	3
15	−	+	+	+	3	1.8
16	+	+	+	+	2.8	3
−1	0.90	Few	High at start	29 min		
+1	1.1	Many	High at end	30 min		

4.2.4 Interpreting the Results

4.2.4.1 Mathematical Model
The a priori linear model chosen is the following:

$$y = a_0 + a_1 x_1 + a_2 x_2 + a_3 x_3 + a_4 x_4$$
$$+ a_{12} x_1 x_2 + a_{13} x_1 x_3 + a_{14} x_1 x_4 + a_{23} x_2 x_3 + a_{24} x_2 x_4 + a_{34} x_3 x_4$$
$$+ a_{123} x_1 x_2 x_3 + a_{124} x_1 x_2 x_4 + a_{134} x_1 x_3 x_4 + a_{234} x_2 x_3 x_4$$
$$+ a_{1234} x_1 x_2 x_3 x_4$$

This model has:

- An intercept a_0
- Four terms with a coefficient (the factor effect) multiplied by the levels of each factor
- Some terms having a coefficient a_{ij} (interactions between two factors) and the product of the levels of the factors taken two at a time
- Some terms having a coefficient a_{ijk} (interactions among three factors), and the product of the levels of the factors taken three at a time
- A term having a coefficient a_{ijkl} (interaction among four factors), and the product of the levels of the factors taken four at a time.

There are 16 coefficients, and therefore 16 unknowns. The 16 trials are going to allow estimation of these 16 unknowns. The solution of the system of equations is carried out using JMP software.

Both responses use the same base model. However, the coefficients are quite different from one response to the other, and therefore the final mathematical representation differs for each response.

4.2.4.2 Preparing for the Calculations
Regardless of the software you use, you have to enter the experimental results into the computer. Take great care to enter the proper result with its corresponding trial from the design. A shift or transcription error would ruin the research and could lead to erroneous interpretation of the results.

For details on entering the data into JMP, see Chapter 14.

4.2.4.3 Examining the Results of the Calculations
The results of the calculations are shown in Table 4.4.

Table 4.4 Effects and interactions of the factors (coded units)

Effect	Separation	Piping
Intercept	2.4	2.16
Layer weight ratio (1)	0.2	0.53
Holes (2)	−0.05	−0.11
Heat profile (3)	0.2	−0.14
Baking time (4)	−0.35	0.19
1×2 Interaction	−0.1	0.11
1×3 Interaction	−0.2	−0.01
1×4 Interaction	0.2	0.11
2×3 Interaction	0.25	0.19
2×4 Interaction	0.05	0.01
3×4 Interaction	0.2	0.09
1×2×3 Interaction	−0.1	−0.14
1×2×4 Interaction	−0.15	−0.01
1×3×4 Interaction	0.05	0.06
2×3×4 Interaction	0.2	0.01
1×2×3×4 Interaction	0	−0.06

Three factors influence the separation:

Layer weight ratio (factor 1)
Heat profile (factor 3)
Baking time (factor 4)

Figure 4.1 shows the values of the model coefficients for the separation response. There are several interactions of order 2 and 3 that are of the same order of magnitude as the main effects. This is not surprising to those who are experts in pastry-making.

Figure 4.1 JMP report and bar chart of the model coefficients for the separation response

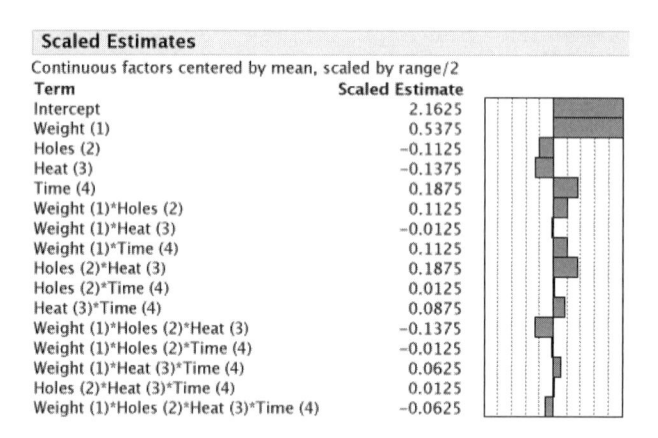

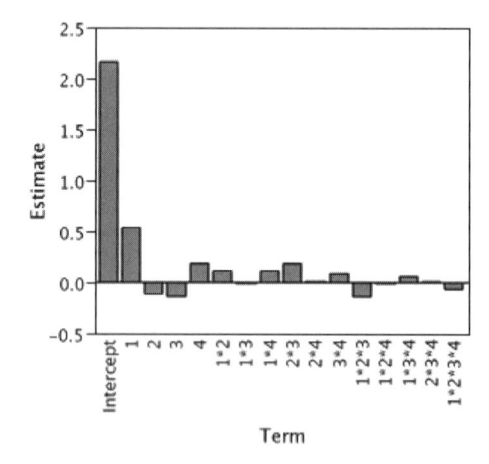

Scaled Estimates
Continuous factors centered by mean, scaled by range/2

Term	Scaled Estimate
Intercept	2.1625
Weight (1)	0.5375
Holes (2)	−0.1125
Heat (3)	−0.1375
Time (4)	0.1875
Weight (1)*Holes (2)	0.1125
Weight (1)*Heat (3)	−0.0125
Weight (1)*Time (4)	0.1125
Holes (2)*Heat (3)	0.1875
Holes (2)*Time (4)	0.0125
Heat (3)*Time (4)	0.0875
Weight (1)*Holes (2)*Heat (3)	−0.1375
Weight (1)*Holes (2)*Time (4)	−0.0125
Weight (1)*Heat (3)*Time (4)	0.0625
Holes (2)*Heat (3)*Time (4)	0.0125
Weight (1)*Holes (2)*Heat (3)*Time (4)	−0.0625

For piping, there is one factor (layer weight ratio, factor 1) that is much more influential than the others. However, none can be ignored, since all are sufficiently strong and must be taken into account. Notice that there are numerous interactions of orders 2 and 3. Figure 4.2 illustrates the piping results from Table 4.4.

Figure 4.2 JMP report and bar chart of the coefficients of piping

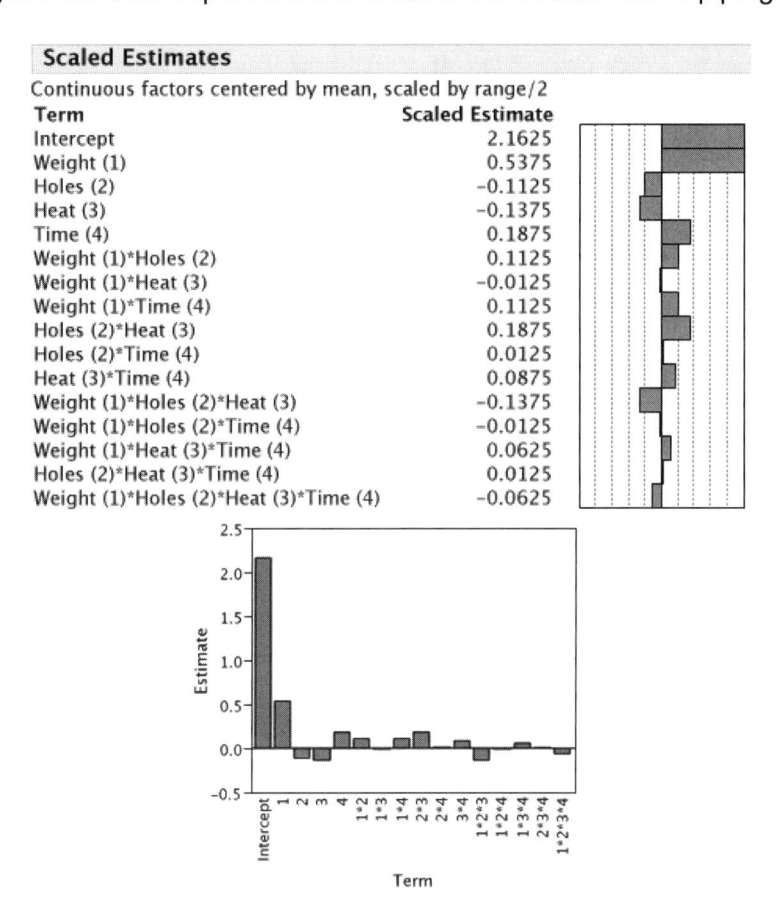

Scaled Estimates

Continuous factors centered by mean, scaled by range/2

Term	Scaled Estimate
Intercept	2.1625
Weight (1)	0.5375
Holes (2)	-0.1125
Heat (3)	-0.1375
Time (4)	0.1875
Weight (1)*Holes (2)	0.1125
Weight (1)*Heat (3)	-0.0125
Weight (1)*Time (4)	0.1125
Holes (2)*Heat (3)	0.1875
Holes (2)*Time (4)	0.0125
Heat (3)*Time (4)	0.0875
Weight (1)*Holes (2)*Heat (3)	-0.1375
Weight (1)*Holes (2)*Time (4)	-0.0125
Weight (1)*Heat (3)*Time (4)	0.0625
Holes (2)*Heat (3)*Time (4)	0.0125
Weight (1)*Holes (2)*Heat (3)*Time (4)	-0.0625

The objective of the study is to increase both responses while at the same time reducing the separation and piping. We are looking for the conditions that allow us to attain a rating of 3 for both responses.

4.2.4.4 Interpreting the Results of the Calculations

The presence of the interactions keeps us from seeing the principal effect of a factor on a response. Interactions mean that when a level of a factor is changed, the effect of other factors also changes. At the center of the study domain, the rating of separation is 2.4 and the rating of piping is 2.1625 (Figure 4.3). An interpretation based only on the principal effects of the factors would cause errors, so interactions must be taken into account. We are going to work progressively, thinking about how, and in what direction (higher or lower) each effect changes the two responses. Calculating the response according to factor levels is carried out in JMP with the prediction profiler.

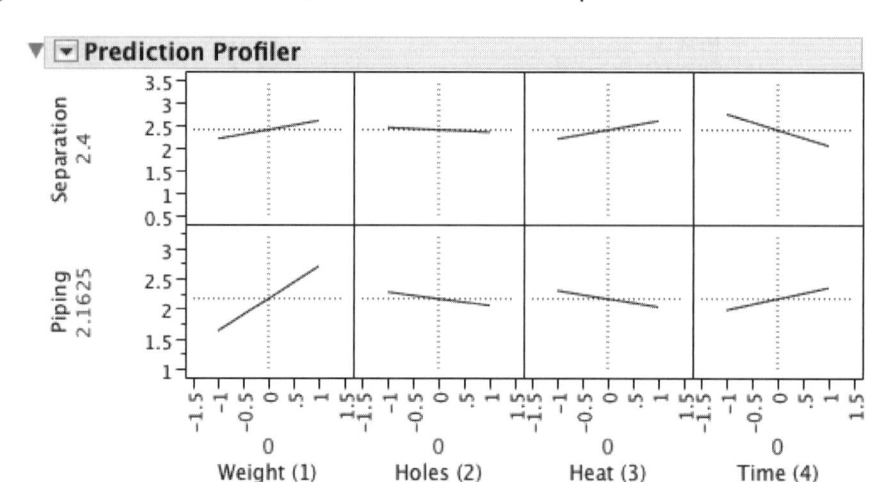

Figure 4.3 Profiles of the four factors for two responses

The direction of the layer weight ratio (factor 1) is the same for both responses. Therefore, improving (i.e., decreasing defects for) one improves (or decreases defects for) the other. This is interesting, since it is the only factor that has higher values associated with improved piping. Using high layer weight ratio levels results in galettes with less separation and fewer pipes. Therefore, we set factor 1 at its high level (Figure 4.4). Note that with this change, separation changes from 2.4 to 2.6, and piping passes from 2.16 to 2.7.

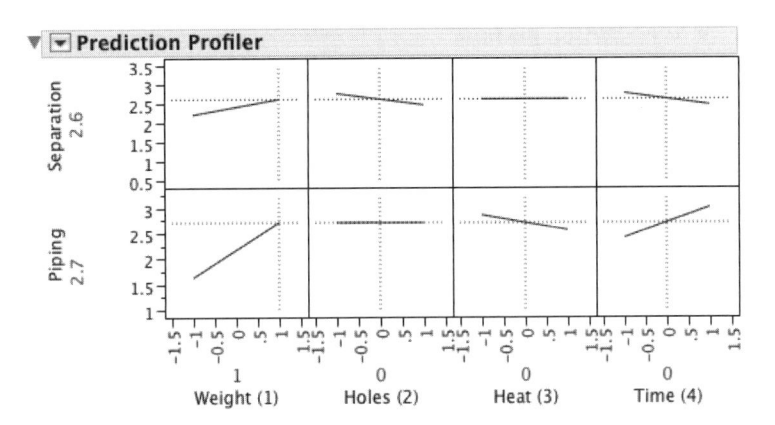

Figure 4.4 Factor 1 set at its high level

When the layer weight ratio (factor 1) is set at its high level, the profiler shows that the number of holes (factor 2) affects only separation and has no effect on piping. So, this factor is set at its lowest level to reduce separation (Figure 4.5). Note that now, the heat profile (factor 3) affects both responses in the same way. This means that changing factor 1 caused the slopes of factors 2, 3, and 4 to change.

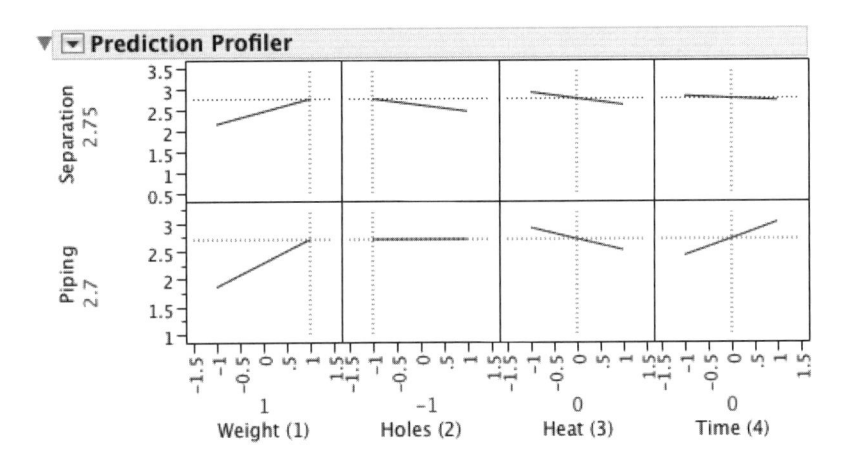

Figure 4.5 Factor 2 set at its low level

Because interaction caused the slope of the heat profile to change to nearly flat, our next choice is straightforward: the heat profile (factor 3) is set at its low level for both responses (Figure 4.6).

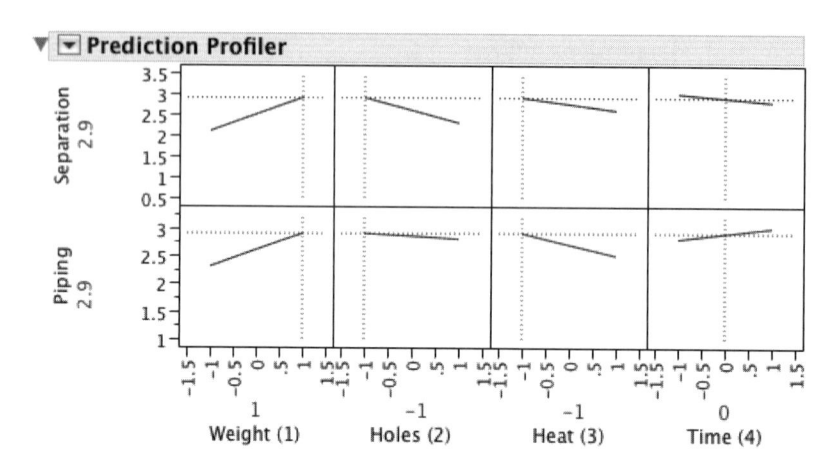

Figure 4.6 Factor 3 set at its low level

[Prediction Profiler showing Separation 2.9 and Piping 2.9 across Weight (1), Holes (-1), Heat (-1), Time (0)]

Adjusting baking time (factor 4) is more delicate. In fact, this factor acts inversely proportional to both responses. Placing baking time at a high level results in a 3 rating for piping, but reduces separation to 2.8. Conversely, placing baking time at a low level results in a 3 rating for separation, but reduces piping to 2.8. When left at its zero level, both responses get a rating of 2.9 (Figure 4.7). Should the baking time remain at 30 minutes, or should it be reduced to eliminate separation or increased to reduce piping? A subject-matter expert or other decision-maker must decide. In this case, a marketing person will have to evaluate which solution is better, given the customer base.

Graphs allow presentation of the different facets of the problem and aid in decision-making. The experimenter has the data and the methods to make a presentation to the decision-makers. Additionally, using a desirability function (detailed in the next section) allows the experimenter a mathematical reason to say that the best solution has been found.

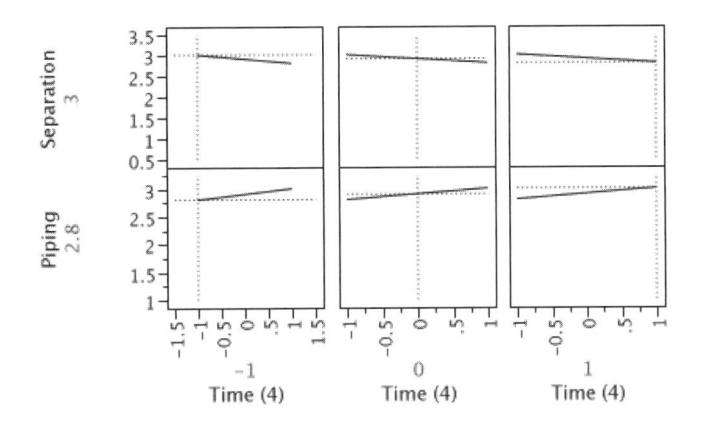

Figure 4.7 Factor 4 can be set at various levels, depending on the research decision.

[Figure: Interaction plots showing Separation and Piping responses vs. Time (4) at three levels (-1, 0, 1)]

The experimenter could also suggest a complementary study to obtain a 3 rating for both responses. Looking at Figure 4.6, note that the situation could be improved by:

- Increasing the layer weight ratio
- Decreasing the number of holes
- Increasing the initial baking temperature of the oven

If these improved results are worth the trouble, the experimenter should have no trouble obtaining a small extra budget to finalize the study.

4.2.5 Desirability Functions

The desirability function is quite useful when it is necessary to find the best compromise among several responses. This function was proposed by Derringer and Suich (1980) and Jones (1990) and appears in several DOE software products like JMP. It gives exceptional results for something that is so easy to use. We use it for several examples.

4.2.5.1 The Desirability Function Applied to a Single Response

Let's start by defining the desirability function for a single response. This function varies between 0 and 1. The value of 1 corresponds to maximum satisfaction. The value of 0 corresponds to complete dissatisfaction (that is, a completely undesirable result).

Maximum Desired Values

Using the galette example, suppose you wanted a separation higher than 2.5. You estimate that any separation score below 2.5 is unacceptable, so the corresponding desirability function should be set to 0 for all separations between 0 and 2.5. On the other hand, separations higher than 2.5 are satisfactory, so the desirability function is set to 1 for all separation values above 2.5.

Figure 4.8 The desirability function is 1 when the response is satisfactory. It is set to 0 when the response is not satisfactory.

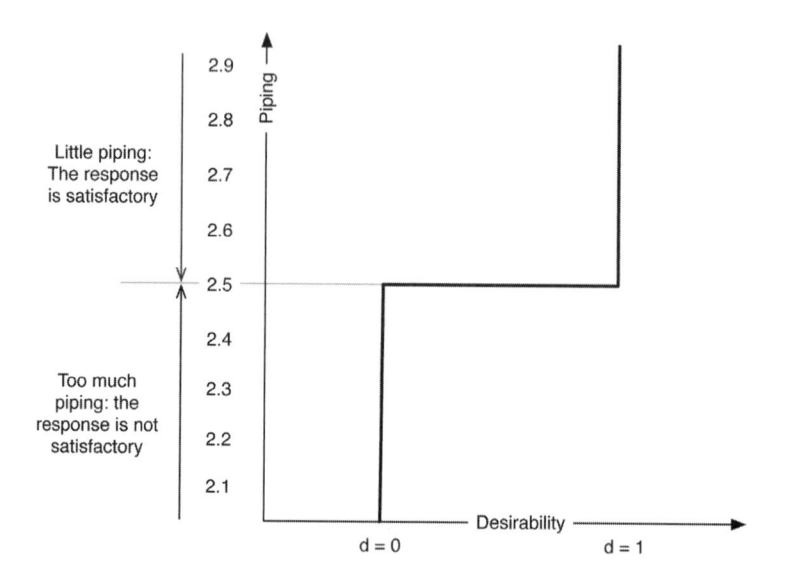

We can represent the desirability function as in Figure 4.8. This function stays at value 0 as long as the response value is unsatisfactory and goes to 1 as soon as the response value is satisfactory. However, this representation is rough and without nuance. A separation rating of 2.49 is nearly identical to a value of 2.51, yet the desirability function designates the first as 0 (no) desirability and the second as 1 (complete) desirability. This is why a certain amount of flexibility and progressiveness needs to be introduced. A separation of 2.6 is better than 2.4, but not as good as 2.7. Introducing intermediate values for desirability between the unacceptable and acceptable values solves this problem. For example, we can choose the following grid:

Desirability = 0 for separations rated 2.3 and lower
Desirability = 0.25 for separations rated 2.4 to 2.5
Desirability = 0.5 for separations rated 2.5 to 2.6

Desirability = 0.75 for separations rated 2.6 to 2.7

Desirability = 1 for separations rated 2.7 or higher.

Figure 4.9 The desirability function takes values between 0 and 1 as the response progressively improves.

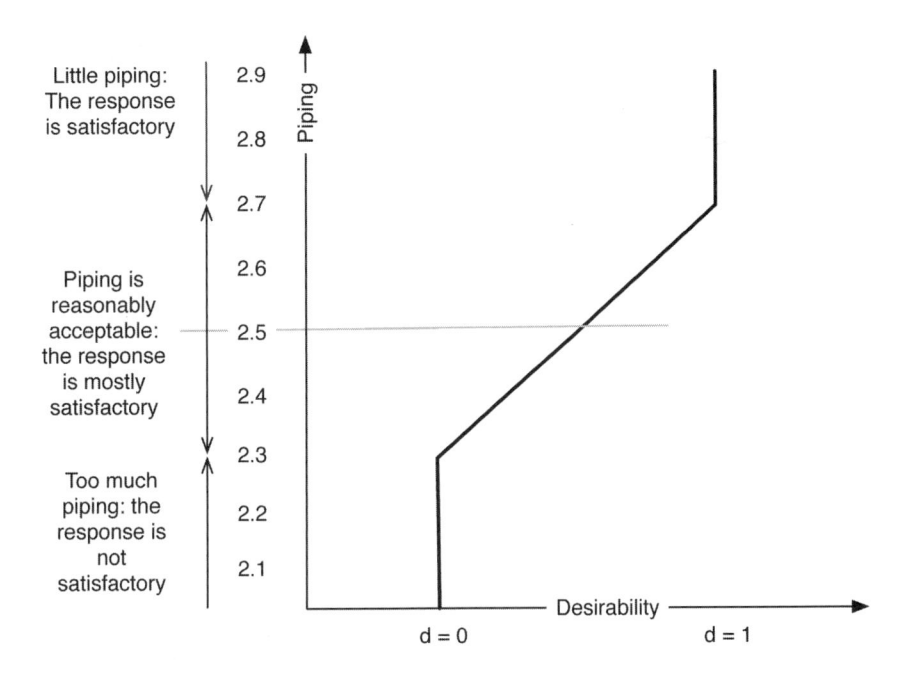

The shape of the function that progressively takes all values between 0 and 1 can take different appearances. Some software offers a wide variety of functions, many of which can be complicated to adapt to a specific study objective. In this book, we consider only two cases:

- Linear piece-wise desirability functions (e.g., Figure 4.9), which are useful for pedagogical examples
- Curved piece-wise functions that are smooth at the boundary points, and which are useful for software that must use well-defined functions in calculating maxima and minima. The functions are used in JMP.

Minimum Desired Values

Figure 4.9 shows a response where high values are considered desirable. However, some experiments want to minimize a value: smaller values are more desirable. For example, if the response concerns impurity, the smallest possible concentration is most desirable. We would therefore adopt a desirability function like the one in Figure 4.10.

Figure 4.10 This desirability function has low response values as most desirable.

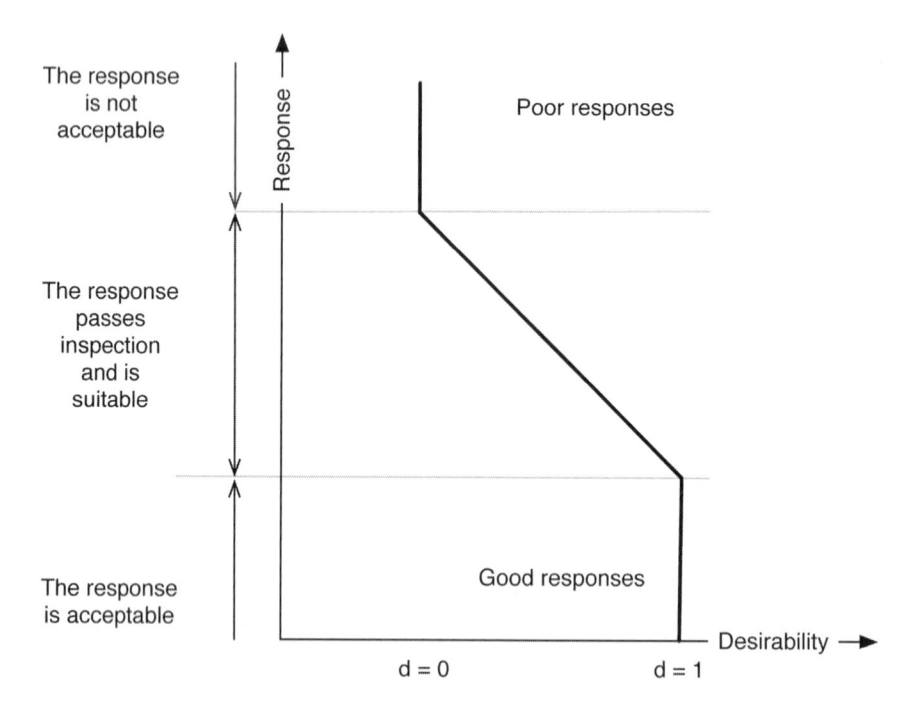

A Target Value

In some cases, a precise target value of the response is desired. Figure 4.11 represents this situation. The desirability function is set to 0 when it is far from the desired value, then it increases gradually as it approaches the target. It has the value 1 for the target value, then decreases, reaching 0 when sufficiently far away from the target. The rates of rise and fall of the desirability function do not have to match.

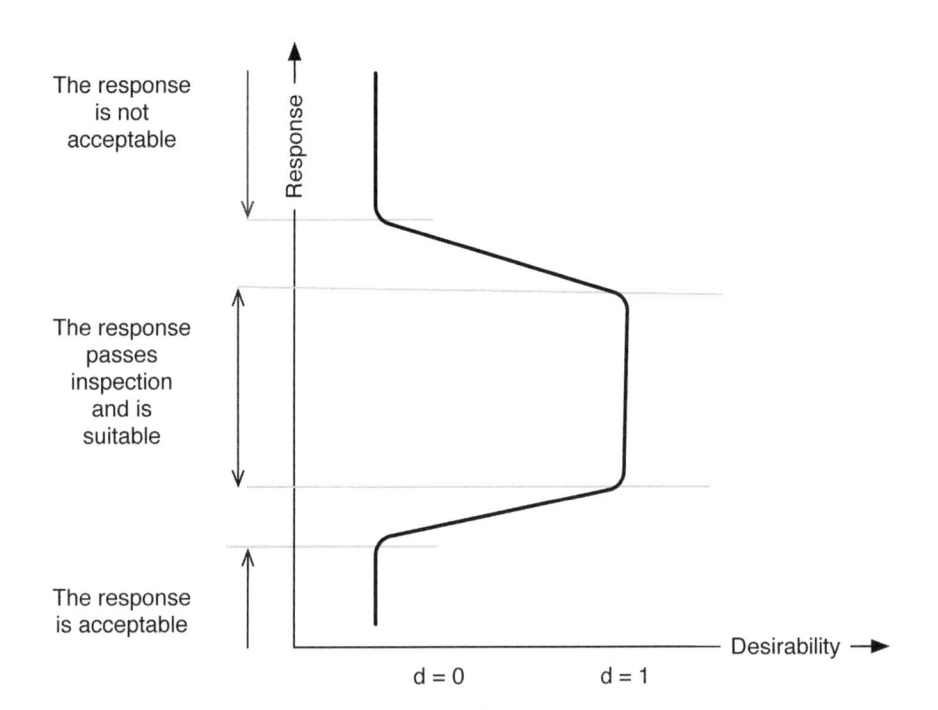

Figure 4.11 Desirability function for a target value

4.2.5.2 A Target Range

Instead of targeting one particular value, a range of values might be equally desirable. Such a desirability function has a plateau. Figure 4.12 shows one such plateau where the slopes of the descending lines are different on the low side and the high side of the plateau. The sharp changes at the endpoints of the lines are softened and rounded. This desirability shape can be fit to all possible situations.

To form desirability functions with this shape in JMP, use two identical columns, one with a desirability function representing the ascending portion of the curve, one representing the descending portion.

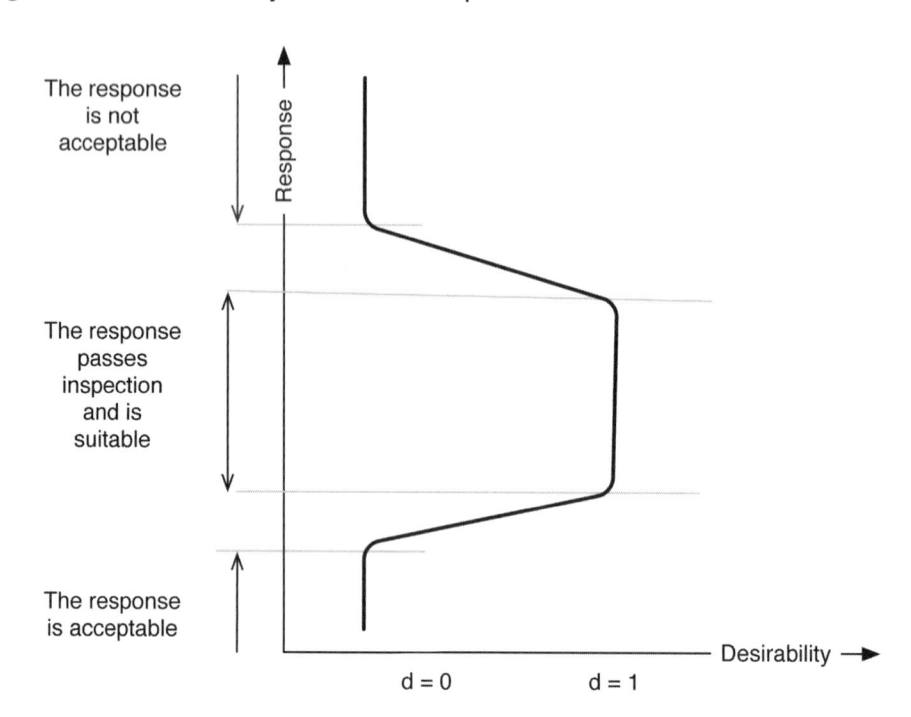

Figure 4.12 Desirability function for a plateau

The response is not acceptable

The response passes inspection and is suitable

The response is acceptable

d = 0   d = 1   Desirability →

4.2.5.3 The Desirability Function Applied to Several Responses

We have examined the desirability function for a single response. However, desirability functions are most interesting when their power is utilized for several responses simultaneously. This makes it possible to find the best compromise when there are constraints on each response.

The global desirability D that takes into account the demands on all the responses at the same time is the geometric mean of the individual desirabilities. That is:

$$D = \sqrt[n]{d_1 d_2 \cdots d_n}$$

This leads to several conclusions:

- The global desirability is equal to 1 when all the objectives are attained. In this case, all the individual desirabilities are equal to 1.

- The global desirability is equal to 0 if at least one of the objectives is totally unacceptable (i.e., zero desirability).

- The global desirability is somewhere between 0 and 1 when all objectives are at least partially obtained (*some* can be completely attained). In this case, all desirabilities are non-zero, and some may be equal to 1.

The best compromise corresponds to the highest global desirability value. The necessary optimization calculations can be complicated and are therefore best left to software. We illustrate this concept by re-examining the galette des rois.

4.2.5.4 Application to the Galette des Rois Example

Suppose that the study objectives are a separation rating higher than 2.5 and a piping rating higher than 2.8. The form of the separation desirability function depends on the levels of the four factors of the study and is illustrated by the curve on the right in Figure 4.13. This curve has a value of 0 until it reaches a separation rating of 2, goes from 0 to 1 for separation ratings between 2 and 2.5, and is 1 for separation ratings higher than 2.5.

Figure 4.13 The value of the separation desirability function varies according to levels of the factors.

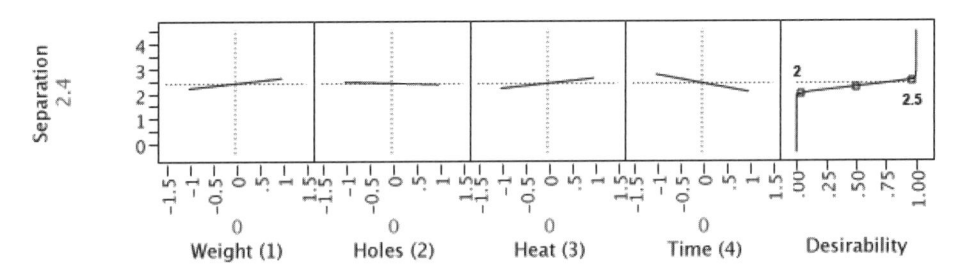

The same idea applies to piping, except that the desirability function is different: 0 up to 2.5, increasing from 2.5 to 2.8 until it reaches its value of 1 at piping rating 2.8 (Figure 4.14).

Figure 4.14 The value of the desirability function of piping varies according to the levels of the factors.

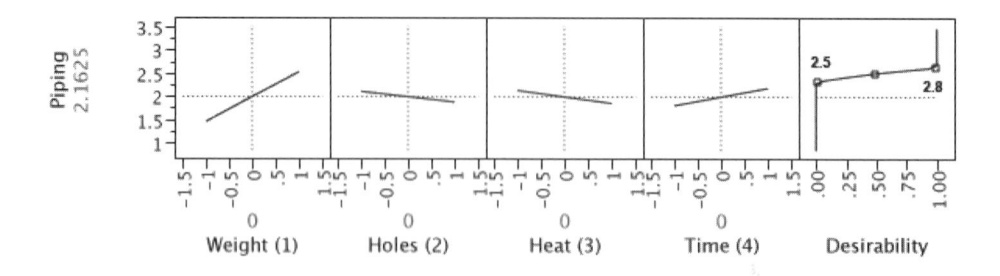

JMP calculates the desirability for each point in the study domain. For example, Figure 4.15 shows that the desirability is valued at 0.996 for the point (in coded units) weight = +1, holes = –1, heat = 0, time = 0.67. JMP also draws slices of the response surface for the fixed levels of the three other factors. For example, for the layer weight ratio factor (factor 1), we have a slice of the response surface for the levels holes = –1, heat = 0, time = 0.67 of the other factors. It is by modifying the levels of the other factors that the maximum desirability is found. JMP has a command (**Maximize Desirability**) that allows this maximum to be found quickly.

Figure 4.15 The global desirability function varies according to the levels of the factors.

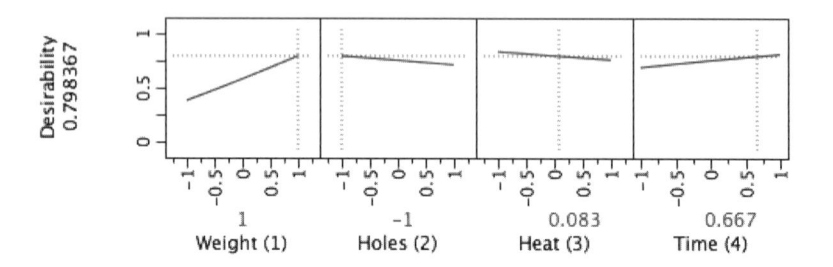

We now have the settings representing the highest desirability. Since there may be several factor-level settings that give a desirability equal to 1, the optimizer does not always give the same solution, but chooses one among the possible solutions. If you searched for an optimal solution manually (using the mouse, as we did in Section 4.2.4.4), the optimizer generally finds the solution closest to this setting.

4.2.6 Study Conclusion

Separation and piping are decreased by setting:

- The layer weight ratio $\left(\dfrac{\text{weight of the upper layer}}{\text{weight of the lower layer}}\right)$ to 1.1

- The number of holes in the upper layer to Few

- The heat profile to apply high heat at start

Separation can be decreased at the expense of piping by baking for 29 minutes. Conversely, piping can be decreased at the expense of separation by increasing the baking time to 31 minutes.

Improvement methods are possible if the study domain defined at the beginning of the study is set aside. Note, for example, that the objectives can be obtained by increasing the layer weight ratio beyond 1.1, by decreasing the number of holes, and by increasing the baking temperature at the beginning of baking. This is a controlled extrapolation: the mathematical model, established within the study domain, is used outside the domain. As usual, it is necessary to confirm any extrapolated forecasts by an experiment. In the case of the galettes des rois, complementary tests were run to establish that a rating of 3 is achieved for both responses by extending the study domain. These new trials were essentially directed toward a gentle increase in the layer weight ratio and an increase in initial baking temperature. The objective was achieved for:

- A layer weight ratio of 1.2

- The number of holes at level Few (no change)

- The oven temperature at level "a little more than before"

Practice shows that controlled extrapolation is an effective means to direct a study toward a desired solution. However, it is essential to ensure these forecasts are checked and confirmed by experiments. Omitting verification can result in nasty surprises indeed.

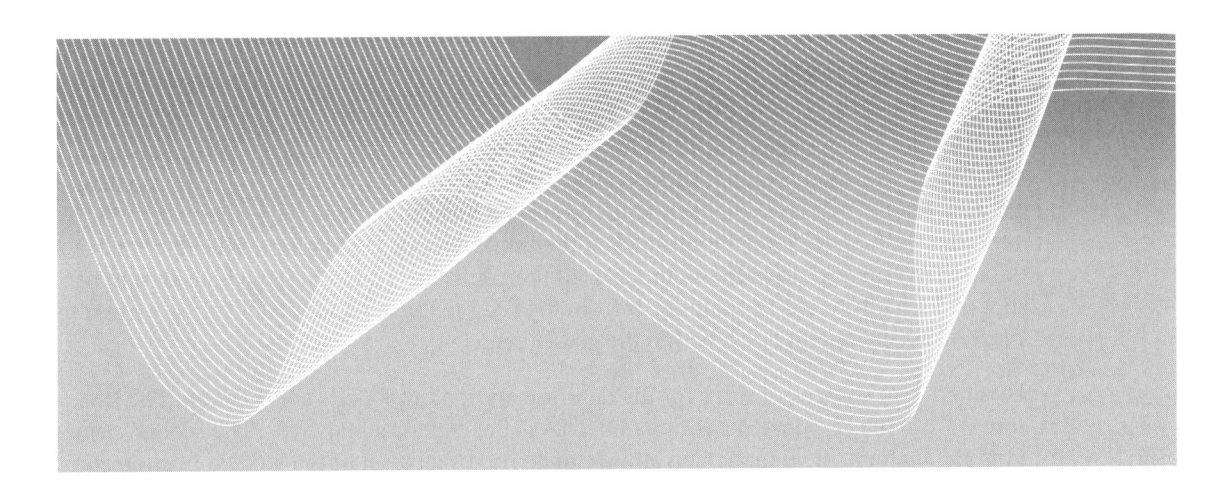

Chapter 5

Statistical Concepts for Designed Experiments

    5.1 Introduction 94
    5.2 Example 4: Lifespan of Disposable Cutting Tools 95
        5.2.1 **Preparing the Designed Experiment** 95
        5.2.2 **Experimentation** 97
        5.2.3 **Intepreting the Results of the Calculations** 98
        5.2.4 **Statistical Concepts Used in DOE** 99
        5.2.5 **Factors and Influential Interactions** 113
        5.2.6 **Analysis of Variance (ANOVA)** 115
        5.2.7 **Application** 119
        5.2.8 **Residual Analysis** 125
        5.2.9 **Study Conclusion** 126

5.1 Introduction

The full-factorial designs that we have seen let us evaluate the influence of factors and their interactions via the coefficients of the postulated model. We were able to see that the coefficients that have the largest value are the most important. We judged the importance of coefficients by comparing them to each other. However, we did not have a standard "yardstick" to help us compare all the coefficients, and judge which should be kept and which should be eliminated from the final mathematical model. We are missing a test of the uncertainty attached to the coefficients.

There are two sources of error for the determination of a model's coefficients. The first comes from the response measurement. This is the experimental error. The second comes from the mathematical model, an approximate representation of the studied phenomenon. This is the lack of fit error. Together, these errors represent the total error, which is the uncertainty of the model.

Total Error = Experimental Error + Lack of Fit Error

When several trials are carried out under the same experimental conditions, errors appear in the measured responses. Values are similar, but not identical to each other; there is a dispersion of the measurements. This dispersion comes from the fact that the responses are from random variables. There is an experimental error attached to each realization of a response, which is transferred to the coefficients.

There is also a difference between the model postulated by the experimenter and the actual model. This difference is the lack of fit between the two models. Lack of fit error transmits itself equally to the coefficients of the model.

Investigating these two types of error, experimental error and lack of fit, allows us to evaluate the importance of the coefficients. For example, if the error on a coefficient is 5 and the coefficient has a value of 4, the factor is considered negligible and not influential. On the other hand, a coefficient of 30 with the same error(s) would be considered as influential.

It is therefore important to know the error that is used in the estimation of the coefficients. To carry through a study, it is necessary to know the fundamental statistical concepts that are used to make the calculations and to apply the correct reasoning. Software relieves us of having to make all the calculations, but we need to be able to interpret the statistical measurements that it provides us.

A disposable cutting tools example illustrates the theoretical concepts developed in this chapter. First, we introduce the two most important statistical measures, mean and standard deviation. Then, we show the concepts of population, sample, and distribution. We emphasize the paramount role of the standard deviation, which is used as a standard to evaluate the importance of a measurement from a random variable. We will see how the standard deviation allows calculation of the *p*-value, which measures the probability that an event is rare.

The primary objective of this chapter is to explain the concepts that make it possible to evaluate, and therefore improve, the postulated model that represents the experimental results. In a word, these ideas help us to find the best possible model that both represents the experimental data and enables us to make accurate predictions.

5.2 Example 4: Lifespan of Disposable Cutting Tools

5.2.1 Preparing the Designed Experiment

5.2.1.1 Description of the Study
The machining of metals requires cutting tools with precise material and behavior. Good tools must cut perfectly, be safe to use, not wear out too quickly, and consistently cut the fabricated objects. The sharpening of such tools poses a number of problems, so a manufacturer decided to study disposable tools that require no sharpening. To assure their profitability, these tools must have a reasonable lifespan.

This study relates to special, intensive-use tools whose lifespan needs to be maximized.

5.2.1.2 Defining the Study Objective
The objective of the study is to define the conditions of use that ensures a lifespan of more than 20 hours for each cutting tool.

5.2.1.3 Choosing a Response That Represents the Objective

The chosen response is the lifespan of the tools.

5.2.1.4 Factors and Study Domain

After considering many factors, we now choose the following for the study:

- Flow of the cutting oil
- Cutting speed of the tool
- The tool's cutting depth
- The forward speed of the tool through material

These four factors and their domains are shown in Table 5.1.

Table 5.1 Factors and study domain

Factors	Low Level (−1)	Middle Level	High Level (+1)
Flow (1)	650	725	800
Cutting speed (2)	10	18	26
Depth (3)	0.05	0.125	0.20
Forward speed (4)	0.5	0.75	1

5.2.1.5 Choosing the Experimental Design

The experimenter decides to conduct a 2^4 full-factorial design, resulting in 16 trials. However, he wants to have an estimation of the experimental error. To do this, he adds four trials situated at the center of the study domain. He is therefore going to carry out 20 trials (Table 5.2).

5.2.2 Experimentation

Table 5.2 Trials and responses for the disposable cutting tools experiment (coded units)

Trial	Flow	Cutting Speed	Depth	Forward Speed	Lifespan
	(1)	(2)	(3)	(4)	Hours
1	− 1	− 1	− 1	− 1	26.1
2	+ 1	− 1	− 1	− 1	22.2
3	− 1	+ 1	− 1	− 1	10.1
4	+ 1	+ 1	− 1	− 1	12.2
5	− 1	− 1	+ 1	− 1	14.2
6	+ 1	− 1	+ 1	− 1	12.7
7	− 1	+ 1	+ 1	− 1	5.9
8	+ 1	+ 1	+ 1	− 1	5.6
9	− 1	− 1	− 1	+ 1	23
10	+ 1	− 1	− 1	+ 1	20.1
11	− 1	+ 1	− 1	+ 1	2.4
12	+ 1	+ 1	− 1	+ 1	3.7
13	− 1	− 1	+ 1	+ 1	11
14	+ 1	− 1	+ 1	+ 1	13.4
15	− 1	+ 1	+ 1	+ 1	0.5
16	+ 1	+ 1	+ 1	+ 1	1.7
17	0	0	0	0	11.1
18	0	0	0	0	12.6
19	0	0	0	0	10.4
20	0	0	0	0	11.9
− 1	650	10	0.05	0.5	
0	725	18	0.125	0.75	
+ 1	800	26	0.2	1	

The center points are grouped together at the end of the design only for the presentation of the trials. However, the execution order of the trials of a design is not dictated by their presentation in our table. For example, a center point may appear first in the study, another at trial 6, a third after trial 12, and the fourth as the last trial.

5.2.3 Interpreting the Results of the Calculations

We adopt a model with the main effects and their second-order interactions. We assume third- and fourth-order interactions do not enter into this model (Why? See Chapter 6). When calculating effects, only use the 16 trials of the factorial design. Don't use the center points, which are control points and not points for calculation. They are used only to calculate an estimation of the experimental error.

Software calculates the intercept, main effects, and six second-order interactions (Table 5.3).

Table 5.3 Model coefficient (coded units)

Term	Value, Estimate	Standard Deviation	t-Ratio	p-Value
Intercept	11.55	0.360902	32.00	<0.0001
Flow (1)	−0.1	0.360902	−0.28	0.7928
Cutting speed (2)	−6.2875	0.360902	−17.42	<0.0001
Depth (3)	−3.425	0.360902	−9.49	0.0002
Forward speed (4)	−2.075	0.360902	−5.75	0.0022
1×2	0.6375	0.360902	1.77	0.1376
1×3	0.325	0.360902	0.90	0.4091
2×3	1.5875	0.360902	4.40	0.0070
1×4	0.35	0.360902	0.97	0.3767
2×4	−1.1125	0.360902	−3.08	0.0274
3×4	0.6	0.360902	1.66	0.1573

To interpret this table correctly, it's important to understand the meaning of the provided information: in particular, the standard deviation, the *t*-ratio, and the *p*-value. This requires a detour to introduce the principal notions of statistics used in DOE. We will see how the properties of a normal distribution are used to estimate errors and probabilities, and how these statistical tools allow us to obtain a method for evaluating the influence of the factors. We will also see how the analysis of variance (ANOVA) provides useful statistical measurements to help us evaluate the mathematical models used in the analysis. Lastly, we show an application that allows us to see how these introductory concepts are used.

5.2.4 Statistical Concepts Used in DOE

First, we examine the experimental error, then the concepts of population and sample.

5.2.4.1 Experimental Error

The four center points have different values. Instead of giving the list of the four values, we could summarize them by stating the central value and the dispersion around the central value. In general, the mean is used as the measure of center and the standard deviation as the dispersion measurement.

Mean

By definition, the arithmetic mean of a group of values is the sum of all the values divided by the number of values. Here, the arithmetic mean is equal to

$$\bar{y} = \frac{1}{4}(11.1 + 12.6 + 10.4 + 11.9) = 11.5$$

Standard deviation

The definition of the standard deviation is a little more complicated than the mean. We are going to describe its calculation step by step:

1. Start by calculating the deviations from the mean, i.e., the difference between each value and the mean.

    $11.1 - 11.5 = -0.4$

    $12.6 - 11.5 = +1.1$

    $10.4 - 11.5 = -1.1$

    $11.9 - 11.5 = +0.4$

Note that the sum of the deviations from the mean is zero:

$$-0.4 + 1.1 - 1.1 + 0.4 = 0$$

This can be shown to be true in general:

$$\sum_{i=1}^{n}(y_i - \bar{y}) = \sum_{i=1}^{n} y_i - \sum_{i=1}^{n} \bar{y} = \frac{n}{n}\sum_{i=1}^{n} y_i - n\bar{y} = n\bar{y} - n\bar{y} = 0$$

Therefore, the sum of deviations from the mean cannot be used as a measure of dispersion. To eliminate this problem, we eliminate the negative signs by taking the squares of the deviations. This is why the squared terms appear in the calculations.

2. Square each deviation from the mean and add them together. This results in the sum of the squared deviations from the mean.

$$(-0.4)^2 + (1.1)^2 + (-1.1)^2 + (0.4)^2$$
$$= 0.16 + 1.21 + 1.21 + 0.16$$
$$= 2.74$$

3. This sum is divided by the number of values minus 1.

$$\frac{2.74}{4-1} = 0.9133$$

This quantity is named the *variance* and is a fundamental measurement in statistical science. It is ubiquitous and frequently used.

4. Finally, the *standard deviation* is obtained by taking the square root of the variance.

$$\text{standard deviation} = \sqrt{0.9133} = 0.9557 \approx 0.96$$

Why take the square root of the variance? When the deviations from the mean are squared, so are their units of measurement. The variance is therefore expressed with a unit that is the square of the original units. We therefore take the square root simply so that dispersion is expressed in the same units as the original data and the mean. This makes comparisons easy.

Fortunately, computers exist to do these calculations, giving the value of the response's standard deviation without any hand computations.

What is the meaning of these measurements "mean" and "standard deviation"? And how will they be used?

If a series of responses are taken from the same experimental point, the mean and standard deviation of the set of points is easy to calculate. But is it possible to predict, with a good chance of being right, the value of another new measurement taken from the same experimental point? It is likely that it will not be much different from the mean.

There is less chance of being wrong if we give an interval that may contain the new value rather than the precise new value itself. If you say, "The value will probably be between such and such value," you increase the chances of being correct over reporting just a mean. A larger interval gives a greater chance of making a good prediction. Statisticians have already calculated the probability that your interval is correct—all by using the standard deviation.

To look deeper into these important questions, we are going to explore the notions of population, sample, distribution, degrees of freedom, and error transmission.

5.2.4.2 Population
Suppose we have made several measurements under the same experimental conditions. We obtain a list of values that are near to one another but not exact matches. Imagine that we continue taking measurements until we have an infinite number of them (key word: imagine). The group of all the values forms a population of random measurements characterized by

- a measure of center, called the *population mean*, which is denoted by the Greek letter μ.
- a measure of dispersion called the *population standard deviation*, which is denoted by the Greek letter σ.
- a distribution.

5.2.4.3 Sample

From a statistical point of view, obtaining a sample of n values is the same as taking n random draws from a population of all possible values. The value of n is small compared to the number of individuals in the population. A sample of n values is characterized by

- a measure of center, the sample mean $\bar{y}$.

    Given a sample of n responses, the mean $\bar{y}$ is calculated using the equation:

    $$\bar{y} = \frac{y_1 + y_2 + ... + y_n}{n}$$

    $$= \frac{1}{n}(y_1 + y_2 + ... + y_n)$$

    $$= \frac{1}{n}\sum_{i=1}^{i=n} y_i$$

- a measure of center, the *sample standard deviation* denoted by s.
- a histogram of values.

A histogram is a graphical representation of a group of sample values. To construct the histogram shown in Figure 5.1, we used a sample of 100 values between 9 and 14. They are distributed as follows:

Range of Values	Number of Points
9 to 9.5	1
9.5 to 10	5
10 to 10.5	8
10.5 to 11	14
11 to 11.5	20
11.5 to 12	22
12 to 12.5	15
12.5 to 13	9
13 to 13.5	5
13.5 to 14	1

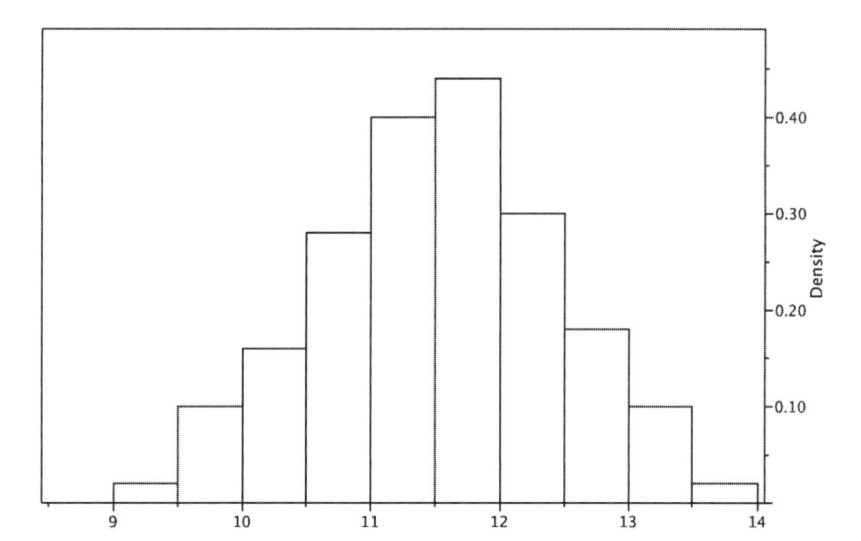

Figure 5.1 Histogram of 100 values

5.2.4.4 From the Sample to the Population

In practice, the characteristics of a population are seldom known. The sample mean $\bar{y}$ is used most often to estimate population characteristics from a sample. Statisticians have taken a great interest in this problem and have concluded:

- The best estimation of the population mean (μ) is the sample mean ($\bar{y}$).

- The best estimator of the population standard deviation is the sample standard deviation (s).

Be sure to note that the denominator for s is $n - 1$ rather than n.

Degrees of freedom

Take n measured responses *independent* of each other, i.e., with no mathematical relation among them. The n deviations from the mean of these responses are not independent. There is, in fact, a mathematical relationship among the deviations. When these $n - 1$ of them are known, the nth can be calculated mathematically. For example, suppose there are four deviations from the mean from the previous standard deviation example (4.1). The first three deviations are

$-0.4 \quad 1.1 \quad -1.1$

The fourth deviation is easily calculated because the sum of the deviations is always equal to zero:

4th deviation = $-0.4 + 1.1 - 1.1 = 0$
4th deviation = 0.4

There are therefore only $n - 1$ independent deviations. We say that the series of n deviations has $n - 1$ *degrees of freedom* (or DF). The number of degrees of freedom is important because it commonly shows up in statistical formulas.

Distribution

Suppose you continually sample from a process, so that the sample grows in size. As values are added to a sample, the sample's histogram becomes more and more regular, and for an infinite number of values (i.e., for a population), the histogram becomes identical to a theoretical *distribution*. It is possible to describe a population's distribution using a mathematical equation. For example, the distribution most often encountered in the realm of DOE is the normal distribution. The normal distribution is sometimes called the *bell curve*, the *Gaussian distribution*, or the *Laplace-Gaussian distribution*. This bell-shaped distribution is given by the equation

$$f(y) = \frac{1}{\sigma\sqrt{2\pi}} e^{-\frac{(y-\mu)^2}{2\sigma}}$$

This distribution is completely defined by its population mean μ and its standard deviation σ. In addition, all normal curves can be translated so that they have a mean of 0 and a standard deviation of 1 (Figure 5.2).

Figure 5.2 Representation of the normal distribution (μ=0, σ=1)

5.2.4.5 Principal Properties of the Normal Distribution

To read probabilities from the normal distribution, examine the surface that is under the curve. The total area under the curve represents all the possible values of the population. The probability that a value is higher than, say, 1.2, is represented by the area under the normal curve between 1.2 and infinity (Figure 5.3).

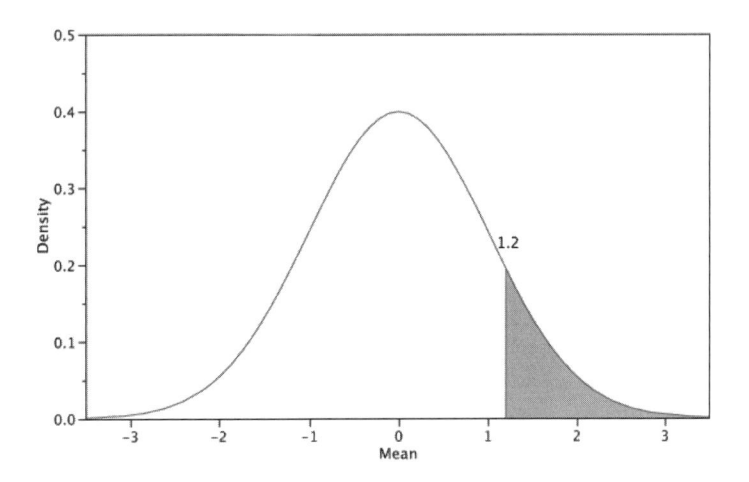

Figure 5.3 The probability of drawing a value larger than 1.2 is proportional to the shaded area.

The probability that a value is smaller than, say, 0.8 is represented by the area under the normal curve between negative infinity and 0.8 (Figure 5.4).

Figure 5.4 The probability of drawing a value less than 0.8 is proportional to the shaded area.

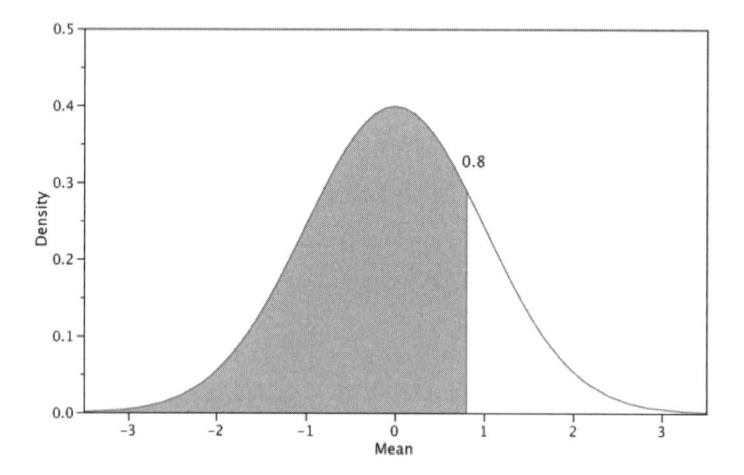

Lastly, the probability that a value is between -0.5 and 1.5 (or any other two given values) is represented by the area under the curve between the two values (Figure 5.5).

Figure 5.5 The probability of drawing a value between -0.5 and 1.5 is proportional to the shaded area.

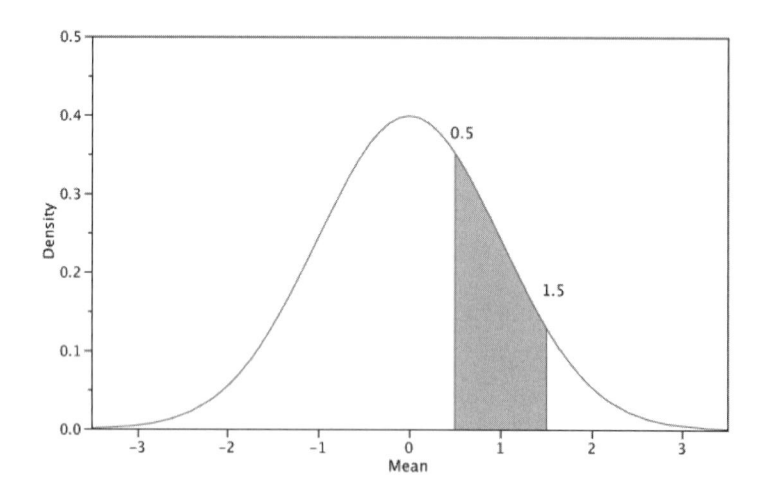

For example, it has been shown that 68.26% of the values of the population lie between one standard deviation below and one standard deviation above the population mean (Figure 5.6). This means that a random draw from a normal distribution has a 68% chance of being in the interval $\mu \pm s$ and a 32% chance of being outside that interval.

Figure 5.6 68.26% of the population is inside the interval $\mu \pm s$.

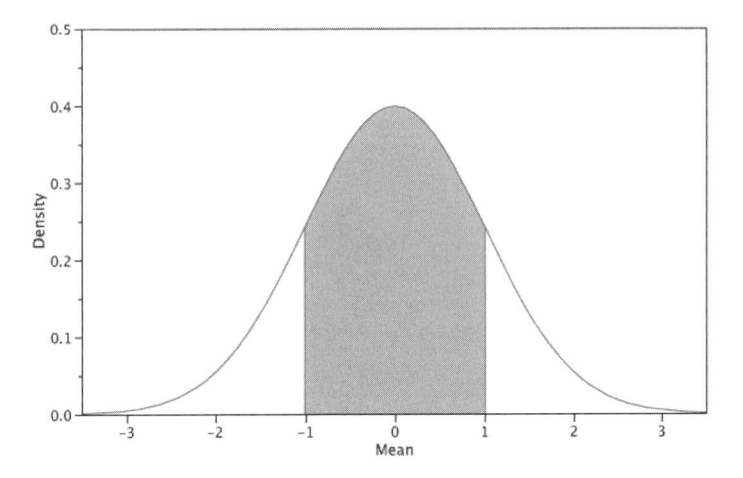

In addition, 95% of the population values lie between 1.96 standard deviations below and 1.96 standard deviations above the population mean. 95% of the time, a random draw from a normal distribution will have a value in the interval $\mu \pm 1.96s$ (Figure 5.7). 5% of the time, the random draw will be outside this interval.

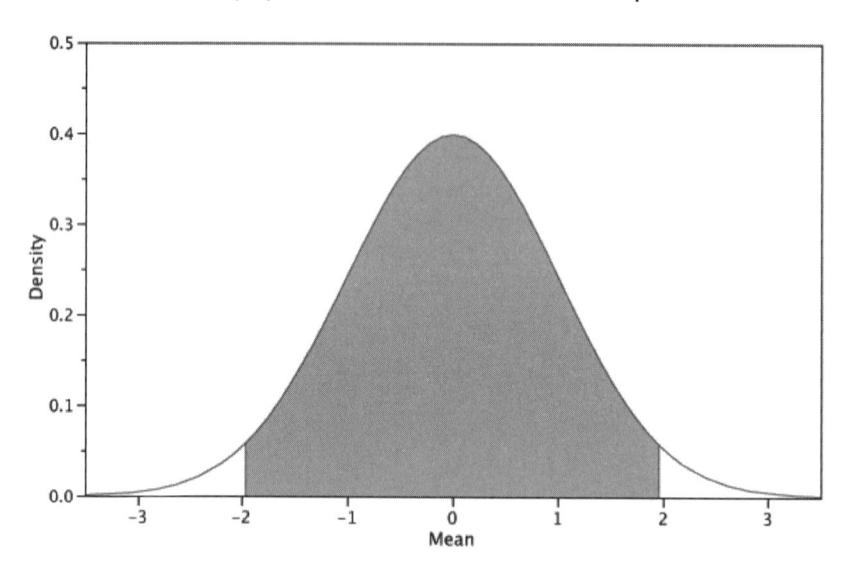

Figure 5.7 95% of the population is inside the interval μ ±1.96s.

Finally, in the interval μ ± 3s, there are 95% of the population's values (Figure 5.8). There is about a 2.5 out of 1000 chance that a random draw will be more than three standard deviations from the mean.

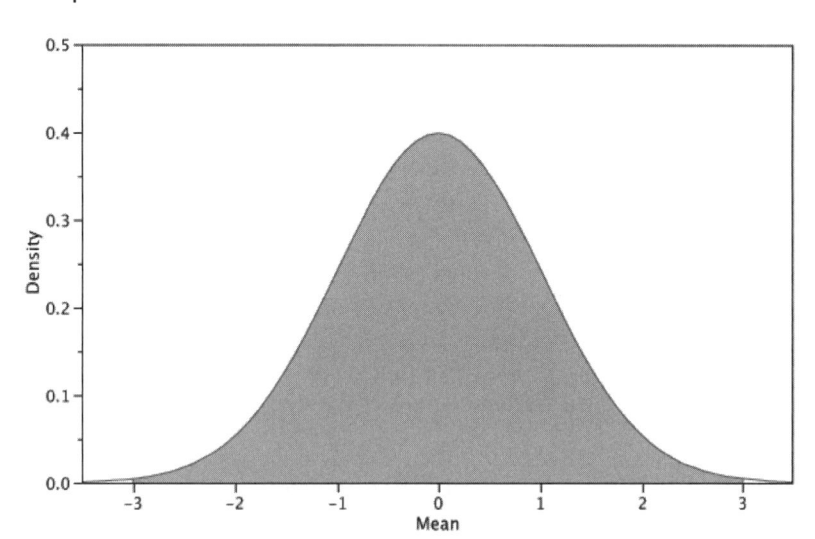

Figure 5.8 99.7% of the population is inside the interval in the interval $\mu \pm 3s$.

In each case, the population standard deviation is taken as the reference. This statistic is therefore quite important because is allows us to estimate the dispersion of the measurements. The estimation of the standard deviation of the population of responses is used as the measure of experimental error.

5.2.4.6 Error Transmission

From a statistical point of view, measuring a response experimentally is the same as randomly selecting a value from the population of responses. This population has a distribution, a mean, and a standard deviation. In many cases, the distribution of the responses is a normal distribution and the standard deviation is a measure of the experimental error. Responses drawn at random are likely to distribute themselves around the mean in a completely predictable manner.

If several trials are taken from the central point of the response distribution, their mean can be calculated. For example, the mean of four trials is

$$\bar{y} = \frac{1}{4}\left[y_1 + y_2 + y_3 + y_4\right]$$

How do the errors made on the responses y_i affect the mean? Statisticians studied this problem and saw that the errors were not additive. The error on our example mean is not four times the error from each response. To solve this problem, we need to use the variance. By definition, the variance of a response, $V(y_i)$ is the square of the standard deviation. That is, if the standard deviation of the response y_1 is σ_y, the variance of the response is σ_y^2. The equation giving an estimation of the response's population variance is

$$s_y^2 = V(y_i) = \frac{1}{n-1}\sum_{i=1}^{n}(y_i - \bar{y})^2$$

Note that the variance is equal to the sum of the squares of the deviations from the mean divided by the number of degrees of freedom of the deviations. That is, divide the sum of the squares of the deviations from the mean by their degrees of freedom. This rule is used extensively in the section describing analysis of variance (ANOVA) where several variances having different degrees of freedom are calculated.

Variances can be added together, and are always positive (since the square of a value is always greater than zero). The variance of a sum is therefore equal to:

$$V(y_1 + y_2 + y_3 + y_4) = V(y_1) + V(y_2) + V(y_3) + V(y_4)$$

The variance of a difference is similarly equal to:

$$V(-y_1 + y_2 - y_3 + y_4) = V(y_1) + V(y_2) + V(y_3) + V(y_4)$$

Also note that a constant c multiplied by a random variable increases the variable's variance by a factor of c^2:

$$V(cy) = \frac{1}{n-1}\sum_{i=1}^{n}(cy_i - c\bar{y})^2$$

$$= \frac{1}{n-1}\sum_{i=1}^{n}\left(c(y_i - \bar{y})\right)^2$$

$$= \frac{1}{n-1}\sum_{i=1}^{n}c^2(y_i - \bar{y})^2$$

$$= c^2\left(\frac{1}{n-1}\sum_{i=1}^{n}(y_i - \bar{y})^2\right)$$

$$= c^2 V(y)$$

Finding the mean of our four values [$\bar{y} = \frac{1}{4}(y_1 + y_2 - y_3 + y_4)$] involves a coefficient of $\frac{1}{4}$. Calculating the variance squares this value, so the variance of the mean is equal to

$$V(\bar{y}) = V\left(\tfrac{1}{4} y_1 + y_2 + y_3 + y_4\right)$$

$$= \left(\frac{1}{4}\right)^2 V(y_1 + y_2 + y_3 + y_4)$$

$$= \left(\frac{1}{4}\right)^2 \left(V(y_1) + V(y_2) + V(y_3) + V(y_4)\right)$$

If the variances of the responses are equal to each other, they are said to possess *homoscedasticity*. If we let $V(y_i)$ represent this constant variance, the preceding equation can be rewritten as

$$V(\bar{y}) = \left(\frac{1}{4}\right)^2 \left(V(y_1) + V(y_2) + V(y_3) + V(y_4)\right)$$

$$= \frac{1}{16}\left(V(y_i) + V(y_i) + V(y_i) + V(y_i)\right)$$

$$= \frac{4}{16} V(y_i)$$

$$= \frac{1}{4} V(y_i)$$

Taking the square root of both sides of this equation and replacing 4 with n, we find that the number of responses involved in taking the mean results in

$$\sqrt{V(\bar{y})} = \sqrt{\frac{V(y_i)}{n}}$$

Recalling that the standard deviation is the same as the square root of the variance, we can see that gives us

$$\sigma_{\bar{y}} = \frac{\sigma_{y_i}}{\sqrt{n}} \tag{5.1}$$

The standard deviation of the means of a series of groups is equal to the standard deviation of the individual groups divided by the square root of the number of individual groups. This relationship illustrates that larger values of n give better precision on the mean's prediction.

The dispersion of the mean of the groups is smaller than the dispersion of the groups themselves. Therefore, there is better precision when estimating the mean of responses than on estimating any particular response.

5.2.4.7 Confidence Interval of the Responses

We have just seen the importance of the standard deviation of the population of responses, which is considered an evaluation of the experimental error or pure error. The estimate of this standard deviation, s, from a sample of the population is obtained using the equation

$$s = \sqrt{\frac{1}{n-1}\sum_{i=1}^{n}(y_i - \bar{y})^2}$$

The precision of this estimate depends on the number of values n, which is used in the calculation. If the sample has a large number of measurements, the calculated standard deviation will be of high precision, i.e., close to the population standard deviation. If the sample contains only a few measurements, the calculated standard deviation will have less precision, and it will need to be used cautiously. The *confidence interval* (CI) depends on:

- the probability chosen by the user. This probability is often 95% or 99%.
- the precision of the calculated standard deviation.

Stated mathematically,

$$CI = ks$$

Table 5.4 shows the values of k according to the chosen probability (percentage of cases where the hypothesis is correct) and the precision of the calculated standard deviation (number of measurements used in calculating s).

When the sample has a large number of independent observations, the precision of the standard deviation is high. This situation is common in factories or laboratories that calculate the same measurements on identical products day after day. Suppose the confidence interval has an associated probability of 95%. If a measurement y_i is taken, you can say that you have a 95% chance that the interval $y_i \pm 1.96s$ contains the mean of the population.

When considering designed experiments, it is rare that n is high. Most often, there are only a few responses measured at the same experimental point, frequently at the center of the experimental domain. These are *replicates*, i.e., measurements carried out in the same experimental conditions.

Suppose that the standard deviation had been calculated with five replicates and that a 95% probability is needed. If a measurement y_i is made, there is a 95% chance that the interval $y_i \pm 2.78s$ contains the mean of the population. With ten replicates in the calculation of the standard deviation, we can say that there is a 95% chance that the interval $y_i \pm 2.26s$ contains the mean of the population.

Table 5.4 Number of standard deviations needed to determine the probability that the mean of the population is inside the confidence interval

		Number of Measurements Used to Calculate s						
		2	3	4	5	10	20	∞
% of cases where the hypothesis is correct	70%	1.96	1.38	1.25	1.19	1.10	1.06	1.03
	90%	6.31	2.92	2.35	2.13	1.83	1.73	1.64
	95%	12.71	4.3	3.18	2.78	2.26	2.06	1.96
	99%	63.66	9.92	5.84	4.60	3.25	2.86	2.58

5.2.5 Factors and Influential Interactions

The influence of factors and their interaction are evaluated through the coefficients of the postulated model. We need to find a standard value to use for judging the importance of a coefficient. This standard is the standard deviation of the coefficient. That is to say, the value of a coefficient (a) is compared with the value of its standard deviation (s_a).

1. $a \gg s_a$: If the coefficient is markedly larger than its standard deviation, we deem the coefficient influential.

2. $a \ll s_a$: If the coefficient is markedly smaller than its standard deviation, we deem that the coefficient is essentially zero and its associated effect can be eliminated.

3. $a \approx s_a$: If the coefficient is of the same order of magnitude of its standard deviation, we must use subject-area knowledge and factor in the risk of omitting a needed effect to make a decision.

To evaluate the importance of a coefficient, we apply statistical theory that compares the coefficient (a) with its standard deviation (s_a) using the ratio $\dfrac{a}{s_a}$. This ratio is called

Student's t or the *t-ratio*. Starting with the *t*-ratio, we can evaluate the probability that the coefficient is different from zero, or, said another way, if it is or is not significant. This probability is the *p-value*. If the *p*-value is close to zero (that is, close to zero probability), the coefficient is influential and therefore is not equal to zero. If the *p*-value is close to one, the coefficient cannot be distinguished from zero and is therefore not influential. If the *p*-value has a value between these two extremes, the coefficient might be marginally significant or not significant.

Knowing whether or not a coefficient is significant requires us to evaluate the coefficient's standard deviation. We know that coefficients depend on the responses, the postulated model, and the calculation method. Similarly, the variance of the coefficients depends on the responses, on the postulated model, and on the calculation method. Statisticians have established formulas giving the variance of the coefficients, $V(a) = s_a^2$, as a function of the variance of the error, $V(e)$, sum of the variance of the experimental error, and the value of the error variance from the postulated model. Therefore,

$$V(a) = K\, V(e)$$

where the constant K depends on the postulated model and experimental matrix. In the most general case, K is hard to calculate and only specialty software has the necessary algorithms to make the calculations. In the case of full-factorial experiments in which the levels –1 and +1 are perfectly respected and where the postulated model is a polynomial, i.e., in the cases that we have seen, the relation simplifies and becomes

$$V(a) = \frac{1}{n} V(e)$$

The variance of the coefficients is therefore directly related to the variance of the error. Remember that the error can be divided into two parts: the *lack of fit* and the *pure error* (also known as the experimental error)

$$e = \Delta + \varepsilon$$

And so

$$V(e) = V(\Delta) + V(\varepsilon)$$

To get the standard measure that we are searching for, we must have a value for the variance of the error. We get this value thanks to the variance.

5.2.6 Analysis of Variance (ANOVA)

5.2.6.1 Principles of Analysis of Variance

Analysis of Variance (ANOVA) consists of finding the source of variation of the responses. Suppose that the responses have been calculated with a postulated model $y_i = f(x_1, x_2, x_3 \cdots, x_n) + e_i$, by using the method of least squares; that is, by minimizing the sum of the squares of the errors. In this case, the responses are written $\hat{y}_i$ and the errors as e. These theoretical errors take particular values, written as r_i, and called *residuals*. The residuals are therefore particular values of the errors. We have

$$\hat{y}_i = f(x_1, x_2, x_3 \cdots, x_n)$$

With the new notation, the equation giving the response can be written as:

$$y_i = \hat{y}_i + r_i$$

Classical analysis of variance uses not only the responses themselves but also the difference between the responses and their mean $(y_i - \bar{y})$ or $(\hat{y}_i - \bar{y})$. This difference is designated as "errors about the mean." In the case of calculated responses, we can also say, "corrected for the mean."

In the case of the method of least squares, the mean of the observed responses is equal to the mean of the observed responses under the postulated model. Therefore, if $\bar{y}$ is the mean of the responses,

$$y_i - \bar{y} = \hat{y}_i - \bar{y} + r_i$$

Squaring both side of the equation gives:

$$\sum (y_i - \bar{y})^2 = \sum (\hat{y}_i - \bar{y})^2 + \sum r_i^2 \tag{5.2}$$

This is the fundamental relation of analysis of variance. The left side is the sum of squares of the errors around the mean of the observed responses. This sum decomposes into two pieces: the sum of squares of the errors around the mean of the responses calculated with the model, and the sum of the squares of the residuals.

The sum of squares of the residuals is the smallest value from the sum of squares of the errors. Therefore,

$$\sum r_i^2 = \text{Minimum of } \sum e_i^2 = \text{Minimum of } \sum (\Delta + \sigma)_i^2$$

Dividing the sum of squares of the residuals by the number of degrees of freedom of the residuals gives the variance of the residuals. The variance of the residuals, $V(r_i)$, is therefore the smallest variance of the errors, $V(e)$. Therefore,

$$V(r_i) = \text{Minimum of } V(e) = \frac{1}{n-p} \sum_{i=1}^{i=n} r_i^2$$

This is the minimum value of the variance of the errors that is the generally adopted standard for evaluating the importance of a coefficient. The variance of the coefficients is calculated by the following general formula, which is used by computers:

$$V(a_i) = KV(e) = KV(r_i)$$

which can be simplified with factorial or polynomial models to:

$$V(a_i) = \frac{1}{n} V(e) = \frac{1}{n} V(r_i) \tag{5.3}$$

In summary, the variance of the residuals of the analysis of variance is used to calculate the variance of the coefficients. This is the variance of the coefficients that are used to find the standard for testing whether a coefficient is significant or not.

Note 1
The n observed responses are completely independent, i.e., there is no mathematical relationship among them. They therefore have n degrees of freedom. One degree of freedom is used to calculate the mean. The error variance of the mean of the observed responses, $y_i - \bar{y}$, has $n - 1$ degrees of freedom.

The calculation of p coefficients takes $p - 1$ degrees of freedom only because the mean has already been calculated. The variance of the errors around the mean of the observed responses $\hat{y}_i - \bar{y}$, therefore, has $p - 1$ degrees of freedom.

There remains $n - 1 - (p - 1) = n - p$ degrees of freedom for calculation of the variance of the residuals.

Note 2
These rules and statistical tests apply only to purely random variables. The lack of fit is not a random measurement, but a systematic error, so the statistical rules of errors are not applicable. However, it is often assumed that the lack of fit is the same order of magnitude as the experimental error. It is a good idea to verify this fact. The measure of

experimental error, $V(\sigma)$, is assured by repetitions. The measure of the residuals, $V(r)$, is taken from the analysis of variance. The lack of fit $V(\Delta)$ can therefore be calculated as:

$$V(r) = V(\Delta) + V(\sigma)$$

By comparing the experimental error variance to the lack of fit, it is possible to see if this hypothesis is valid.

Note 3

Do not confuse the errors, the residuals, and the deviations from the mean.

The *errors* are the differences, e, between the observed responses and the mathematical model postulated before calculating the coefficients by the method of least squares:

$$y_i = f(x_1, x_2, x_3 \cdots, x_n) + e_i$$

The *residuals* are the differences, r_i, between the observed responses and the predicted responses with the coefficients obtained by the method of least squares:

$$r_i = y_i - \hat{y}_i$$

The *errors around the mean* are the differences, $y_i - \bar{y}$ or $(\hat{y}_i - \bar{y})$, between the responses and the mean of the responses.

Note 4

The mean square of the residuals is obtained by dividing the sum of squares of the residuals by its corresponding number of degrees of freedom. It is therefore a measurement analogous to the variance. Consequently, the square root of this variance is analogous to a standard deviation. This is why the expressions *residual variance* and *standard deviation of the residuals* are found to qualify these quantities. However, since these errors are not entirely random, some authors prefer to use the term *mean square of the residuals* instead of *residual variance* and *root square of the mean square of the residuals* instead of *standard deviation of the residuals*. The expression *square root of the mean square of the residuals* is a little long, so the abbreviation RMSE (*root mean square error*) is usually used.

When the model is well fit, the RMSE is used to calculate the error on the coefficients of the postulated model.

Regardless of the units used for the measurements, long calculations are inevitable. Luckily, computers carry out all the calculations and provide the results of the analysis of variance in tabular form. The only element chosen by the experimenter is the *a priori* model used to calculate the answers. The results of the analysis are dependent on the model choice. You are invited to redo the calculations of the analysis of variance by utilizing different postulated models to see the influence of the model choice on the RMSE.

5.2.6.2 Presentation of the Analysis of Variance (ANOVA)

Software, even spreadsheets, can construct ANOVA tables. The simplest of these tables has five columns (source of variation, sum of squares, degrees of freedom (DF), mean square, and F-ratio) and four lines (column titles, model corrected for the mean, residuals and observed responses corrected for the mean) similar to Table 5.5. The first column shows the sources of variation. The second column shows the DF of each sum of squares. Note also that the sum of the DF from the model and residuals is equal to the DF of the observed responses. The third column gives the sums of squares of the errors around the mean. Note that the sum of squares of the observed responses (corrected for the mean) is equal to the sum of the two other columns. The mean squares of the fourth column are the sums of squares divided by their DF. Note that the square root of the mean squares of the residuals serves to calculate the standard, allowing for testing of the coefficients. It is therefore a very important statistic. Finally, the fifth column shows the F-ratio, which is the ratio of the mean square of the model to the mean square of the residuals. This ratio allows the calculation of the probability that the two mean squares are not equal. In other words, if the F-ratio is high (small probability that the model is only due to the effect of the mean), the variations of the observed responses are likely due to variations in the factors. If the F-ratio is near 1 (strong probability that the model is not due to the effects), the variations of the observed responses are comparable to those of the residuals. The p-value corresponding to the F-ratio is also shown.

Table 5.5 Analysis of variance (ANOVA) table

Analysis of Variance				
Source	DF	Sum of Squares	Mean Square	F Ratio
Model	10	965.30000	96.5300	46.3196
Error	5	10.42000	2.0840	Prob > F
C. Total	15	975.72000		0.0003*

The coefficient of determination R^2

The analysis of variance allows the calculation of a very useful statistic: R^2. This statistic is the ratio of the sum of squares of the predicted responses (corrected for the mean) to the sum of squares of the observed responses (also corrected for the mean):

$$R^2 = \frac{\text{Sum of squares (Model)}}{\text{Sum of Squares (Total)}}$$

In our disposable cutting tools example,

$$R^2 = \frac{965.30}{975.72} = 0.9893$$

How do we evaluate the value of 0.9893? We know the following about R^2.

- If the model reproduces the observed responses exactly, the sum of squares of the calculated responses is equal to the sum of squares from the model and to the total sum of squares. R^2 is equal to 1.

- If the model gives predictions equal to the mean, the sum of squares of the model is equal to zero. R^2 is equal to zero. The model has no explanatory power.

R^2 is therefore a measure of the quality of the model. In practice, it is difficult to say what a good value of R^2 is. For example, an R^2 of 0.8 may be considered poor by an engineer, yet a psychologist considers an R^2 of 0.3 highly significant.

R^2 plays the role of indicating the quality of a linear model, provided that the residuals are not zero. If the residuals are zero, R^2 is equal to 1, regardless of the quality of the model. It is therefore a good indicator of the quality of a model if there are more experimental points than there are coefficients in the postulated model.

5.2.7 Application

We now construct an ANOVA table for the disposable cutting tools example and deduce from it the significance of each coefficient. First, we gather the necessary data: the observed responses, the predicted responses with a model, and the corresponding residuals (Table 5.6). The chosen model is the model of factorial designs having second-order interactions. It has 11 coefficients:

$$\hat{y} = 11.55 - 0.1x_1 - 6.2875x_2 - 3.425x_3 - 2.075\,x_4 \\ + 0.6375x_1x_2 + 0.325x_1x_3 + 0.35x_1x_4 + 1.5875x_2x_3 - 1.1125x_2x_4 + 0.6x_3x_4$$

Table 5.6 Data used to calculate the ANOVA table, where lifespan of the tool is the response

Trial	Observed Lifespan	Predicted Lifespan	Residual
1	26.1	25.825	0.275
2	22.2	23	−0.8
3	10.1	11.025	−0.925
4	12.2	10.75	1.45
5	14.2	13.95	0.25
6	12.7	12.425	0.275
7	5.9	5.5	0.4
8	5.6	6.525	−0.925
9	23	22	1
10	20.1	20.575	−0.475
11	2.4	2.75	−0.35
12	3.7	3.875	−0.175
13	11	12.525	−1.525
14	13.4	12.4	1
15	0.5	−0.375	0.875
16	1.7	2.05	−0.35

Model sum of squares corrected for the mean

The mean of the responses is 11.

1. Start by calculating the deviations from the mean of the 16 observed responses from the factorial design:

$$26.1 - 11.55 = +14.55$$
$$22.2 - 11.55 = +10.65$$
$$10.1 - 11.55 = -1.45$$
$$\vdots$$
$$0.5 - 11.55 = -11.05$$
$$1.7 - 11.55 = -9.85$$

2. Then, square these deviations and add them up. This gives the sum of squares around the mean of the observed responses corrected for the mean:

$$(14.55)^2 + (10.65)^2 + \cdots + (-11,05)^2 + (-9,85)^2 =$$
$$211.7025 + 113.4225 + \cdots + 122.1025 + 97.0225 = +975.72$$

Mean square for the model (variance of the predictions or model variance)

1. First, calculate the 16 responses for the model specified above. Verify that their mean is equal to 11.55.

2. Then calculate the 16 prediction's deviations from the mean:

$$25.825 - 11.55 = +14.275$$
$$23.0 - 11.55 = +11.45$$
$$11.025 - 11.55 = -0.525$$
$$\vdots$$
$$-0.375 - 11.55 = -11.925$$
$$2.05 - 11.55 = -9.5$$

3. These deviations from the mean are squared and summed. This gives the error sum of squares about the mean.

$$(14.275)^2 + (11.45)^2 + \cdots + (-11.925)^2 + (-9.5)^2 =$$
$$+203.775625 + 131.1025 + \cdots + 142.205625 + 90.25 = +965.30$$

4. This sum is divided by its corresponding degrees of freedoms, i.e., the number of coefficients minus one. This gives the mean square of the error (or the variance of the observed responses or the model variance).

$$\frac{965.30}{11-1} = 96.53$$

Mean square of the errors (variance of the residuals)

Remember that a residual is equal to

$$r_i = y_i - \hat{y}_i$$

1. Calculate the 16 residuals:

    $26.1 - 25.825 = +0.275$

    $22.2 - 23 = -0.8$

    $10.1 - 11.025 = -0.925$

    $\vdots$

    $0.5 - (-0.375) = -0.875$

    $1.7 - 2.05 = -0.35$

2. These residuals are squared and summed. This gives the sum of squares of the errors:

    $+0.075625 + 0.64 + \cdots + 0.765625 + 0.1225$

    $= +10.42$

3. This sum is divided by its corresponding degrees of freedom; that is, $n - p = 16 - 11 = 5$ DF for error:

    $$\frac{10.42}{16 - 11} = 2.084$$

This results in the mean square for the error. Its square root is the RMSE, which serves as the standard for evaluating the importance of the coefficients. The RMSE here is 1.4436 when the postulated model contains only main effects and second-order interactions.

Note that R^2 and the RMSE are displayed in the Summary of Fit portion of a standard JMP model report.

Summary of Fit	
RSquare	0.989321
RSquare Adj	0.967962
Root Mean Square Error	1.443607
Mean of Response	11.55
Observations (or Sum Wgts)	16

Standard deviation of the coefficients

In our example, we have a factorial design where the levels are coded only as –1 and 1. Also, the model is a polynomial as well, so the simple formula is appropriate for finding a standard of comparison.

Each coefficient has been calculated with 16 responses.

$$V(a_i) = \frac{1}{n} V(r_i) = \frac{1}{16} 2.084 = 0.13025$$

$$\sigma_{a_i} = \sqrt{0.13025} = 0.3609$$

This is the comparison value that we have been searching for.

p-value

The *p*-value is the probability that a coefficient is not significant. It is calculated from the ratio of the coefficient to its standard deviation (i.e., the *t*-ratio). For example, the *t*-ratio of the flow coefficient is – 0.1/0.3609 = – 0.28, and the associated *p*-value is 0.7928.

It is now possible to construct a table where each coefficient is shown along with its value, its standard deviation, its *t*-ratio, and its *p*-value (Table 5.7). This table is identical to Table 5.3. Now, however, we can understand the significance of the numbers.

Table 5.7 Significance of the model coefficients (coded units)

Coefficient	Value	Standard Deviation	t-Ratio	p-Value
Intercept	11.55	0.3609	32	< 0.0001
Flow (1)	− 0.1	0.3609	− 0.28	0.7928
Cutting speed (2)	− 6.2875	0.3609	− 17.42	< 0.0001
Depth (3)	− 3.425	0.3609	− 9.49	0.0002
Forward speed (4)	− .075	0.3609	− 5.75	0.0022
1×2	0.6375	0.3609	1.77	0.1376
1×3	0.325	0.3609	0.90	0.4091
1×4	0.35	0.3609	0.97	0.3767
2×3	1.5875	0.3609	4.40	0.0070
2×4	− 1.1125	0.3609	− 3.08	0.0274
3×4	0.6	0.3609	1.66	0.1573

The intercept has less than one chance in 10,000 to be equal to zero. It is certainly not equal to zero, and it is significant, and is saved in the final model.

Flow (factor 1) has a p-value of 0.79. That is, repeated experiments would show this coefficient to be essentially zero 79% of the time. There is therefore no evidence to say it is not zero. Therefore, it is considered as zero and eliminated from the final model. This means that the observed responses are not much different from those obtained when a final model is used omitting this effect.

If the acceptance probability for the coefficients is set at a p-value of 0.1, we keep cutting speed (factor 2), depth (factor 3) and forward speed (factor 4), as well as the cutting speed×depth and cutting speed×forward speed interactions. The final model can be written as

$$y = 11.55 - 6.29 x_2 - 3.42 x_3 - 2.1 x_4 + 1.6 x_2 x_3 - 1.1 x_2 x_4 \qquad (5.4)$$

We check to see that the model has a good R^2 (0.97) and that the *p*-values of the coefficients are all less than 0.1. If we had fixed the acceptance probability at another level, a different final model would have been obtained. The choice of the final model is left to the discretion of the experimenter, who knows the risks and rewards of the study.

5.2.8 Residual Analysis

If the interpretation is done correctly, the model represents the observed values well. R^2 is near 1 and the RMSE is of the same order of magnitude as the experimental error. To make sure that there is no structural information in the results, it is common to examine a graph of the residuals. It is therefore important to look at how the residuals are structured according to different criteria. If they seem to be distributed randomly, there is no more information to extract. This is the case in the example of this chapter (Figure 5.9).

Figure 5.9 Residual analysis for the cutting tools example

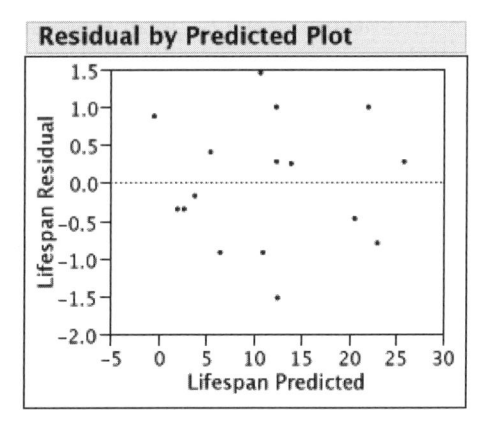

On the other hand, if the residual analysis showed a marked pattern, there is still some information to extract. For example, graphs will sometimes show a pattern where the residuals are more and more spread out as the response gets larger are encountered (Figure 5.10A). In this case, the hypothesis of homoscedasticity has been violated. Also, graphs where the residuals are negative for small and large response values and positive for intermediate values appear (Figure 5.10B). In this case, the hypothesis of an underlying linear model with or without interactions is doubtful, and a model of second or higher degree should be investigated.

Figure 5.10A Examples of a residual analysis showing particular structures. The dispersion increases with the response (non-homoscedastic data).

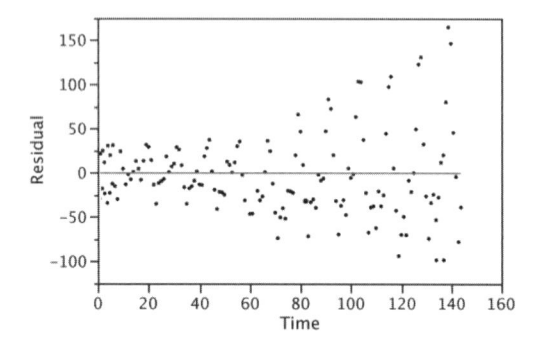

Figure 5.10B Examples of a residual analysis showing particular structures. The residuals support a second-degree model.

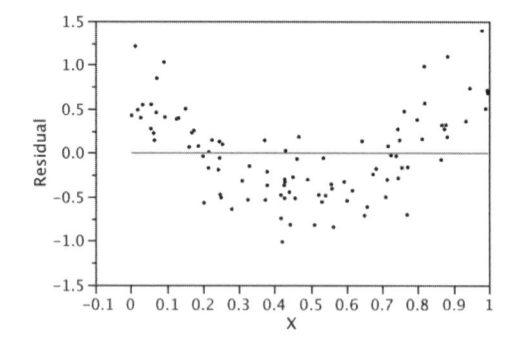

5.2.9 Study Conclusion

The lifetime of disposable cutting tools is influenced by the speed and depth of cutting. To increase the lifespan of the tools, it is necessary to work at low cutting speeds and not to use the tools to cut deeply.

However, to ensure profitability, the output must be sufficiently high. Therefore, a compromise must be made that ensures a profitable production with a controlled wear of the tools. This compromise is obtained if the lifespan is at least 20 hours. The established model (which is in coded units) allows predictions to be made.

$$y = 11.55 - 6.29x_2 - 3.42x_3 - 2.1x_4 + 1.6x_2x_3 - 1.1x_2x_4$$

The graph in Figure 5.11, drawn for a flow of 725 and a forward speed of 0.75, shows a potentially favorable zone that is in the lower left corner, i.e., low cutting speeds and small depths. After the results of the designed experiment, the trials 1, 2, 9, and 10 correspond to these requirements and verify that lifespans are more than 20 hours long (Table 5.2).

Figure 5.11 Iso-response curves for tool lifetime as a function of the cutting speed and the depth. The flow and the forward speed are set at 725 and 0.75, respectively.

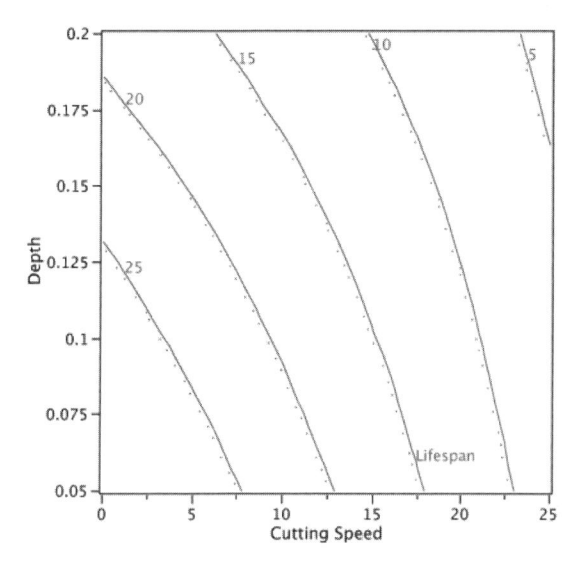

Table 5.8 Trials where the lifespan is longer than 20 hours

Trial #	Flow	Cutting Speed	Depth	Forward Speed	Lifespan (Response)
	(1)	(2)	(3)	(4)	
1	650	10	0.05	0.5	26.1
2	800	10	0.05	0.5	22.2
9	650	10	0.05	1	23
10	800	10	0.05	1	20.1

Before making proposals, it is wise to carry out confirmatory experiments to verify the predictions. Therefore, three tests were carried out (Table 5.9), one at the domain boundary and others at the 20-hour limit (trials 22 and 23).

Table 5.9 Verification trials

Trial	Flow	Cutting Speed	Depth	Forward Speed	Predicted Lifespan	Measured Lifespan
	(1)	(2)	(3)	(4)		
21	725	10	0.05	0.75	22.86	23.1
22	725	13	0.05	0.75	19.90	20.2
23	725	10	0.09	0.75	20.18	19.8

After comparing the predictions made with the simplified model (5.4) with the new measurements, agreement is noted. The model is therefore validated and recommendations can be as follows.

In order to preserve the cutting tools and to ensure them a lifespan of (about) 20 hours or more, it is necessary to cut with a speed of 11, with a cutting depth of less than 0.07, and a forward speed that is less than 0.75 (Figure 5.12). These recommendations are easy to find using the desirability functions and the **Maximize Desirability** command shown in Chapter 4.

Figure 5.12 The desirability allows rapid discovery of the best operating conditions.

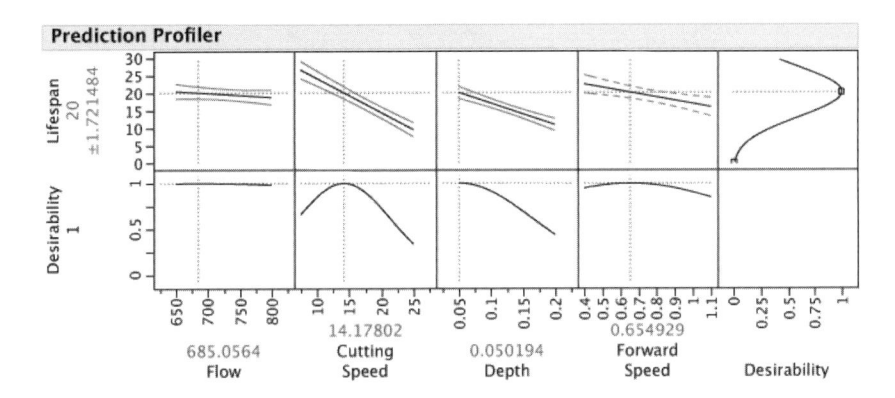

Chapter 6

Fractional Factorial and Screening Designs

6.1 Introduction   132
6.2 Example 5: Measuring Tellurium Concentration   133
    6.2.1 Preparing the Designed Experiment   133
    6.2.2 Running the Experiment   135
    6.2.3 Interpreting the Results   136
6.3 Alias Theory   137
    6.3.1 Definition of Contrasts   138
    6.3.2 New Interpretation Hypotheses   140
6.4 Box Calculations   141
    6.4.1 Box Notation   141
    6.4.2 Operations on the Column of Signs   142
    6.4.3 Rules to Remember   144
6.5 Equivalence Relation   144
    6.5.1 Basic Design   144
    6.5.2 Equivalence Relation   146

6.6 Alias Generating Functions 147
    6.6.1 Alias Generating Function of the Upper Half Design 147
    6.6.2 Alias Generating Function of the Lower Half Design 148
    6.6.3 Reading Aliases in Software 149
6.7 Practical Construction of a Fractional Factorial Design 149
    6.7.1 2^3 Full Factorial Design 151
    6.7.2 2^{4-1} Fractional Factorial 152
    6.7.3 2^{5-2} Fractional Factorial 154
    6.7.4 2^{7-4} Fractional Factorial 156
6.8 Maximum Number of Factors from a Base Design 157
6.9 Aliasing Theory with the Tellurium Example 157
    6.9.1 Confounding in the Tellurium Example 158
    6.9.2 Application of the Interpretation Assumption to the Tellurium Example 158
    6.9.3 Study Conclusion 159

6.1 Introduction

Like full-factorial designs, fractional factorial designs deal with factors having two levels, a low level and a high level. However, unlike full-factorial designs, all combinations of these levels are not used in the experiment. As seen in Chapter 4, the number of trials for a full factorial experiment rises rapidly with the number of factors.

Although it's not uncommon to find experiments using seven or eight factors, it is unreasonable to execute $2^7 = 128$ or $2^8 = 256$ trials. In these cases, a fraction of the trials from a full factorial is chosen to make a fractional factorial design. This selection is based on mathematical principals that are applied using Box's method. It's also possible to utilize DOE software like JMP to put these mathematical principals into practice.

It is more difficult to interpret fractional factorial plans than it is to interpret full factorials, since there is less information. However, we can often be satisfied by finding out which of the main effects are significant and, in some cases, which second-order interactions come into play. This is the reason that these designs are often called *screening designs*. These designs let us determine which of a large number of factors are influential. This is often the single goal of these experiments, so they are not often carried through to the stage of mathematical modeling and coefficient interpretation. Therefore, the mathematical models used are themselves far simpler. The most common models are those having only main effects (first-degree terms) or models with main effects and second order interactions, depending on the objectives of the study.

Instead of carrying out a 2^4 full factorial of 16 trials, we can carry out only 8 trials, half the number of runs. The corresponding fractional design is a 2^4 design divided in half (by 2), or a $2^4/2$ design, or simply a 2^{4-1} design. The meaning of the notation 2^{4-1} is the following: the 2 shows that the factors each take only two levels. The 4 shows that the study has four factors. Finally, $4 - 1 = 3$ shows that we are using a design analogous to a 2^3 full factorial that only has 8 runs. This notation works mathematically as well, since it indicates the number of trials to be used in our plan: $2^{4-1} = 8$ trials.

The interpretation of fractional factorial designs requires us to introduce the theory of aliases and to apply interpretation hypotheses. The first of these interpretation hypotheses is the following:

Assumption 1
Third- and higher-than-third-order interactions are not significant.

6.2 Example 5: Measuring Tellurium Concentration

6.2.1 Preparing the Designed Experiment

6.2.1.1 The Tellurium Study
In this study, chemists are trying to determine the tellurium content of seawater. However, the nature and concentration of metals aside from tellurium can distort measurements. The tellurium content may read as too high or too low, depending on the presence of other metals and their concentrations. Some problematic metals are sodium (Na), potassium (K), calcium (Ca), and magnesium (Mg).

6.2.1.2 Defining the Study Objectives
Chemists want to know which metals distort their measurements, and they want to have an idea of the importance of the difference between the measured tellurium concentration and the real tellurium concentration. They want to be able to answer the question "Is the

measurement of tellurium content distorted a little, some, or a lot by the presence of Na, K, Ca, or Mg?" To carry out this study, the chemists prepare solutions containing identical quantities of tellurium, into which they add the contents of the (possibly) distorting metals.

This study does not try to find precise corrections for solutions containing Na, K, Ca, and Mg. To do so would require a complete factorial design of 16 studies, possibly followed by a quadratic design, if the linear model proved insufficient. The chemists simply want to know the magnitude of error caused by the presence of the four metals tested.

6.2.1.3 Choosing the Response

The chosen response is the difference between the true tellurium concentration and the observed concentration, measured by atomic spectrometry.

6.2.1.4 Search for Factors That May Influence the Response

For the four distorting metals, we'll keep:

- Sodium concentration
- Potassium concentration
- Calcium concentration
- Magnesium concentration

Table 6.1 shows the concentrations inside the study domain. Note that the central (0) point is not the middle of the interval [2.5, 250]. The reason is that chemists know that it's necessary to use logarithms of concentrations rather than concentration measurements directly. The zero level is a natural center point for this logarithmic scale.

Table 6.1 Factors retained in the domain

Factors	−1 level	0 level	+1 level
	µg/ml	µg/ml	µg/ml
Na concentration (1)	2.5	25	250
K concentration (2)	2.5	25	250
Ca concentration (3)	2.5	25	250
Mg concentration (4)	2.5	25	250

The factors studied and used in the mathematical model are:

- The logarithm of the sodium (Na) concentration
- The logarithm of the potassium (K) concentration
- The logarithm of the calcium (Ca) concentration
- The logarithm of the magnesium (Mg) concentration

6.2.1.5 Choosing the Design

The experimenter could do a complete factorial design, with 16 trials. This allows estimation of the main effects, second-order interactions, as well as third- and fourth-order interactions. However, there are probably only second-order interactions among the distorting metals. The experimenter therefore decides to do an eight-run design, that is, a 2^{4-1} design. This allows evaluation of the main effects of each factor and shows if second-order interactions are likely to be influential.

Table 6.2 shows the details of the design and the responses measured during the experiment.

6.2.2 Running the Experiment

Table 6.2 Trials and responses of the tellurium experiment

Trial	Na	K	Ca	Mg	Tellurium
	(1)	(2)	(3)	(4)	
1	−1	−1	−1	−1	128
2	+1	−1	−1	+1	153
3	−1	+1	−1	+1	104
4	+1	+1	−1	−1	130
5	−1	−1	+1	+1	86
6	+1	−1	+1	−1	109

(continued)

Table 6.2 (*continued*)

Trial	Na	K	Ca	Mg	Tellurium
7	−1	+1	+1	−1	66
8	+1	+1	+1	−1	96

−1	Log 2.5	Log 2.5	Log 2.5	Log 2.5
0	Log 25	Log 25	Log 25	Log 25
+1	Log 250	Log 250	Log 250	Log 250

6.2.3 Interpreting the Results

To interpret the experimental results, we can treat the raw data in several ways. We could eliminate some of the coefficients of the model so that the number of parameters that we need to estimate matches the number of coefficients. We could also regroup the coefficients to achieve the same goal. We could also use a mixed method, based on both a simplified model and the theory of aliases. In the first case, the theory of aliases must be used to understand the significance of the calculated values.

This interpretation of results is facilitated by the interpretation assumption. We will examine several fractional factorial designs, and we will see how simple reasoning allows us either to conclude that the study is finished, or to decide if more trials are needed.

6.2.3.1 Mathematical Model

Using the first assumption of interpretation, "Interactions of third or higher order are not significant," we choose a model using all the main effect (first degree) terms and all the first-order interaction terms.

$$y = a_0 + a_1 x_1 + a_2 x_2 + a_3 x_3 + a_4 x_4 + a_{12} x_1 x_2 + a_{13} x_1 x_3 + a_{14} x_1 x_4 \\ + a_{23} x_2 x_3 + a_{24} x_2 x_4 + a_{34} x_3 x_4 \quad (6.1)$$

There are therefore 11 coefficients. Software can calculate the intercept, main effects, and the three interaction groups. If the calculated interaction terms are weak, they can be eliminated from the model. If they are strong, they cannot be eliminated, and the interpretation becomes quite delicate. We then need to use the theory of aliases and a new assumption of interaction.

Note in Table 6.3 that one factor is particularly weak: magnesium (factor 4). The three other metals (sodium, potassium, and calcium) are significant, i.e., they distort the tellurium concentration.

The sums of the interactions are smaller than the main effect values and can be considered negligible.

Table 6.3 Model coefficients (coded units)

Effect	Value
Intercept	109
Na (1)	13
K (2)	−10
Ca (3)	−19.75
Mg (4)	−0.75
Na K (12) + Ca Mg (34)	1
Na Ca (13) + K Mg (24)	0.25
K Ca (23) + Na Mg (14)	−1.75

In JMP, the model coefficients are displayed in a report similar to the following, which uses the Screening platform.

Figure 6.1 JMP Screening Platform Output

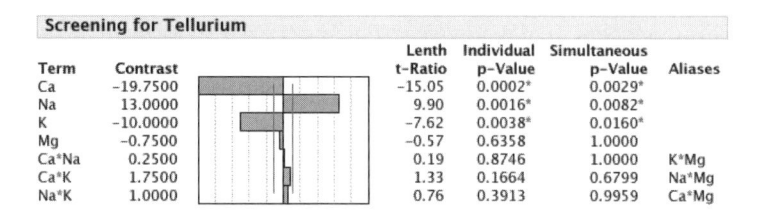

Screening for Tellurium

Term	Contrast		Lenth t-Ratio	Individual p-Value	Simultaneous p-Value	Aliases
Ca	−19.7500		−15.05	0.0002*	0.0029*	
Na	13.0000		9.90	0.0016*	0.0082*	
K	−10.0000		−7.62	0.0038*	0.0160*	
Mg	−0.7500		−0.57	0.6358	1.0000	
Ca*Na	0.2500		0.19	0.8746	1.0000	K*Mg
Ca*K	1.7500		1.33	0.1664	0.6799	Na*Mg
Na*K	1.0000		0.76	0.3913	0.9959	Ca*Mg

6.3 Alias Theory

The theory of aliases is useful for understanding and interpreting the results of a fractional factorial design. We have divided the study of this theory into five parts:

1. Definition of contrasts

2. Interpretation hypotheses

3. Box calculations

4. Equivalence relation

5. Alias generators

Following the theory of aliases, we will see two important aspects of fractional factorial designs:

- Construction of fractional factorial designs
- Maximum number of studied factors in a design of given data

6.3.1 Definition of Contrasts

When interpreting the results of a fractional factorial, the usual, full-factorial calculation rules apply. The postulated model for analyzing the tellurium data is

$$y = a_0 + a_1 x_1 + a_2 x_2 + a_3 x_3 + a_4 x_4$$
$$+ a_{12} x_1 x_2 + a_{13} x_1 x_3 + a_{14} x_1 x_4 + a_{23} x_2 x_3 + a_{24} x_2 x_4 + a_{34} x_3 x_4$$
$$+ a_{123} x_1 x_2 x_3 + a_{124} x_1 x_2 x_4 + a_{123} x_1 x_3 x_4 a_{234} x_2 x_3 x_4$$
$$+ a_{124} x_1 x_2 x_3 x_4$$

(6.2)

This model has 16 unknown coefficients. To calculate them, 16 equations are needed, as in the case of factorial designs. However, with a fractional factorial design, there are only eight equations. The design matrix therefore has 8 rows and 16 columns, and the columns are arranged so that they have identical levels in groups of two. The unknowns are therefore regrouped in groups of two. This gives us a system of eight groups of unknowns for eight equations. For the tellurium example, the levels of magnesium (factor 4) are the same as the levels of the third order Na×K×Ca interaction, so the magnesium column is the same as the Na×K×Ca interaction column. In this design, we would write Mg=Na×K×Ca or $x_4 = x_1 x_2 x_3$. We will see how to associate columns, and therefore their coefficients, according to the experimental points used in the fractional factorial plan. We now have eight groups of two unknown factors, so the system of equations is solvable. These regroupings of coefficients are called aliases or contrasts and are written as ℓ_i. In the tellurium example, the contrast ℓ_1 groups the coefficient a_1 from factor 1 with the coefficient a_{234} from the 2×3×4 interaction. We say, "a_1 is aliased with the interaction a_{234}."

In the same way,

- a_2 is aliased with the interaction a_{134}.
- a_3 is aliased with the interaction a_{124}.
- a_4 is aliased with the interaction a_{123}.
- a_{12} is aliased with the interaction a_{34}.
- a_{13} is aliased with the interaction a_{24}.
- a_{23} is aliased with the interaction a_{14}.
- a_0 is aliased with the interaction a_{1234}.

Equation (6.2) can be rewritten (to follow alias groupings):

$$y = (a_0 + a_{1234}) + (a_1 + a_{234})x_1 + (a_2 + a_{134})x_2 + (a_3 + a_{124})x_3 + (a_4 + a_{123})x_4 \\ + (a_{12} + a_{34})(x_1x_2 \text{ or } x_3x_4) + (a_{13} + a_{24})(x_1x_3 \text{ or } x_2x_4) + (a_{14} + a_{23})(x_1x_4 \text{ or } x_2x_3)$$

The numeric value of these regroupings is the sum of the values of the coefficients. For example, the contrast ℓ_1 is equal to the effect of factor 1 added to the value of the 2×3×4 interaction.

$$\ell_1 = a_1 + a_{234}$$

If the 2×3×4 interaction is weak, the contrast ℓ_1 is equal to the effect of factor 1. Since we have assumed assumption 1, which dictates that third-order interactions are negligible, we can say that the contrast ℓ_1 is equal only to the effect of factor 1.

Now, consider the 1×2 interaction, which is aliased with the 3×4 interaction.

$$\ell_{12} = \ell_{34} = a_{12} + a_{34}$$

The numeric value of this contrast ℓ_{12} (or ℓ_{34}) is due to both the 1×2 interaction and the 3×4 interaction. There is no way to separate out the contributions of the individual interactions to the contrast. They are grouped into the same contrast, and we know only the value of the group.

However, through practical experience, experimenters noticed that, most of the time, if a contrast had a small numeric value, the aliases involved in the contrast were also weak. They also noted that when two factors were strong, there may be a strong interaction between them. On the other hand, if two factors were weak, it was unlikely that there was a real interaction between them. From these observations, some new assumptions for interpreting fractional factorial designs were developed.

6.3.2 New Interpretation Hypotheses

To analyze the results of a fractional factorial design, assumption 1 must be supplemented by some new assumptions.

Assumption 1

Third- and higher-order interactions are not significant.

Assumption 2

All the coefficients aliased in a weak (negligible) contrast are themselves weak (negligible).

Assumption 3

If two contrasts are strong, their interaction may be strong (but it may not).

Assumption 4

If two contrasts are weak, we assume their interactions are weak as well.

Assumption 5

A weak main effect and a strong main effect sometimes (but not always) generate a weak interaction.

The five assumptions presented here are often true, but sometimes they are shown to be false. They are valid about 95% of the time, but invalid about 5% of the time.

For example, assumption 4 is sometimes risky if two factors are simultaneously present that trigger the same response: the process of a thermo-hardening resin is activated by the simultaneous presence of a catalyst (first factor) and an accelerator (second factor). Alone, the catalyst or the accelerator would not change the resin, but together their behavior is quite different.

It is always possible to adopt another assumption according to the problem at hand and the incurred risks. For a good analysis, it's a good idea to always specify the assumptions of hypothesis that have been used. These assumptions are excellent guides for analyzing the results of a fractional factorial design. They allow us to discover deficiencies in the experimentation and to specify any complementary trials needed to obtain a complete interpretation.

We have just seen that a contrast is the sum of two coefficients. However, it can also be a succession of sums or differences (that is, more than two), because the association among coefficients depends on the position of the experimental points that were chosen during the construction of the fractional design. The ability to find the elements that make up contrasts is crucial in correctly interpreting a fractional factorial design.

The mathematics of alias theory is beyond the scope of this book. However, there is a much simpler theory, based on *Box calculations*. This theory is appropriate only for fractional factorial designs with two levels fixed exactly at coded levels −1 and +1. Of course, computer software can be used to directly find the alias decomposition.

For information about the general mathematical theory of aliases, see the bibliography. We give an outline of the Box calculation here because it, along with the equivalence relation, is used to understand the construction and interpretation of fractional factorial designs.

6.4 Box Calculations

Box calculations make it possible to quickly find how effects and interactions are aliased in contrasts. This theory, as we have already stated, is appropriate only for fractional factorial designs with two levels fixed at exactly −1 and +1.

6.4.1 Box Notation

In Box notation, the number **1** (in boldface) represents factor 1 with its signs in Yates order. For a 2^2 design, we have:

$$\mathbf{1} = \begin{bmatrix} -1 \\ +1 \\ -1 \\ +1 \end{bmatrix}$$

Similarly, factor 2's column is designated as:

$$\mathbf{2} = \begin{bmatrix} -1 \\ -1 \\ +1 \\ +1 \end{bmatrix}$$

We also have unit vectors of positive and negative signs.

$$\mathbf{I} = \begin{bmatrix} +1 \\ +1 \\ +1 \\ +1 \end{bmatrix} \quad -\mathbf{I} = \begin{bmatrix} -1 \\ -1 \\ -1 \\ -1 \end{bmatrix}$$

6.4.2 Operations on the Column of Signs

Box calculations consist of carrying out operations on these columns using rules that we now define. Signs are multiplied term-by-term by applying the sign rule. For example, the multiplication of **1** and **2** is

$$\mathbf{1} \times \mathbf{2} = \begin{bmatrix} -1 \\ +1 \\ -1 \\ +1 \end{bmatrix} \times \begin{bmatrix} -1 \\ -1 \\ +1 \\ +1 \end{bmatrix} = \begin{bmatrix} +1 \\ -1 \\ -1 \\ +1 \end{bmatrix}$$

The +1 sign from the first term of the column-product is the result of the multiplication of −1 (first term from **1**) by −1 (first term of **2**). The other signs of the column-product are obtained in the same way.

We now show the most useful operations used on columns of signs.

Multiplication of a column by itself

For example, multiply column **1** by itself:

$$\mathbf{1} \times \mathbf{1} = \begin{bmatrix} -1 \\ +1 \\ -1 \\ +1 \end{bmatrix} \times \begin{bmatrix} -1 \\ +1 \\ -1 \\ +1 \end{bmatrix} = \begin{bmatrix} +1 \\ +1 \\ +1 \\ +1 \end{bmatrix} = \mathbf{I}$$

We obtain a column of plus signs. The multiplication of column **2** by itself gives the same result. In general, the multiplication of a column by itself gives a column of plus signs.

Multiplication of a column by a column of plus signs
Multiplying column **2** by **I**:

$$2 \times \mathbf{I} = \begin{bmatrix} -1 \\ -1 \\ +1 \\ +1 \end{bmatrix} \times \begin{bmatrix} +1 \\ +1 \\ +1 \\ +1 \end{bmatrix} = \begin{bmatrix} -1 \\ -1 \\ +1 \\ +1 \end{bmatrix} = \mathbf{2}$$

The multiplication of a column by a column of positive signs gives the initial column. Said another way, the multiplication of a column by a column of plus signs does not change the multiplied column.

Multiplication of a column by a column of negative signs
Multiplying column **2** by **− I**:

$$2 \times (-\mathbf{I}) = \begin{bmatrix} -1 \\ -1 \\ +1 \\ +1 \end{bmatrix} \times \begin{bmatrix} -1 \\ -1 \\ -1 \\ -1 \end{bmatrix} = \begin{bmatrix} +1 \\ +1 \\ -1 \\ -1 \end{bmatrix} = \mathbf{-2}$$

The multiplication of a column by a column of negative signs gives a column of opposite signs from the original.

Multiplication of a column of plus signs by itself
For example,

$$\mathbf{I} \times \mathbf{I} = \begin{bmatrix} +1 \\ +1 \\ +1 \\ +1 \end{bmatrix} \times \begin{bmatrix} +1 \\ +1 \\ +1 \\ +1 \end{bmatrix} = \begin{bmatrix} +1 \\ +1 \\ +1 \\ +1 \end{bmatrix} = \mathbf{I}$$

Multiplication of a column of plus signs by itself results in an identical column of plus signs.

Commutatively of multiplication

$$1 \times 2 = \begin{bmatrix} -1 \\ +1 \\ -1 \\ +1 \end{bmatrix} \times \begin{bmatrix} -1 \\ -1 \\ +1 \\ +1 \end{bmatrix} = \begin{bmatrix} +1 \\ -1 \\ -1 \\ +1 \end{bmatrix} = \begin{bmatrix} -1 \\ -1 \\ +1 \\ +1 \end{bmatrix} \times \begin{bmatrix} -1 \\ +1 \\ -1 \\ +1 \end{bmatrix} = \mathbf{2 \times 1}$$

The result of multiplying **1** by **2** is the same as multiplying **2** by **1**. This is the *commutative* property.

6.4.3 Rules to Remember

Simply remember the following rules to master Box calculations. For simplicity, the multiplied signs have been omitted from the formulas.

Rule 1: Commutatively

    1 2=2 1

Rule 2: Multiplication of a column by itself

    1 1=I   2 2=I

Rule 3: Multiplication of a column by **I** or **– I**

    1 I=1   2 I=2
    1 (–I)= – 1   2 (–I)= – 2
    I I=I

6.5 Equivalence Relation

6.5.1 Basic Design

Consider a 2^3 design and its postulated model.

$$y = a_0 + a_1 x_1 + a_2 x_2 + a_3 x_3 + a_{12} x_1 x_2 + a_{13} x_1 x_3 + a_{23} x_2 x_3 + a_{123} x_1 x_2 x_3$$

The term $x_1 x_2$ is the product of the levels of factors 1 and 2, i.e., the interaction 1×2. We can therefore construct a column of signs corresponding to the 1×2 interaction by multiplying, using Box calculation rules, the columns of factor 1 and factor 2. We can do the same for the 1×3, 2×3, and 1×2×3 interactions. We can also add a column of positive signs to introduce the intercept into the calculations. This gives a table, called the *base matrix* or *base design*, which is composed of 8 lines and 8 columns (Table 6.4).

Table 6.4 Base matrix for a 2^3 design

Trial	I	1	2	3	12	13	23	123
1	+	−	−	−	+	+	+	−
2	+	+	−	−	−	−	+	+
3	+	−	+	−	−	+	−	+
4	+	+	+	−	+	−	−	−
5	+	−	−	+	+	−	−	+
6	+	+	−	+	−	+	−	−
7	+	−	+	+	−	−	+	−
8	+	+	+	+	+	+	+	+

This base matrix corresponds to the matrix that is used to calculate the effects and interactions of a full factorial design. However, for a fractional factorial, only half of the trials are used. Divide this base matrix into two pieces: a half-design consisting of trials 5, 2, 3, and 8 (shaded rows of Table 6.5) and a half-design consisting of trials 1, 6, 7, and 4.

Table 6.5 Base matrix cut into two fractional designs

Trial	I	1	2	3	12	13	23	123
5	+	−	−	+	+	−	−	+
2	+	+	−	−	−	−	+	+
3	+	−	+	−	−	+	−	+
8	+	+	+	+	+	+	+	+
1	+	−	−	−	+	+	+	−
6	+	+	−	+	−	+	−	−
7	+	−	+	+	−	−	+	−
4	+	+	+	−	+	−	−	−

Initially, consider the shaded half design. It contains eight columns of four signs where each column has a duplicate. In Box notation we can write, for example, that the column of four signs of factor 1 is equal to that of the interaction 2×3. That is:

$$1 = 23$$

We saw that in this half-design, factor 1 was confounded with the 2×3 interaction, and that the contrast ℓ_1, calculated with column 1 (or with column 23), was the sum of the coefficients a_1 and a_{23}.

$$\ell_1 = \ell_{23} = a_1 + a_{23}$$

6.5.2 Equivalence Relation

Note that the aliased coefficients in a contrast are those that have the same column of signs in the considered half-design. This is a general rule: A contrast is the algebraic sum of the coefficients that have the same column of signs. That is, **1 = 23** in Box notation implies the contrast calculated with column **1** is the sum $\ell_1 = a_1 + a_{23}$, and the contrast calculated with column **23** is the sum $\ell_{23} = a_1 + a_{23}$.

We can therefore say

1 = 23   is equivalent to $\ell_1 = \ell_{23} = a_1 + a_{23}$

This is the equivalence relation. It is useful in both notations and it forms the base of the theory of aliases. An examination of Table 6.5 shows that we also have

2 = 13   is equivalent to $\ell_2 = \ell_{13} = a_2 + a_{13}$

3 = 12   is equivalent to $\ell_3 = \ell_{12} = a_3 + a_{12}$

I = 123   is equivalent to $\ell_0 = \ell_{123} = a_0 + a_{123}$

The importance of these equations lies in the fact that they enable the discovery of interactions and aliasing in each contrast. To know the aliasing structure, we could proceed as above: write a basic design, slice it into fractions, and search for columns with equal signs. Although useful for understanding the equivalence relation, this process takes too long and makes the aliasing structure difficult to discover. It is by using Box calculations and introducing alias generating functions that we can easily find the aliasing structure.

Note
The term *contrast* is not universally used. Some books use the term *confounding*. Equally, the term *alias* is often used. Finally, the word *concomitance* is sometimes used to show the simultaneous estimation of a coefficient in the same structure. All these terms are synonymous and translate the two aspects of the equivalence relation by highlighting that the effects and interactions are amalgamated into a single unknown and that the columns of signs correspond to half-designs. The notion of contrasts itself is delicate and the differently used terms express the difficulty in finding the best word. These different names are used synonymously in this book.

6.6 Alias Generating Functions

6.6.1 Alias Generating Function of the Upper Half Design

Consider the upper half design from Table 6.5. The two columns of + signs let us write the following in Box notation:

$$I = 123 \tag{6.2}$$

By multiplying both sides of this equation by **1** and using the rules for Box multiplication, we get identical columns of the upper half design.

1. Multiply both sides of equation (6.3) by **1**.

    1×I = 1×123

2. Apply rule 2

    1×I = I×23

3. Apply rule 3

    1 = 23

By multiplying both sides of equation (6.3) successively by **2** and **3**, we get the two equations

$2 = 13$

$3 = 12$

The equation **I = 123** therefore allows recovery of all the columns that are equal in the upper half design. By knowing these equalities and by applying the equivalence relation, we recover how the coefficients are aliased in the contrasts.

The equation **I = 123** is called the *alias generating function*.

6.6.2 Alias Generating Function of the Lower Half Design

Examine the lower half design in Table 6.5 to see that columns correspond in pairs, but with opposite signs. The column of plus signs corresponds to the column of minus signs of the 1×2×3 interaction. Therefore, in Box notation, we have

$$I = -123 \tag{6.3}$$

This is the alias generating function of the lower half plan.

By multiplying into both sides of equation (6.4) and using the Box multiplication rules, we have

$1 \times I = 1 \times -123$

$1 = -I \times 23$

$1 = -23$

The 2×3 interaction column has exactly the opposite signs of column 1. To find the structure of the contrast of column 1, apply the equivalence relation

$$\ell'_1 = -\ell'_{23} = a_1 - a_{23}$$

The calculated contrasts with the lower half design are differences of coefficients. In the same way, we can calculate

$2 = -13$ giving $\ell'_2 = -\ell'_{13} = a_2 - a_{13}$

$3 = -12$ giving $\ell'_3 = -\ell'_{12} = a_3 - a_{12}$

$I = -123$ giving $\ell'_0 = -\ell'_{123} = a_0 - a_{123}$

6.6.3 Reading Aliases in Software

Good DOE software always shows how the coefficients are aliased in the contrasts. For example, JMP shows the aliasing alongside the results of the experiment when the Screening platform is used (see Figure 6.1). The Fit Model platform shows them in an outline node titled **Singularity Details**. Columns that are equal are shown as in Box calculations. Other software shows the aliased coefficients in each contrast.

6.7 Practical Construction of a Fractional Factorial Design

Looking at the four first columns of the upper half design (Table 6.5), we see that we have the column of signs from a 2^2 factorial design. This design is made up of columns 1 and 2, with column 12 made by using the rule of signs and a column of plus signs (Table 6.6).

Table 6.6 Base 2^2 design

Trial	I	1	2	12
1	+	-	-	+
2	+	+	-	-
3	+	-	+	-
4	+	+	+	+

The 1×2 interaction could be used to study an extra factor, say, factor 3. Levels for this additional factor are similar to the signs of the 1×2 interaction column (Table 6.8). This allows us to easily build fractional factorial designs. In Box notation, factor 3 has levels that are equal to the signs of the 1×2 interaction

$3 = 12$

When we multiply each side of this equation by **3**, the alias generating function appears.

3×3 = 3×123

I = 123×3

I = 123

This generator allows us, via Box calculations and the equivalence relation, to see how the coefficients are aliased in the contrasts.

Table 6.7 2^{3-1} design built with the generator I = 123

Trial	1	2	3
1	−	−	+
2	+	−	−
3	−	+	−
4	+	+	+

In the place of the generator **I = 123**, we can write the generator **I = −123**. In this case, the third factor is studied using the opposite signs of the 1×2 interaction (Table 6.8).

Table 6.8 2^{3-1} built from the generator I = −123

Trial	1	2	3
1	−	−	−
2	+	−	+
3	−	+	+
4	+	+	−

The practical construction of fractional factorials that we have just seen is from a basic 2^2 design, which can be generalized to all 2^k designs as follows:

1. Choose a full factorial design and write the corresponding base design by applying the sign rule.

2. In the base design, choose a column of signs corresponding to an interaction and designate it as an additional factor. Use either the column with identical signs or the column with opposite signs.

3. Find the alias generator function using Box calculations.

4. By multiplying the alias generating function by the equivalence relation, find the structure of the contrasts.

Let's complete these steps using a 2^3 base design (Table 6.9). There are four available columns for studying additional factors: 1×2, 1×3, 2×3, and 1×2×3 interactions. Therefore, several fractional factorial plans can be constructed that will have eight trials, but which will make it possible to study several additional factors.

Table 6.9 Basic 2^3 design

Trial	I	1	2	3	12	13	23	123
1	+	−	−	−	+	+	+	−
2	+	+	−	−	−	−	+	+
3	+	−	+	−	−	+	−	+
4	+	+	+	−	+	−	−	−
5	+	−	−	+	+	−	−	+
6	+	+	−	+	−	+	−	−
7	+	−	+	+	−	−	+	−
8	+	+	+	+	+	+	+	+

From this base design, we are going to repeatedly extract full factorial designs, from which we can build fractional factorial designs.

6.7.1 2^3 Full Factorial Design

Columns 1, 2, and 3 are from a full factorial design for studying three factors (Table 6.10).

Table 6.10 2^3 Full factorial design

Trial	1	2	3
1	−	−	−
2	+	−	−
3	−	+	−
4	+	+	−
5	−	−	+
6	+	−	+
7	−	+	+
8	+	+	+

6.7.2 2^{4-1} Fractional Factorial

This is the design used for the tellurium example. We want to study four factors, but only use eight runs. Give the name **4** to the additional factor, and choose one of the four interaction columns. For example, let us choose the 1×2×3 interaction (Table 6.11). The levels used to study factor 4 are those of the 1×2×3 interaction column. We build the fractional factorial by extracting the four columns **1**, **2**, **3**, and **123** from the base design.

Table 6.11 2^{4-1} design

Trial	1	2	3	4 = 123
1	−	−	−	+
2	+	−	−	−
3	−	+	−	−
4	+	+	−	+
5	−	−	+	+
6	+	−	+	−
7	−	+	+	−
8	+	+	+	+

Since the fourth factor is being studied using the levels of the 1×2×3 interaction, we can write

I = 1234

This is the alias generating function that allows the calculation of the contrast structure. By multiplying the generator successively by 1, 2, 3, and 4, we get the equalities of the columns. Then, by utilizing the equivalence relation, we get the contrasts.

$1 = 234$ is equivalent to $\ell_1 = a_1 + a_{234}$

$2 = 134$ is equivalent to $\ell_2 = a_2 + a_{134}$

$3 = 124$ is equivalent to $\ell_3 = a_3 + a_{124}$

$4 = 123$ is equivalent to $\ell_4 = a_4 + a_{123}$

$I = 1234$ is equivalent to $\ell_0 = a_0 + a_{1234}$

We could have aliased factor 4 with another interaction, giving other contrast structures. For example, if we chose to study factor 4 with the 1×2 interaction, we would have had

4 = 12

which gives an alias generating function of

I = 124

By multiplying this generator successively by **1, 2, 3,** and **4**, we get equivalence relations and the structure of the corresponding contrasts.

$1 = 24$ is equivalent to $\ell_1 = a_1 + a_{24}$

$2 = 14$ is equivalent to $\ell_2 = a_2 + a_{14}$

$3 = 1234$ is equivalent to $\ell_3 = a_3 + a_{1234}$

$4 = 12$ is equivalent to $\ell_4 = a_4 + a_{12}$

$I = 124$ is equivalent to $\ell_0 = a_0 + a_{124}$

In the same way, we could have chosen the 1×3 interaction or the 2×3 interaction to study factor 4. These choices, however, are not equivalent. The first choice, **4 = 123**, is much better than the others because the main effect is completely aliased with the third-order interaction, i.e., with the interaction having the best chance of being insignificant. This is not the case with 2^{4-1} designs where some main effects are confounded with second-order interactions.

6.7.3 2^{5-2} Fractional Factorial

It's completely possible to study two additional factors. We choose two columns that are not already occupied by main effects (here, columns 1, 2, and 3). For example, we could choose the 1×2 interaction for the fourth factor and the 1×3 interaction for the fifth factor (Table 6.12). The corresponding fractional factorial is a 2^{5-2} design because it is a full factorial of 32 trials cut into fourths. The 2^3 design was divided by 2^2, which is equal to writing 2^{5-2}. Table 6.12 shows the 2^{5-2} fractional factorial.

Table 6.12 2^{5-2} Fractional factorial

Trial	1	2	3	4 = 12	5 = 13
1	-	-	-	+	+
2	+	-	-	-	-
3	-	+	-	-	+
4	+	+	-	+	-
5	-	-	+	+	-
6	+	-	+	-	+
7	-	+	+	-	-
8	+	+	+	+	+

We now find the aliasing structure using Box calculations. We have two equations

$$4 = 12 \qquad 5 = 13$$

so, of course, two alias generating functions

$$I = 124 \qquad I = 135$$

These two alias generating functions give the choice of two independent interactions from the base design. Such generators are *independent* generating functions.

If both independent alias generating functions are multiplied through, a third generator appears.

$$I \times I = 124 \times 135$$

$$I = 2345$$

This new alias generator is a *dependent* alias generator. Note that two additional factors introduce a *group of generating functions* (GGF) rather than a single one. This GGF has four terms:

$$I = 124 = 135 = 2345$$

This GGF is used to establish the aliasing structure of the fractional factorial design. For example, the contrast ℓ_1 is found by multiplying all the terms of the GGF by the **1** column.

$$1 \times I = 1 \times 124 = 1 \times 135 = 1 \times 2345$$

Simplifying gives:

$$1 = 24 = 35 = 12345$$

The four columns **1**, **24**, **35**, and **12345** are identified in the quarter base design. The equivalence relation gives the four aliased coefficients in the contrasts ℓ_1, ℓ_{24}, ℓ_{35} and ℓ_{12345}:

$$\ell_1 = \ell_{24} = \ell_{35} = \ell_{12345} = a_1 + a_{24} + a_{35} + a_{12345}$$

The equation is simplified by writing only one of the contrasts.

$$\ell_1 = a_1 + a_{24} + a_{35} + a_{12345}$$

Other contrasts are calculated in the same way and incorporate all four coefficients.

Note
The term *alias generating function* (AGF) is also known as the *defining equation*. It is this relation that allows the definition of the fractional factorial plan with precision and that gives the aliasing structure.

6.7.4 2^{7-4} Fractional Factorial

The most general use of this method is to use all the columns of the base design (Table 6.13). Starting from a $2^3 = 8$ run full factorial, we can study up to seven factors since there are four interaction columns. In this case, we divide a 128-run design (2^7) into sixteenths (2^4).

Table 6.13 2^{7-4} fractional factorial

Trial	1	2	3	4 = 123	5 = 12	6 = 13	7 = 23
1	−	−	−	−	+	+	+
2	+	−	−	+	−	−	+
3	−	+	−	+	−	+	−
4	+	+	−	−	+	−	−
5	−	−	+	+	+	−	−
6	+	−	+	−	−	+	−
7	−	+	+	−	−	−	+
8	+	+	+	+	+	+	+

The alias generator is obtained by first taking the four independent generators:

    4 = 123   5 = 12
    6 = 13   7 = 23

The two dependent generators are obtained by multiplying them in pairs, then three at a time, and finally four at a time. The AGF contains 16 terms and is multiplied successively by **1, 2, 3, 4, 5, 6,** and **7**. The resulting equations allow us to establish the contrast structure that show each of the 16 terms in the 2^{7-4} fractional factorial. In the general case, the contrasts of a 2^{k-p} fractional factorial contain 2^p terms. Calculating each contrast is tedious, tiring, and the results are prone to mistakes, so we will see how to get them from software.

6.8 Maximum Number of Factors from a Base Design

You can study as many additional factors as there are interactions in the base design (Table 6.14).

For a 2^2 base design, there is one interaction. Therefore, three factors can be studied, two for columns 1 and 2, and a third for the interaction column.

For a 2^3 base design, there are four interactions. Therefore, seven factors can be studied: three for columns 1, 2, and 3, and four others for the interaction columns 1×2, 1×3, 2×3, and 1×2×3.

Table 6.14 shows the maximum number of factors that can be studied for a given base design.

Table 6.14 Maximum number of factors that can be studied for a given base design

Base Design	Number of Factors in the Full Factorial Design	Number of Interactions	Maximum Number of Factors That Can Be Studied
2^2	2	1	3
2^3	3	4	7
2^4	4	11	15
2^5	5	26	31
2^6	6	57	63
2^7	7	120	127

6.9 Aliasing Theory with the Tellurium Example

Let's see how these recently learned ideas are put into practice in the chapter's example.

6.9.1 Confounding in the Tellurium Example

The tellurium design is a 2^{4-1} fractional factorial where the alias generating function is

$$I = 1234$$

By applying Box calculations, we get the following for the main effects:

$$1 = 234 \qquad 2 = 134 \qquad 1 = 234$$

If a mathematical model is chosen with negligible third-order interactions, we have equivalence relations

$$\ell_1 = a_1 \qquad \ell_2 = a_2 \quad \text{and} \qquad \ell_3 = a_3$$

For these interactions, we get

$$12 = 34 \qquad 13 = 24 \qquad 23 = 14$$

So

$$\ell_{12} = \ell_{34} = a_{12} + a_{34} \qquad \ell_{13} = \ell_{24} = a_{13} + a_{24} \qquad \text{and} \qquad \ell_{23} = \ell_{14} = a_{23} + a_{14}$$

6.9.2 Application of the Interpretation Assumption to the Tellurium Example

Assumption 1 was applied in the choice of the model. The main effects are obtained directly, and they are not confounded with interactions. To analyze the results, re-examine the contrasts in Table 6.3 in the form of a bar chart (Figure 6.2) and analyze them.

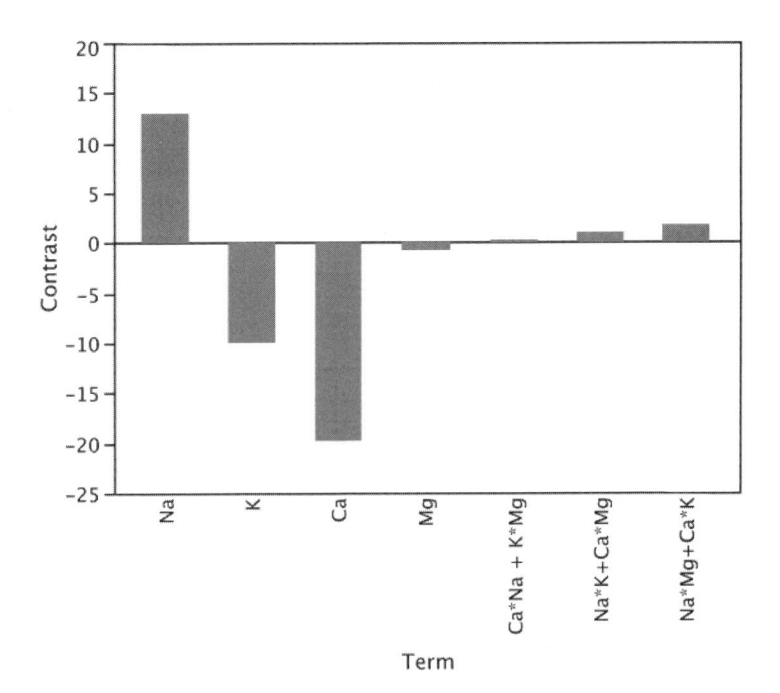

Figure 6.2 Bar chart of the coefficients

Apply assumption 2 (All coefficients in a negligible contrast are themselves negligible) by assuming that a contrast lower than 2 is negligible.

Since ℓ_{13} is equal to 0.25, we consider it insignificant. Therefore, the coefficients a_{13} and a_{24} are also insignificant. Using the same reasoning, we can deduce from contrast ℓ_{14} that the coefficients a_{14} and a_{23} are close to zero and therefore negligible. The same goes for a_{12} and a_{34}.

6.9.3 Study Conclusion

Only the salts of calcium, potassium, and sodium affect the measurement of the tellurium concentration of seawater. There is no interaction among the metals. Everything happens as if each metal were the only one affecting the saltwater tellurium measure.

- Magnesium does not affect the measurements, so a correct tellurium content can be measured.

- The most influential factor is calcium. The apparent tellurium content is much smaller than the real tellurium content. In the presence of calcium, the measurements are defective.

- Potassium has the same effect as calcium. That is, in the presence of potassium, the values are also defective.

- Sodium causes tellurium readings to be higher than real values.

To make accurate measurements, these interferences must be taken into account. Potassium and calcium salts decrease the real values, while sodium increases them.

This measurement study shows that corrections must be made to the actual readings. A more complete study is necessary to give more precise direction on what these corrections should be. One or more designs should be considered to model the phenomenon. We will see that composite designs become invaluable for such situations, allowing models of the second degree (Chapter 9).

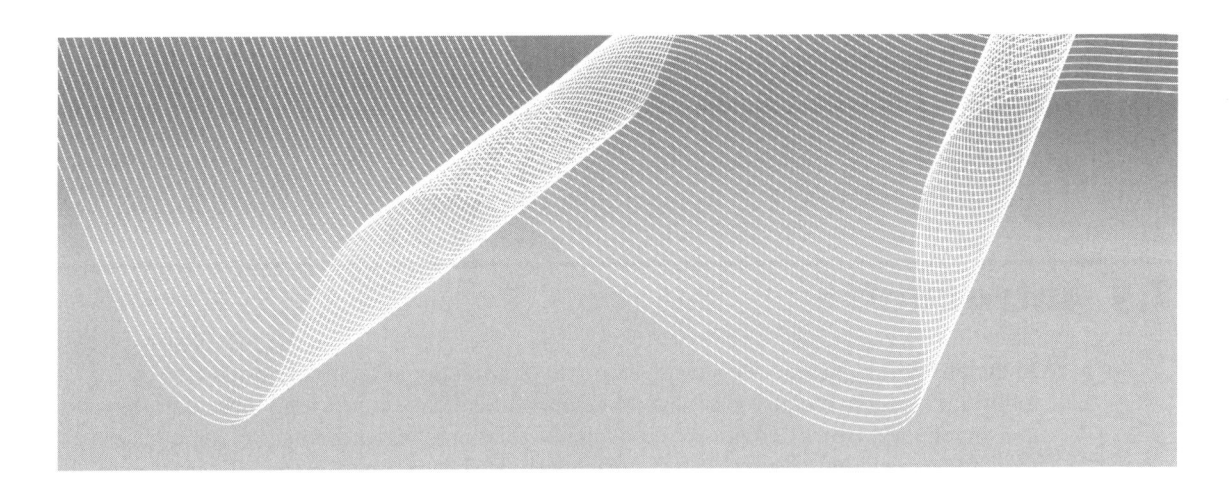

Chapter 7

Examples of Fractional Factorial Designs

7.1 Introduction 162
7.2 Example 6: Sulfonation 163
    7.2.1 Preparing the Designed Experiment 163
    7.2.2 Carrying Out the Experiment 165
    7.2.3 Interpreting the Results 166
    7.2.4 Study Conclusion 173
7.3 Example 7: Spectrofluorimetry 174
    7.3.1 Preparing the Designed Experiment 174
    7.3.2 Carrying Out the Experiment 180
    7.3.3 Interpreting the Results 180
    7.3.4 Building the Complementary Design 190
    7.3.5 Study Conclusion 196
7.4 Example 8: Potato Chips 198
    7.4.1 Preparing the Designed Experiment 198
    7.4.2 Carrying Out the Experiment 201

7.4.3 Interpreting the Results 201
7.4.4 Study Conclusion 204

7.1 Introduction

In the preceding chapter, we saw an example of a fractional factorial design (the tellurium design). We also saw several facets of the theory concerning these designs: aliasing theory, Box calculations, equivalence relations, the interpretation hypotheses, and the construction of fractional factorial designs. The comparison and illustration of all this theory is impossible with a single example. So, in this chapter, we examine several examples of fractional factorial designs. The number of factors for these designs increases, but the number of runs remains small. The interpretation of these plans starts with first postulating a model and then applying aliasing theory and the interpretation hypotheses. We then see (perhaps surprisingly) that we can gain a lot of information with a very few well-placed runs.

We say that with a 2^{k-p} base design we can theoretically study k factors where p of them have study levels calculated from columns of certain interactions. Negative signs are used as low levels and positive signs as high levels. Until now, we have used only one interaction of the base design as an additional study column. With a 2^3 base plan, there are four interactions, so we could study from four to seven additional factors with eight trials. The latter is a 2^{7-4} fractional design. Since all the interactions are used to study the main effects, we refer to this plan as *saturated*. Is it truly possible to study seven factors with only eight runs? We are going to see that it is possible and, in practice, experimenters often use such plans. The only conditions for success are to carry out all the trials and to use alias theory and the interpretation hypotheses correctly. Frequently, this initial experiment must be followed up with an augmented design, whose runs are specifically chosen to untangle the ambiguities which appear (by design) in the initial experiment. However, even if the initial design has eight runs, followed up by a design with eight runs, we have saved considerable resources. In effect we've examined seven factors, but instead of using 128 runs in a full 2^7 factorial design, we only used 16. It's hard to lose when you take a chance with a fractional design.

7.2 Example 6: Sulfonation

7.2.1 Preparing the Designed Experiment

7.2.1.1 The Study: Sulfonation of a BTX Mixture
Sulfonation of aromatic compounds produces surface-active compounds that are the foundations of many commercial detergents. Aromatic compounds that are studied are benzene, toluene, and xylenes (BTX mixtures), by-products of processing crude oil. Only toluene and xylenes provide interesting surfactants. To obtain the surfactant products, sulfuric acid (H_2SO_4) is added to a BTX mixture and left for a time so that the components react with each other. In the presence of sulfuric acid, benzene, toluene, and xylenes transform themselves progressively into sulfonic acids, which are used to make sulfonates. The sulfonation reaction can be accelerated either by adding sulfur anhydride (SO_3), or by eliminating the formed water, or by doing both. The BTX chemical reaction with sulfuric acid is called *sulfonation*, and we say that the BTX mixture has been *sulfonated*. The formed sulfonates contain the surfactants.

7.2.1.2 Defining the Objective of the Study
We want to produce toluene and xylene sulfonates that allow us to make high-quality detergents. On the other hand, we want to avoid benzene sulfonates, since they are not of interest. We therefore are searching for operating conditions that allow the sulfonation of toluene and the xylenes while avoiding the sulfonation of benzene.

The study will be considered a success if we can design a process that achieves these two goals:

- Sulfonation of toluene and the xylenes
- Sulfonation of as little benzene as possible

7.2.1.3 Choosing the Response to Measure
The chosen response is the ratio of sulfonation defined as:

$$\rho = \frac{\text{sulfonated toluene} + \text{sulfonated xylenes}}{\text{sulfonated benzene}}$$

A large value of this ratio is most desirable.

7.2.1.4 Searching for Factors That May Influence the Response

Among all the factors that might influence the sulfonation reaction, the experimenter has selected six:

- Duration of the addition of the sulfuric acid
- Percentage of sulfur anhydride (SO_3) in the sulfuric acid
- Temperature of the reaction
- Elimination of water during the reaction
- Time that the sulfuric acid remains in contact with the BTX mixture
- The ratio $\dfrac{acid}{toluene + xylenes}$

The study domain for these six factors is shown in Table 7.1.

Table 7.1 Factors and their study domain

Factors	−1 Level	+1 Level
Reaction duration (1)	5 hours	9 hours
SO_3 in H_2SO_4 (2)	0%	10%
Reaction temperature (3)	95°C	110°C
Water elimination (4)	Yes	No
Duration of the addition of acid (5)	10 min	30 min
Ratio $\dfrac{acid}{toluene + xylenes}$ (6)	0.8	1.2

7.2.1.5 Choosing the Design

If the experimenter had conducted a full factorial for these two-level factors, he would have had to carry out 64 trials. This is a considerable number. Therefore, he has decided to reduce the number of trials and to complete a fractional factorial design. The factors all have two study levels. The experimental budget allows for 16 trials, or four (2^2) times fewer than a full-factorial plan. With a 2^{6-2} fractional factorial with 16 trials, it is possible to study six factors with their second-order interactions.

7.2.1.6 Constructing the Design

The base design is a 2^4 factorial. The experimenter chooses to alias the duration of the acid addition (factor 5) with the 1×2×4 interaction, and the acid-response ratio (factor 6) with the 2×3×4 interaction. That is, the study levels of duration of the acid addition (factor 5) are the same as those of the 1×2×4 interaction. Likewise, the study levels of the acid-response ratio (factor 6) are the same as the signs of the 2×3×4 interaction. In Box notation, we write:

$$5 = 124$$

$$6 = 234$$

We write the four columns of the 2^4 design and calculate the signs of the 1×2×4 interactions and the 2×3×4 interactions by using the sign rules (Table 7.2).

7.2.2 Carrying Out the Experiment

Table 7.2 Trials and responses for the sulfonation experiment

Trial	Time	SO$_3$	Temperature	Water	Acid	Ratio	Response (ρ)
	1	2	3	4	5 = 124	6 = 234	
1	−1	−1	−1	−1	−1	−1	11.76
2	+1	−1	−1	−1	+1	−1	12.55
3	−1	+1	−1	−1	+1	+1	7.89
4	+1	+1	−1	−1	−1	+1	8.20
5	−1	−1	+1	−1	−1	+1	12.35
6	+1	−1	+1	−1	+1	+1	13.98
7	−1	+1	+1	−1	+1	−1	7.25
8	+1	+1	+1	−1	−1	−1	10.10
9	−1	−1	−1	+1	+1	+1	13.06
10	+1	−1	−1	+1	−1	+1	13.40

(continued)

Table 7.3 (continued)

Trial	Time 1	SO₃ 2	Temperature 3	Water 4	Acid 5 = 124	Ratio 6 = 234	Response (ρ)
11	− 1	+ 1	− 1	+ 1	− 1	− 1	12.10
12	+ 1	+ 1	− 1	+ 1	+ 1	− 1	8.91
13	− 1	− 1	+ 1	+ 1	+ 1	− 1	13.65
14	+ 1	− 1	+ 1	+ 1	− 1	− 1	16.10
15	− 1	+ 1	+ 1	+ 1	− 1	+ 1	11.09
16	+ 1	+ 1	+ 1	+ 1	+ 1	+ 1	9.86
− 1	5	0	95	Yes	10	0.8	
+ 1	9	10	110	No	30	1.2	

7.2.3 Interpreting the Results

To interpret the results of a fractional factorial design, it is best to understand the way the coefficients are aliased in the contrasts. Most often, it is only a question of the second-order interactions because the first interpretation hypothesis assumes that interactions higher than second-order are negligible.

7.2.3.1 Mathematical Model

We use a model with an intercept, coefficients for main effects, and coefficients for second-order interactions. This gives a system of 16 equations having 22 unknowns. We know that the second-order interactions are confounded and the Box calculations tell us how these interactions are grouped in the aliases.

$$y = a_0 + a_1 x_1 + a_2 x_2 + a_3 x_3 + a_4 x_4 + a_5 x_5 + a_6 x_6 + a_{12} x_1 x_2 + a_{13} x_1 x_3 + \ldots + a_{56} x_5 x_6 \tag{7.1}$$

7.2.3.2 Alias Structure
We have already written:

$$5 = 124 \qquad 6 = 234$$

That is,

$$\mathbf{I} = 1245 \qquad \mathbf{I} = 2346$$

Multiply **1245** by **2346** to get **1356**, which is also equal to **I**. This gives us the alias-generating function

$$\mathbf{I} = 1245 = 2346 = 1356$$

This group shows that the main effects are aliased with third-order interactions. If assumption 1 is respected, we can directly calculate the main effects. The second-order interactions are aliased with themselves. Multiply the generating function by **12**, **13**, and so on to get the contrasts. The fifteen second-order interactions regroup into the following contrasts:

$$\ell_{12} = \ell_{45} = a_{12} + a_{45}$$

$$\ell_{13} = \ell_{56} = a_{13} + a_{56}$$

$$\ell_{14} = \ell_{25} = a_{14} + a_{25}$$

$$\ell_{15} = \ell_{24} = \ell_{36} = a_{15} + a_{24} + a_{36}$$

$$\ell_{16} = \ell_{35} = a_{16} + a_{35}$$

$$\ell_{23} = \ell_{46} = a_{23} + a_{46}$$

$$\ell_{26} = \ell_{34} = a_{26} + a_{34}$$

7.2.3.3 Value of the Effects
Table 7.3 shows the results of the calculations of the effects and the aliases. A bar chart is shown in Figure 7.1 to illustrate this table. In addition, JMP output for the same results is shown.

Table 7.3 Effects and aliases in coded units

Effect	Value
Intercept	11.39
Reaction duration (1)	0.25
SO_3 in H_2SO_4 (2)	−1.96
Reaction temperature (3)	0.41
Water elimination (4)	0.88
Duration of the addition of acid (5)	−0.49
ratio $\dfrac{\text{acid}}{\text{toluene + xylenes}}$ (6)	−0.16
$\ell_{12} = a_{12} + a_{45}$	−0.40
$\ell_{13} = a_{13} + a_{56}$	0.46
$\ell_{14} = a_{14} + a_{25}$	−0.45
$\ell_{15} = a_{15} + a_{24} + a_{36}$	0.18
$\ell_{16} = a_{16} + a_{35}$	−0.11
$\ell_{23} = a_{23} + a_{46}$	−0.26
$\ell_{26} = a_{26} + a_{34}$	−0.003

Figure 7.1 Bar chart and JMP output for the sulfonation experiment

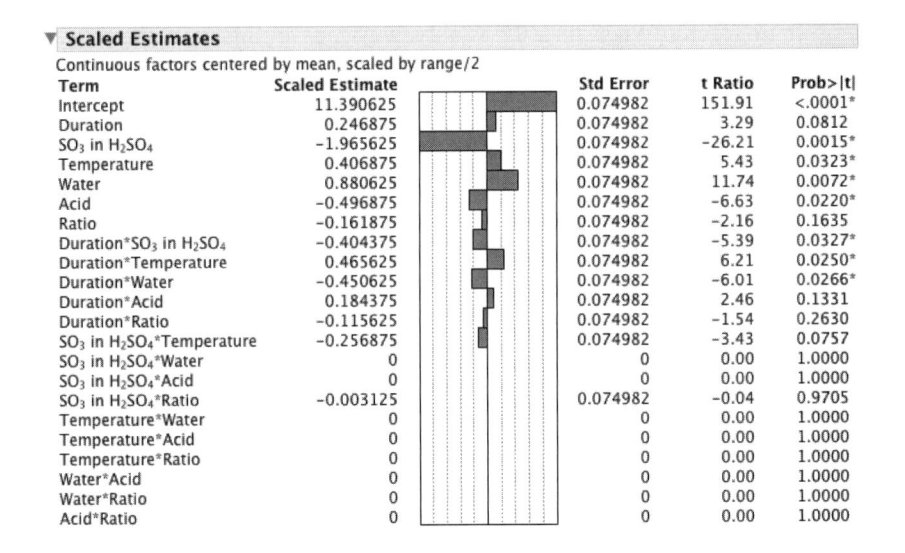

▼ Scaled Estimates
Continuous factors centered by mean, scaled by range/2

Term	Scaled Estimate	Std Error	t Ratio	Prob>|t|
Intercept	11.390625	0.074982	151.91	<.0001*
Duration	0.246875	0.074982	3.29	0.0812
SO_3 in H_2SO_4	-1.965625	0.074982	-26.21	0.0015*
Temperature	0.406875	0.074982	5.43	0.0323*
Water	0.880625	0.074982	11.74	0.0072*
Acid	-0.496875	0.074982	-6.63	0.0220*
Ratio	-0.161875	0.074982	-2.16	0.1635
Duration*SO_3 in H_2SO_4	-0.404375	0.074982	-5.39	0.0327*
Duration*Temperature	0.465625	0.074982	6.21	0.0250*
Duration*Water	-0.450625	0.074982	-6.01	0.0266*
Duration*Acid	0.184375	0.074982	2.46	0.1331
Duration*Ratio	-0.115625	0.074982	-1.54	0.2630
SO_3 in H_2SO_4*Temperature	-0.256875	0.074982	-3.43	0.0757
SO_3 in H_2SO_4*Water	0	0	0.00	1.0000
SO_3 in H_2SO_4*Acid	0	0	0.00	1.0000
SO_3 in H_2SO_4*Ratio	-0.003125	0.074982	-0.04	0.9705
Temperature*Water	0	0	0.00	1.0000
Temperature*Acid	0	0	0.00	1.0000
Temperature*Ratio	0	0	0.00	1.0000
Water*Acid	0	0	0.00	1.0000
Water*Ratio	0	0	0.00	1.0000
Acid*Ratio	0	0	0.00	1.0000

7.2.3.4 Distinguishing the Influential Factors

The coefficients of two factors, sulfur anhydride (factor 2) and the elimination of water (factor 4), are much larger than the others. These are therefore the ones that are most influential in achieving our goal. But are there other influential factors? Knowing where to draw the line between influential and non-influential factors is a delicate question that uses the value of the experimental error (Chapter 5). Since the number of trials in a fractional factorial is limited, this value is not always available. Analysis of variance (ANOVA) gives an initial answer, but we should not forget that the residuals contain interactions that have not been taken into account. We assume the model is proper, but in fact it may not be.

According to the chosen model, we can obtain an RMSE (root mean square error) of reasonable size. The analysis of variance is a partial response to the problem of other inflated factors. There are two other tools that allow us to have an idea of the relative importance of the coefficients. These are the *Pareto diagram* and the *Daniel (Normal) chart*. These tools help the experimenter to draw a line between influential and non-influential factors. In this situation, we can use several types of reasoning that complement each other, using them in concert to develop a final answer.

One method of reasoning says that all effects lower than a certain value don't influence the response noticeably. For example, the experimenter may say that a variation of the ratio (factor 6) less than 0.5 is not significant. In this case, there are only two influential factors. If the experimenter decides to put the limit at 0.25, there are four influential factors.

A second method uses the Pareto diagram (Figure 7.2). All coefficient values are placed in decreasing order of the absolute value of their coefficients. This facilitates the choice of the limit between significance and non-significance: save the coefficients that are above a certain value, and throw out those that are below it. There is not a big difference between the two methods, except the second uses a picture, which makes the comparisons easier.

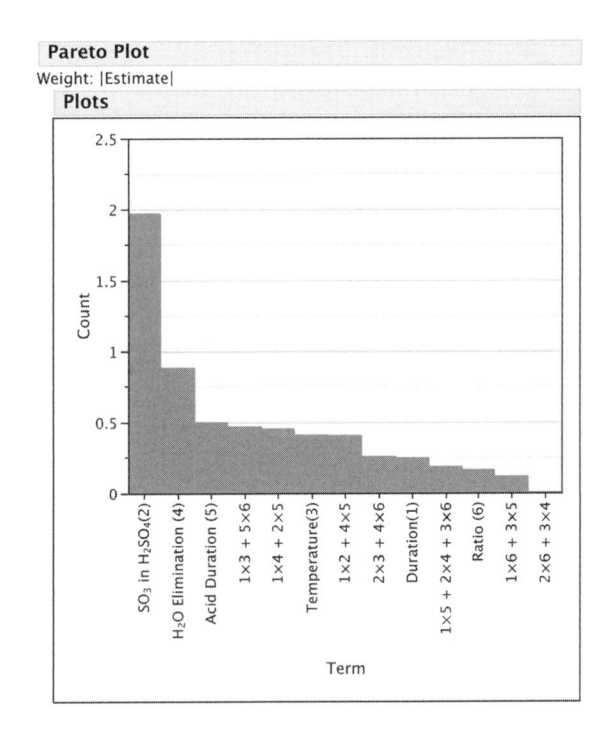

Figure 7.2 Pareto chart of the sulfonation experiment

[Pareto Plot showing terms from largest to smallest: SO₃ in H₂SO₄(2), H₂O Elimination (4), Acid Duration (5), 1×3 + 5×6, 1×4 + 2×5, Temperature(3), 1×2 + 4×5, 2×3 + 4×6, Duration(1), 1×5 + 2×4 + 3×6, Ratio (6), 1×6 + 3×5, 2×6 + 3×4]

A third method supports both previous modes of reasoning. We use a Daniel diagram, implemented in JMP as the Normal Plot. The small-valued coefficients follow a normal distribution, are assimilated into the experimental error, and align along a line called the Henry line. High-value coefficients do not follow a normal distribution, so they don't follow the Henry line. This partitions the two populations, the experimental error and the effects we need to take into account (Figure 7.3). With the Daniel diagram, the arbitrariness of the decision is considerably diminished.

If possible, its best to use other statistical techniques that help to make a good decision. For example, if the experimenter has made repetitions (duplicate runs under the same experimental conditions), a real estimate of experimental error can be calculated to obtain the limit between significant and non-significant factors. A commonly chosen limit is two or three times the standard deviation. The decision of how many standard deviations to use is based on the experimental error and the knowledge of the risks of incorrect conclusions.

Regardless of the reasoning you use, it is always a good idea to examine a Pareto chart and a Daniel diagram. They are good decision-making tools.

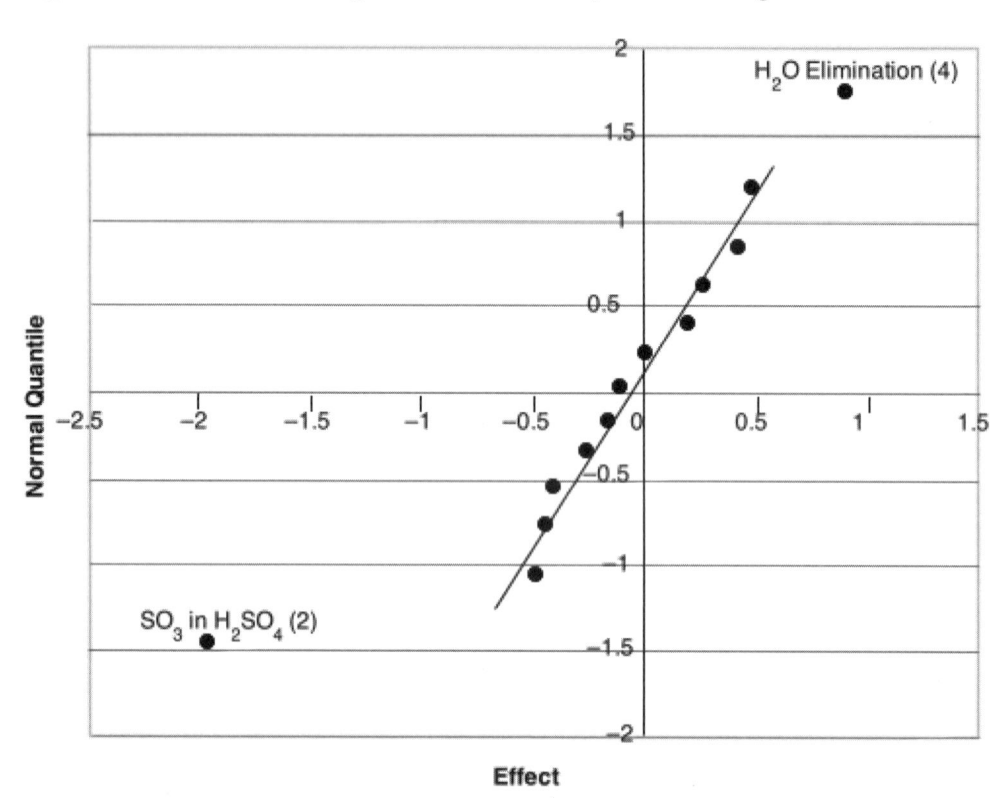

Figure 7.3 The Daniel diagram shows the separation of significant effects

[Normal Quantile plot with Effect on x-axis, showing H_2O Elimination (4) as a high outlier and SO_3 in H_2SO_4 (2) as a low outlier, with other points falling along a line]

The examination of the Pareto and Daniel diagrams shows that we should retain a single influential factor: the sulfuric anhydride concentration in the sulfuric acid (factor 2).

This experiment also shows that the elimination of water (factor 4) is slightly influential. The decision to keep or eliminate this factor is not based on statistics. Here, reasoning based on chemical best practice must be the guide. Since the drainage of water affects the concentration of the sulfuric acid, it is chemically sound to regard water elimination (factor 4) as slightly influential, and to keep it.

The other factors and interactions are too small and do not contribute much to explaining the response.

In a choice, there is always an arbitrary element, but in the case of designed experiments, the choice is never absolute and can always be modified later in a new analysis.

7.2.4 Study Conclusion

The relative importance of the contrasts is indicated by the bar chart (Figure 7.1), the Pareto Plot (Figure 7.2), and the Daniel plot (Figure 7.3).

The contrasts ℓ_{12}, ℓ_{13}, ℓ_{14}, ℓ_{15}, ℓ_{16}, ℓ_{23} and ℓ_{26} are small. Using the second assumption, we see that all the coefficients aliased in these contrasts are negligible. There are therefore no second-order interactions among the factors.

Two influential factors remain (Figure 7.4): the quantity of sulfur anhydride present in the sulfuric acid (factor 2) and the elimination of water during the reaction (factor 4).

Figure 7.4 Effects of the two influential factors

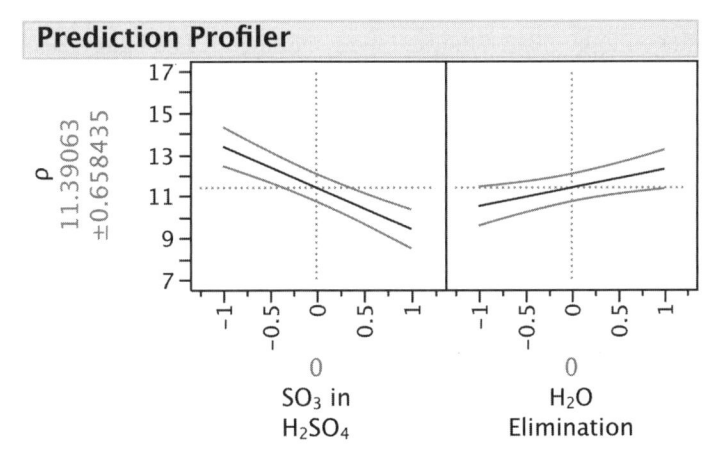

The amount of sulfur anhydride (SO_3) present in the sulfuric acid has a negative effect. The response is high if we choose the low level; that is, we shouldn't add SO_3 to the sulfuric acid.

Water elimination during the reaction has a positive effect. Therefore, the response will be higher if we choose its high level—that is, if we eliminate the water. This effect is only slightly elevated and might be ignored if we relied simply on statistics. However, from reasoning based on chemical best practice, the elimination or water raises the acid concentration and helps the reaction form sulfonic acids. The influence of this factor cannot be ignored.

The sulfonation of benzene, in the presence of toluene and of xylenes, is therefore minimized if water is eliminated from concentrated sulfuric acid that does not include sulfur anhydride.

7.3 Example 7: Spectrofluorimetry

7.3.1 Preparing the Designed Experiment

7.3.1.1 Study Description

Benzopyrene is categorized as a carcinogen. Its content in lubricating oils must be less than an infinitesimal quantity. Its analysis is therefore delicate, and requires important methods. Specialists developing the method to measure proportion chose spectrofluorimetry. Fiture 7.5 shows the set-up of the apparatus: a beam of light from a xenon light falls on the first monochromater. The light is diffracted. A light of well-defined wavelength reflects from the monochromater and goes through a slit, the excitation slit. This ray falls on the sample, which absorbs some of it and re-emits fluorescent light in all directions. This light is to be analyzed. It passes, therefore, through a second monochromater, which resolves it into different wavelengths. These light waves pass through another slit, the emission slit, and are detected by a photomultiplier. Finally, a recorder fitted on the photomultiplier saves the corresponding spectrum. One of the peak wavelengths of the spectrum is characteristic of benzopyrene. This peak is at 481 nanometers and its height is proportional to the benzopyrene concentration. The objective of the study is to obtain a spectrum of good quality, allowing us to measure quantitatively the proportion of benzopyrene. To do so, we need the height of the peak at 481 nanometers to be as great as possible, and also we need the small peak at 489 nanometers to be separated from the peak at 481 nm (Figure 7.5). Finally, the background noise cannot hide the 481 nm-benzopyrene peak when the content is small and when, therefore, the height of the peak is small.

An apparatus of this sophistication requires precise adjustments so that the benzopyrene concentration is measured with reliability and precision.

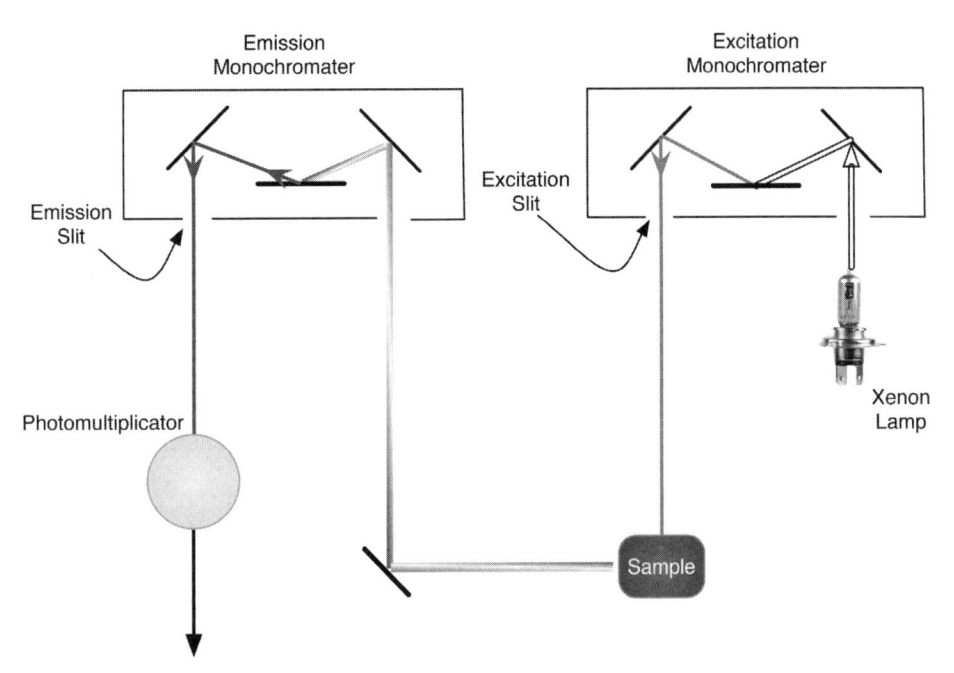

Figure 7.5 Spectrofluoriometer diagram

7.3.1.2 Responses
The experimenters have defined three responses (Figure 7.6).

- Sensitivity (A), evaluated by the height of the peak at 481 nm.
- Background noise (B), evaluated by the distance between the lower envelope and upper envelope of the recorded curve at the lowest wavelengths
- Selectivity (C), evaluated by the width at the mid-height of the peak at 481 nm.

Sensitivity and background noise are expressed in optical density.

Figure 7.6 Definition of the responses on the recorded spectrum: sensitivity (A), background noise (B), and selectivity (C)

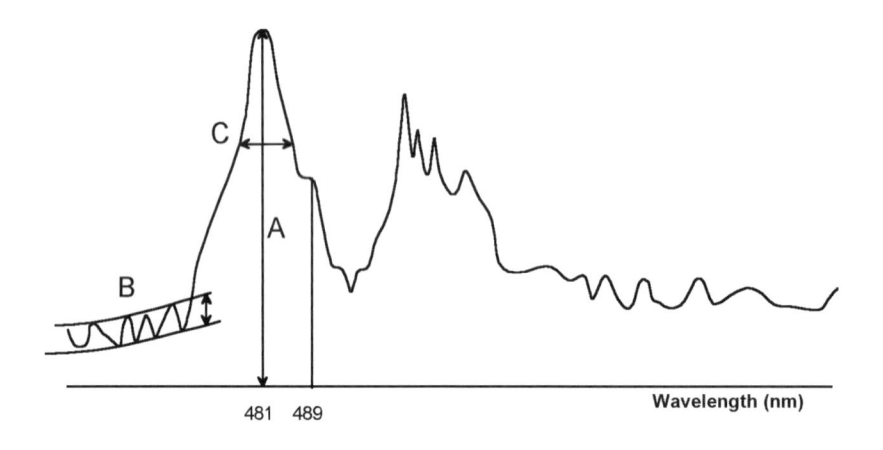

7.3.1.3 Study Objective
The target values for each response are as follows:

- Sensitivity: the height of the peak at 481 nm must be as high as possible.

- Background noise: the distance between the lower and upper envelopes must be as small as possible.

- Selectivity: the width at the mid-height of the 481 mn peak must be as small as possible.

These objectives are useful when setting up desirability functions.

7.3.1.4 Factors and Study Domain
Following experts in spectrofluorimetry, seven factors may change the chosen responses.

- Factor 1: width of the excitation slit
- Factor 2: width of the emission slit
- Factor 3: temperature of the sample
- Factor 4: scanning speed
- Factor 5: apparatus gain

- Factor 6: photomultiplier voltage
- Factor 7: damping of the recording pen

The study domain is a space of seven dimensions, defined by the high and low levels of each factor (Table 7.4).

Table 7.4 Study domain

Factors	−1 Level	+1 Level
Excitation slit width (1)	2.5 nm	7.5 nm
Emission slit width (2)	2.5 nm	7.5 nm
Temperature (3)	20°C	40°C
Scanning speed (4)	20	100
Gain (5)	1	10
Voltage (6)	310 volts	460 volts
Dampening (7)	2	4

7.3.1.5 Mathematical Model

We are looking for the influential factors, their direction of variation, and their second-order interactions.

We choose a classic linear model with second-order interaction terms, which in total has 29 coefficients.

7.3.1.6 Choosing the Design

With eight trials, we can solve for eight unknowns—that is, eight contrasts. To win our bet (that a fractional factorial can give us the necessary information), for each response, we can determine without ambiguity the important coefficients. If not, we run the risk of needing a complementary design.

We alias the first additional factor (scanning speed, factor 4) with the 1×2×3 interaction from the base design. In Box notation, we can write

4 = 123

Then, we alias the following factors as

   5 = 12

   6 = 23

   7 = 13

From these, we deduce the four independent alias generators:

   I = 1234 = 125 = 236 = 137

A control point is not added, since the experimenter knows that this model is not intended to make forecasts.

7.3.1.7 Constructing the Design

To construct a 2^{7-4} design, take the 2^3 base plan (Table 6.9 from Chapter 6) and assign the additional factors to the interactions.

Table 7.5 2^{7-4} Fractional factorial design

Trial	1	2	3	4=123	5=12	6=23	7=13
1	−	−	−	−	+	+	+
2	+	−	−	+	−	+	−
3	−	+	−	+	−	−	+
4	+	+	−	−	+	−	−
5	−	−	+	+	+	−	−
6	+	−	+	−	−	−	+
7	−	+	+	−	−	+	−
8	+	+	+	+	+	+	+

7.3.1.8 The Confounding

The four independent alias generators, **I = 1234 = 125 = 236 = 137**, allow the calculation of the dependent alias generators. We multiply (using Box multiplication) the independent alias generators two at a time, three at a time, and four at a time. We get

$$1234 \times 125 = 345 \qquad 1234 \times 236 = 146 \qquad 1234 \times 137 = 247$$
$$125 \times 236 = 12356 \qquad 125 \times 137 = 2357 \qquad 236 \times 137 = 1267$$

$$1234 \times 125 \times 236 = 2456 \qquad 1234 \times 125 \times 137 = 1457 \qquad 1234 \times 236 \times 137 = 3467$$

$$125 \times 236 \times 137 = 567$$

$$1234 \times 125 \times 236 \times 137 = 1234567$$

So the complete generator has 16 terms.

I = 1234 = 125 = 236 = 137 = 345 = 146 = 247 = 12356 = 2357 = 1267 = 2456 = 1457 = 3467 = 567 = 1234567

To get the coefficients in the contrast ℓ_1, multiply the alias generators by **1**. The generators lose a number if they contain a **1**, or add a number if they don't possess a **1**. Since we have assumed that third-order interactions are negligible, we can remove any terms that have more than four numbers from the generators. This gives a complete simplified generator as

I = 234 = 125 = 236 = 137 = 345 = 146 = 247 = 567

This simplified generator makes it possible to know how the main effects are aliased with the second-order interactions of the fractional design

$$\ell_2 = a_2 + a_{15} + a_{36} + a_{47}$$

$$\ell_3 = a_3 + a_{17} + a_{26} + a_{45}$$

$$\ell_4 = a_4 + a_{16} + a_{27} + a_{35}$$

$$\ell_5 = a_5 + a_{12} + a_{34} + a_{67}$$

$$\ell_6 = a_6 + a_{14} + a_{23} + a_{57}$$

$$\ell_7 = a_7 + a_{13} + a_{24} + a_{56}$$

7.3.2 Carrying Out the Experiment

The experimental runs were carried out according to the designed experiment, and the results are shown in Table 7.6.

Table 7.6 Initial responses from the design

Trial	Sensitivity	Selectivity	Background Noise
1	1.22	5.5	−1.47
2	0.9	9	−1.47
3	5.33	20	2.3
4	5.64	12	−0.69
5	3.89	7.5	0.69
6	3.88	8	0.4
7	2.82	13	0.26
8	2.33	23	−3.91

7.3.3 Interpreting the Results

7.3.3.1 Calculations

A quick examination shows that there are no marked correlations among the three responses, so they are analyzed one after the other. We choose a model containing main effects and second-order interactions. First, we examine sensitivity.

7.3.3.2 Sensitivity

We know that the values shown are those of contrasts (Table 7.7 and Figure 7.7). We do the interpretation by looking at the structure of these aliases and by observing the interpretation assumptions.

Table 7.7 Coefficients of the model for sensitivity (coded units)

Effect	Value
ℓ_0 (Intercept)	3.25
ℓ_1	−0.06
ℓ_2	0.78
ℓ_3	−0.02
ℓ_4	−0.14
ℓ_5	0.018
ℓ_6	−1.43
ℓ_7	−0.06

Two contrasts are strong: ℓ_2 and ℓ_6.

Take special note of the 2×6 interaction (assumption 3). The 2×6 interaction is aliased with the effect of factor 3, the 1×7 interaction, and the 4×5 interaction in the ℓ_3 contrast. The ℓ_3 contrast is practically zero. Using assumption 2, we see that all the coefficients of this contrast are also zero. The 2×6 interaction is therefore non-significant.

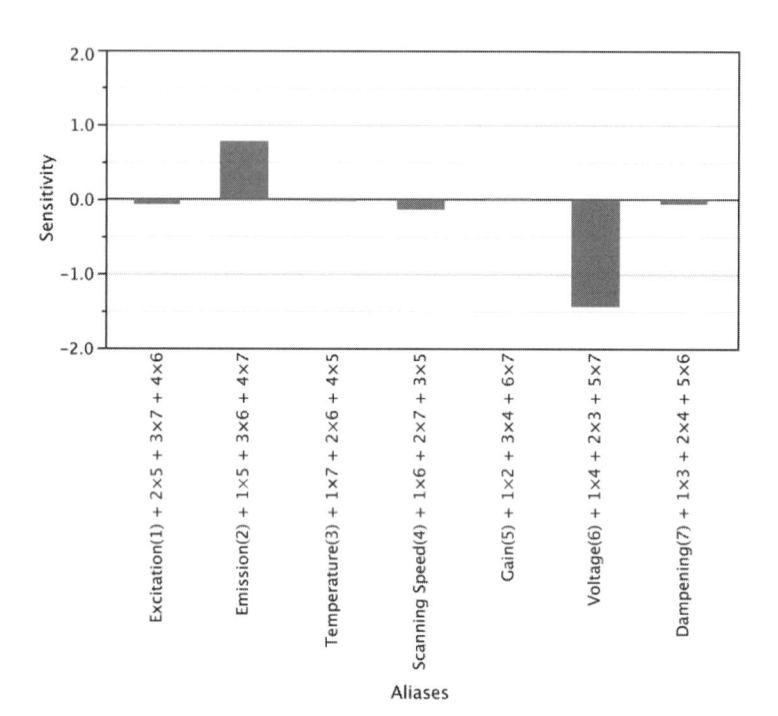

Figure 7.7 Bar chart for sensibility aliasing

If sensitivity were the only response, the study would be over, and we would know the two influential factors: the emission slit width (factor 2) and the voltage of the photomultiplier (factor 6). We can verify this conclusion by examining a model with these two factors and their interaction.

Figure 7.8 Model with two factors

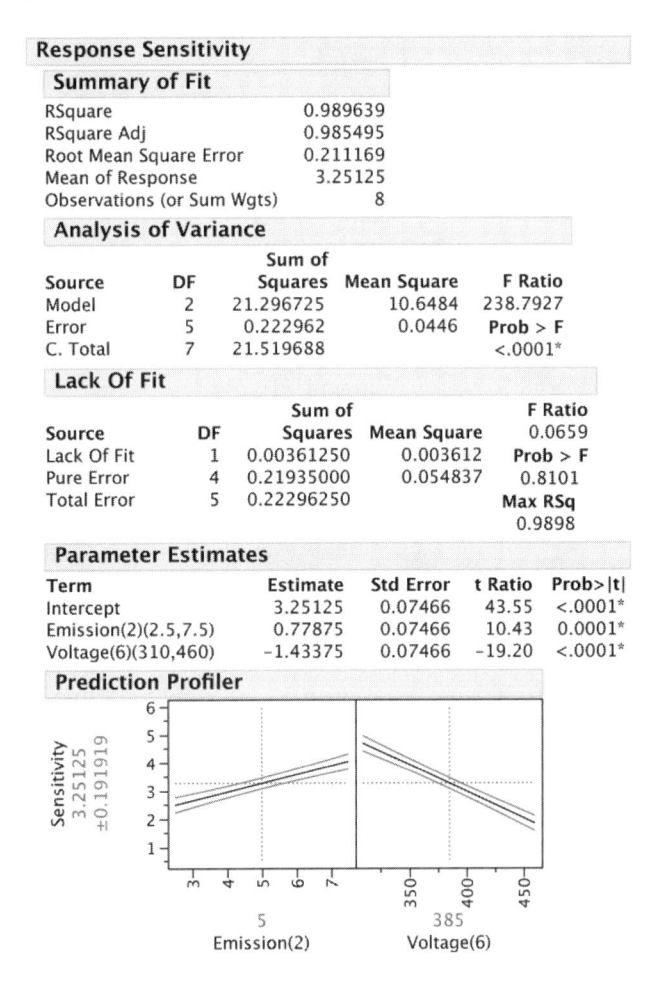

Response Sensitivity

Summary of Fit

RSquare	0.989639
RSquare Adj	0.985495
Root Mean Square Error	0.211169
Mean of Response	3.25125
Observations (or Sum Wgts)	8

Analysis of Variance

Source	DF	Sum of Squares	Mean Square	F Ratio
Model	2	21.296725	10.6484	238.7927
Error	5	0.222962	0.0446	Prob > F
C. Total	7	21.519688		<.0001*

Lack Of Fit

Source	DF	Sum of Squares	Mean Square	F Ratio
Lack Of Fit	1	0.00361250	0.003612	0.0659
Pure Error	4	0.21935000	0.054837	Prob > F
Total Error	5	0.22296250		0.8101
				Max RSq
				0.9898

Parameter Estimates

Term	Estimate	Std Error	t Ratio	Prob>|t|
Intercept	3.25125	0.07466	43.55	<.0001*
Emission(2)(2.5,7.5)	0.77875	0.07466	10.43	0.0001*
Voltage(6)(310,460)	-1.43375	0.07466	-19.20	<.0001*

Prediction Profiler

This model has an R^2 of 0.989. The profiler shows that the levels that support a strong sensitivity are a high level for the emission slit and a low level for voltage (Figure 7.8).

7.3.3.3 Background Noise

Calculations proceed just like they did with sensitivity—that is, with a model containing main effects and second-order interactions. The aliasing structure is the same as for sensibility. The analysis results, too, proceed in the same way.

Table 7.8 Background noise coefficients (coded units)

Effect	Value
ℓ_0 (Intercept)	−0.486
ℓ_1	−0.931
ℓ_2	−0.024
ℓ_3	−0.154
ℓ_4	−0.111
ℓ_5	−0.858
ℓ_6	−1.161
ℓ_7	−0.183

- Three contrasts are strong: ℓ_1, ℓ_5, and ℓ_6 (Table 7.8 and Figure 7.8).
- We must take special note of the interactions 1×5, 1×6, and 5×6 (assumption 3).
- The 1×5 interaction is aliased with the effect of factor 2, the 3×6 interaction, and the 4×7 interaction in the contrast ℓ_2. Since ℓ_2 is practically zero, using assumption 2, we see that all the coefficients of the contrast are zero. The 1×5 interaction is therefore negligible.

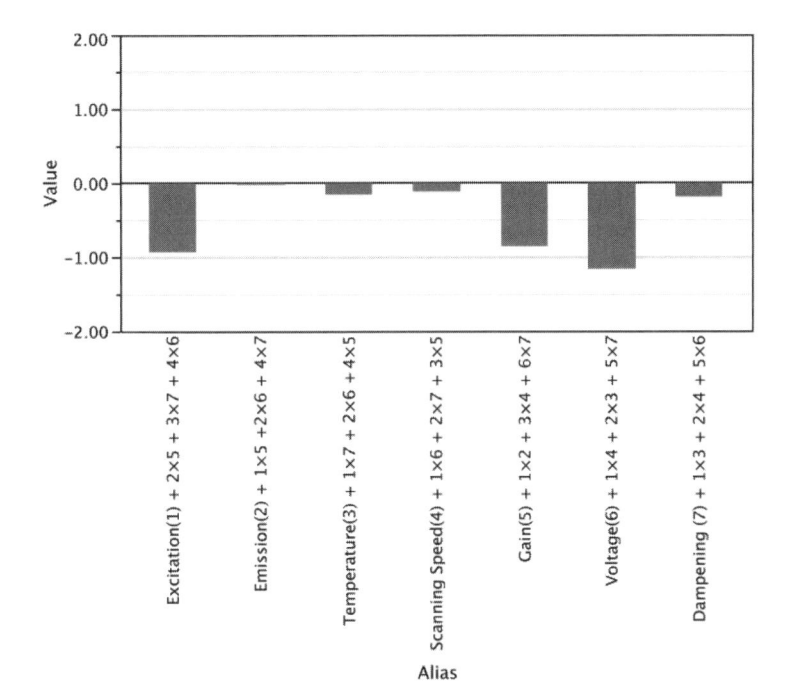

Figure 7.9 Diagram of background noise aliases

- The 1×6 interaction is aliased with the effect of factor 4, the 2×7 interaction, and the 3×5 interaction in contrast ℓ_4. Since ℓ_4 is practically zero, assumption 2 says that all the coefficients in the contrast are also zero. The 1×6 interaction is therefore negligible.
- The 5×6 interaction is aliased with the effect of factor 7, the 1×3 interaction, and the 2×4 interaction in contrast ℓ_7. Since ℓ_7 is practically zero, assumption 2 tells us that the coefficients of the contrast are also zero. The 5×6 interaction is therefore negligible.

Background noise is influenced by the excitation slit (factor 1), by the gain of the apparatus (factor 5), and by the voltage in the photomultiplier (factor 6). There are apparently no interactions among the factors.

We can verify this conclusion by choosing a model with the three previously mentioned active factors and their interactions.

Figure 7.10 Model with three factors

Response Noise

Summary of Fit

RSquare	0.976735
RSquare Adj	0.959285
Root Mean Square Error	0.375083
Mean of Response	-0.48625
Observations (or Sum Wgts)	8

Analysis of Variance

Source	DF	Sum of Squares	Mean Square	F Ratio
Model	3	23.625438	7.87515	55.9762
Error	4	0.562750	0.14069	Prob > F
C. Total	7	24.188188		0.0010*

Parameter Estimates

Term	Estimate	Std Error	t Ratio	Prob>|t|
Intercept	-0.48625	0.132612	-3.67	0.0215*
Excitation(1)(2.5,7.5)	-0.93125	0.132612	-7.02	0.0022*
Gain(5)(1,10)	-0.85875	0.132612	-6.48	0.0029*
Voltage(6)(310,460)	-1.16125	0.132612	-8.76	0.0009*

Prediction Profiler

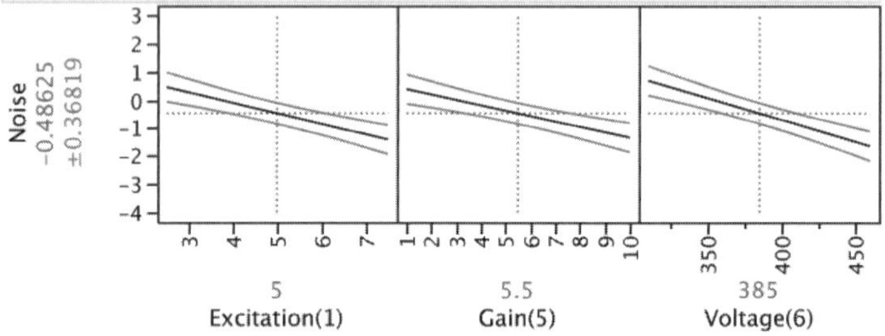

The high levels of all three factors—excitation slit, gain, and voltage—produce a low background noise (Figure 7.10).

If there were only the two responses, sensitivity and background noise, the study would be over and we would know that there are:

- Two influential factors on sensitivity: excitation slit and voltage. There is no interaction among these factors.
- Three influential factors in background noise: excitation slit, gain, and voltage. There is no interaction among these factors.

7.3.3.4 Selectivity

The calculations and analysis proceed in the same way: a model with main effects and second-order interactions. The alias structure and analysis methods are well known by now:

Table 7.9 Selectivity coefficients (coded units)

Effect	Value
ℓ_0 (Intercept)	12.25
ℓ_1	0.75
ℓ_2	4.75
ℓ_3	0.625
ℓ_4	2.625
ℓ_5	−0.25
ℓ_6	0.375
ℓ_7	1.875

- Three contrasts are strong: ℓ_2, ℓ_4, and ℓ_7 (Table 7.9 and Figure 7.11).

- We must be careful with the 2×4, 2×7, and 4×7 interactions (assumption 3).

- The 2×4 interaction is aliased with the effect of factor 7, the 1×3 interaction, and the 5×6 interaction in the ℓ_7 contrast. Since ℓ_7 is not small, we cannot apply assumption 2. We do not know if ℓ_7 is strong because of the effect of factor 7 or the 2×4 interaction. There is an ambiguity.

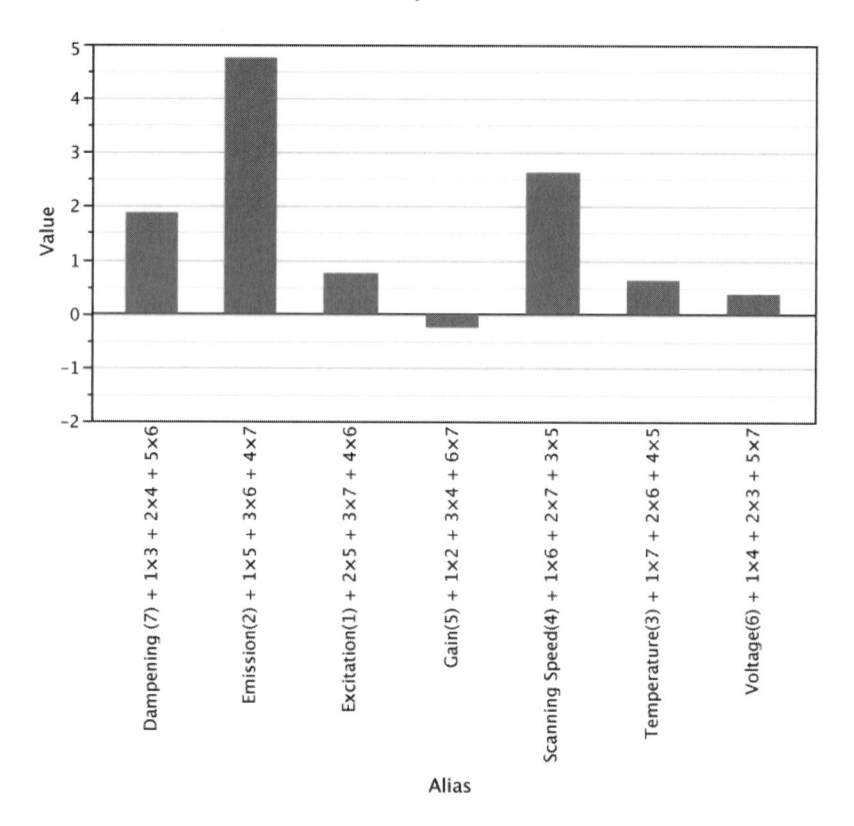

Figure 7.11 Bar chart of the selectivity aliases

- The 2×7 interaction is aliased with the effect of factor 4, the 1×6 interaction, and the 3×5 interaction in contrast ℓ_4. Since ℓ_4 is strong, we know that assumption 2 does not hold. We do not know if the strong ℓ_4 contrast is due to the effect of factor 4 or the 2×7 interaction. Again, there is ambiguity.
- The 4×7 interaction is aliased with the effect of factor 2, the 1×5 interaction, and the 3×6 interaction in contrast ℓ_2. Again, ℓ_2 is not small, and assumption 2 is not tenable. We do not know if ℓ_2 is strong because of the effect of factor 2 or the 4×7 interaction. A third ambiguity exists.

The selectivity response forces us to consider a complementary design for de-aliasing:

- The effect of factor 2 (emission slit width) on the 4×7 interaction
- The effect of factor 4 (scanning speed) on the 2×7 interaction
- The effect of factor 7 (dampening) on the 2×4 interaction

7.3.3.5 Provisional Assesssment of Results

Before tackling the complementary plan, we can give a summary of the information that has been determined so far. Table 7.10 shows favorable levels of the factors for the objectives.

Table 7.10 Favorable levels of the influential factors on the responses

Factors	Sensitivity	Background Noise	Selectivity
Excitation slit width (1)		+	
Emission slit width (2)	+		?
Temperature (3)			
Scanning speed (4)			?
Gain (5)		+	
Voltage (6)	-	+	
Dampening (7)			?

Note that

- Excitation slit width (1) affects only background noise.
- Emission slit width (2) affects sensitivity and perhaps selectivity.
- Temperature (3) doesn't affect any of the responses.
- If scanning speed (4) affects anything, it is sensitivity.
- Gain (5) affects only background noise.

- Voltage (6) affects both sensitivity and background noise. However, they affect the two responses in opposite ways. This is not a surprise, since an increase (or decrease) in the optical density also increases (or decreases) the 481 nm peak in the background noise.
- If Dampening (7) affects anything, it is only selectivity.

7.3.4 Building the Complementary Design

The complementary design must allow the measurement of factor 2's effect without the 1×5, 3×6, and 4×7 interactions; i.e., we want a design that has a contrast.

$$\ell'_2 = a_2 - a_{15} - a_{36} - a_{47}$$

This contrast corresponds to the confoundings

2 = –15 = –36 = –47

By multiplying by **2**, we get three generators of the desired design

I = –125 = –236 = –247

Since four generators are needed, we start again with

I = 1234

To associate the generator **–247** with an interaction from the base design, we can replace **4** by **123**:

–247 = –21237 = –137

This gives us the four independent generators for the complementary design

I = –125 = –236 = –137 = 1234

From here, we can deduce the signs of the complementary design. Apply Box calculations by multiplying the independent generators by **4**, **5**, **6**, and **7**:

4 = 123

5 = –12

6 = –23

7 = –13

Therefore, we must change the signs of the columns of factors 5, 6, and 7.

Let's verify that this choice really de-aliases factor 2 with the 4×7 interaction. The initial design had a contrast ℓ_2 whose structure is

$$\ell_2 = a_2 + a_{15} + a_{36} + a_{47}$$

The complementary design has a contrast ℓ'_2 whose structure is

$$\ell'_2 = a_2 - a_{15} - a_{36} - a_{47}$$

The analysis of both designs will give the sum and the difference these contrasts. The sum gives us the effect of factor 2 only, and the difference gives us the sum of the three interactions.

$$\frac{\ell_2 + \ell'_2}{2} = a_2 \qquad \frac{\ell_2 - \ell'_2}{2} = a_{15} + a_{36} + a_{47}$$

The effect of factor 2 is therefore de-aliased from the 4×7 interaction.

We have shown this technique specifically for factor 2, but it is true for other factors. In general, factor effects are de-aliased from second-order interactions and stay aliased with themselves.

7.3.4.1 Constructing the Complementary Design

To construct the complementary design, simply change the signs of the 1×2. 1×3, and 2×3 interactions.

Table 7.11 Complementary 2^{7-4} fractional factorial design

Trial	1	2	3	4 = 123	5 = –12	6 = –23	7 = –13
9	−	−	−	−	−	−	−
10	+	−	−	+	+	−	+
11	−	+	−	+	+	+	−
12	+	+	−	−	−	+	+
13	−	−	+	+	−	+	+
14	+	−	+	−	+	+	−
15	−	+	+	−	+	−	+
16	+	+	+	+	−	−	−

We carry out these eight new trials and measure the three responses.

Table 7.12 Complementary design responses

Trial	Sensitivity	Selectivity	Background Noise
9	4.14	3.5	3.56
10	3.18	12	−2.41
11	2.82	14	1.39
12	2.74	14	−1.9
13	2.44	8	−0.62
14	0.98	6	−3.22
15	5.66	14	0.02
16	5.63	14	−1.61

7.3.4.2 Confoundings (Initial Design and Complementary Design)

Now, we have a 2^{7-3} design of 16 trials with an independent generator

$$I = 1234 = 3467 = 1356 = 1457 = 1267 = 1356 = 2357$$

Notice that the main effects are aliased with third-order or higher interactions. Using assumption 1, we see that these interactions are negligible, and the contrasts of the main effects are simply equal to the effects.

Second-order interactions are aliased with themselves three at a time.

$$\ell_{12} = a_{12} + a_{34} + a_{67}$$

$$\ell_{13} = a_{13} + a_{24} + a_{56}$$

$$\ell_{14} = a_{14} + a_{23} + a_{57}$$

$$\ell_{15} = a_{15} + a_{36} + a_{47}$$

$$\ell_{16} = a_{16} + a_{35} + a_{27}$$

$$\ell_{17} = a_{17} + a_{26} + a_{45}$$

$$\ell_{25} = a_{25} + a_{37} + a_{46}$$

In particular, we have de-aliased the effect of factor 2 from the 4×7 interaction, the effect of factor 4 from the 2×7 interaction, and the effect of factor 7 from the 2×4 interaction.

We first analyze selectivity to see if the extended designs sufficiently explain this response. If so, we can stop. If not, we continue the experiment by adding trials that resolve any new ambiguities.

Finally, we check that the analysis of sensitivity and background noise are confirmed using 16 runs.

7.3.4.3 The Three Responses Analyzed with 16 Trials

We redo the calculations using all 16 trials. We now have the coefficients (not the contrasts) for the main effects. The interactions are regrouped in the contrasts (Table 7.13).

Table 7.13 Coefficients (sensitivity, background noise, selectivity)

Effect	Sensitivity	Background Noise	Selectivity
Intercept	3.35	−0.54	11.47
Excitation slit (1)	−0.19	−1.31	0.78
Emission slit (2)	0.77	0.02	4.03
Temperature (3)	0.10	−0.46	0.22
Scanning speed (4)	−0.035	−0.16	1.97
Gain (5)	−0.13	−0.66	0.28
Voltage (6)	−1.32	−0.82	0.09
Dampening (7)	−0.002	−0.41	1.59
$\ell_{12} = 12 + 34 + 67$	0.15	−0.20	−0.53
$\ell_{13} = 13 + 24 + 56$	−0.058	0.22	0.28
$\ell_{14} = 14 + 23 + 57$	−0.115	−0.34	0.28
$\ell_{15} = 15 + 36 + 47$	0.007	−0.05	0.72
$\ell_{16} = 16 + 27 + 35$	−0.10	0.05	0.66
$\ell_{17} = 17 + 26 + 45$	−0.12	0.30	0.41
$\ell_{25} = 25 + 37 + 46$	0.126	0.38	−0.03

The experimenters considered that all the interactions were not important enough to modify the settings of the apparatus (Figure 7.12). In this case, only the main effects are taken into account. There are therefore only three influential factors on selectivity and no important interactions among the factors.

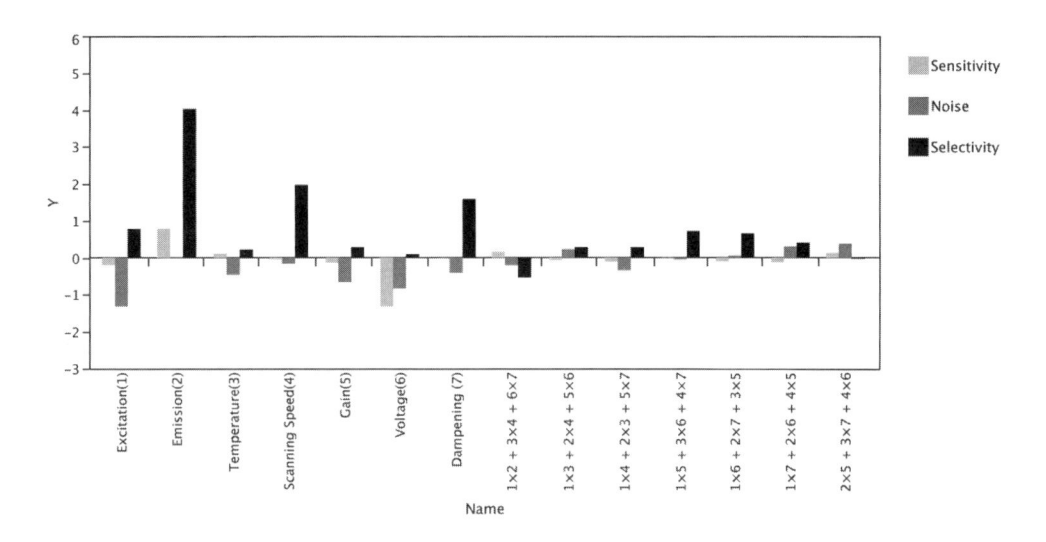

Figure 7.12 Bar chart of the effects and aliases for the three responses

Selectivity, which is measured by the size of the peak at mid-height, is good when this size is small. Therefore, we leave factors 2, 4, and 7 at their low levels (Figure 7.13).

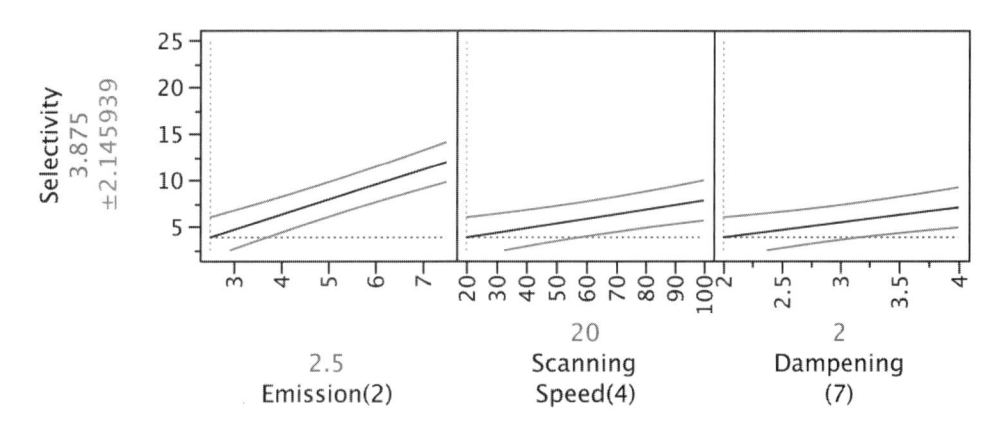

Figure 7.13 Effect diagram for the factors affecting selectivity

For sensitivity, we again see the two important factors: emission slit (2) and voltage of the photomultiplier (6). There are no important interactions among the factors. To get the best sensitivity, set the emission slit at its high setting and the voltage of the photomultiplier at its low setting.

For background noise, three important factors were again found: the excitation slit (1), the gain of the photomultiplier (5) and the voltage of the photomultiplier (6). There are no important interactions among these factors. For optimum (i.e., minimum) background noise, set factors 1, 5, and 6 at their high levels.

7.3.5 Study Conclusion

Now, we gather the conclusions for the three responses to interpret them together. The results that we had written in Table 7. are confirmed for sensitivity and background noise. We can now complete the table for selectivity (Table 7.14).

Table 7.14 Factor settings giving favorable responses for the influential factors

Factors	Sensitivity	Background Noise	Selectivity
Excitation slit (1)		+	
Emission slit (2)	+		−
Temperature (3)			
Scanning speed (4)			−
Gain (5)		+	
Voltage (6)	−	+	
Dampening (7)			−

Of these seven factors, five are easy to set:

- The emission slit (factor 1) must be set at 7.5 nm to diminish background noise.
- The temperature of the sample (factor 3) has no effect on the responses. It can therefore be set anywhere between 20°C and 40°C.
- The scanning speed (factor 4) must be set at 20 to reduce the size of the peak at mid-height (selectivity).
- Gain (factor 5) must be set at 10 to lower background noise.
- Dampening (factor 7) must be set at 2 to increase selectivity.

Two factors are harder to set:

- If the voltage of the photomultiplier (factor 6) is set at 310 volts, sensitivity will be elevated, but the background noise will be prominent. Conversely, if the voltage of the photomultiplier is set at 460 volts, there will be little background noise, but the sensitivity will be diminished. A compromise must be reached between these two responses.
- A wide emission slit (factor 2) raises the sensitivity but degrades the selectivity. A narrow emission slit improves the selectivity, but degrades the sensitivity. A compromise width will have to be found that gives the best compromise between the two responses.

A spectrum was examined with these settings (Figure 7.14). The peak at 481 nm is high and distinct from the peak at 489 nm, and background noise practically disappeared.

In practice, the first five factors would be used at the advised levels, and another design would be carried out to find good settings for the last two to find the best compromise according to the concentration of benzopyrene and the presence of impurities in the analyzed solution.

Figure 7.14 Spectrum of the optimal conditions defined with the aid of a designed experiment

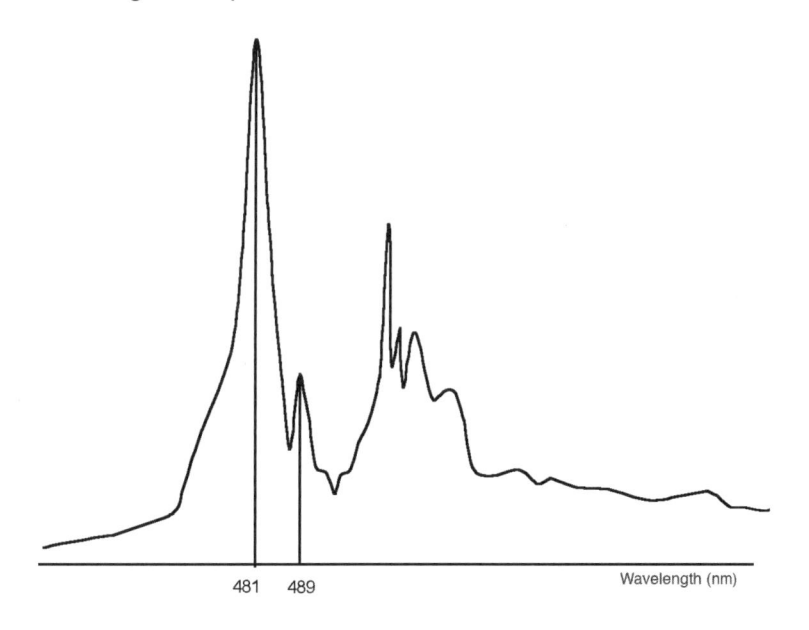

7.4 Example 8: Potato Chips

7.4.1 Preparing the Designed Experiment

7.4.1.1 Description of the Study
Potato chips are thin potato slices that are fried in an oil bath. Potato chips are pleasant to eat as long as they don't have a residual smell from this oil. After cooking, most of the oil is extracted under 40 MPa pressure during a one-hour period at 60° C (140° F). Then, in an attempt to extract as much oil as possible, the chips are subjected to a final treatment under 10 MPa pressure for 30 minutes under a flow of supercritical carbon dioxide at 700 Kg/h. Finally, the chips are dried and packaged. Several types of chips are manufactured: large and small, flat and with ridges.

7.4.1.2 Responses
The manufacturer has defined two responses:

- Amount of recovered oil, measured in pounds
- Taste of the chips, evaluated by a panel consisting of experts, who grade the chips from 0 (bad taste) to 10 (delicious).

7.4.1.3 Study Objective
The objective of the study is to select the factors that have the most influence on the two chosen responses. First, a preliminary study is completed to prepare an initial model. A screening design is carried out so we can bring a large number of factors into play.

7.4.1.4 Factors and Study Domain
The factors selected for this study cover the whole process from oil removal to salting. Nine factors that may influence the responses are listed.

- Factor 1: Pressure of the extraction of the oil
- Factor 2: Temperature of the extraction of the oil
- Factor 3: Duration of the extraction of the oil

- Factor 4: Pressure of the separation of the oil
- Factor 5: Temperature of the separation of the oil
- Factor 6: Rate of supercritical carbon dioxide gas
- Factor 7: Quantity of salt added to the chips
- Factor 8: Size of the chips
- Factor 9: Type of chip

The study domain is defined for the low and high levels of each factor (Table 7.15).

Table 7.15 Study domain

Factors	Units	−1 Level	+1 Level
Oil extraction pressure (1)	MPa	30	50
Oil extraction temperature (2)	°C	50	70
Oil extraction duration (3)	min	45	75
Oil separation pressure (4)	MPa	5	15
Oil separation temperature (5)	°C	25	40
CO_2 rate (6)	Kg/h	600	800
Salt (7)	g	0	1
Size (8)		small	large
Type (9)		flat	ridged

7.4.1.5 Mathematical Model

We are looking for influential factors and the direction of their variation. The postulated mathematical model is a simple polynomial using only terms of the first degree.

$$y = a_0 + a_1 x_1 + a_2 x_2 + a_3 x_3 + a_4 x_4 + a_5 x_5 + a_6 x_6 + a_7 x_7 + a_8 x_8 + a_9 x_9 \quad (7.2)$$

The same model is used for both responses.

7.4.1.6 Choosing the Design

There are ten unknowns to determine: the intercept and nine main effects. Therefore, we need at least ten trials. The closest classical design is a Placket-Burman design with 12 trials.

Although these designs can be constructed by hand using Placket and Burman's rules, it is much easier to use statistical software such as JMP. Placket-Burman designs have numbers of runs that are equal to a multiple of four. Factorial designs also have numbers of runs that are a multiple of four. This arises mathematically because all these two-level designs are built on Hadamard matrices that have a number of rows that is a multiple of 4. Hadamard matrices have the important property of orthogonality; i.e., the scalar product of any two columns is zero.

In practice, *factorial designs* are all those that have 2^k trials, where Placket-Burman designs have $4k$ trials where $4k$ is not a power of two. Thus, a 12-run design is a Placket-Burman design, but a 16-run design is a factorial design. This distinction is necessary because the properties of the two design types are slightly different. For example, the aliases of factorial designs can be calculated using Box calculations, but Placket-Burman aliases cannot.

Table 7.16 12-run Placket-Burman design

Trial	OEP	OET	OED	OSP	OST	CO2	Salt	Size	Type
1	1	−1	1	−1	−1	−1	1	1	−1
2	1	1	−1	1	−1	−1	−1	1	−1
3	−1	1	1	−1	1	−1	−1	−1	−1
4	1	−1	1	1	−1	1	−1	−1	1
5	1	1	−1	1	1	−1	1	−1	1
6	1	1	1	−1	1	1	−1	1	1
7	−1	1	1	1	−1	1	1	−1	−1
8	−1	−1	1	1	1	−1	1	1	1
9	−1	−1	−1	1	1	1	−1	1	−1
10	1	−1	−1	−1	1	1	1	−1	−1
11	−1	1	−1	−1	−1	1	1	1	1
12	−1	−1	−1	−1	−1	−1	−1	−1	1
−	30	50	45	5	25	600	0	small	flat
+	50	70	75	15	40	800	1	large	ridged

7.4.2 Carrying Out the Experiment

The results of the experiment are shown in Table 7.17.

Table 7.17 Design responses

Trial	Oil	Taste
1	50.4	8
2	53.9	1
3	45.8	5
4	55.4	1
5	53.35	4
6	50.1	2
7	50.4	7
8	49.8	7
9	49.2	3
10	50.6	7
11	44.9	9
12	45.7	5

7.4.3 Interpreting the Results

7.4.3.1 Oil Response

Starting with the experimental results obtained with oil, we calculate the value of the coefficients of each factor by using the simplified model (7.2). These values are shown in Table 7.18 and are illustrated in Figure 7.15. Two factors are clearly influential: oil extraction pressure (1) and oil separation pressure (4). The other factors do not seem to play an important role in oil elimination.

Table 7.18 Coefficients for oil model (in coded units)

Effect	Value	p-value
Intercept	49.96	<0.0001
Oil extraction pressure (1)	2.32	0.0025
Oil extraction temperature (2)	−0.22	0.1943
Oil extraction duration (3)	0.36	0.0921
Oil separation pressure (4)	2.04	0.0033
Oil separation temperature (5)	−0.16	0.3085
CO_2 Rate (6)	0.14	0.3495
Salt (7)	−0.06	0.6674
Size (8)	−0.24	0.1748
Type (9)	−0.09	0.5153

Figure 7.15 Coefficients for the oil model

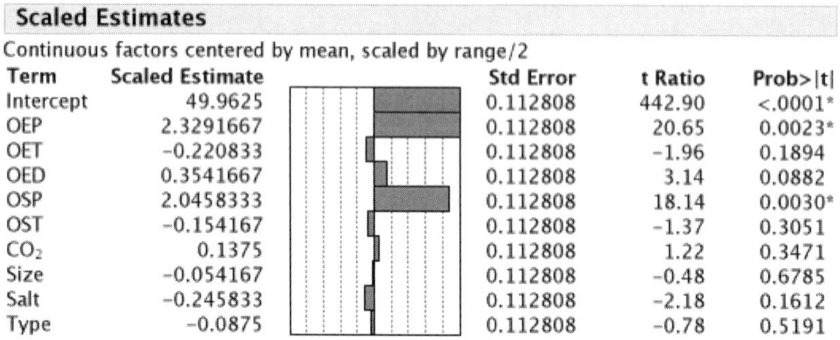

Scaled Estimates
Continuous factors centered by mean, scaled by range/2

Term	Scaled Estimate	Std Error	t Ratio	Prob>|t|
Intercept	49.9625	0.112808	442.90	<.0001*
OEP	2.3291667	0.112808	20.65	0.0023*
OET	−0.220833	0.112808	−1.96	0.1894
OED	0.3541667	0.112808	3.14	0.0882
OSP	2.0458333	0.112808	18.14	0.0030*
OST	−0.154167	0.112808	−1.37	0.3051
CO_2	0.1375	0.112808	1.22	0.3471
Size	−0.054167	0.112808	−0.48	0.6785
Salt	−0.245833	0.112808	−2.18	0.1612
Type	−0.0875	0.112808	−0.78	0.5191

Since the effects are positive, more oil can be extracted at high pressure than at low pressure.

7.4.3.2 Taste Response

The taste response is treated in the same manner as the oil response. Table 7.19 and Figure 7.16 show that there is only one strikingly influential factor, salt (7), and two slightly influential factors, oil extraction pressure (7) and oil separation pressure (4).

Table 7.19 Coefficients for the taste model (coded units)

Effect	Value	p-value
Intercept	4.9	0.0003
Oil extraction pressure (1)	−1.08	0.0059
Oil extraction temperature (2)	−0.25	0.0955
Oil extraction duration (3)	0.08	0.4226
Oil separation pressure (4)	−1.08	0.0059
Oil separation temperature (5)	−0.25	0.0955
CO_2 Rate (6)	−0.08	0.4226
Salt (7)	2.08	0.0016
Size (8)	0.08	0.4226
Type (9)	−0.25	0.0955

Figure 7.16 Coefficients of the taste response

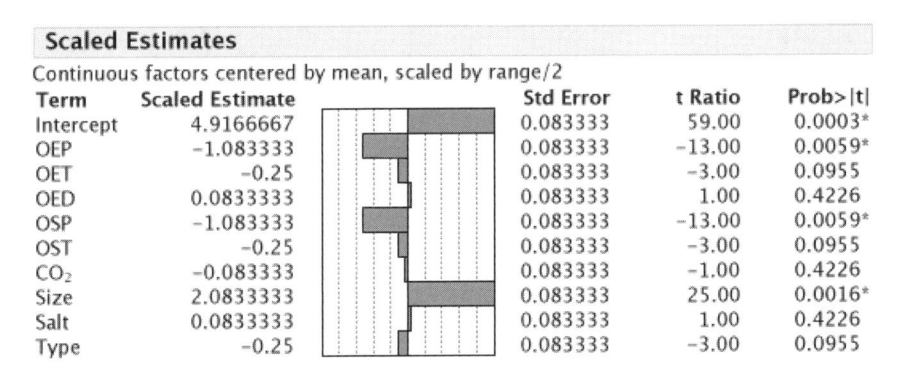

```
Scaled Estimates
Continuous factors centered by mean, scaled by range/2
Term      Scaled Estimate    Std Error   t Ratio   Prob>|t|
Intercept    4.9166667       0.083333    59.00     0.0003*
OEP         -1.083333        0.083333   -13.00     0.0059*
OET         -0.25            0.083333    -3.00     0.0955
OED          0.0833333       0.083333     1.00     0.4226
OSP         -1.083333        0.083333   -13.00     0.0059*
OST         -0.25            0.083333    -3.00     0.0955
CO₂         -0.083333        0.083333    -1.00     0.4226
Size         2.0833333       0.083333    25.00     0.0016*
Salt         0.0833333       0.083333     1.00     0.4226
Type        -0.25            0.083333    -3.00     0.0955
```

Therefore, to improve the taste, add salt.

7.4.4 Study Conclusion

The chips are therefore better using the lower levels of extraction and separation pressures. However, these levels result in lower oil extraction. The chips therefore have a greasier taste than they do when lots of oil is withdrawn. It's easy to see the conundrum here: if there is too much oil, the chips are fatty, but if there is not enough oil, richness is lost. The amount of oil that remains on the chips must therefore be balanced. It's now clear why an optimization plan is necessary: to find a good balance between salt and residual oil in the chips. A design utilizing these three factors (salt, extraction pressure, and separation pressure) should give us the correct solution. Through this example, we see why screening designs are important. They eliminate the factors that play a minor role (or even no role) in the response under study.

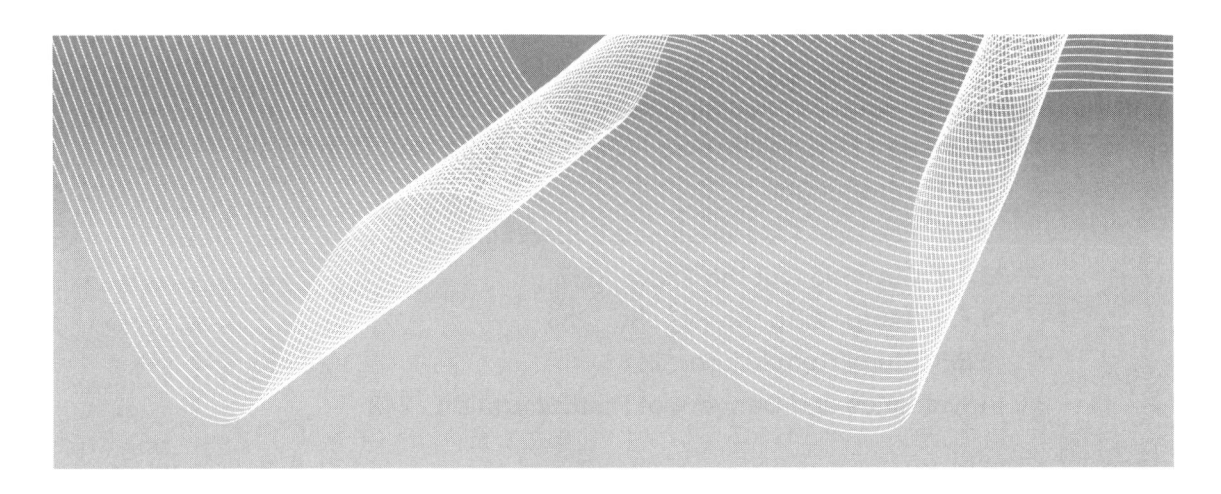

Chapter 8

Trial Order and Blocking

8.1 Introduction   206
8.2 The Nature of Errors   207
    8.2.1 Blocking   208
    8.2.2 Anti-Drift Designs   209
    8.2.3 Random Variation   210
    8.2.4 Small Systematic Variations   211
8.3 Example 9: Penicillium Chrysogenum (Blocking Example)   212
    8.3.1 Preparing the Designed Experiment   212
    8.3.2 Constructing the Plan and Checking the Blocking Advantage   214
    8.3.3 Carrying Out the Trials   217
    8.3.4 Interpreting the Results   218
    8.3.5 Study Conclusion   224
8.4 Example 10: Yates's Beans   225
    8.4.1 Preparing the Designed Experiment   225
    8.4.2 Running the Experiment   228

   8.4.3 Interpreting the Results 230
   8.4.4 Study Conclusion 232
  8.5 Example 11: "The Crusher" (Example of an Anti-Drift Design) 233
   8.5.1 Introduction 233
   8.5.2 Preparing the Designed Experiment 236
   8.5.3 Carrying Out the Trials 237
   8.5.4 Interpreting the Results 238
   8.5.5 Study Conclusion 241
  8.6 Advantages and Dangers of Randomization 242

8.1 Introduction

Is there any advantage in carrying out experimental trials in one order over another? To answer this question, we must take several elements into account: some practical, others theoretical. Here are some common considerations that fall into both categories.

Experimental requirements may impose an order. For example, a manufacturing process might require a glass part, and that part may take two positions in a designed experiment. To avoid breaking the part by moving it several times, it may be advantageous to carry out the trials at one level then the other. The glass needs to be moved only once. Another designed experiment might involve heating a furnace. The thermal equilibrium of a furnace can take a long time to establish, and the experimenter certainly doesn't want to reheat it several times. Other examples can be found where the same experimental conditions impose a trial order, whether they are material constraints, time constraints, or others.

The experimenter could suspect a change in the studied phenomenon's time or space, and therefore also suspect systematic variations in the response or responses. These must be taken into account. If the change is regular, such as the wear and tear of a mechanical element, or the aging of a product, there is *drift,* and the designed experiment must be ordered to measure or infer the important results. To measure these results, we could utilize certain anti-drift designs, add control points to follow the change of this drift, or both.

It's possible that the place or the moment where the tests are carried out affects the experimental results. For example, measures carried out in the morning could be systematically stronger than those in the afternoon. The experimenter, therefore, has to structure the experiments acordingly. Additionally, two different lots of different substances may be required in an experiment. How can we obtain effects that are not marred by the systematic error that exists between the morning and afternoon measurements or between the two different lots? In each case, systematic error must be accounted for. We will see that *blocking* is the means to fight against systematic error.

It could equally be true that small systematic errors change the results by trial groups. Randomization lets us report these systematic errors as random errors, so typical statistical tests remain valid.

Finally, observed variation might be due only to natural randomness.

To answer these questions relating to the possible effect of order, we start by studying the nature of the different errors. We then give examples of different strategies that can be adopted according to what we learn from the disturbances that intervene during the experiment.

8.2 The Nature of Errors

When you carry out the same measurement several times under the same operating conditions, there are always small differences among the measurements. These small variations form the *experimental error.*

The origin of these errors is found in the variations of the levels of all the factors that may modify a response. We can classify these active factors into two categories: *controlled factors* and *uncontrolled factors.*

Controlled factors are those whose levels are set by the experimenter. These are both the factors taken into account for the execution of the design and also all the factors fixed at a constant level throughout the experiment. We consider (according to the linear regression hypothesis) that these factors do not introduce error. Figure 8.1 illustrates the change in level undertaken by a controlled factor (factor 1) during the execution of a 2^3 design.

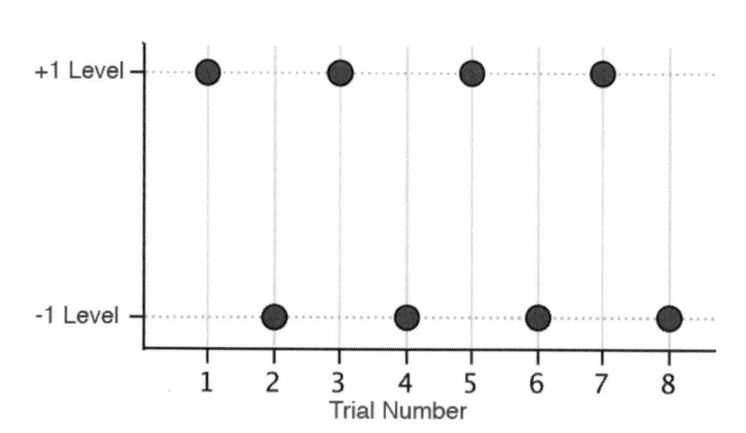

Figure 8.1 Controlled factor: The experimenter imposes any changes in level.

Uncontrolled factors are the others, those whose levels are not fixed by the experimenter. These factors can make the response vary because of unforeseen and unknown variations. We distinguish among several types of uncontrolled factors according to three ways of fighting them: blocking, anti-drift designs, and randomization.

8.2.1 Blocking

Consider factors whose levels stay constant during a series of trials. For example, if you carry out the first part of a designed experiment during the summer, and the second part during winter, there are two trial stages. We assume that an uncontrolled factor stays at "level a" during the first stage and "level b" during the second stage. However, the two levels "a" and "b" are different. It's easy to imagine situations where two levels appear: the design was executed for the same period of time, but by two different operators, or in two different laboratories. A common situation in agriculture arises when tests must be carried out on two separate plots of land. There can be a constant difference between the responses measured at two times or by two operators or by two laboratories or from two plots. Figure 8.2 shows the level variations of an uncontrolled factor during the execution of a two-stage 2^4 design.

Figure 8.2 Uncontrolled factor (blocking): The levels of the first stage are constant, but different from the second.

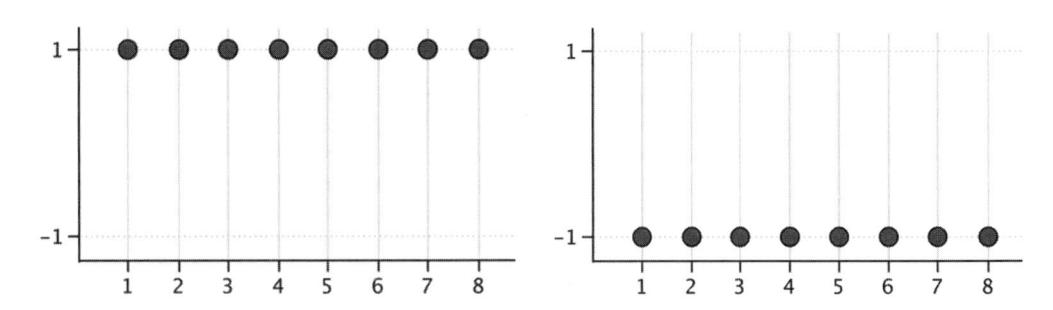

This is a commonly encountered situation, and luckily factorial designs give a method to fight against this type of systematic error. This method is *blocking*. Despite the disturbance introduced by the uncontrolled factor, it is possible to obtain the undistorted factor effects.

Blocking is the technique most often employed to address this situation.

8.2.2 Anti-Drift Designs

The level of an uncontrolled factor can diminish or increase in a regular way according to the trial. Responses are modified by this level variation and the factor effects are distorted if precautions are not taken. This progressive variation is called a *drift* and is illustrated in Figure 8.3. As examples, we could cite the activity of a progressively diminishing catalyst, the flow of a liquid that is slowly reduced because of the gradual stopping of a pipe, a soda solution whose deterioration gets worse over time, or the aging of a chromatographic column, which separates less and less effectively.

Figure 8.3 Uncontrolled factor (drift): The changes in level are progressive from one trial to the next.

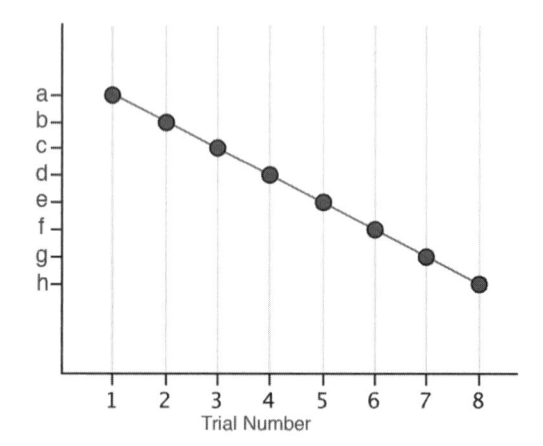

Here, too, factorial designs offer a method to battle against drift. There are anti-drift designs that allow us to obtain the values of the main effects as if there were no drift.

8.2.3 Random Variation

A factor's level can vary in a perfectly random manner from one trial to the next (Figure 8.4). There is no way to battle against such perturbations of a factor. It is part of the experimental error. Tiny variations do not introduce a big problem. If it introduces strong variation to the response, it must be controlled, or its influence must be reduced.

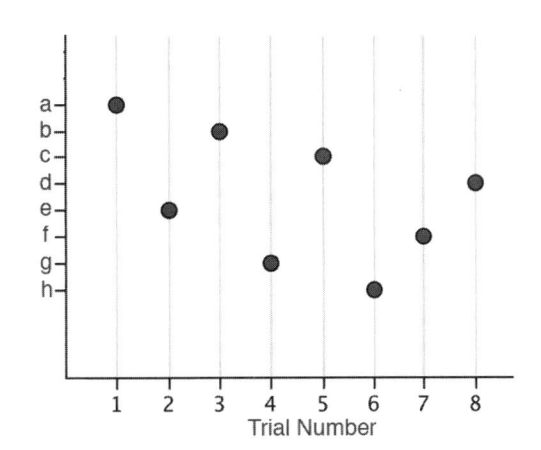

Figure 8.4 Uncontrolled factor: Random level changes

8.2.4 Small Systematic Variations

An uncontrolled factor level may stay stable during two or three trials, then change abruptly to another level, then change after two or three runs to yet another level, and so on. The factor introduces systematic error that is incompatible with traditional statistical tests. To be able to use the traditional tests, we must transform these systematic errors into random errors. For this, we use *randomization* (Figure 8.5).

Figure 8.5 Uncontrolled factor (randomization): Changes in level are in batches.

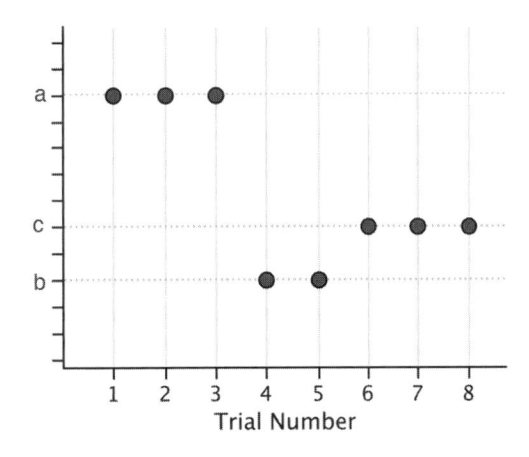

Randomization consists of choosing the trial order in a random manner. Employing randomization would transform Figure 8.5 into Figure 8.4. Traditional statistical tests are then appropriate. The transformation of systematic errors into random errors is both a good and bad choice. It is a good choice regarding statistical tests, but a bad choice because the random error value is increased. This makes it more difficult to detect factors that are only slightly influential. The correct procedure is first to eliminate the systematic errors that are most important by using blocking or anti-drift plans, and then to use randomization.

8.3 Example 9: Penicillium Chrysogenum (Blocking Example)

8.3.1 Preparing the Designed Experiment

8.3.1.1 Description of the Study

Penicillin is made from penicillium chrysogenum. Manufacturers look for the nutritive medium that is most favorable to fast stock development. They undertake a complete factorial design on the five factors that they want to know the influence of. Therefore, there are $2^5 = 32$ runs to be carried out. The duration of trials and the material constraints do not allow them to carry out all the trials at one time. They must split the experiment into two pieces, each carried out at a different time. Scheduling allows them first to carry out 16 trials, and then, after a break of several weeks, to carry out the remaining 16 trials.

The problem is in the two separate realizations. Many uncontrolled factors may change their levels: the stock, the temperature, the operators, and so on. In spite of these possible (and unforeseeable) changes, the experimenters wish to obtain the effect values as if the uncontrolled factors didn't exist. They therefore use a design with blocking.

8.3.1.2 Responses

The response is the number of pounds of penicillin obtained for each trial.

8.3.1.3 Study Objectives
The objective is to learn the composition of the nutritive solution that results in the best penicillin yield.

8.3.1.4 Factors
Factors of study, i.e., the factors whose levels are controlled during the experimental design, are the concentrations of the following products:

- Corn liquor (factor 1)
- Lactose (factor 2)
- Precursor (factor 3)
- Sodium nitrate (factor 4)
- Glucose (factor 5)

8.3.1.5 Study Domain
The study domain is shown in Table 8.1.

Table 8.1 Study domain

Factors	−1 Level	+1 Level
Corn liquor (1)	2%	3%
Lactose (2)	2%	3%
Precursor (3)	0	0.05%
Sodium nitrate (4)	0	0.3%
Glucose (5)	0	0.5 %

8.3.1.6 The Blocking Factor
In addition to the five factors detailed above, we must consider the fact that the experiment is completed in two shifts. An additional factor is thus introduced: the shift. The first 16 trials are at the low level of shift, and the second 16 are at the high level. This extra factor is the *blocking* factor. The blocking factor's level stays constant at a given, but unknown, level during the entire first shift and stays constant at another level (also unknown) during the entire second shift. It is an additional factor where the values are unknown.

8.3.1.7 Choosing the Design

Actually, the plan is not a 2^5 full factorial, but a 2^{6-1} fractional factorial. We need to alias the blocking factor with an interaction factor. Since there is only one extra factor, we choose the highest order interaction to confound with blocking (factor 6):

$$6 = 1 \times 2 \times 3 \times 4 \times 5$$

The trials of the 2^5 full factorial are divided into two groups, one where the $1 \times 2 \times 3 \times 4 \times 5$ interaction is positive, and the other where it is negative. Of course, we make this assignment before we carry out any trials, so that they can be properly assigned to the correct shift.

8.3.1.8 Confounding

The alias generating function allows us, using Box calculations and the equivalence relation, to know how the model coefficients are regrouped into aliases. In particular, the blocking factor is aliased with the $1 \times 2 \times 3 \times 4 \times 5$ interaction:

$$\ell_{1 \times 2 \times 3 \times 4 \times 5} = a_6 + a_{1 \times 2 \times 3 \times 4 \times 5}$$

The $1 \times 2 \times 3 \times 4 \times 5$ interaction has a chance of being quite large. If there are interactions between the blocking factor and the studied factor, there is also a risk of seeing second-order interactions that are large.

$$\ell_{16} = a_{16} + a_{2345} \qquad \ell_{26} = a_{26} + a_{1345} \qquad \text{etc.}$$

8.3.2 Constructing the Plan and Checking the Blocking Advantage

8.3.2.1 Constructing the Plan

Construction of blocking plans is exactly the same as constructing fractional factorials. Here, we write the base plan (2^5) and calculate the signs of the $1 \times 2 \times 3 \times 4 \times 5$ interaction (Table 8.2). However, for blocking plans, we regroup the trials according to the sign of this interaction. The first blocks are those where the $1 \times 2 \times 3 \times 4 \times 5$ interaction is at its low level. It consists of 16 trials numbered 1, 18, 19, 4, 21, 6, 7, 24, 25, 10, 11, 28, 13, 30, 31, and 16. The second block consists of the trials where the $1 \times 2 \times 3 \times 4 \times 5$ interaction is at its high level. It also has 16 trials, numbered 17, 2, 3, 20, 5, 22, 23, 8, 9, 26, 27, 12, 29, 14, 15, and 32.

Table 8.2 Construction of a blocking plan

Trial	1	2	3	4	5	Block = 1×2×3×4×5
1	−1	−1	−1	−1	−1	−1
18	1	−1	−1	−1	1	−1
19	−1	1	−1	−1	1	−1
4	1	1	−1	−1	−1	−1
21	−1	−1	1	−1	1	−1
6	1	−1	1	−1	−1	−1
7	−1	1	1	−1	−1	−1
24	1	1	1	−1	1	−1
25	−1	−1	−1	1	1	−1
10	1	−1	−1	1	−1	−1
11	−1	1	−1	1	−1	−1
28	1	1	−1	1	1	−1
13	−1	−1	1	1	−1	−1
30	1	−1	1	1	1	−1
31	−1	1	1	1	1	−1
16	1	1	1	1	−1	−1
17	−1	−1	−1	−1	1	1
2	1	−1	−1	−1	−1	1
3	−1	1	−1	−1	−1	1
20	1	1	−1	−1	1	1
5	−1	−1	1	−1	−1	1
22	1	−1	1	−1	1	1
23	−1	1	1	−1	1	1
8	1	1	1	−1	−1	1
9	−1	−1	−1	1	−1	1
26	1	−1	−1	1	1	1
27	−1	1	−1	1	1	1
12	1	1	−1	1	−1	1
29	−1	−1	1	1	1	1
14	1	−1	1	1	−1	1
15	−1	1	1	1	−1	1
32	1	1	1	1	1	1

8.3.2.2 Verification of the Blocking Advantage

We can check the advantage of blocking on this example. If, during the second shift, all the responses are increased by 10 points compared to the first shift because of uncontrolled factors, the influence of this shift on the coefficients can be calculated by allotting the value of 10 to all the tests in the second shift. The file **Penicillin_verif.jmp** was constructed so that you can make this check yourself. Calculate the estimates for a model with all first-, second-, third-, fourth-, and fifth-order interactions. Note (Figure 8.6) that only the intercept and the interaction chosen to represent the blocking factor are affected by the change between the two shifts.

Figure 8.6 Full model estimates

Term	Estimate	Std Error	t Ratio	Prob>|t|
Intercept	5	.	.	.
1	0	.	.	.
2	0	.	.	.
3	0	.	.	.
4	0	.	.	.
5	0	.	.	.
1*2	0	.	.	.
1*3	0	.	.	.
1*4	0	.	.	.
1*3*4*5	0	.	.	.
2*3*4*5	0	.	.	.
1*2*3*4*5	5	.	.	.

The other coefficients are not affected. For these runs, it is as if the test were carried out only once, erasing the influence of the shift change (Figure 8.7) for all the effects except for the intercept and blocking interaction.

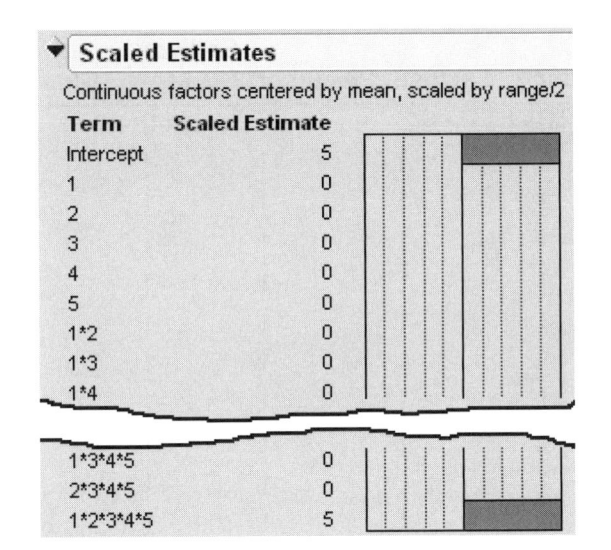

Figure 8.7 Influence of blocking on the coefficients

```
Scaled Estimates
Continuous factors centered by mean, scaled by range/2
Term          Scaled Estimate
Intercept           5
1                   0
2                   0
3                   0
4                   0
5                   0
1*2                 0
1*3                 0
1*4                 0
⋮
1*3*4*5             0
2*3*4*5             0
1*2*3*4*5           5
```

8.3.3 Carrying Out the Trials

The first run is carried out according to the experimental design (Table 8.3). The 16 trials of the first design are executed in a random order. Although blocking allows the systematic error to be absorbed in the blocking term, the experimenters add an additional precaution: a randomization of the trials to free the study from any eventual small systematic errors. Beside the number of each trial, there is a number in parentheses. This number shows the execution order of the trial. For example, trial 12 was executed in the 13th position.

At this stage, it is possible to interpret the first results because we can calculate the five main effects and their ten second-order interactions. We have carried out half of a 2^5 full factorial plan, that is, a 2^{5-1} with the alias generator **I = −1×2×3×4×5.**

Table 8.3 First set of trials

Trial	Corn Liquor (1)	Lactose (2)	Precursor (3)	Sodium Nitrate (4)	Glucose (5)	Pounds
1 (5)	−1	−1	−1	−1	−1	142
18 (16)	1	−1	−1	−1	1	106
19 (11)	−1	1	−1	−1	1	88
4 (10)	1	1	−1	−1	−1	109
21 (6)	−1	−1	1	−1	1	113
6 (9)	1	−1	1	−1	−1	162
7 (1)	−1	1	1	−1	−1	200
24 (3)	1	1	1	−1	1	79
25 (7)	−1	−1	−1	1	1	101
10 (2)	1	−1	−1	1	−1	108
11 (13)	−1	1	−1	1	−1	146
28 (15)	1	1	−1	1	1	72
13 (4)	−1	−1	1	1	−1	200
30 (14)	1	−1	1	1	1	83
31 (8)	−1	1	1	1	1	145
16 (12)	1	1	1	1	−1	118

8.3.4 Interpreting the Results

The second shift of trials is carried out at a later time. Table 8.4 shows the results of the measurements.

Table 8.4 Second set of trials

Trial	Corn Liquor	Lactose	Precursor	Sodium Nitrate	Glucose	Pounds
	(1)	(2)	(3)	(4)	(5)	
17 (23)	−1	−1	−1	−1	1	106
2 (31)	1	−1	−1	−1	−1	114
3 (18)	−1	1	−1	−1	−1	129
20 (28)	1	1	−1	−1	1	98
5 (25)	−1	−1	1	−1	−1	185
22 (17)	1	−1	1	−1	1	88
23 (30)	−1	1	1	−1	1	166
8 (20)	1	1	1	−1	−1	172
9 (26)	−1	−1	−1	1	−1	148
26 (22)	1	−1	−1	1	1	114
27 (19)	−1	1	−1	1	1	140
12 (32)	1	1	−1	1	−1	95
29 (21)	−1	−1	1	1	1	130
14 (27)	1	−1	1	1	−1	164
15 (24)	−1	1	1	1	−1	215
32 (29)	1	1	1	1	1	110

For the complete interpretation of the design, we combine the 32 trials and analyze them as one global experiment. We chose a model with all possible interactions, and therefore have 32 coefficients.

We see quickly that Corn liquor (1), Precursor (3), and Glucose (5) are very influential (Table 8.5 and Figure 8.8). The 3×5 interaction is also strong. And, completely unexpectedly, some high-order interactions are influential too: 1×2×3×4, 1×3×4×5, and 1×2×3×4×5.

Table 8.5 Model coefficients (coded variables)

Effect	Value	Effect	Value
Intercept	129.56		
		1×2×3	−1.31
Corn liquor (1)	−17.56	1×2×4	−2.87
Lactose (2)	0.56	1×2×5	−1.62
Precursor (3)	16.06	1×3×4	1.75
Sodium Nitrate (4)	1	1×3×5	−3.25
Glucose (5)	−20.87	1×4×5	2.81
		2×3×4	−2.62
1×2	−5.94	2×3×5	2.75
1×3	−6.06	2×4×5	2.31
1×4	−5	3×4×5	0.56
1×5	2.62	1×2×3×4	4
2×3	4.44	1×2×3×5	2.62
2×4	−1	1×2×4×5	1.81
2×5	3	1×3×4×5	4.19
3×4	−1	2×3×4×5	1.06
3×5	−10.5		
4×5	2.19	1×2×3×4×5	6.31

Figure 8.8 Principal factor effects and their interactions

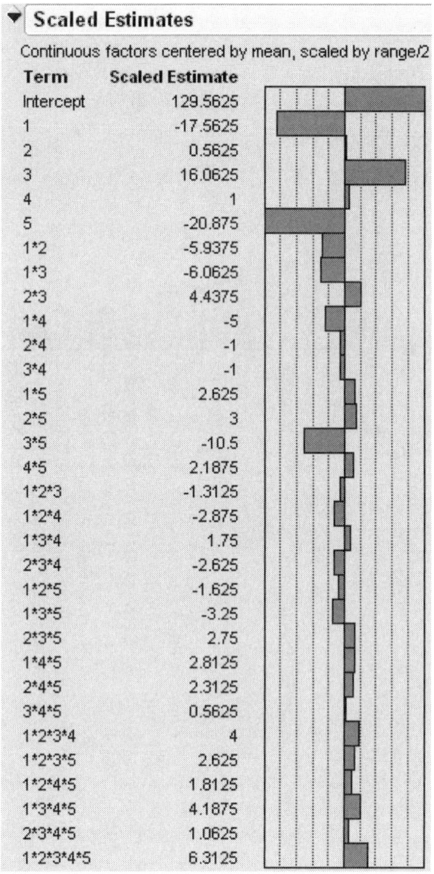

Term	Scaled Estimate
Intercept	129.5625
1	-17.5625
2	0.5625
3	16.0625
4	1
5	-20.875
1*2	-5.9375
1*3	-6.0625
2*3	4.4375
1*4	-5
2*4	-1
3*4	-1
1*5	2.625
2*5	3
3*5	-10.5
4*5	2.1875
1*2*3	-1.3125
1*2*4	-2.875
1*3*4	1.75
2*3*4	-2.625
1*2*5	-1.625
1*3*5	-3.25
2*3*5	2.75
1*4*5	2.8125
2*4*5	2.3125
3*4*5	0.5625
1*2*3*4	4
1*2*3*5	2.625
1*2*4*5	1.8125
1*3*4*5	4.1875
2*3*4*5	1.0625
1*2*3*4*5	6.3125

Scaled Estimates — Continuous factors centered by mean, scaled by range/2

To try to distinguish among those effects that we should retain and those that we can ignore, both a Pareto diagram and a half-normal plot are useful (see Figure 8.9 and Figure 8.10).

Figure 8.9 Pareto diagram of the effects of the penicillin example

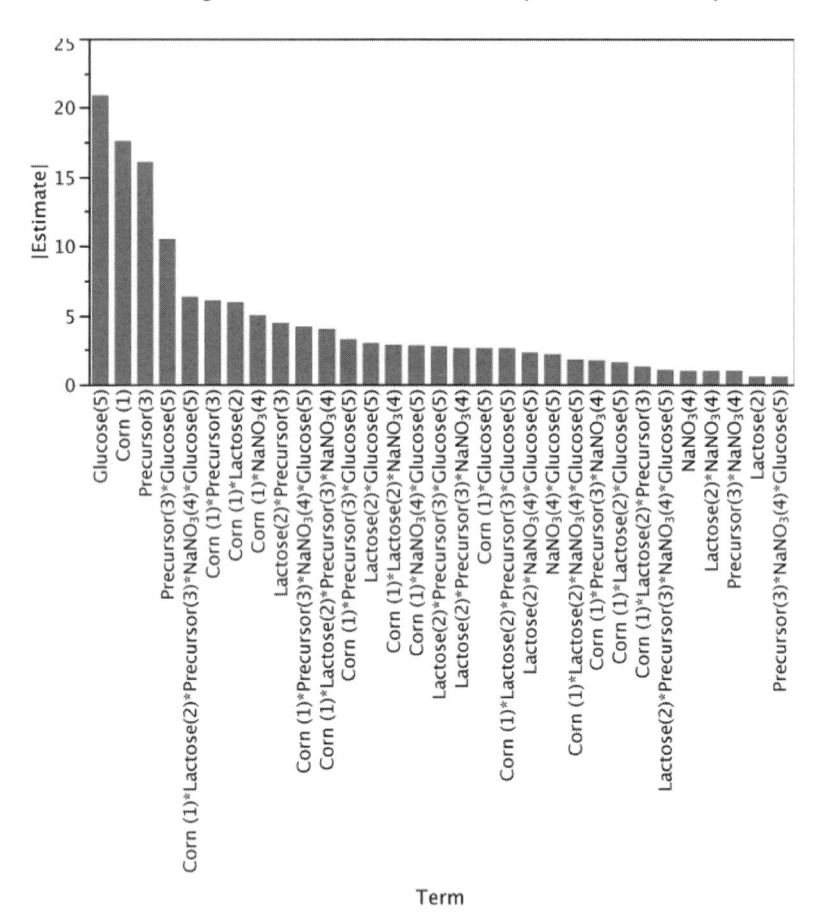

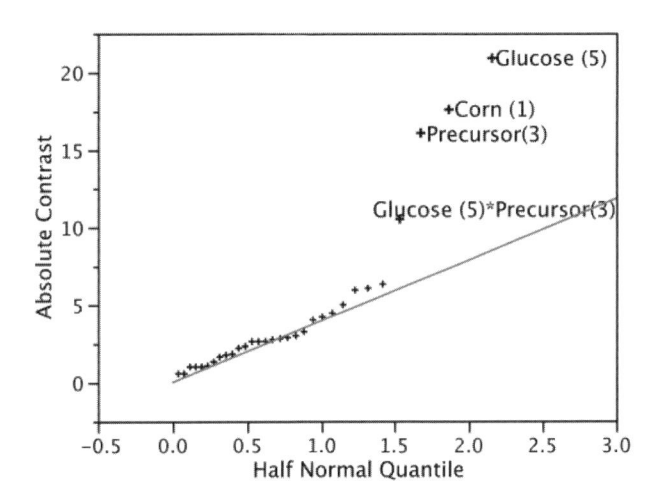

Figure 8.10 Half-normal plot showing the important effects

Examining the Pareto and Daniel diagrams shows that we should retain as influential factors:

- Corn liquor (1)
- Precursor (3)
- Glucose (5)
- The 3×5 (Precursor × Glucose) interaction

The cut between those coefficients that are kept and those that are rejected seems to be in the neighborhood of six. This choice may seem arbitrary, but it is never final and is open to revision with new analyses. What, then, do we think of the 1×2×3×4×5 interaction, which is right on the cutoff point but, by the usual interpretation assumption for high order interaction terms, should be very weak? Remember, this is the interaction that we aliased with the blocking factor.

$$6 = 1 \times 2 \times 3 \times 4 \times 5$$

The equivalence relation shows us that the blocking factor is aliased with the 1×2×3×4×5 interaction:

$$\ell_6 = \ell_{1 \times 2 \times 3 \times 4 \times 5} = a_6 + a_{1 \times 2 \times 3 \times 4 \times 5}$$

In this contrast, it is not the 1×2×3×4×5 interaction that is high, but actually the effect of factor 6. There is a difference of 12 points between the results from the first shift and the second shift. This is certainly not a negligible difference, and would have dramatically distorted the results had the experimenters not taken the precaution of using blocking.

8.3.5 Study Conclusion

How should we set the three influential factors in order to obtain the best possible production for penicillin? See Figure 8.11.

- The corn liquor concentration is set at 2% (-1 level).
- The precursor concentration is set at 0.05% (+1 level).
- No glucose is needed.

If we want to slightly increase the production, we could set

- The lactose concentration (factor 2) at 3% (+1 level).
- The sodium nitrate concentration (factor 4) at 0.3% (+1 level).

Figure 8.11 Factor settings to optimize penicillin output

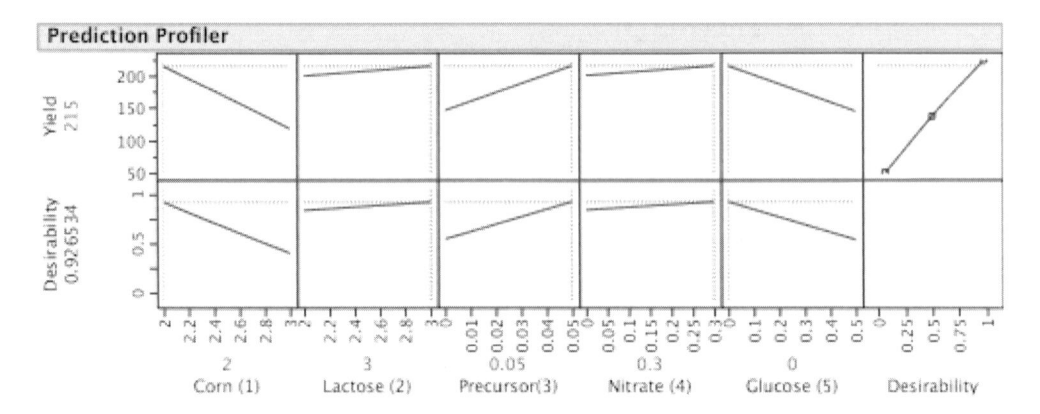

8.4 Example 10: Yates's Beans

8.4.1 Preparing the Designed Experiment

8.4.1.1 Study Description
Yates worked with Fisher at the Rothamsted experimental station in Hertfordshire, England. In 1935, he started researching the effect of fertilizers on the yield of a certain species of bean, publishing his results in 1937. It is one of the oldest experimental designs, and it's interesting to see that even in his era, researchers knew to use the science behind designed experiments to their advantage, especially in the agricultural area. In particular, these scientists used blocking to correct for the many uncontrolled factors that were involved in their research. Since their experiments were long, and their physical space was large, they frequently didn't have to constrain the number of tests they carried out and could consider fractional factorial designs. The precautions they took were of another kind. For example, it is impossible to know if two tracts of land have exactly the same fertility. On one, plants grow exuberantly, while on the other, they are puny and poorly developed. How is it possible to measure the influence of a certain fertilizer in spite of the differing soil fertilities of the experimental tracts? First, the tracts should be as similar as possible fertility-wise. Then blocking should be used to further reduce the influence of its variability.

Yates wanted to study four fertilizers, and he had chosen four tracts of land for his experiment. How should the tracts be organized so that, after the experiments have finished, he had a correct view of the influence of each tested fertilizer? He did not choose the naïve method of assigning one fertilizer to each tract. Instead, he laid out the trials according to a designed experiment that took the differences in fertility of the tracts into account.

8.4.1.2 Responses
The response is measured in pounds of beans harvested for each trial.

8.4.1.3 Study Objective
We want to find the influence of fertilizer alone or associated within the trials.

8.4.1.4 Factors
Yates studied the following factors:

- Space between the rows of beans (factor 1)
- Quantity of manure (factor 2)
- Quantity of nitrate (factor 3)
- Quantity of superphosphate (factor 4)
- Quantity of potash (factor 5)

8.4.1.5 Study Domain
The study domain is specified in Table 8.6.

Table 8.6 Study domain

Factors	−1 Level	+1 Level
Space between rows (1)	18 inches	24 inches
Manure (2)	0 tons/acre	10 tons/acre
Nitrate (3)	0 pounds/acre	50 pounds/acre
Superphosphate (4)	0 pounds/acre	60 pounds/acre
Potash (5)	0 pounds/acre	100 pounds/acre

8.4.1.6 Choosing the Design
Since there are five factors, which each take two levels, Yates decided to carry out a 2^5 full factorial plan. However, he took the precaution of using blocking to give insight into the differences of fertility on the interactions and therefore obtain the true values of the design's five factors.

The 32 tests must be spread over four tracts whose samples can have different fertilities. This is accomplished with eight tests per tract. To divide 32 by 4, we need to introduce two blocking factors, factor 6 and factor 7. The column of factor 6 should have as many minus signs (−) as plus signs (+), which allows division into two blocks. The same holds for column 7. By grouping columns 6 and 7, we get four blocks ++, +−, −+, and − −, each containing eight tests.

It appears, then, that Yates did not carry out a 2^5 full-factorial design, but rather a 2^{7-2} fractional factorial. Since there are two blocking factors, two interaction terms need to be chosen. Yates aliased blocking factor 6 with the 1×2×4 interaction and blocking factor 7 with the 1×3×5 interaction, giving

$$6 = 124 \qquad 7 = 135$$

These two independent generators give the generating function

$$I = 1246 = 1357 = 234567$$

It is possible to calculate the distribution of tests by hand (in fact, Yates had to do that since computers weren't around then). He wrote all the signs of the 1×2×4 and 1×3×5 interactions and grouped them as in Table 8.7. Block 1 contains all tests where 1×2×4 has a minus sign and 1×3×5 has a minus sign. Therefore, block 1 is composed of trials 1, 8, 11, 14, 20, 21, 26, and 31.

This block is given to one of the four tracts. He worked in the same way for the other three blocks. Today, we use software for this work, which causes it to go much more quickly.

Table 8.7 Definition of the levels of the blocking factors for each tract

Terrain	124	135
Block 1	−1	−1
Block 2	+1	−1
Block 3	−1	+1
Block 4	+1	+1

8.4.1.7 Checking the Blocking's Value

We use the model of a 2^5 full factorial with all interactions, knowing that some are distorted by the presence of blocking.

Let's check that a difference in fertility between the tracts does not modify the effects of the factors under consideration. To do this, suppose that the fertility of the first block shifts the responses by 5, that the fertility of the second block shifts the response by 10, that the fertility of the third block shifts the response by 15, and that the fourth block shifts the responses by 20.

Only the intercept and the two interactions chosen for blocking are affected by the change in the fertility of the four tracts (Figure 8.12). The others are not affected by the change. By using blocking, Yates's experiment can therefore be carried out as if the soil samples have the same fertility.

Figure 8.12 Blocking check

Sorted Parameter Estimates				
Term	Estimate	Relative Std Error	Pseudo t-Ratio	Pseudo p-Value
1*3*5	5	0.176777	0.67	0.5196
1*2*4	2.5	0.176777	0.33	0.7455
1	0	0.176777	0.00	1.0000
2	0	0.176777	0.00	1.0000
3	0	0.176777	0.00	1.0000
4	0	0.176777	0.00	1.0000
5	0	0.176777	0.00	1.0000
1*2	0	0.176777	0.00	1.0000

8.4.1.8 Preparing the Trials

To begin, we divide the first tract into eight parcels and assign it randomly to one of the four blocks. We then lay out the eight trials corresponding to the block. Finally, we do the same for the three other tracts.

How are the trials laid out on each tract? It is probable that there are, on any small parcel, some small variations of fertility. It is also possible that this variation is not random. The fertility might diminish progressively as you move from north to south or from east to west. Many other variations are possible. In these conditions, if we lay out the trials in numerical order from north to south, we will have a correlation between the error introduced by the variation in fertility and the trial number. This situation creates difficulty in applying statistical tests that assume that the deviations (fertility variation) are independent, i.e., uncorrelated with each other. In order to apply statistical tests, we usually distribute the trials randomly within the blocks. In this example, the blocks are on the ground. That is exactly what Yates did.

8.4.2 Running the Experiment

After the preparations, shoots were planted and watched until the beans were harvested. The collected quantities were weighed and the pounds of beans from each trial were recorded. These results are shown in Table 8.8.

Table 8.8 Designed experiment and results

Trial	1	2	3	4	5	6=124	7=135	Block	Pounds
1	−1	−1	−1	−1	−1	−1	−1	1	66.5
2	1	−1	−1	−1	−1	1	1	4	36.2
3	−1	1	−1	−1	−1	1	−1	2	74.8
4	1	1	−1	−1	−1	−1	1	3	54.7
5	−1	−1	1	−1	−1	−1	1	3	68
6	1	−1	1	−1	−1	1	−1	2	23.3
7	−1	1	1	−1	−1	1	1	4	67.3
8	1	1	1	−1	−1	−1	−1	1	70.5
9	−1	−1	−1	1	−1	1	−1	2	56.7
10	1	−1	−1	1	−1	−1	1	3	29.9
11	−1	1	−1	1	−1	−1	−1	1	76.7
12	1	1	−1	1	−1	1	1	4	49.8
13	−1	−1	1	1	−1	1	1	4	36.3
14	1	−1	1	1	−1	−1	−1	1	45.7
15	−1	1	1	1	−1	−1	1	3	60.8
16	1	1	1	1	−1	1	−1	2	64.6
17	−1	−1	−1	−1	1	−1	1	3	63.6
18	1	−1	−1	−1	1	1	−1	2	39.3
19	−1	1	−1	−1	1	1	1	4	51.3
20	1	1	−1	−1	1	−1	−1	1	73.3
21	−1	−1	1	−1	1	−1	−1	1	71.2
22	1	−1	1	−1	1	1	1	4	60.5
23	−1	1	1	−1	1	1	−1	2	73.7
24	1	1	1	−1	1	−1	1	3	92.5
25	−1	−1	−1	1	1	1	1	4	49.6
26	1	−1	−1	1	1	−1	−1	1	74.3
27	−1	1	−1	1	1	−1	1	3	63.6
28	1	1	−1	1	1	1	−1	2	56.3
29	−1	−1	1	1	1	1	−1	2	48

(*continued*)

Table 8.8 (*continued*)

Trial	1	2	3	4	5	6=124	7=135	Block	Pounds
30	1	−1	1	1	1	−1	1	3	47.9
31	−1	1	1	1	1	−1	−1	1	77
32	1	1	1	1	1	1	1	4	61.3

8.4.3 Interpreting the Results

The analysis of the design starts, as usual, with the calculations of the coefficients of the polynomial model where all interactions are included (Table 8.9).

Table 8.9 Model coefficients (coded units)

Effect	Value	Effect	Value
Intercept	58.91		
		1×2×3	0.99
Space between rows (1)	−3.90	1×2×4	−5.85
Manure (2)	7.85	1×2×5	−0.76
Nitrate (3)	1.62	1×3×4	0.45
Superphosphate (4)	−2.75	1×3×5	−3.08
Potash (5)	3.8	1×4×5	−1.74
		2×3×4	0.54
1×2	2.52	2×3×5	1.12
1×3	1.66	2×4×5	−0.87
1×4	1.47	3×4×5	−2.42
1×5	4.37	1×2×3×4	−0.31
2×3	2.57	1×2×3×5	−1.02
2×4	−0.24	1×2×4×5	−1.86
2×5	−1.94	1×3×4×5	−3.17
3×4	−2.58	2×3×4×5	1.56
3×5	2.175		
4×5	−0.21	1×2×3×4×5	2.39

This table is illustrated by the bar chart in Figure 8.13.

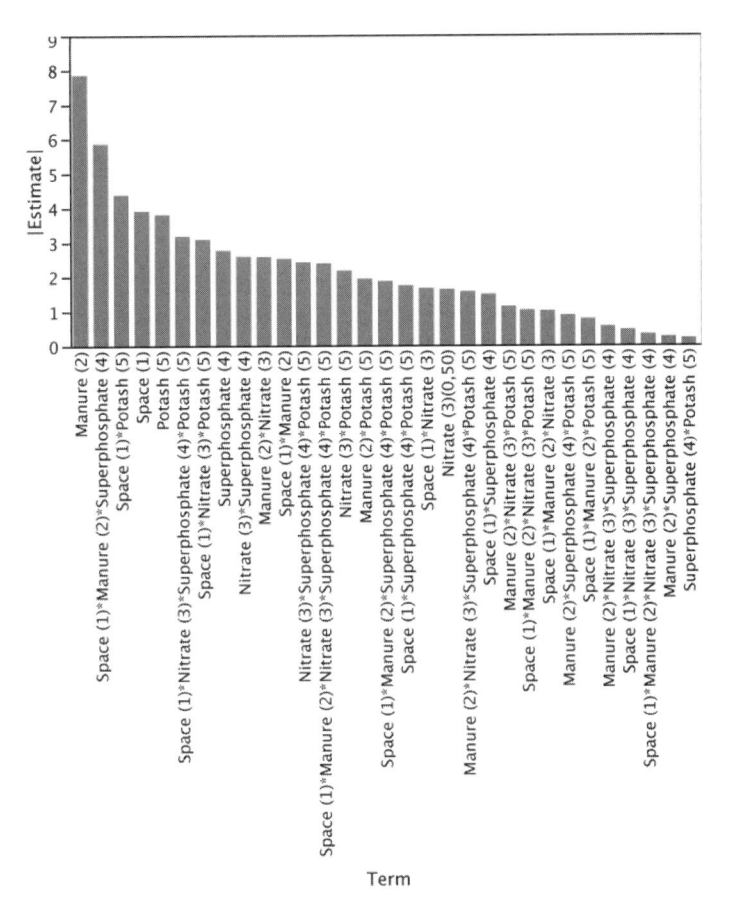

Figure 8.13 Coefficients of the Yates bean experiment

We have calculated 32 coefficients, the strongest being:

- Manure, factor 2. This factor is by far the most influential.
- The 1×2×4 interaction. Don't be too surprised to find a third-order interaction that is this large. It is actually one of the blocking factors. This result proves that the soil fertility was quite different from one tract to another. Without the precaution of blocking, the interpretation of the design would have been completely erroneous since some of the variations in fertility would have been attributed to one of the factors.

- The 1×5 interaction. The influence of potash is not the same for narrow and wide rows.
- The space between the rows (factor 1).
- Potash (factor 5).
- The 1×3×5 interaction, which is the other blocking factor. The high value of this interaction confirms the strong disparity of soil fertility among the tracts.
- The 1×3×4×5 interaction, which is the interaction between superphosphate (factor 4) and the fertility of the terrain. This interaction says that soil fertility did not have the same influence among the tracts.

The influence of the other factors and interactions are weaker and weaker. We decide to keep three influential factors:

- Space between rows (1)
- Quantity of manure (2)
- Quantity of potash (5)

8.4.4 Study Conclusion

If you recalculate the model with the three preceding factors and their second-order interactions, you get the results shown in Figure 8.14.

Figure 8.14 Bean yield according to the three most influential factors

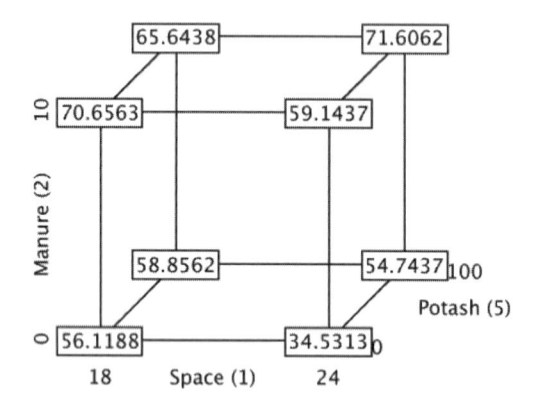

```
                  65.6438 ─────── 71.6062
                 ╱              ╱
         70.6563 ─────── 59.1437
  10    │              │
Manure (2)            │
        │    58.8562 ─────── 54.7437  100
        │   ╱              ╱         Potash (5)
   0    56.1188 ─────── 34.5313      0
            18    Space (1)    24
```

If there is neither manure (lower grade of factor 2) nor potash (lower grade of factor 5), and the rows are spaced (high level of factor 1), the yield is bad—34.5. The yield can be increased in two ways:

1. Decrease the space between the rows and add manure, which doubles the output (70.6).

2. Leave the row spacing as-is, but add manure and potash. This, too, doubles the output (71.6).

Both rules give almost exactly the same yield. Therefore, choose either the most economical or the most practical solution.

8.5 Example 11: "The Crusher" (Example of an Anti-Drift Design)

8.5.1 Introduction

We have just seen an example of systematic variations with blocks. There are also systematic variations when the response drifts. Drift occurs when the response of each trial increases (or decreases) by an increasing quantity proportional to the response without drift. For example, the progressive wear of a machine element or of a material can cause a systematic variation of the response during an experiment. Two types of drift are examined: linear drift and unspecified drift. It is necessary to protect yourself against both.

8.5.1.1 Linear Drifts

The response of the first trial is, say, y_1 when there is no drift. When there is drift, we have y_1' such that $y_1' = y_1 + h$

For the second trial, the response without drift is, say, y_2. The response with drift y_2' is expressed as $y_2' = y_2 + 2h$

Table 8.10 summarizes the data for a 2^3 design, assuming that the order of trials is the same as the rest we have seen, that is, in Yates order.

Table 8.10 Linear drift

Trial	Response without Drift	Response with Drift
1	y_1	$y'_1 = y_1 + h$
2	y_2	$y'_2 = y_2 + 2h$
3	y_3	$y'_3 = y_3 + 3h$
4	y_4	$y'_4 = y_4 + 4h$
5	y_5	$y'_5 = y_5 + 5h$
6	y_6	$y'_6 = y_6 + 6h$
7	y_7	$y'_7 = y_7 + 7h$
8	y_8	$y'_8 = y_8 + 8h$

The effect matrix of a 2^3 design allows us to calculate the influence of drift on each effect and each interaction.

Table 8.11 shows the calculation.

Table 8.11 Influence of drift on the effects of a 2^3 design

Trial	I	1	2	3	1×2	1×3	2×3	1×2×3	Responses
1 (1)	+1	-1	-1	-1	+1	+1	+1	-1	1 h
2 (2)	+1	+1	-1	-1	-1	-1	+1	+1	2 h
3 (3)	+1	-1	+1	-1	-1	+1	-1	+1	3 h
4 (4)	+1	+1	+1	-1	+1	-1	-1	-1	4 h
5 (5)	+1	-1	-1	+1	+1	-1	-1	+1	5 h
6 (6)	+1	+1	-1	+1	-1	+1	-1	-1	6 h
7 (7)	+1	-1	+1	+1	-1	-1	+1	-1	7 h
8 (8)	+1	+1	+1	+1	+1	+1	+1	+1	8 h
Drift Influence	36h	4h	8h	16h	0	0	0	0	

We can conclude that the effects are modified as follows:

$$E'_1 = E_1 + 0.5h \quad E'_2 = E_2 + 1h \quad E'_3 = E_3 + 2h \quad E'_{12} = E_{12}$$

$$E'_{13} = E_{13} \quad E'_{23} = E_{23} \quad E'_{123} = E_{123} \quad I' = I + 4.5h$$

Drift does not influence the four interactions, but does influence the main effects. Can we make the inverse be true? The problem becomes easy if we notice that it is the order of the + and – signs of the interactions that cancel out the influence of the drift. Therefore, we must organize the trials so that the principal effects use the signs of the interactions. For example, factor 1 is studied using the signs of the interaction 1×2×3, factor 2 using factor 1×2, and factor 3 using 2×3.

This leads us to a new experimental matrix with the same trials as the original matrix, but with a different order. With the given assumptions, we must adopt the order 7, 6, 2, 3, 4, 1, 5, 8. The main effects are therefore independent of drift, but the interactions are obviously tainted with an error like those shown in Table 8.12.

Table 8.12 Influence of drift on the effects of a 2^3 reordered design

Trial	I	1'	2'	3'	1'2'	1'3'	2'3'	1'2'3'	Responses
7 (1)	+1	-1	-1	-1	+1	+1	+1	-1	1 h
6 (2)	+1	+1	-1	-1	-1	-1	+1	+1	2 h
2 (3)	+1	-1	+1	-1	-1	+1	-1	+1	3 h
3 (4)	+1	+1	+1	-1	+1	-1	-1	-1	4 h
4 (5)	+1	-1	-1	+1	+1	-1	-1	+1	5 h
1 (6)	+1	+1	-1	+1	-1	+1	-1	-1	6 h
5 (7)	+1	-1	+1	+1	-1	-1	+1	-1	7 h
8 (8)	+1	+1	+1	+1	+1	+1	+1	+1	8 h
Drift influence	36h	0	0	0	16h	4h	0	8h	

It is important to remember that when there is a drift, the order of the trials affects the responses, and that it is necessary to choose the run order carefully to arrive at relevant conclusions about the main effects and interactions.

In particular, be wary of interactions which, like those in this case, are distorted by drift. There is a means to detect this drift, because there are three values in proportion: 1, 2, 4.

8.5.1.2 Unknown Drift

In some cases, the experimenter fears a drift may influence his experiment, but does not have any reason to think that it is linear. He wants, of course, to estimate the effects as if there is no drift at all.

8.5.2 Preparing the Designed Experiment

8.5.2.1 Describing the Study

An experimenter wants to increase the quantity of powder that is produced by a crusher. Wear on the jaws may introduce drift to the process, and therefore distorted effects may be a problem.

8.5.2.2 Objective of the Study

We want to get estimates of the main effects as if there were no drift.

8.5.2.3 Responses

The response is the mass of powder (in grams) that the crusher produces with good granularity, from tests of the same duration.

8.5.2.4 Factors
The factors to be taken into account are:

- Rotation speed (factor 1)
- Crushing pressure (factor 2)
- Height of the air gap (factor 3)

8.5.2.5 Choosing an Experimental Design
Since there are three factors to study, the simplest design choice is a 2^3 full factorial. However, the presence of an eventual drift makes the experimenter choose an anti-drift plan. Even if the drift is not linear, the main effects are little affected by the drift error. Moreover, it is better still if we can evaluate the influence of the drift. To do so, we must add some replicate points in order to follow the evolution of the drift and to be able to make the necessary corrections to measure the effects as if there were no drift. The number of replicate points depends on the importance (or stakes) of the study and the cost of the trials. At the very least, we need a point at the beginning, middle, and end of the design. In fact, it would be better if we could put one point in between each point of the design. Depending on the importance and the budget of this study, the experimenter can choose between three and nine points at the center to follow the drift. This example is developed with nine points at the center.

So, the experimenter draws the order randomly from an anti-drift plan and adds a replicate point between each trial of the design.

The randomly drawn order is 6, 7, 3, 2, 4, 1, 5, 8. The center points are numbered with a 0 in front of their trial number. The complete anti-drift design has therefore $9 + 8 = 17$ trials. Table 8.13 shows the trials and their associated experimental results.

8.5.3 Carrying Out the Trials
The trials are scrupulously carried out in the order specified by the designed experiment, and the results are shown in Table 8.13.

Table 8.13 Experimental matrix and raw results of the measurements

Trial	Rotation Speed (1)	Pressure (2)	Air Gap (3)	Mass (g)
01	0	0	0	500
6 (1)	+	−	+	493
02	0	0	0	460
7 (2)	−	+	+	410
03	0	0	0	426
3 (3)	−	+	−	402
04	0	0	0	393
2 (4)	+	−	−	410
05	0	0	0	363
4 (5)	+	+	−	434
06	0	0	0	335
1 (6)	−	−	−	261
07	0	0	0	309
5 (7)	−	−	+	216
08	0	0	0	285
8 (8)	+	+	+	338
09	0	0	0	263
− Level	40	4	0.20	
0 Level	50	6	0.25	
+ Level	60	8	0.30	

8.5.4 Interpreting the Results

Examination of the succession of values obtained for the center points shows clearly that there is drift in the experiment. When graphed with the response values as y and the trial number as x, the pattern is clear. On the same graph, we draw the responses corresponding to the points of the 2^3 experimental design.

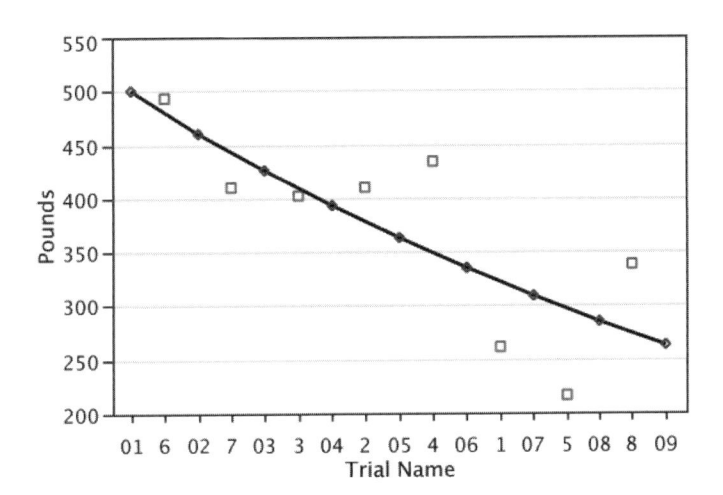

Figure 8.15 Replicates at the center point allow us to see the drift.

Although the drift is not linear, the calculation of the effects (Table 8.14) reveals relationships close to 0, 1, 2, and 4. The main effects should not be too far from their true values. It is clear in this example that the interactions are not, in any case, estimations of the error on the coefficients. Only the 1×3 interaction could be considered as such. (Remember that the calculation of effects and interactions is done without using the control points at the center.)

Table 8.14 Coefficients without corrections (coded units)

Effect	Value
Intercept	370.47
Rotation speed (1)	48.25
Pressure (2)	25.5
Air-gap (3)	−6.25
1×2	−58.25
1×3	3
2×3	−15.75
1×2×3	−29

Since the drift is not completely linear, we can't use the formulas in Table 8.10 to make corrections. We are going to adopt a graphical method. Between trials 01 and 02, the deviation is 20 grams, that is, 20 grams on each side of trial 6. We assume that if there were no drift, the response would have been more than 20 grams (493 + 20 = 513 grams). For trial 7 (carried out second), the mean value at the midpoint was 0.5(460 + 426) = 443 grams instead of 500 grams, 57 grams smaller. The response for trial 7 must be increased by the same amount: 410 + 57 = 467 grams (Table 8.15).

Table 8.15 Response corrected for the drift

Trial	Corrected Mass (in grams)
6	513
7	467
3	492
2	530
4	584
1	438
5	420
8	566

Corrections for the rest of the factorial design responses are carried out in the same way. The main effects and interactions are recomputed with these corrected answers. In this way, we get the value of the coefficients as if there had been no drift. Table 8.15 shows the drift-corrected responses, and Table 8.16 shows the effects recalculated with the corrected responses.

Table 8.16 Drift-corrected coefficients (coded units)

Effect	Value
Intercept	501.25
Rotation speed (1)	47
Pressure (2)	26
Air gap (3)	−9.75
1×2	0.75
1×3	1
2×3	−1
1×2×3	0.75

8.5.5 Study Conclusion

The three factors involved in the study are influential on powder yield. Most important is the number of revolutions, which must be at least 60 turns/minute. The pressure of the spring must be set as high as possible, here at 8. The air gap must be 0.20, the lower level of the settings.

There is no interaction among the factors.

Day by day, a strong reduction in the output is noticed, due to wear on the jaws. So, the nature of the jaws needs to be changed to avoid this reduction in output. Whether a higher number of revolutions or a stronger pressure may affect the output are also questions for further study.

8.6 Advantages and Dangers of Randomization

We have already defined randomization as the choice of the order of trials in a random way. The essential goal is to be able to use standard statistical tests despite some small, systematic errors. However, the transformation of systematic errors into random errors is not necessarily a good thing. In fact, the systematic error increases the random error. Then, it becomes more difficult to detect the weakly influential factors. If the systematic errors are important, randomization can be a catastrophic technique.

The systematic errors must be eliminated before the randomization.

The correct procedure is first to eliminate the most important systematic errors by using blocking or an anti-drift design, and then to follow that with randomization.

What would have been the results of the design with drift if the experimenters had simply randomized their trials without being wary of the drift? Suppose that the trials were randomly drawn (in order 1, 5, 8, 7, 4, 6, 2, 3) and that no replicate control points were carried out.

In such as case, using the results we have above, we can recalculate the responses that the experimenter would have measured. The experimental matrix would have looked like Table 8.17 and the experimenter would have then gotten the effects shown in Table 8.18. These effects are completely false, as are their interactions.

Table 8.17 Raw results of the measures from a simply randomized design

Trial	Rotation Speed (1)	Pressure (2)	Air Gap (3)	Mass of Powder
1 (1)	+	−	+	415
5 (2)	−	+	+	358
8 (3)	−	+	−	474
7 (4)	+	−	−	342
4 (5)	+	+	−	433
6 (6)	−	−	−	337
2 (7)	−	−	+	332
3 (8)	+	+	+	259
− Level	40	4	0.20	
0 Level	50	6	0.25	
+ Level	60	8	0.30	

Table 8.18 Coefficients of a simply randomized plan (coded units)

Effect	Value
Intercept	368.75
Rotation speed (1)	25.25
Pressure (2)	8.25
Air gap (3)	9
1×2	51.25
1×3	2.5
2×3	22
1×2×3	−13

Comparing methods

In order to compare the various techniques on the organization of trial order, we summarize the effects in Table 8.19 and illustrate them in Figure 8.16.

Table 8.19 Comparison of the three techniques

Effects	Anti-Drift Design	Responses Corrected for the Drift	Randomization
Intercept	370.5	501.25	368.75
Rotation speed (1)	48.25	47	25.25
Pressure (2)	25.5	26	8.25
Air gap (3)	−6.25	−9.75	9
1×2	−58.25	0.75	51.25
1×3	3	1	2.5
2×3	−15.75	−1	22
1×2×3	−29	0.75	−13

1. Anti-drift design

   The effects of the principal factors are purely obtained without influence of the drift. But the interactions are tainted. The experimenter suspected the drift, but he could carry out only eight trials. He chose the best experimental conditions, but he could not draw conclusions from the interactions.

Figure 8.16 Bar chart for comparison of the methods

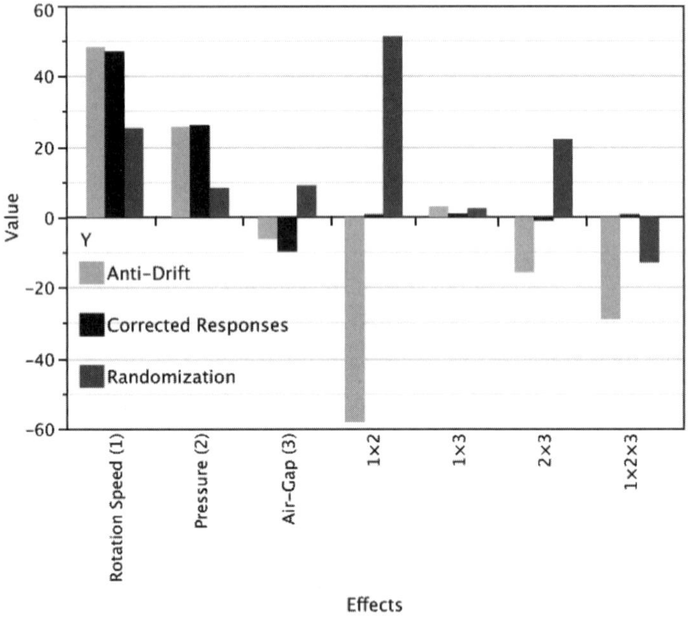

2. Complete correction of the drift on the responses

   The effects and the interactions are estimated well, but at the expense of a higher number of trials.

3. Simple randomization without taking drift into account

   Neither main effects nor interactions are correctly estimated. This lack of foresight of the experimenter can be catastrophic.

Remember this example, where it was necessary to control for the systematic errors by using blocking or an anti-drift design, and then by using randomization.

Chapter 9

Response Surface Designs

9.1 Introduction 247
9.2 Composite Designs 247
9.3 Box-Behnken Designs 249
9.4 Doehlert Designs 250
9.5 Example 12: The Foreman's Rectification (Example of a Composite Design) 255
    9.5.1 Preparing the Designed Experiment 255
    9.5.2 Responses and Objectives of the Study 256
    9.5.3 Factors 257
    9.5.4 Study Domain 257
    9.5.5 Choosing the Design 257
9.6 Experimentation (Factorial Design) 258
9.7 Interpreting the Factorial Design Results 258
    9.7.1 Verification of the Linear Model 259
    9.7.2 Positions of Star Points 260
9.8 Second-Degree Complementary Design 262

9.9 Interpreting the Results 263
    9.9.1 Modeling 263
    9.9.2 Graphical Representation of the Results 264
    9.9.3 Confirming the Results 268
9.10 Study Conclusion 268
9.11 Example 13: Soft Yogurt (Box-Behnken Design Example) 269
    9.11.1 Preparing the Design Experiment 269
    9.11.2 Factors 270
    9.11.3 Study Domain 271
    9.11.4 Responses 271
    9.11.5 Choosing the Design 271
9.12 Experimentation 271
9.13 Interpreting the Design 272
    9.13.1 Model 272
    9.13.2 Interpreting the Results 274
9.14 Study Conclusions 276
9.15 Example 14: Insecticide (Example of a Doehlert Design) 277
    9.15.1 Preparing the Designed Experiment 277
    9.15.2 Factors and Study Domain 277
    9.15.3 Responses 278
    9.15.4 The Designed Experiment 278
9.16 Experimentation 278
9.17 Interpreting the Results 279
    9.17.1 Calculating the Coefficients 279
    9.17.2 Modeling 281
    9.17.3 Residual Analysis 282
    9.17.4 Graphical Representation of the Results 282
9.18 Study Conclusion 286

9.1 Introduction

The designs in preceding chapters had only two levels per factor, and the mathematical models were the first degree in each factor. These designs are the most commonly used because they allow the screening of the factors and often lead to simple but sufficient models. However, in many cases, we must move up to models of the second degree in order to have a good model of the studied phenomenon. These quadratic models are *response surface models*. This chapter covers the three most important designs of this type: composite designs, Box-Behnken designs, and Doehlert designs.

The postulated mathematical model used with response surface designs is a second-degree model with second-order interactions. For two factors,

$$y = a_0 + a_1 x_1 + a_2 x_2 + a_{12} x_1 x_2 + a_{11} x_1^2 + a_{22} x_2^2 + e$$

For three factors,

$$y = a_0 + a_1 x_1 + a_2 x_2 + a_3 x_3 + a_{12} x_1 x_2 + a_{13} x_1 x_3 + a_{23} x_2 x_3 + a_{11} x_1^2 + a_{22} x_2^2 + a_{33} x_3^2 + e$$

9.2 Composite Designs

Composite designs lend themselves well to a sequential study. The first part of the study is a full- or fractional-factorial design supplemented by center points to check the validity of the first-degree, factorial model. If the validation tests are positive (the response measures at the center of the field are statistically equal to the predicted value at the same point), the study is generally completed. If the tests are negative, supplementary trials are undertaken to establish a second-degree model. The additional trials are represented by the design points located on the axes of the coordinates and by new central points. The points located on the coordinate axes are called *star points*. Composite plans therefore have three parts (Figure 9.1):

- Factorial design
  This is a full- or fractional-factorial design with two levels per factor. The experimental points are at the corners of the study domain.
- Star design
  The points of a star design are on the axes and are, in general, all located at the same distance from the center of the study domain.

- Center points
  There are usually center points, at the center of the study domain, for both the factorial designs and the star designs.

To calculate the total number of trials, n, to carry out, sum the following:

- The trials from the factorial design (n_f)
- The trials from the star plan (n_α)
- The trials at the center (n_0)

So, the number of trials for a composite design is given by the equation

$$n = n_f + n_\alpha + n_0$$

Figure 9.1 Composite design for studying two factors. The factorial points are black, the star points are gray, and the center points are white.

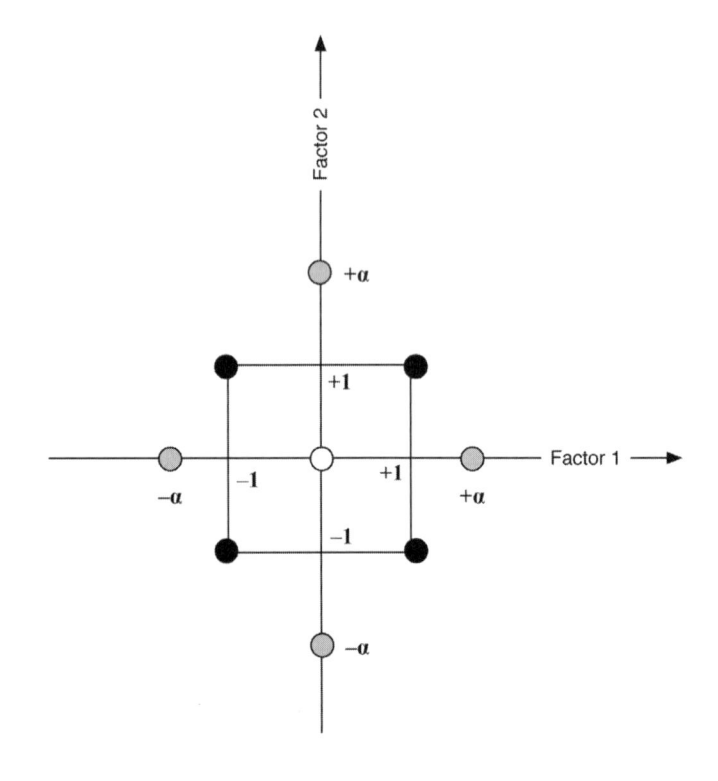

Each factor has five levels. For face-centered designs (where the star points are at the center of each face of the design space, that is, on the square's edge), there are only three levels per factor.

9.3 Box-Behnken Designs

In 1960, Box and Behnken proposed designs that allow us to directly implement second-degree models. All the factors have three levels: −1, 0, and 1. These designs are easy to carry out and have the property of *sequentiality*. It is possible to study k factors and still have the option to add new ones without losing the results from the trials already carried out.

The Box-Behnken design for three factors is constructed on a cube. For four factors, the design is constructed on a four-dimensional hypercube. The experimental points are placed not at the corners of the hypercube, but in the middle of the edges, in the center of the faces (squares), or the center of the cube. This arrangement means that all experimental points are placed equidistant from the center of the study domain, that is, on a sphere or hypersphere, depending on the number of dimensions. Center points are added to the sphere center.

The Box-Behnken design for three factors is shown in Figure 9.2. The cube has 12 edges. Traditionally, three experimental points are placed at the center of the study. Box-Behnken designs for three factors therefore have 12 + 3 = 15 trials. Note that with four center points instead of three, the design respects the so-called *near-orthogonality* criterion.

Figure 9.2 Illustration of the Box-Behnken design for three factors. There are twelve experimental points at the center of each edge, and three points at the center of the cube.

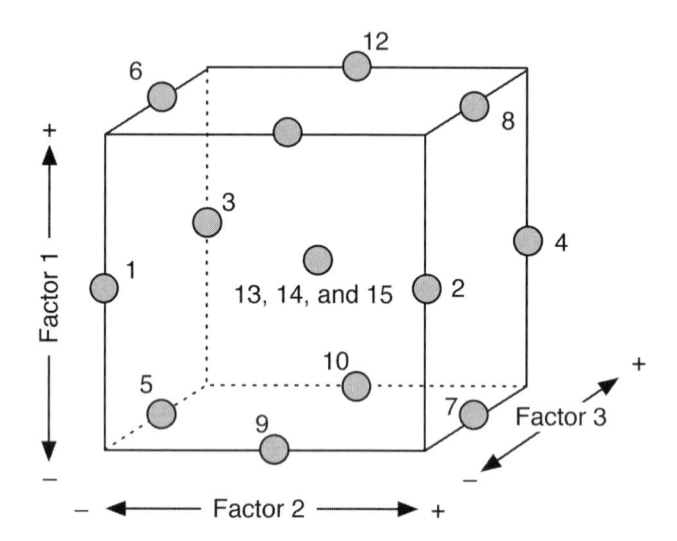

9.4 Doehlert Designs

The experimental points of the designs proposed by David H. Doehlert in 1970 fill the experimental space uniformly. For two factors, the experimental points are placed at the vertices of a regular hexagon. There is one center point (Figure 9.3).

Having seven experimental points, this plan allows the calculation of at least seven unknowns, therefore seven coefficients. Since the experimental points are evenly spread in the experimental space, it is easy to extend the design into any direction by adding more regularly distributed points.

These designs also make it easy to introduce new factors. New trials can be directly added to the existing ones, so no trials are lost. The only precaution to take is to make sure the non-studied factors stay at a constant value (zero-level) while studying the active factors.

Figure 9.3 Doehlert design for the study of two factors. The points are regularly distributed on a hexagon, along with a single center point.

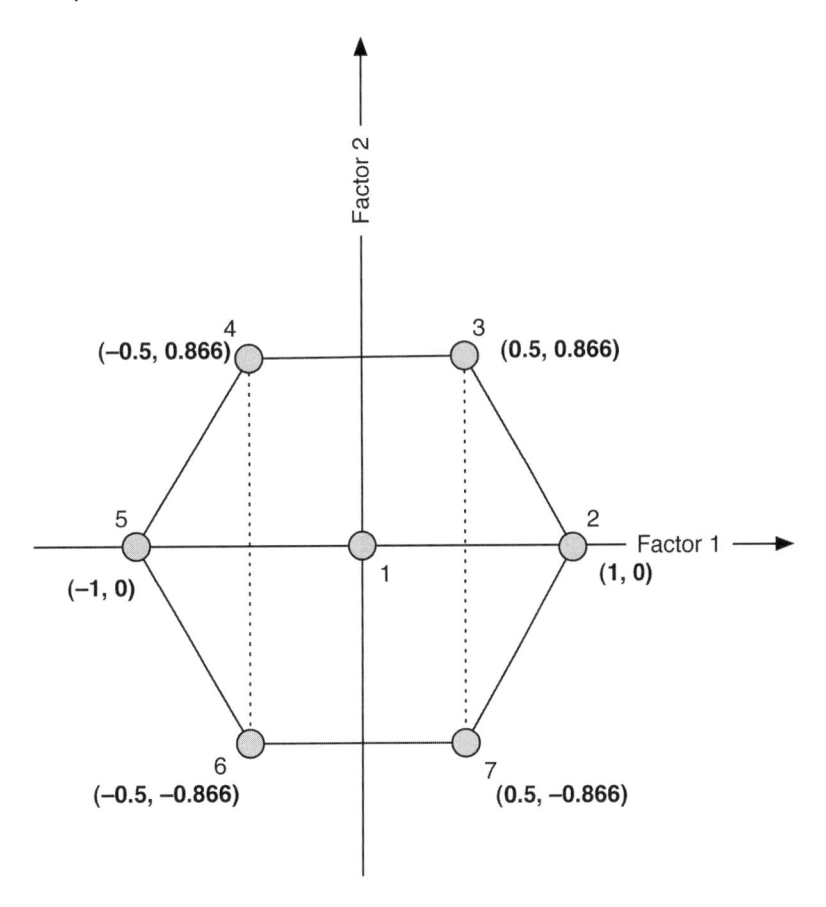

Table 9.1 is the translation, in the form of an experimental matrix, of Figure 9.3.

Table 9.1 Doehlert design for two factors

Trial	Factor 1	Factor 2
1	0	0
2	+ 1	0
3	+ 0.5	+ 0.866[1]
4	− 0.5	+ 0.866
5	− 1	0
6	− 0.5	− 0.866
7	+ 0.5	− 0.866

The arrangement of the points in Figure 9.3 leads to five levels for factor 1 and three levels for factor 2. Before assigning values to the factor levels, check that they are compatible with these numbers of levels. If difficulties arise, rotating the hexagon easily generates a new Doehlert design. Figure 9.4 shows another arrangement of the same design after a 90-degree rotation. Now, factor 1 has three levels, and factor 2 has five.

---

[1] $0.866 = \dfrac{\sqrt{3}}{2}$

Figure 9.4 Another possible arrangement of points in a Doehlert design to study two factors. The points are always evenly arranged in the experimental space.

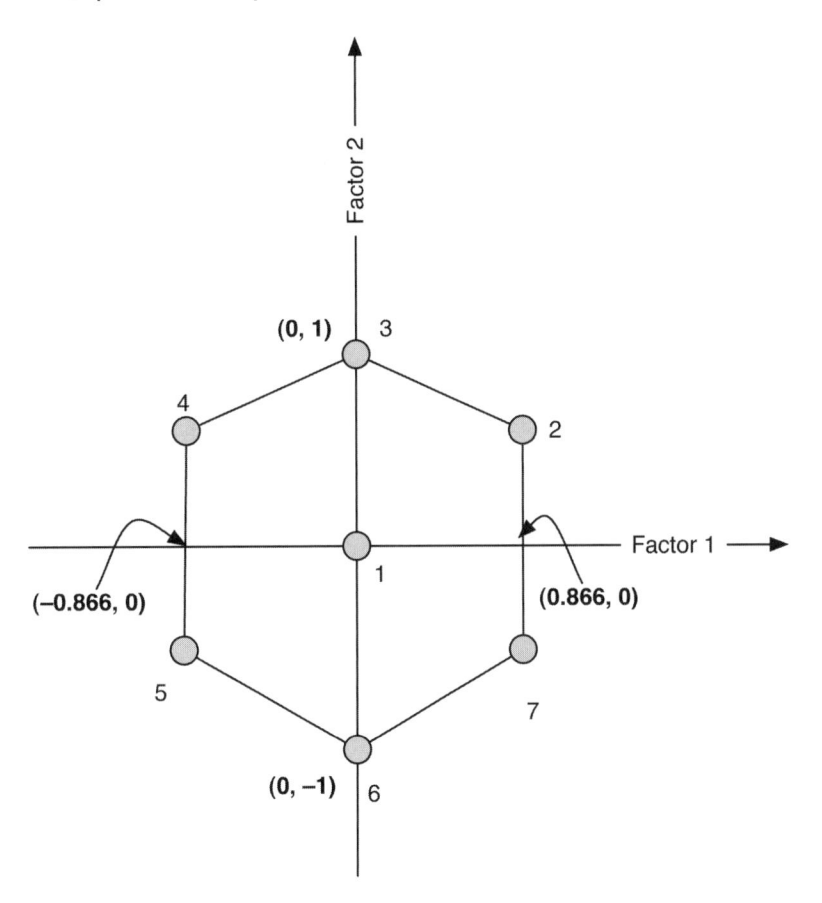

All the points in the Doehlert design are on a unit circle (in centered and scaled units). The domain defined by Doehlert designs is spherical: a circle in two dimensions, a sphere in three dimensions, a hypersphere in more than three dimensions.

If the desired results are not found in this study domain, the domain can be extended in the direction where most of the desired points are likely to be. Just add three experimental points (Table 9.2) to find a new Doehlert design (Figure 9.5). The points 2, 1, 7, 8, 9, 10, and 3 form a new hexagon. Of course, the design can be extended in other directions in the same way.

Table 9.2 Extension points for a two-factor Doehlert design

Trial	Factor 1	Factor 2
8	+ 1.5	− 0.866
9	+ 2	0
10	+ 1.5	+ 0.866

Figure 9.5 Extension of a two-factor Doehlert design. Three points are all that is needed to make a new Doehlert design.

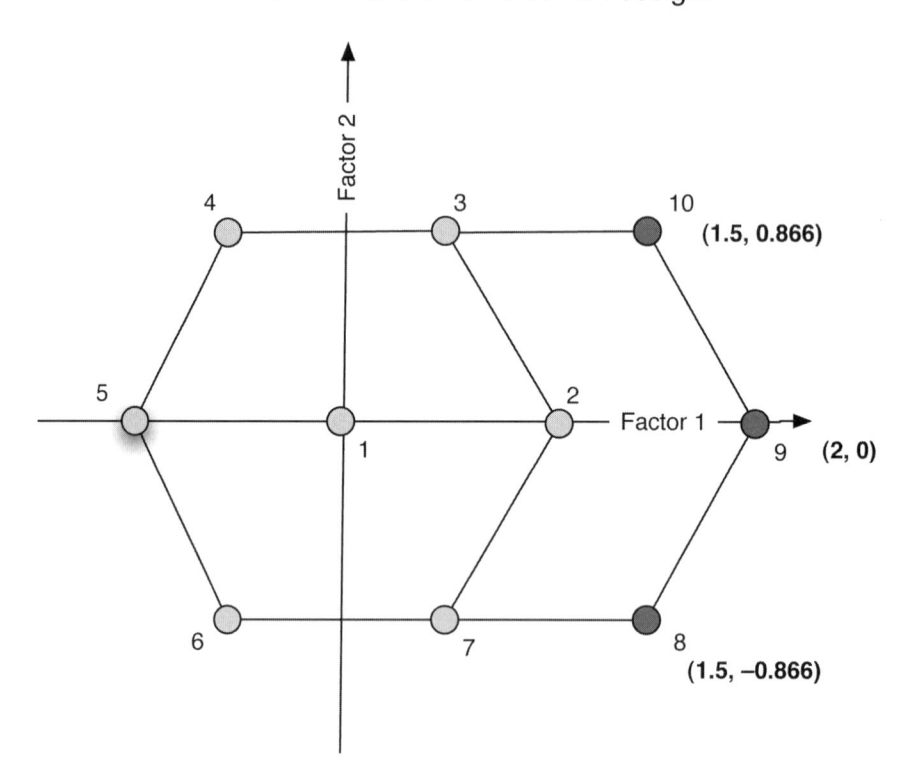

9.5 Example 12: The Foreman's Rectification (Example of a Composite Design)

9.5.1 Preparing the Designed Experiment

9.5.1.1 Describing the Study

A foreman is not happy with the surface quality of the metal parts that are manufactured in his workshop. The last machined step, which gives the part its final appearance, is *rectification*. This is therefore the technique that the foreman wants to improve. Two factors, roughness and the number of peaks per unit of length, characterize the parts' surface quality. The foreman would be happy if he could make parts that had a measured roughness lower than 0.150 and fewer than 50 peaks. If he achieves this goal, the surface quality of his parts would be regarded as perfect and all his customers would be satisfied.

To obtain the desired surface quality, the foreman carried out tests, changing settings by relying on his common sense and his experience. However, all his attempts failed, and the results seemed, well, contradictory. Sometimes, an increased cutting speed made better quality parts, sometimes worse quality. Not knowing what to do, the foreman decided to carry out the recommendations from the training course in DOE that he had just taken.

In rectification, the metal part is seated firmly in a support. A grinding stone removes a fine metal film from the surface of the part. This tool is an abrasive disk that spins at high speed and moves forward slowly to remove thin layers of metal (Figure 9.6). The thickness of the metal layer to be removed can be adjusted for each pass. The last pass is the one that contributes the most to the final appearance of the part. It is therefore important to avoid putting too much stress on the grinder, and instead to remove only a very fine layer of metal.

The workshop manufacturing rules are

- Fast, tangential cutting speed (20 m/s)
- Slow advance (0.9 m/min)

Figure 9.6 Schematic of machining a part by rectification. The grinding stone rotates and advances to level the surface.

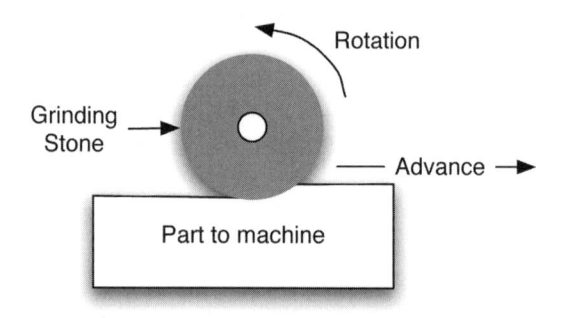

9.5.2 Responses and Objectives of the Study

Recall that the factors chosen by the foreman are the roughness and the number of peaks per unit length (Figure 9.7). They are defined as follows:

Roughness
Roughness is measured by a standardized method. The smallest possible value is desired. A value smaller than 0.15 is considered a success. The standard deviation of this measure is 0.002 units.

Figure 9.7 Enlargement of the rectified surface. During machining, peaks are created because metal is removed from the surface of the part. The peaks' number and height determine the roughness and appearance of the part's surface.

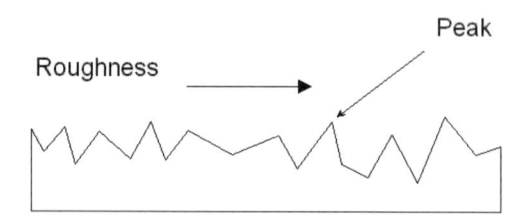

Peaks per unit length
The foreman counts the number of peaks per unit length. This number should be as small as possible. The goal is to have fewer than 50 peaks per unit length. The standard deviation of this measurement is 2 units.

9.5.3 Factors

The foreman uses two factors:

- Factor 1: forward speed of the grinding wheel (in meters/minute).
- Factor 2: tangential cutting speed (in meters/second). This speed is related to the number of revolutions and the diameter of the grinding stone.

Many other factors are fixed: the shape and material of the grinding wheel, the quality of the grinding abrasion, worked metal, depth of the final pass (0.02 mm), and so on.

9.5.4 Study Domain

The upper and lower levels of each factor are defined in Table 9.3.

Table 9.3 Study domain

Factor	−1.21 Level	−1 Level	0 Level	+1 Level	+1.21 Level
Forward speed (1)	0.74	0.9	1.65	2.4	2.56
Cutting speed (2)	13.95	15	20	25	26.05

9.5.5 Choosing the Design

The foreman starts with a traditional factorial design, but he suspects that he will have to continue the study with a response surface design. Therefore, he plans to have two control points at the center of the domain.

9.6 Experimentation (Factorial Design)

The results of the trials are shown in Table 9.4.

Table 9.4 Factorial design and results

Trial	Advancement (1)	Cutting (2)	Roughness×1000	Peaks
1	− 1	− 1	194	77.8
2	+ 1	− 1	282	68.4
3	− 1	+ 1	120	65.3
4	+ 1	+ 1	91	96.1
5	0	0	233	63.8
6	0	0	235	61.9
−Level	0.9	15		
0 Level	1.65	20		
+1 Level	2.4	25		

9.7 Interpreting the Factorial Design Results

The results of the calculations are shown in Table 9.5. Remember that the coefficients are calculated only with the four trials of the design and not with the control points.

Table 9.5 Model coefficient (coded units)

Effect	Roughness×1000	Peaks
Intercept	171.75	76.9
Advancement (1)	14.75	5.35
Cutting (2)	−66.25	3.8
1×2	−29.25	10.05

9.7.1 Verification of the Linear Model

We can check the validity of the linear model by comparing the predicted response of the control point to the observed response at the same point.

For roughness, the predicted response at the center of the domain is equal to the intercept of the model. We use a 3 standard deviation margin of error:

$$\hat{a}_0 = 171.75 \pm 3 \times \frac{2}{\sqrt{4}} = 171.75 \pm 3$$

There is therefore a 99.74% chance that the mean of the predicted response lies in the interval (168.75, 174.75).

The observed response is

$$y_0 = \frac{233 + 235}{2} = 234 \pm 3 \times \frac{2}{\sqrt{2}} = 234 \pm 4.24$$

There is therefore a 99.74% chance that the mean of the observed population lies in the interval (229.76, 238.24).

The intervals do not intersect (Figure 9.8). Therefore, we conclude that the two values are not equal. Considering the above percentages, we are fairly certain that we are observing a real difference rather than a fluke.

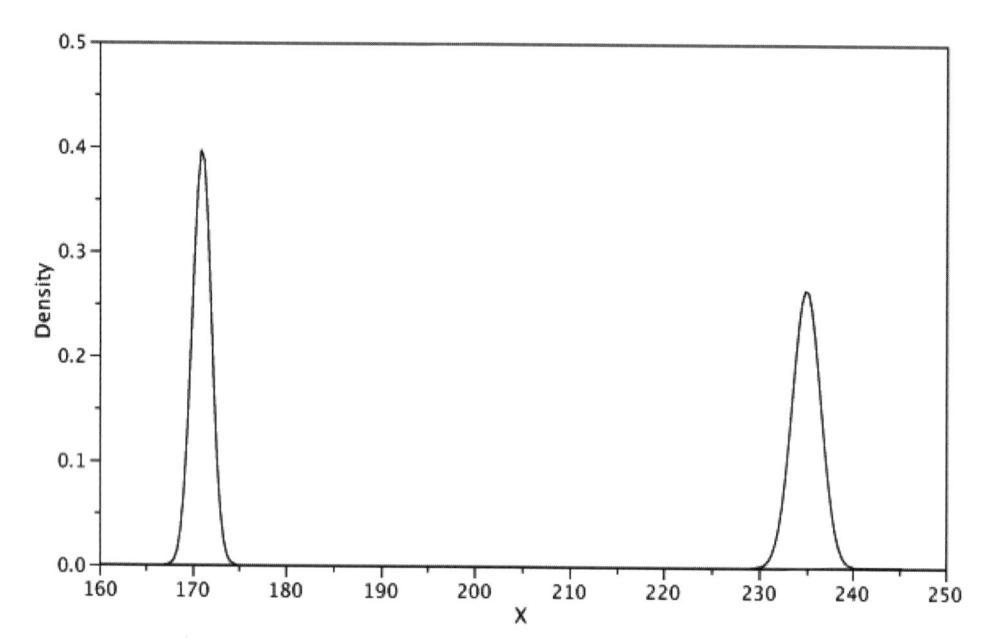

Figure 9.8 Comparison of the predicted responses and observed responses

Alternatively, we could use the formula for comparison of means (see Appendix B).

$$t = \frac{|\hat{a}_0 - y_0|}{\sqrt{\sigma_{a_0}^2 + \sigma_{y_0}^2}} = \frac{171.75 - 234}{\sqrt{1+2}} = \frac{62.25}{1.732} = 35.94$$

The difference between the two responses is 35.94 standard deviations of the difference. The corresponding probability is so small that we can conclude with certainty that the two values are not equal.

The conclusion is that the linear model is not sufficient and that we must use a second-degree model. To do so, we must add some star points and some center points.

9.7.2 Positions of Star Points

The best positioning of star points is still hotly debated among statisticians, and there are entire books devoted to this question. Indeed, it's important to know that the precision of the coefficients in the postulated model is influenced by the position of the points in the designed experiment. Depending on whether these points are well or poorly placed, the coefficients can have good or bad precision. With two-level designs based on Hadamard matrices (that is, full-factorial designs, fractional-factorial designs, and Plackett-Burman designs), the best placement of the points is assured. With quadratic (i.e., second-degree) designs, this is no longer true. A criterion of quality for the point placement must be chosen. This criterion allows the calculation of the best possible star point position. We assume that the axial points are at the same distance (in centered and scaled units) from the center of the study domain, and that this distance is notated α.

For example, we may want the prediction error to be the same for points that are equally distant from the domain center. In this case, we would choose an *isovariance* criterion by rotation. The value of α is

$$\alpha = n_f^{\frac{1}{4}}$$

To make the composite design satisfy the rotation criterion, the star points must be placed at a distance α equal to the fourth root of the number of points of the factorial design.

Alternatively, we may want the coefficients to respect the *near orthogonality* criterion. The value of α must be chosen such that

$$\alpha = \left(\frac{n_f \left(\sqrt{n_0 + n_f + n_\alpha} - \sqrt{n_f} \right)^2}{4} \right)^{\frac{1}{4}}$$

The value of α is a function of the number of points at the center, the number of points in the factorial design, and the number of star points in the design. Table 9.6 lets you choose the value of α for the most common cases.

Table 9.6 Value of α as a function of the number of points in the factorial design (n_f), star points (n_α), and center points (n_0) for the *near orthogonality* criterion

Number of factors	2	3	4	5	5	6	6
Design	2^2	2^3	2^4	2^{5-1}	2^5	2^{6-1}	2^6
n_f	4	8	16	16	32	32	64
n_α	4	6	8	10	10	12	12
$n_0 = 1$	1	1.215	1.414	1.547	1.596	1.724	1.761
$n_0 = 2$	1.078	1.287	1.483	1.607	1.662	1.784	1.824
$n_0 = 3$	1.147	1.353	1.547	1.664	1.724	1.841	1.885
$n_0 = 4$	1.210	1.414	1.607	1.719	1.784	1.896	1.943

9.8 Second-Degree Complementary Design

The foreman plans to add two new center points. In order for the two-factor composite plan to respect the criterion of near orthogonality, he must choose $\alpha = 1.21$, since there are four points in the factorial design, four star points, and four center points. The design is run and the results are shown in Table 9.7.

Table 9.7 Complementary designed experiment and results

Trial	Advancement (1)	Cutting (2)	Roughness × 1000	Peaks
7	−1.21	0	154	52.3
8	+1.21	0	195	60.4
9	0	−1.21	278	87.0
10	0	+1.21	122	95.7
11	0	0	232	61.5
12	0	0	230	60.5
−1.21 Level	0.74	13.95		
0 Level	1.65	20		
+1.21 Level	2.56	26.05		

9.9 Interpreting the Results

To interpret the results, we join the two designs: the initial factorial design and the complementary star design. For this interpretation, the center points are no longer control points. They are used in the calculation of the coefficients.

9.9.1 Modeling

We use a second-degree (quadratic) mathematical model. The same model is used for both responses:

$$y = a_0 + a_1 x_1 + a_2 x_2 + a_{12} x_1 x_2 + a_{11} x_1^2 + a_{22} x_2^2 + e$$

Table 9.8 Model coefficients (centered and scaled units)

Coefficients	Roughness x 1000	Peaks
a_0 (Intercept)	232.4	62.1
a_1	15.7	4.5
a_2	−65.5	3.7
a_{12}	−29.2	10
a_{11}	−39.2	−4.3
a_{22}	−21.8	19.6

These coefficients (Table 9.8) let us write a model for roughness ($R^2 = 0.9993$) and for the number of peaks ($R^2 = 0.9937$) in coded units:

$$\hat{y}_{Roughness} = 232.4 + 15.7x_1 - 65.5x_2 - 29.2x_1x_2 - 39.2x_1^2 - 21.8x_2^2$$

$$\hat{y}_{Peaks} = 62.1 + 4.5x_1 + 3.7x_2 + 10.0x_1x_2 - 4.3x_1^2 + 19.6x_2^2$$

9.9.2 Graphical Representation of the Results

These two models can be used to show the results inside the study domain.

Residual analysis

The residuals are plotted as a function of the predicted responses (Figure 9.9). The points seem to be distributed randomly, without any of the structures shown in Chapter 5. Given this information, we assume that there is no more information to be extracted from the data.

Figure 9.9 Residual plots for the roughness and peak models

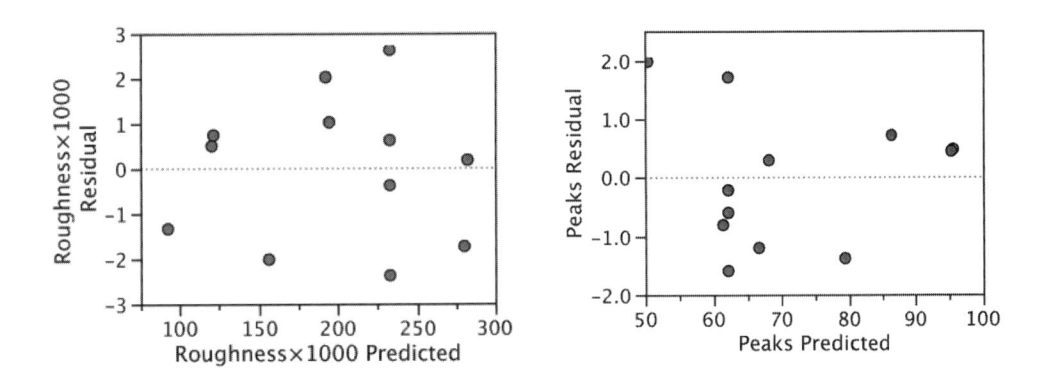

Response surfaces

The model for roughness lets us draw corresponding response surfaces (Figure 9.10). We see that the objective of having a roughness lower than 0.150 can be obtained in the study domain. We must merely choose a forward speed and a cutting speed that together give a response along the line representing the 150-roughness level.

Figure 9.10 Response surface for roughness. This surface shows a maximum, but it is not of interest here because we want a roughness less than 0.15. (The values for roughness have been multiplied by 1000.)

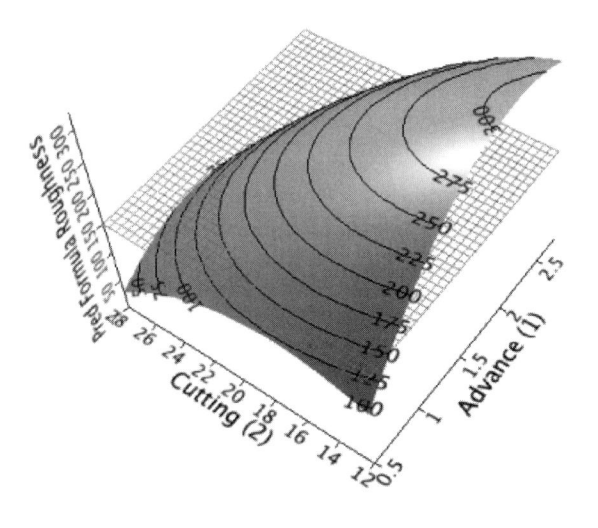

The model for peaks also lets us draw a response surface (Figure 9.11). Note that the objective of a number of peaks less than 50 can be attained within the study domain but at the boundaries.

Figure 9.11 Response surface for peaks. Fewer than 50 peaks are reachable on this surface.

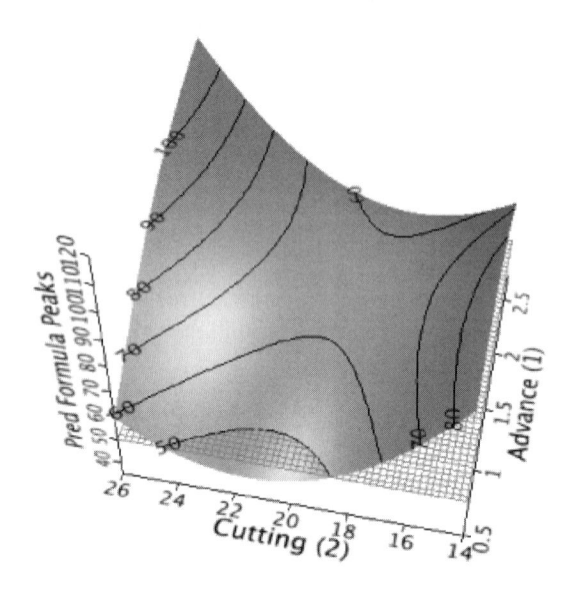

By examining these two response surfaces, the foreman can see that his objectives can be reached. He must choose regulations for cutting speed and forward speed that take the constraints for both responses into account. To see the situation clearly, he draws contour curves for both responses on the same graph (Figure 9.12).

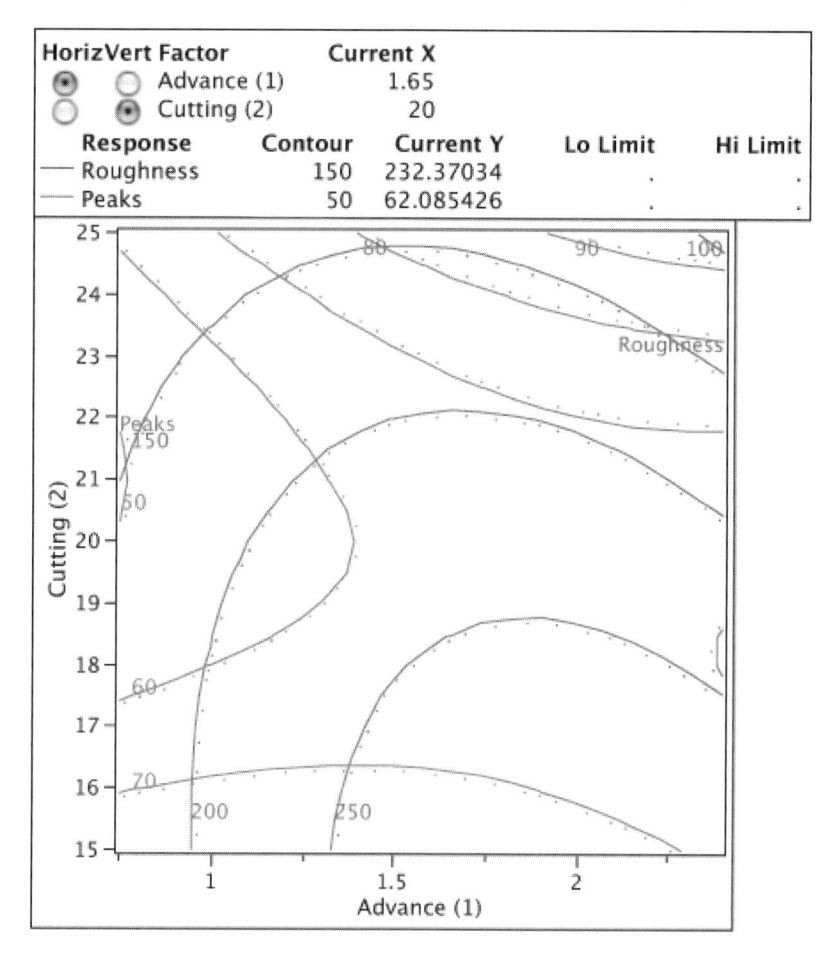

Figure 9.12 Contour curves for roughness and number of peaks

He sees that there is a small window corresponding to

- Forward speed of –1.2
- Cutting speed of 0.2

9.9.3 Confirming the Results

Since the solution is on the edges of the study domain, the prediction precision is not high. These process refinements are not good enough to give to his workmen. The foreman decides to make some confirmatory trials. He calculates (in engineering units) the cutting speed and forward speed corresponding to the centered and scaled values:

- Forward speed of 0.75 meters/minute
- Cutting speed of 21 meters/second

He makes several test parts according to these rules and obtains surfaces that conform to his expectations perfectly. By taking measurements of roughness and number of peaks, he sees that the model is satisfactory.

9.10 Study Conclusion

The quality of the manufactured parts can be improved if the manufacturing conditions are correctly set. For a cutting depth of 0.02 mm, the forward speed of the grinding stone must be 0.75 meters per minute and its forward speed must be 21 meters per second. These rules are strict because they were made from results on the edge of the response surface and are consequently unstable. That is, these rules are not robust, so the workmen will have to pay close attention to them, strictly following them. Any increase in forward speed lowers the surface quality. Similarly, a reduction in forward speed improves the surface quality, but is not economically feasible. An increase or reduction in cutting speed reduces the surface quality.

Therefore, the foreman gives these rules with the following note placed on a display board:

Precision Grinding:

The conditions for the final manufacturing step must be precisely:

- Forward speed: 0.75 meters/minute
- Cutting speed of 21 meters/second
- Cutting depth of 0.02mm

9.11 Example 13: Soft Yogurt (Box-Behnken Design Example)

9.11.1 Preparing the Designed Experiment

9.11.1.1 Describing the Design
In an industrial laboratory, a researcher wants to study the influence of several factors likely to decrease the acidity of yogurt. Lactic leaveners transform lactose into lactic acid and produce acidity. A particularly strong concentration of acid is characteristic of Bulgarian yogurts. The aim of this study is to decrease the acidic taste of the fermented milk. For this reason, stabilized milk is produced from a natural stabilizer, which attenuates the variations of acid in the final product in spite of the presence of lactic leaveners.

The first step of this process (Figure 9.13) is to dilute the raw milk with water, since undiluted milk is not amenable to the manufacturing process. The second stage of the process is to concentrate the mixture by removing some of the lactose and the water. With less available lactose, the leaveners produce less lactic acid. Both of these stages produce milk that must be stabilized. So, a further treatment that involves the injection of a stabilizer is needed. This treatment does not modify the volume of the mixture. This results in stabilized milk that is ready to use.

Figure 9.13 Preparation diagram of the milk used to make reduced-acidity yogurt

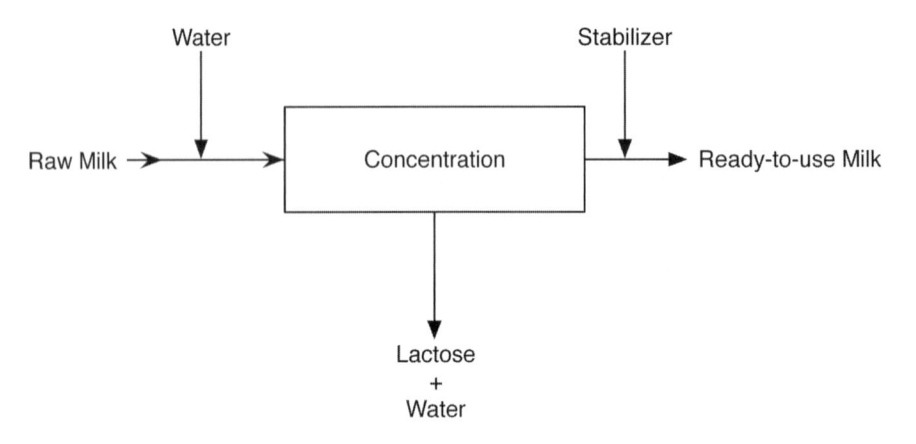

9.11.2 Factors

The three factors used in this experiment are:

- Factor 1: Dilution ratio. This is the ratio of added water to raw milk.

- Factor 2: pH, which is related to the injected stabilizer. Enough stabilizer is added to get a certain pH after the injection. It is the pH that is controlled.

- Factor 3: Milk ratio. This is the ratio of raw milk to stabilized milk. The volume of stabilized milk is smaller than that of the raw milk. This ratio is therefore greater than one.

9.11.3 Study Domain

The high and low levels of each factor are shown in Table 9.9.

Table 9.9 Study domain

Factor	−1 Level	+1 Level
Dilution (1)	0.5	2
pH (2)	6	5
Concentration (3)	1.5	2.5

9.11.4 Responses

The response chosen by the researcher is acid loss, which measures the loss of lactic acid. Higher values of acid loss are better. Therefore, the researcher looks for preparation rules that lead to a high value of this response. The goal is to get stabilized milk with an acid loss of at least 48.

9.11.5 Choosing the Design

The researcher expects to see response variations that require a second-degree model. After thinking about the problem in detail, the researcher chooses a Box-Behnken design, since it allows estimation of a second-degree model without a restriction on the number of tests.

9.12 Experimentation

Results of the 15 trials are shown in Table 9.10. These trials are reordered into the classical presentation of a Box-Behnken design. The numbers in parentheses show the trial run order. For example, trial 1(5) is trial number 1 in the classical design, but was executed fifth.

Table 9.10 Trial matrix and experimental results

Trial	Dilution (1)	pH (2)	Concentration (3)	Responses
1 (5)	−	−	0	51.3
2 (9)	+	−	0	42.6
3 (7)	−	+	0	42.2
4 (12)	+	+	0	50.4
5 (6)	−	0	−	40.7
6 (2)	−	0	+	41.5
7 (13)	+	0	−	41.3
8 (10)	+	0	+	40.8
9 (4)	0	−	+	35.2
10 (11)	0	+	−	35.3
11 (3)	0	−	−	39.5
12 (14)	0	+	+	39.8
13 (1)	0	0	0	50.8
14 (8)	0	0	0	50.1
15 (15)	0	0	0	49.4
−1 level	0.5	6	1.5	
0 level	1.25	5.5	2	
+1 level	2	5	2.5	

9.13 Interpreting the Design

9.13.1 Model

The postulated mathematical model is quadratic:

$$y = a_0 + a_1 x_1 + a_2 x_2 + a_3 x_3 + a_{12} x_1 x_2 + a_{13} x_1 x_3 + a_{23} x_2 x_3 + a_{11} x_1^2 + a_{22} x_2^2 + a_{33} x_3^2 + e$$

The interpretation starts by calculating the coefficients of the model (Table 9.11).

Table 9.11 Model coefficients (coded units)

Coefficients	Acid Loss		Coefficients	Acid Loss
Intercept a_0	50.10		a_{12}	4.22
			a_{13}	−0.32
a_1	−0.07		a_{23}	2.20
a_2	−0.11		a_{11}	0.07
a_3	0.06		a_{22}	−3.55
			a_{33}	−9.10

Using these coefficients, we have the following second-degree model (with an $R^2 = 0.9968$).

$$\hat{y} = 50.1 - 0.07x_1 - 0.11x_2 + 0.06x_3 + 4.22x_1x_2 - 0.32x_1x_3 + 2.2x_2x_3 + 0.07x_1^2 - 3.55x_2^2 - 9.1x_3^2$$

The center points let us calculate one estimate of experimental error, the pure error. The sum of squares of the experimental error is 0.98 with 2 degrees of freedom (Table 9.12). The corresponding standard deviation is 0.7.

The sum of squares due to the lack-of-fit is 0.3825 with 3 degrees of freedom. The lack of fit is 0.357, which is much less than the pure error. This model is, statistically speaking, indistinguishable from other models that have a lack-of-fit error of the same order of magnitude as the experimental error.

Table 9.12 Comparison of the lack of fit with the pure error

Variation Source	Sum of Squares	DF	Mean Square
Lack of fit	0.3825	3	0.1275
Pure error	0.9800	2	0.4900
Residuals	1.3625	5	0.2725

Residual analysis

The scatter of the residuals does not show any particular patterns or tendencies (Figure 9.14). There is nothing special appearing in this plot that makes us suspect anything but a random dispersion of residuals.

Figure 9.14 Residual plot for the acid loss response

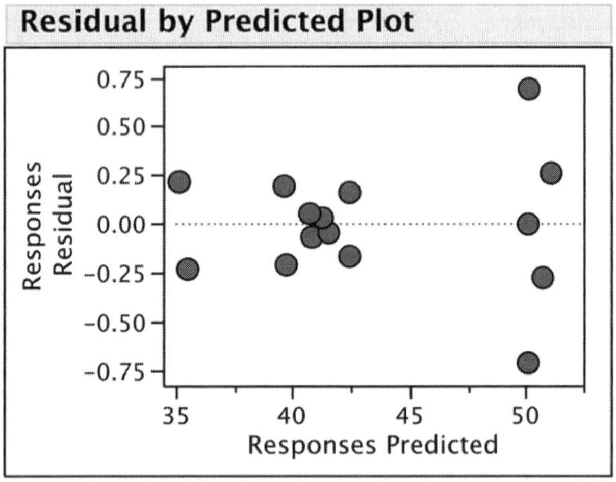

Residual by Predicted Plot

Our chosen model explains the experimental variation well. This result is confirmed by all follow-up tests. However, before using this model, we must validate it.

9.13.2 Interpreting the Results

We want to get an acid loss that is higher than 48. Looking at this model, we see immediately that our objective can be reached inside the study domain since the central point has an acid loss of 50. We want the region of the study domain to be where this condition is respected.

From an economic point of view, we are interested in choosing the weakest possible dilution, that is, the −1 level. At this level, the smallest amount of water is added, which means that there is less water to extract from the raw milk and thus smaller production costs. The selected dilution is therefore 0.5.

Figure 9.15 Contour curve for the pH by concentration design for a dilution rate of 0.5 (-1 in coded variable)

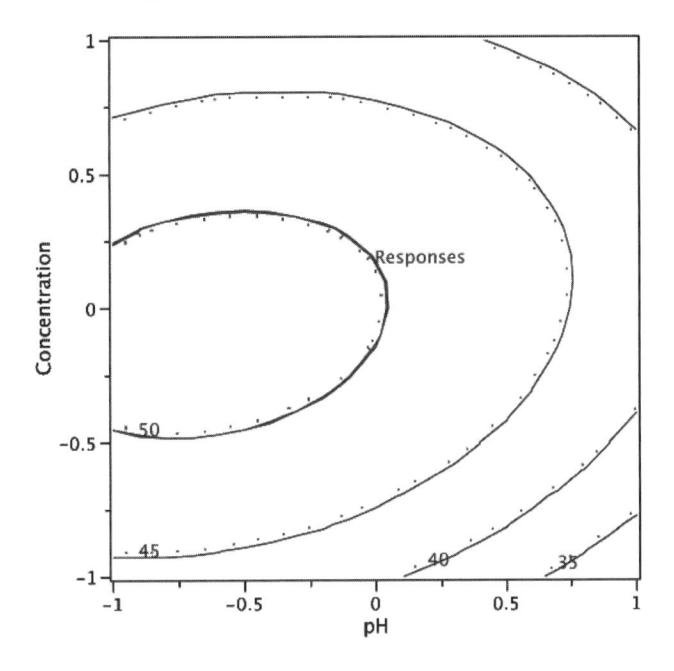

To find the pH and the concentration, look at Figure 9.15. The contour curves show that there is a maximum response. The coordinates of this maximum are found using software such as JMP.

$x_2 = -0.62$

$x_3 = -0.05$

The predicted response at this point is 51.6.

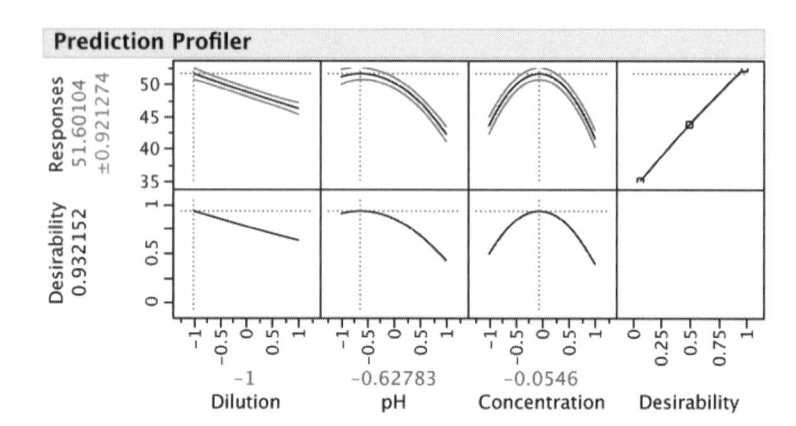

Figure 9.16 Factor values for maximum response

[Prediction Profiler showing: Dilution -1, pH -0.62783, Concentration -0.0546, Desirability 0.932152; Responses 51.60104 ±0.921274]

Converting back to natural units, the optimal conditions are:

- Dilution ratio set at 0.5 (−1 level)
  This means that water equal to half the volume of raw milk is added to the mixture at the beginning of the treatment.

- pH is fixed at 5.8 (−0.61 level)
  Stabilizer is added to obtain a pH of 5.8 at the end of the injection.

- Concentration ratio of the milk is set at almost 2 (level −0.05)
  The concentration ratio of the milk is defined as the ratio of raw milk volume/stabilized milk volume. The stabilized milk volume will be equal to half of the volume of raw milk.

9.14 Study Conclusions

Stabilized milk has the best possible acid loss under these conditions:

- The raw milk is diluted with the following proportions: one unit of water for two units of raw milk.
- The injection is stabilized at a pH of 5.8.

Under these conditions, two units of raw milk produce one unit of stabilized milk, and the acid loss is at least 50.

9.15 Example 14: Insecticide (Example of a Doehlert Design)

9.15.1 Preparing the Designed Experiment

9.15.1.1 Description of the Study
An insecticide maker wants to adapt his product to the desires of his customers. This requires a balance of concentrations of several ingredients to obtain optimal results. Three base commodities make up the commercial product:

- The insecticide itself.
  This is the lethal product used to kill pests.
- The "knock-down."
  This is a substance that puts the pests to sleep quickly.
- The synergist.
  This is a compound that prepares and reinforces the action of the insecticide.

These three products are diluted in a compound that keeps them in suspension and allows them to vaporize at the moment of use. Perfume is added to mask the unpleasant odor of the raw ingredients.

9.15.2 Factors and Study Domain
The researcher keeps, as factors, the concentration of each base product:

- Factor 1: Insecticide concentration
- Factor 2: Knock-down concentration
- Factor 3: Synergist concentration

The high and low levels of these factors are shown in Table 9.13.

Table 9.13 Study domain

Factor	−1 Level	0 Level	+1 Level
Insecticide (1)	0.01 %	0.03 %	0.05 %
Knock-down (2)	0.1 %	0.4 %	0.7 %
Synergist (3)	0 %	1 %	2 %

9.15.3 Responses

The experimenter chose M24 and KT50 as responses.

M24

M24 is the percentage of dead pests after 24 hours. The objective is to have this value be as high as possible. We try for 95% as a goal.

KT50

KT50 is the time, in minutes, when 50% of the observed population is asleep. The objective is to have the smallest KT50 possible. A KT50 of 5 minutes or less would be excellent. A KT50 between 5 and 10 minutes would also be a good result.

9.15.4 The Designed Experiment

The biologists, through past experience, know that the responses need a second-degree model. A Doehlert plan with three factors seems perfectly appropriate.

9.16 Experimentation

The three factors, insecticide, knock-down, and synergist are studied. The experimenters also plan three center points. The trial results are collected in Table 9.14.

Table 9.14 Designed experiment and results

Trial	Insecticide (1)	Knock-down (2)	Synergist (3)	KT50	M24
1	0	0	0	11	75
2	+1	0	0	15	57
3	+0.5	+0.866	0	11	56
4	−0.5	+0.866	0	6	65
5	−1	0	0	8	60
6	−0.5	−0.866	0	14	66
7	+0.5	−0.866	0	15	72
8	0	0	0	10	75
9	−0.5	+0.289	+0.816	2	91
10	0	−0.577	+0.816	8	99
11	+0.5	+0.289	+0.816	10	81
12	−0.5	−0.289	−0.816	11	72
13	0	+0.577	−0.816	8	81
14	+0.5	−0.289	−0.816	11	80
15	0	0	0	12	74

−1 Level	0.01 %	0.1 %	0 %
0 Level	0.03 %	0.4 %	1 %
+1 Level	0.05 %	0.7 %	2 %

9.17 Interpreting the Results

9.17.1 Calculating the Coefficients

We carry out calculations for both responses (Table 9.15) illustrated in Figure 9.17. Notice the very strong curvatures induced by coefficients a_{11} and a_{33} of M24 and the coefficient a_{33} of KT50.

Table 9.15 Coefficients of the MT24 and KT50 models (coded units)

Coefficients	M24	KT50
Intercept a_0	74.7	11
a_1	−1.4	3.5
a_2	−4.8	−3.32
a_3	7.7	−2.04
a_{12}	−8.7	2.31
a_{13}	−7.9	4.08
a_{23}	−9.8	0.71
a_{11}	−16.2	0.50
a_{22}	−7.8	0.50
a_{33}	20	−4.25

Figure 9.17 Model coefficient bar graphs of M24 and KT50

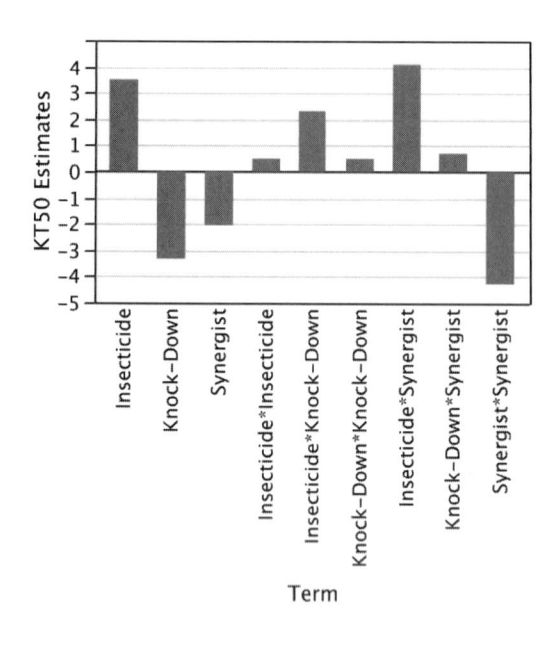

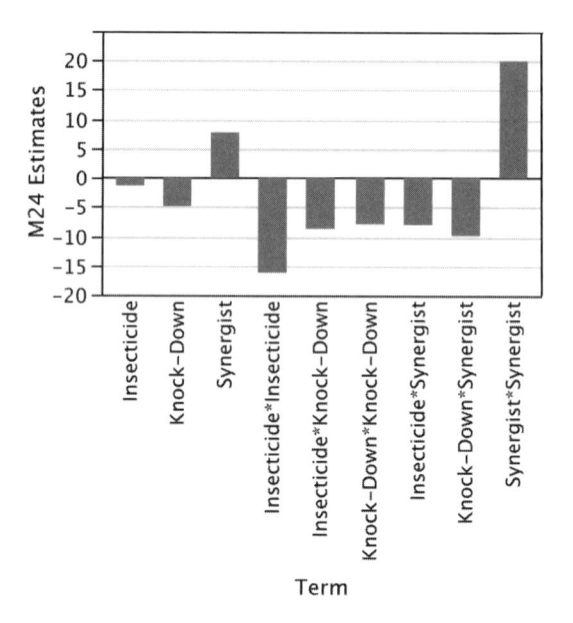

9.17.2 Modeling

These coefficients result in models (in coded units) of M24 ($R^2 = 0.9995$) and KT50 ($R^2 = 0.983$):

$$\hat{y}_{M24} = 74.7 - 1.4x_1 - 4.8x_2 + 7.7x_3 - 8.7x_1x_2 - 7.9x_1x_3 - 9.8x_2x_3 - 16.2x_1^2 - 7.8x_2^2 + 20x_3^2$$

$$\hat{y}_{KT50} = 11 + 3.50x_1 - 3.32x_2 - 2.04x_3 + 2.31x_1x_2 + 4.08x_1x_3 + 0.71x_2x_3 + 0.50x_1^2 + 0.50x_2^2 - 4.25x_3^2$$

Figure 9.18 Variation of the responses for each factor

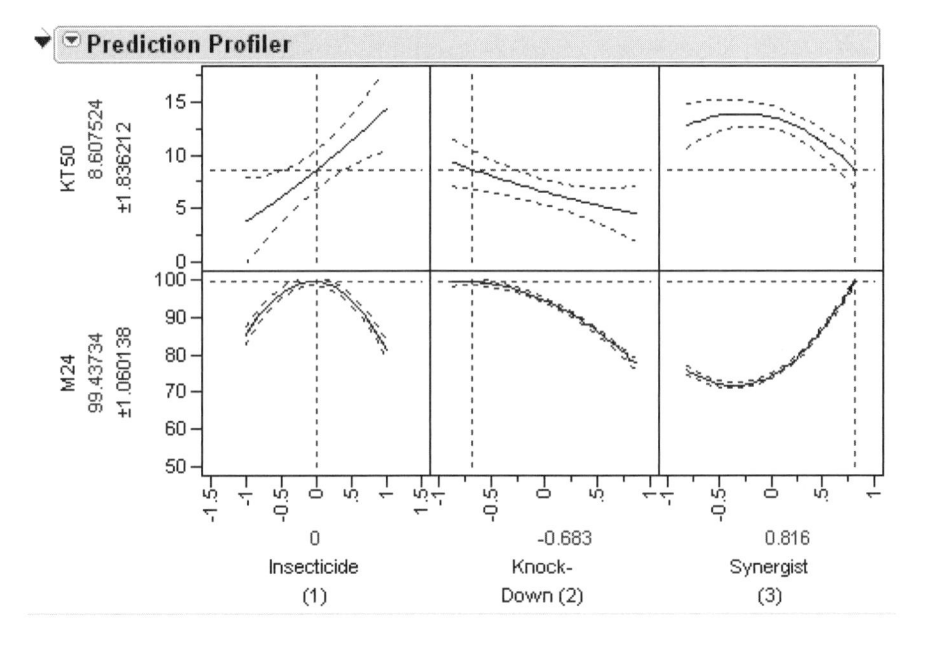

We can see that M24 is maximized when the synergist content is +0.816, that is, for a 1.8% concentration. Since we want to get rid of as many vermin as possible, we use this concentration.

Before using this model, however, we must analyze the residuals and carry out a control experiment to validate the conclusions.

9.17.3 Residual Analysis

Nothing abnormal appears in the residual plots (Figure 9.19).

Figure 9.19 Residual diagram for M24 and KT50 models

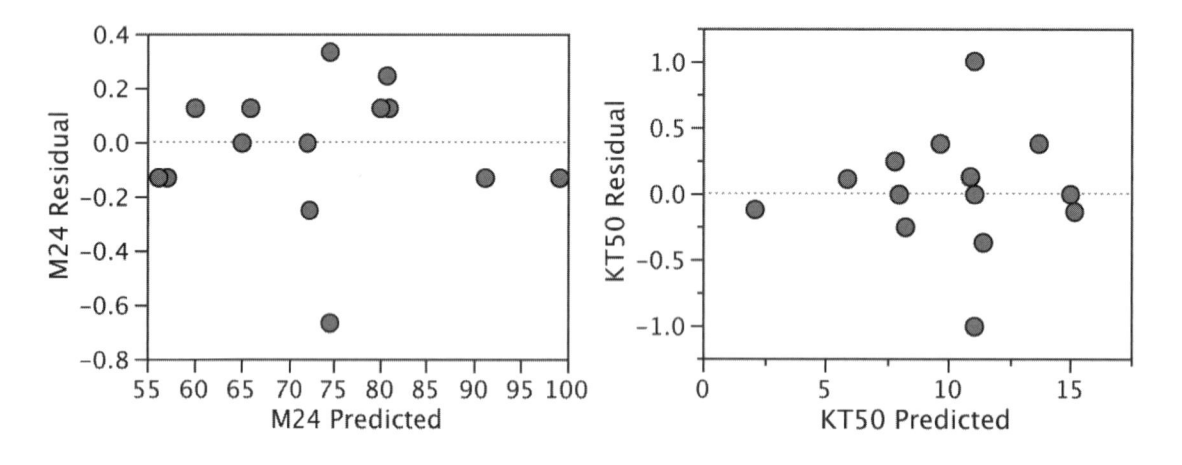

9.17.4 Graphical Representation of the Results

In the M24 model, by replacing x_3 with the value +0.816, we obtain the M24 model for the level $x_3 = +0.816$:

$$\hat{y}_{M24} = 94.3 - 7.8x_1 - 12.8x_2 - 8.7x_1x_2 - 16.2x_1^2 - 7.8x_2^2$$

This model lets us draw a response surface (Figure 9.20). We can see that the objective can be attained. The predictions obtained with this model show that we can exceed a mortality of 90%. The highest mortality rate is obtained for:

$x_1 = -0.02$, i.e., insecticide at 0.03%

$x_2 = -0.8$, i.e., knock-down at 0,16%.

The associated response is 99.5%.

Figure 9.20 Response surface for M24 with a 1.8% synergist concentration (0.816 level)

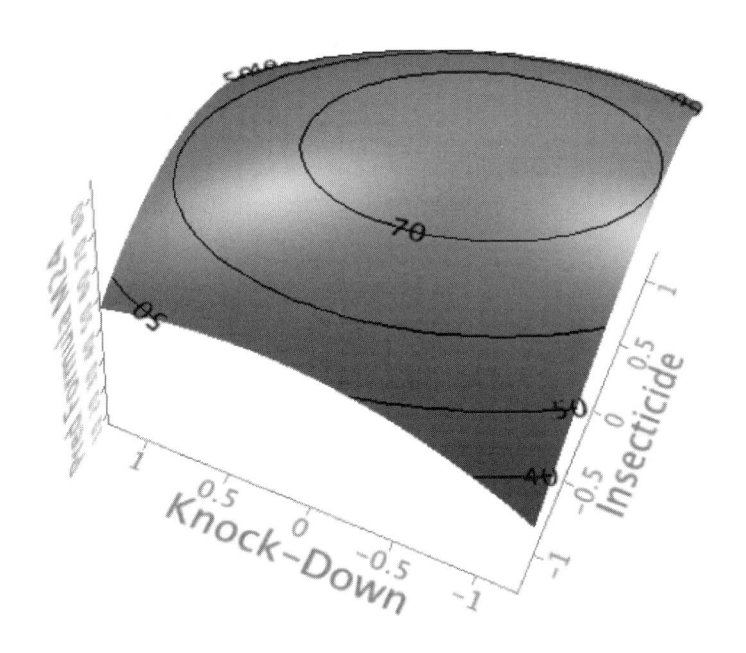

Let's draw the response surface for KT50 (Figure 9.21) for the same level of x_3, +0.816 (i.e., 1.8% synergist content). The model is

$$\hat{y}_{KT50} = 6.6 + 6.8x_1 - 2.7x_2 + 2.3x_1x_2$$

Figure 9.21 KT50 response surface for a 1.8% synergist concentration

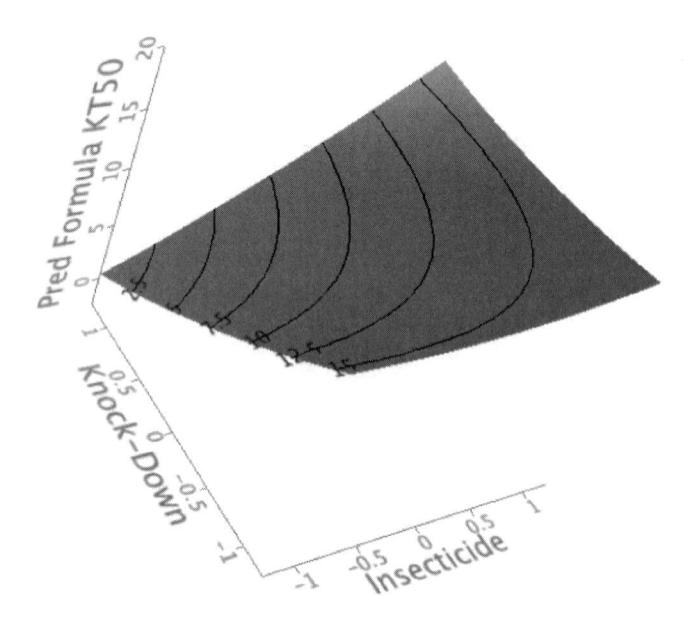

We can draw the contour curves for M24 and KT50 on the same graph (Figure 9.22). KT50 is slightly less than 10 minutes when M24 reaches 99.5%.

Figure 9.22 Contour curves for KT50 (hyperbolic curves) and M24 (ellipses) for the level $x_3 = 0.816$

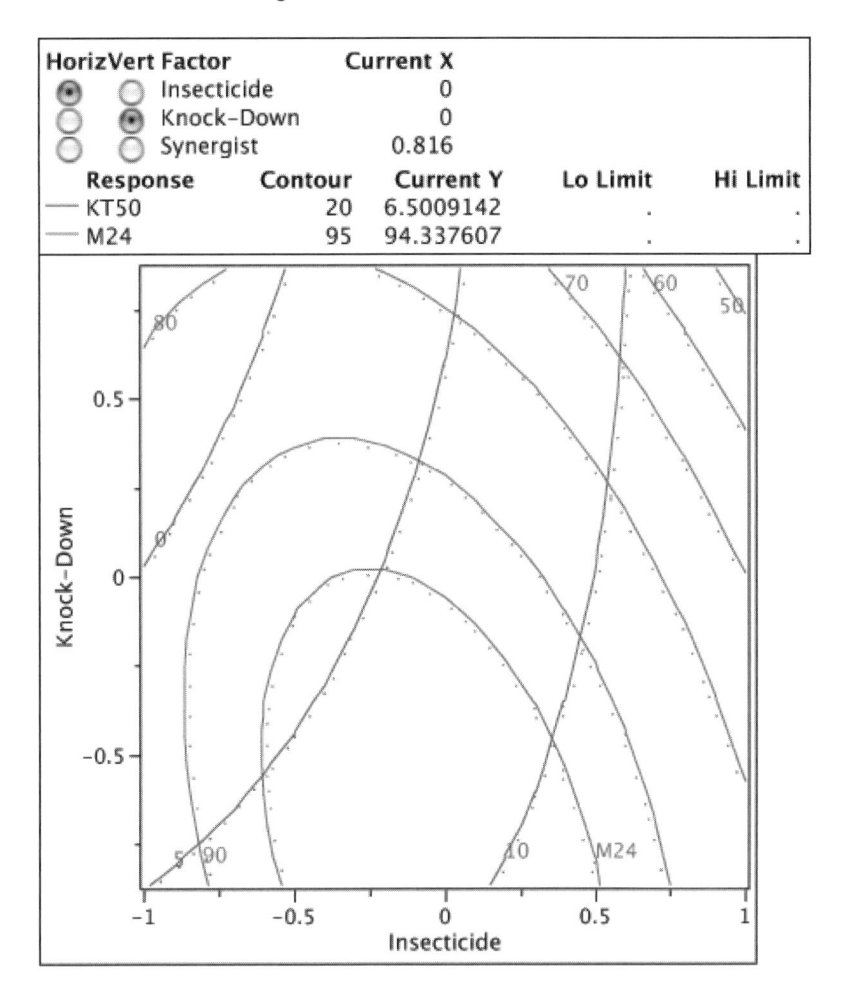

9.18 Study Conclusion

The M24 model allowed us to precisely find the region of the highest mortality. The commercial product's composition, at this stage of the study, is:

- Insecticide concentration 0.03% (0 level)
- Knock-down concentration 0.16% (– 0.8 level)
- Synergist concentration 1.8% (+0.8 level)

Using these proportions, we can expect a KT50 slightly less than 10 minutes and an M24 of more than 95% (Figure 9.22). The study objectives can be achieved. Control experiments were later carried out, which confirmed these conclusions.

Chapter 10

Mixture Designs

10.1 Introduction   288
10.2 Fundamental Constraint of Mixtures   289
10.3 Geometric Representation of a Mixture   289
    10.3.1 Two-Component Mixtures   289
    10.3.2 Reading a Binary Mixture Plot   291
    10.3.3 Reading a Ternary Mixture Plot   293
    10.3.4 Four-Component Mixture   294
10.4 Classical Mixture Designs   295
    10.4.1 Simplex-Lattice Designs   295
    10.4.2 Simplex-Centroid Designs   297
    10.4.3 Augmented Simplex-Centroid Designs   298
10.5 Mixture Design Mathematical Models   299
    10.5.1 First-Degree Models   299
    10.5.2 Second-Degree Models   300
    10.5.3 Third-Degree Models   301

10.6 Example 15: Three Polymers 302
    10.6.1 Preparing the Designed Experiment 302
    10.6.2 Running the Experiment 303
    10.6.3 Interpreting the Results 304
    10.6.4 Study Conclusion 306

10.1 Introduction

In classical non-mixture designs (factorial designs and response surface designs), all factors are independent. This means that it is possible to freely choose the level of a factor regardless of the other factors' levels. For example, having chosen the levels of the first three factors of a 2^4 design, it is possible to choose the levels of the fourth factor without constraint. This freedom does not exist for mixture designs, because the factors are constituent proportions of a mixture. Since these proportions must always sum to 100%, the last component percent is dictated by the sum of all the others. In this mixture situation, the factors are not independent, which has consequences on the design process.

The methodology used to design experiments involving mixtures is the same as for classical designs.

A mixture design is appropriate when the response depends on the component *proportions* of the mixture and not on the component *quantities*. For example, a cocktail recipe is usually written using proportions of each ingredient. Methodically adjusting the cocktail (for a better taste, perhaps) by varying ingredient proportions is a mixture design. On the other hand, adjusting the cocktail by adding fixed amounts, ignoring the cocktail quantity, is not a mixture design. If the response depends on the quantity of the mixture, it requires a classical design and the choice of all factor levels is free. If the response depends on the proportions of a mixture, it requires a mixture design, and there is a constraint on the factors.

We begin by studying the factor constraint that causes the fundamental difference between mixture and classical designs.

10.2 Fundamental Constraint of Mixtures

Consider a mixture with n components. The first component makes up a given percentage of the mixture. The second component makes up another percentage of the mixture. Continuing in the same manner, each component is a certain percentage of the full mixture. However, all the components form a whole and the sum of the component mixtures must equal 100%. If the proportions of the first $n-1$ components are defined, the proportion of the nth component cannot be freely chosen. It is already determined.

If x_i is the percentage content of component i, the sum of all the mixture components is given by the relationship

$$\sum_{i=1}^{n} x_i = 100\ \%$$

The content of each component must stay between 0% and 100%. Increasing the proportion of one component automatically decreases the proportion of the other components so that that the sum of all the proportions stays equal to 100%.

The 100% percentage can also be expressed as the proportion 1, giving

$$\sum_{i=1}^{n} x_i = 1$$

This relationship is named the *fundamental mixture constraint.*

It is because of this constraint that mixture experiments must be studied as a separate subject. This also means that the geometric representations and the mathematical models are not the same for mixtures as they are for classical experimental designs.

10.3 Geometric Representation of a Mixture

10.3.1 Two-Component Mixtures

Suppose the proportion of the first component is x_1 and the proportion of the second component is x_2. For a Cartesian representation, let the axis Ox_1 be orthogonal to the axis Ox_2 (Figure 10.1). Axes are scaled from 0 to 1. A mixture which contains x_a of product

A and x_b of product B is represented by a point situated at the intersection of the coordinates x_a and x_b.

This point corresponding to a specific mixture is called a *composition point,* a *mixture point,* or simply a *point*.

Figure 10.1 Representation of a mixture in a Cartesian system

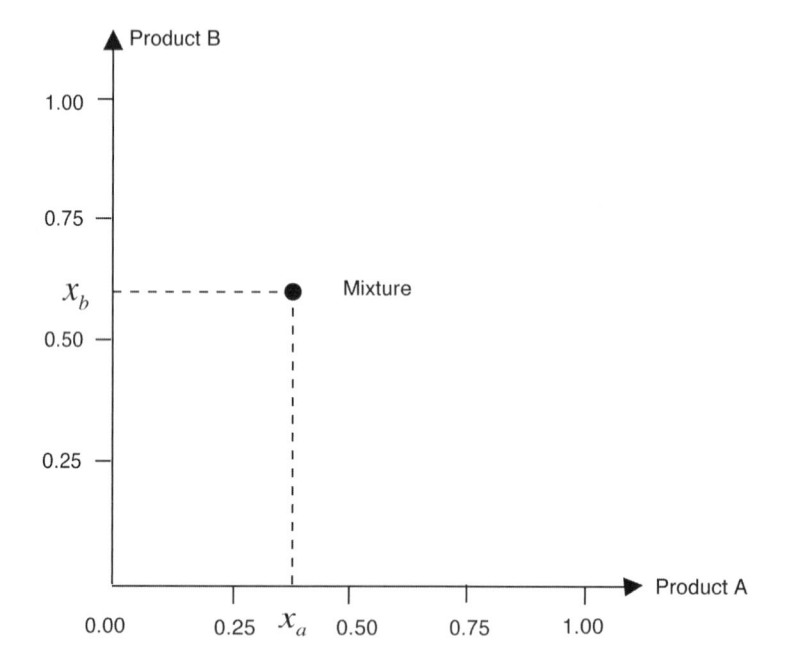

The *fundamental mixture constraint* adds a relationship between x_a and x_b:

$$x_a + x_b = 1$$

which can be written

$$x_b = -x_a + 1$$

This last relationship shows that points with coordinates x_a and x_b are on a straight line with slope −1, cutting the axis of product A at 1.00 (point A in Figure 10.2) and axis of product B at 1.00 (point B in Figure 10.2). Since the proportions x_a and x_b vary from 0 to 1, only the segment $\overline{AB}$ is useful. The points of this segment represent all possible mixtures of the two products A and B.

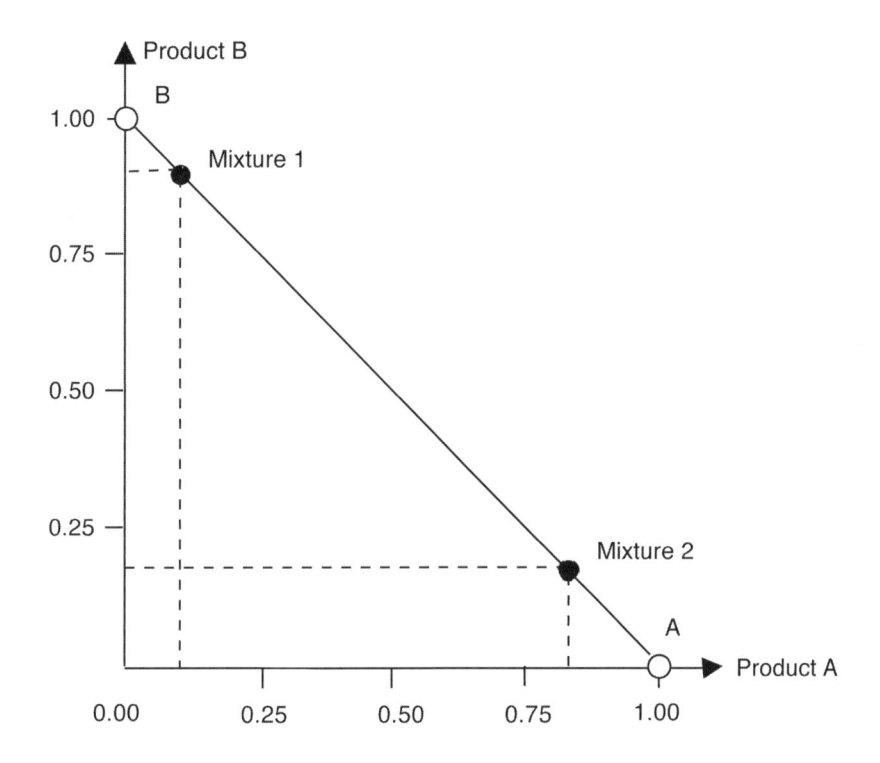

Figure 10.2 Segment $\overline{AB}$ represents the components of a two-component mixture.

Therefore, this segment can be kept, and the axes Ox_1 and Ox_2 are not needed.

Product A is at one end of segment $\overline{AB}$, and product B is at the other. This segment has a double scale (Figure 10.3), one scale representing product A's contribution, the other showing product B's. Reading mixture compositions requires training and practice. These scales can be read from left to right or from right to left.

10.3.2 Reading a Binary Mixture Plot

The segment in Figure 10.3 represents mixtures of the two components A and B. Product A is on the right, and product B is on the left. The lower scale represents product A and varies from 0 on the left to 1 on the right. The upper scale is the scale of product B, and it varies from 0 on the right to 1 on the left.

Figure 10.3 Two-component mixture represented by a straight line segment

```
                    Scale of product B
        ←─────────────────────────────────────────
        1.00        0.75        0.50        0.25        0.00
    B ├──────────────┼───────────┼───────────┼───────────┤ A
        0.00        0.25        0.50        0.75        1.00
        ─────────────────────────────────────────→
                    Scale of product A
```

These scales can be read from left to right or from right to left. The sum of the component percentage at any point of the scale is always equal to 1.

An example mixture (Mixture 1) is represented by a point located at a point 20% along A's axis and 80% along B's. This point is close to B and away from A. This is expected because there is more B than A in the mixture (Figure 10.4).

Figure 10.4 Mixture 1 contains 20% A and 80% B. Mixture 2 contains 77% A and 23% B.

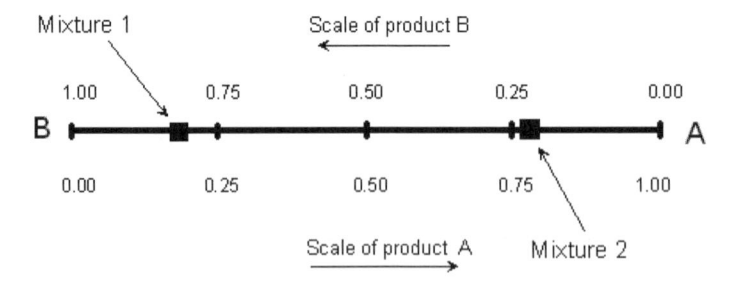

```
        Mixture 1              Scale of product B
              \                ←──────────────
        1.00   \    0.75        0.50        0.25        0.00
    B ├─────────■────┼───────────┼───────────■───┤ A
        0.00        0.25        0.50        0.75  \     1.00
                                                   \
                                Scale of product A   Mixture 2
                                ──────────────→
```

A second mixture (Mixture 2) is represented by a point located at a point 77% along A's axis and 23% along B's. This point is close to A because A is the more prominent mixture constituent.

Either of the two scales can be suppressed since the sum of the proportions is always equal to 1. If we know the content of one component, a simple subtraction gives the content of the other. This suppression is common.

10.3.3 Reading a Ternary Mixture Plot

Following the same line of argument, a three-component mixture can be represented by an equilateral triangle. The pure products are at the triangle's vertices. Binary mixtures are located on the triangle sides. For instance, the left side $\overline{AB}$ (Figure 10.5) shows mixtures containing only products A and B and no product C.

Figure 10.5 Three-component mixture represented by an equilateral triangle

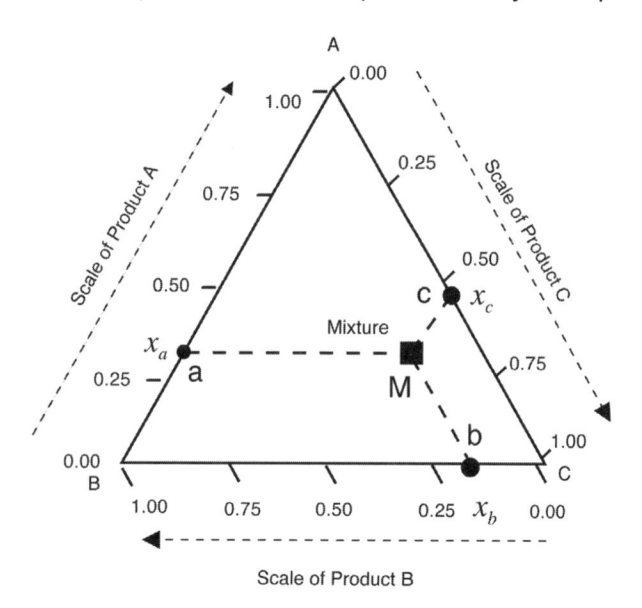

Each side of the equilateral triangle is scaled from 0 to 1. Each side has a single product scale. The scale of the other product can be deduced by subtracting from 1. The proportion of product A is found on side $\overline{AB}$. Similarly, $\overline{BC}$ represents product B's proportion, and $\overline{CA}$ represents product C's.

A point in the inner part of triangle represents a ternary (i.e., three-part) mixture. The contribution of each product to the mixture can be read from the triangle sides. To find the content of product A on side $\overline{AB}$, project point M onto side $\overline{AB}$ parallel to $\overline{BC}$ (the side opposite vertex A). The content of products B and C are found by similar projections.

Therefore, the three-product contributions are given by

bM = Ba = proportion of A in mixture M

cM = Cb = proportion of B in mixture M

aM = Ac = proportion of C in mixture M

The geometric properties of the equilateral triangle ensure that these relationships respect the fundamental mixture constraint.

Ma + Mb + Mc = Ac + Ba + Cb = AB = AC = BC = 1

10.3.4 Four-Component Mixture

Four pure products are at the vertices of a regular tetrahedron (Figure 10.6). The tetrahedron edges represent binary mixtures. The faces, equilateral triangles, represent ternary mixtures, and points inside the tetrahedron represent quaternary mixtures. Mixture contents are obtained by projecting the mixture point onto the faces and edges of the tetrahedron.

Figure 10.6 Four-component mixture represented by a tetrahedron

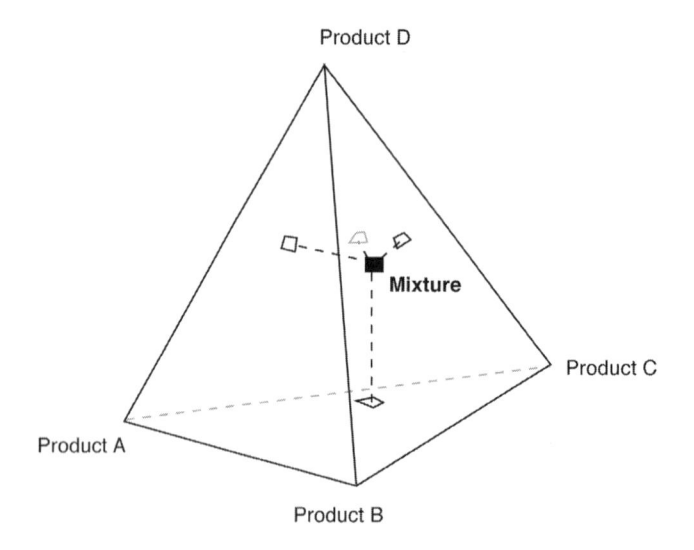

To avoid mistakes in reading mixture proportions, we must scale the tetrahedron carefully so that the projections sum to one.

Beyond four factors, geometric representations are not possible. For these cases tabular representations are used.

10.4 Classical Mixture Designs

In classical mixture designs, it is assumed that pure products have the same usage rules as mixtures and that there are no constraints on the content mixture.

Main kinds of mixture designs are classified by the location of the mixture points. There are

- Simplex-lattice designs
- Simplex-centroid designs
- Augmented simplex-centroid designs

10.4.1 Simplex-Lattice Designs

Simplex-lattice designs were the first mixture designs, introduced by Scheffé in 1958–1965. Mixture points are regularly spaced in the study domain. For three components, the simplex-lattice design includes the three pure products. Mixture points are at the vertices of an equilateral triangle (Figure 10.7) with coordinates 0 and 1.

Figure 10.7 Simplex-lattice designs with the three pure products

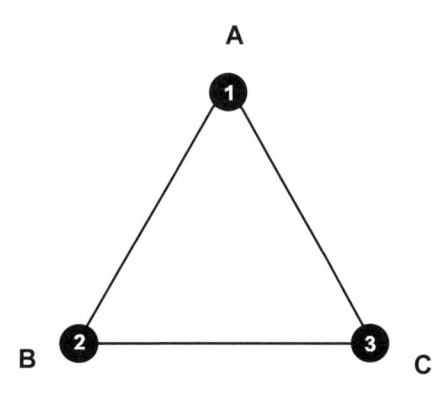

A mixture design containing only the three points representing pure products can be extended by adding points for mixtures containing 50% of each constituent. These new mixtures are illustrated by points located at the midpoint of each of the triangle's sides. Their coordinates are 0 and 1/2. These points (4, 5, and 6) form a lattice. The length of a side of the original triangle is 1; therefore, the coordinates of points 4, 5, and 6 are 1/2.

If a more compact lattice is needed, the side length can be divided by 3. The lattice step of this new design is 1/3.

In the same way, it is possible to build denser and denser lattices by dividing each side by m. The lattice step is $1/m$, and coordinates of the experimental points are 0, $1/m$, $2/m$, to $m/m = 1$.

We adopt the following notation to express these mixture designs. Two digits are used, where the first is the number of components and the second is the divisor (m) that is used to construct the lattice. These two digits are separated by a comma and placed between curly brackets.

Therefore, the design of Figure 10.8 is a mixture lattice design {3,2}: three components, with a step of 1/2. The design of Figure 10.9 is a mixture lattice design {3,3}, with three components and a step of 1/3.

Figure 10.8 Simplex-lattice designs with three pure products and half-and-half mixtures. This design is denoted {3,2}.

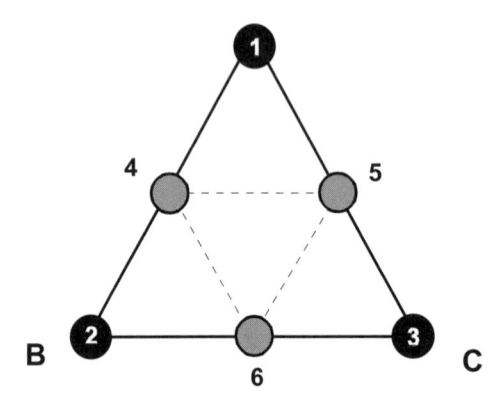

This notation allows quick calculation of the number of mixtures needed for a study, given the number of components and m. For a design $\{q,m\}$, the number of different mixtures is equal to

$$C_{q+m-1}^{m} = \frac{(q+m-1)!}{m!(q-1)!}$$

Figure 10.9 Simplex-lattice designs for three pure products and mixtures 1/3-2/3 and 1/3-1/3-1/3. This is a {3,3} design.

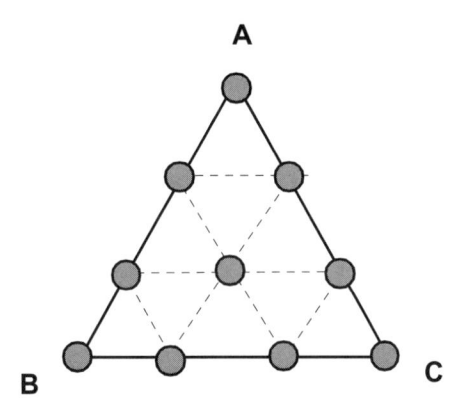

10.4.2 Simplex-Centroid Designs

A central point can be systematically added to a simplex-lattice design to obtain a simplex-centroid design. This central point contains an equal amount of each factor (Figure 10.10). Thus a centroid design for three components is composed of

- Pure products
- Fifty-fifty mixtures of two pure products
- A mixture with an equal amount of the three pure products (central point)

Figure 10.10 Simplex-centroid designs with three pure products, fifty-fifty mixture of two pure products, and mixture with an equal amount of the three pure products

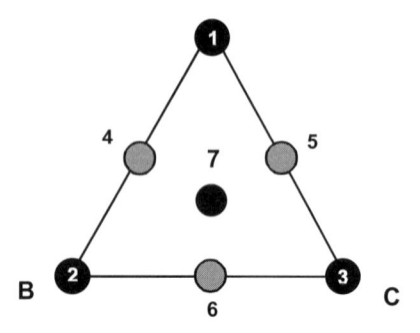

The number of different mixtures needed to study a simplex-centroid design with q components is given by the following equation:

$$N = 2^q - 1$$

For example, a three-component centroid design requires seven different compositions:

$$N = 2^q - 1 = 8 - 1 = 7$$

10.4.3 Augmented Simplex-Centroid Designs

Augmented simplex-centroid designs are centroid designs with new experimental points located at the center of gravity of the individual simplexes. To illustrate a simplex, consider the three-component centroid design, which contains four individual simplexes (Figure 10.11). They are the smallest individual triangles that make up the lattice The center of gravity of the central simplex is already occupied by run 7 (center black point). Three new points are added in the center of the other three individual simplexes: white points 8, 9, and 10.

Figure 10.11 Augmented simplex-centroid design for three components: pure products, half-and-half mixtures, mixture with an equal amount of each product, and mixtures located at the center of gravity of the individual simplexes

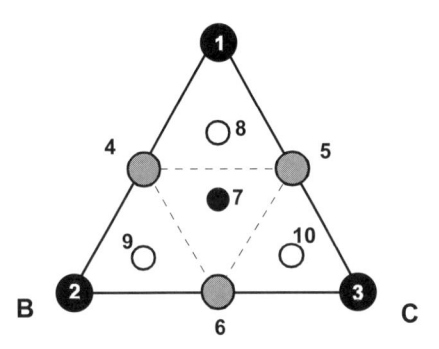

10.5 Mixture Design Mathematical Models

Mathematical models for mixture designs take the fundamental mixture constraint into account. Polynomial models have specific forms which are introduced below.

10.5.1 First-Degree Models

We assume that changes in the response depend only on the product proportions in the mixture. To develop the model for mixtures, start with the polynomial model used for classical factorial designs (whose factors are independent). For example, for a three-component mixture, in a given point, the model can be written:

$$y = a_0 + a_1 x_1 + a_2 x_2 + a_3 x_3 \tag{10.1}$$

But the fundamental mixture constraint must be taken into account. The proportions x_i are not independent. Using the constraint, we know

$$x_1 + x_2 + x_3 = 1$$

We can multiply any term by one, and so we do so with a_0. Equation (10.1) becomes

$$y = a_0(x_1 + x_2 + x_3) + a_1 x_1 + a_2 x_2 + a_3 x_3$$

Or, after regrouping the parameters

$$y = (a_0 + a_1)x_1 + (a_0 + a_2)x_2 + (a_0 + a_3)x_3$$

This model has no constant and if we write

$$b_1 = a_1 + a_0 \qquad b_2 = a_2 + a_0 \qquad b_3 = a_3 + a_0$$

the model takes the following form:

$$y = b_1 x_1 + b_2 x_2 + b_3 x_3 \tag{10.2}$$

This model has neither intercept nor constant. Their disappearance is a direct consequence of the fundamental mixture constraint.

10.5.2 Second-Degree Models

The second-degree mathematical model contains first degree terms, crossed terms, and squared terms. As in the linear case, we start with the factorial design's mathematical model and examine the consequences of the fundamental mixture constraint. For a two-component mixture, knowing that there is no constant or intercept, we can write the model:

$$y = a_1 x_1 + a_2 x_2 + a_{12} x_1 x_2 + a_{11} x_1^2 + a_{22} x_2^2 \tag{10.3}$$

Taking into account the fundamental mixture constraint

$$x_1 + x_2 = 1$$

which can be written in terms of x_1

$$x_1 = 1 - x_2$$

multiplying each side by x_1 gives

$$x_1^2 = x_1(1 - x_2)$$

$$x_1^2 = x_1 - x_1 x_2$$

This shows that the squared term is in fact equal to a first-degree term and a crossed term. Squared terms therefore vanish from the initial relationship. So, the second-degree model therefore contains only first-degree and crossed terms, and can be written

$$y = b_1 x_1 + b_2 x_2 + b_{12} x_1 x_2 \tag{10.4}$$

For a three-component mixture, we have

$$y = b_1 x_1 + b_2 x_2 + b_3 x_3 + b_{12} x_1 x_2 + b_{13} x_1 x_3 + b_{23} x_2 x_3$$

10.5.3 Third-Degree Models

The third-degree mathematical model, specific to mixture designs, can be obtained starting with a third-degree polynomial model and using the fundamental mixture constraint. This model is named the *complete cubic model*:

$$y = b_1 x_1 + b_2 x_2 + b_3 x_3 + b_{12} x_1 x_2 + b_{13} x_1 x_3 + b_{23} x_2 x_3$$
$$b'_{12} x_1 x_2 (x_1 - x_2) + b'_{13} x_1 x_3 (x_1 - x_3) + b'_{23} x_2 x_3 (x_2 - x_3) + b_{123} x_1 x_2 x_3$$

A simplified cubic mathematical model is commonly used. This simplified model contains first-degree terms, crossed terms, and a supplementary term which is the product of the three components. The simplified model, called the *restricted cubic model*, corresponding to a three-component mixture is

$$y = b_1 x_1 + b_2 x_2 + b_3 x_3 + b_{12} x_1 x_2 + b_{13} x_1 x_3 + b_{23} x_2 x_3 + b_{123} x_1 x_2 x_3 \tag{10.5}$$

10.6 Example 15: Three Polymers

10.6.1 Preparing the Designed Experiment

10.6.1.1 Defining the Study Objective
An experimenter is studying the link between the thread elongation of a yarn composed of three polymers (polyethylene, polystyrene, and polypropylene) by studying the composition of their blends. Earlier experiments show that the first-degree model was not sufficient to explain experimental results and the experimenter wants to test the second-degree model.

10.6.1.2 Choosing the Response
The response is the thread elongation of yarns prepared with different polymer mixtures.

10.6.1.3 Factors and Study Domain
Factors are proportions of each polymer:

- Polyethylene
- Polystyrene
- Polypropylene

Proportions can vary from 0% to 100% because the thread elongation property is as valuable for pure products as it is for their mixtures. The study domain is the complete equilateral triangle.

10.6.1.4 Design
The experimenter chooses an augmented simplex-centroid design. The blends of this mixture design are indicated in Table 10.1. The experimenter uses points 8, 9, and 10 as control points (Figure 10.12). These control points are not used to establish the fitted model, but instead to verify the predictive power of the model.

Figure 10.12 Location of the experimental points (black) and of the control points (gray) used to study the thread elongation of three-polymer yarn.

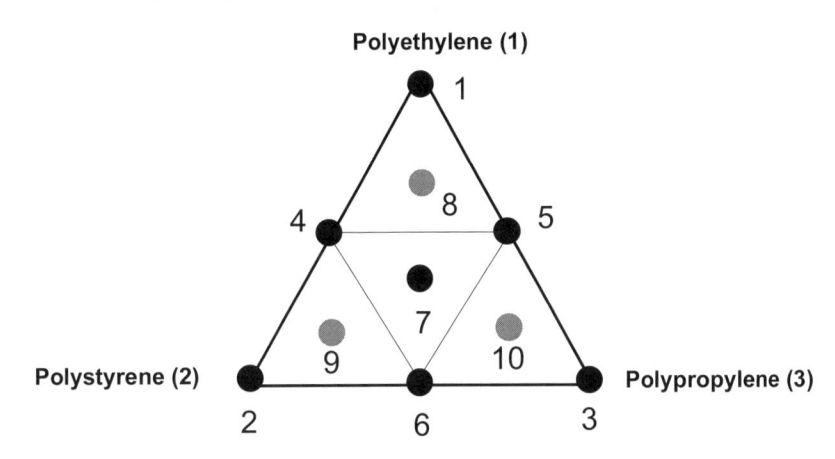

10.6.2 Running the Experiment

The observed results are shown in Table 10.1.

Table 10.1 Mixture design and control points

Trial	Polyethylene (1)	Polystyrene (2)	Polypropylene (3)	Responses
1	1	0	0	32
2	0	1	0	25
3	0	0	1	42
4	1/2	1/2	0	38
5	1/2	0	1/2	39
6	0	1/2	1/2	30.5
7	1/3	1/3	1/3	37
8	2/3	1/6	1/6	37
9	1/6	2/3	1/6	32
10	1/6	1/6	2/3	38

10.6.3 Interpreting the Results

10.6.3.1 Coefficient Calculation and Modeling

A three-component augmented simplex-centroid design lets the experimenter calculate the seven coefficients of the restricted cubic model (Table 10.2).

Table 10.2 Coefficients of restricted cubic model (coded units)

Coefficient	Value
b_1	32
b_2	25
b_3	42
b_{12}	38
b_{13}	8
b_{23}	−12
b_{123}	6

These coefficients specify a model that can be used to calculate predicted responses for each study point:

$$\hat{y} = 32 x_1 + 25\ x_2 + 42 x_3 + 38 x_1\ x_2 + 8 x_1 x_3 - 12 x_2 x_3 + 6 x_1 x_2 x_3$$

10.6.3.2 Validity of the Restricted Cubic Model

There are three control mixtures, represented by points 8, 9, and 10 (Table 10.3). The response at these points is calculated with the model and compared to the observed response at these points.

Table 10.3 Observed and predicted responses at the control points

Trial	Observed Response	Predicted Response
8	37	37.38
9	32	32.22
10	38	38.22

Comparing the observed and predicted responses shows that there is almost no variability left to model. Therefore, the restricted cubic model is sufficient for modeling the thread elongation of yarns containing these three polymers.

10.6.3.3 Graphical Illustration of the Results

Since we have validated the model, we can use it to draw a contour plot that illustrates how the response varies with respect to the proportions of each constituent (Figure 10.13).

Figure 10.13 Contour plot of the response (thread elongation) using the second degree model

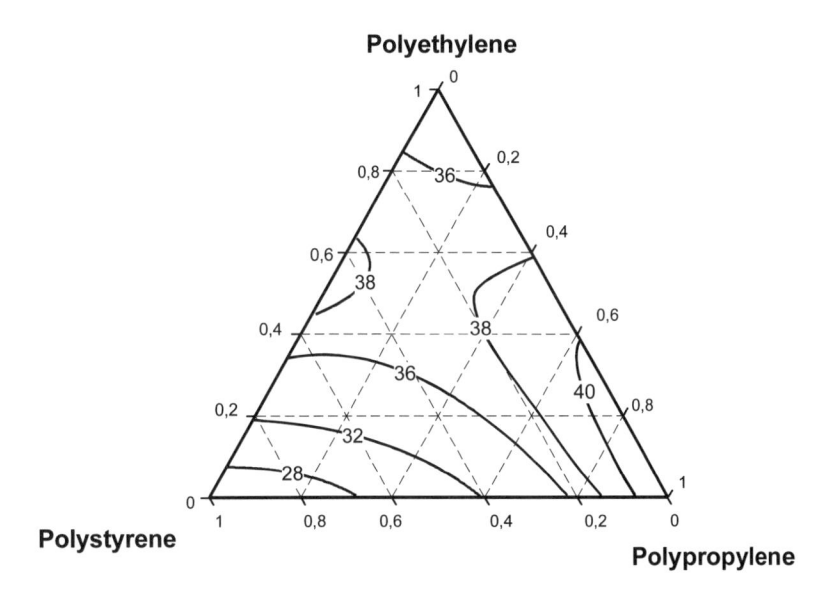

10.6.4 Study Conclusion

The objective, knowledge of the properties of thread elongation, is obtained. Thread elongation can be calculated for any composition of the three polymer mixtures (polyethylene/polystyrene/polypropylene). If the experimenter wants a high value of thread elongation, mixtures with high polypropylene and low polystyrene contents should be chosen. For a thread elongation independent of the composition, choose a mixture near the stationary point: around 20% polypropylene, 30% polystyrene, and 50% polyethylene. For a low value of thread elongation, mixtures with high polystyrene content should be chosen.

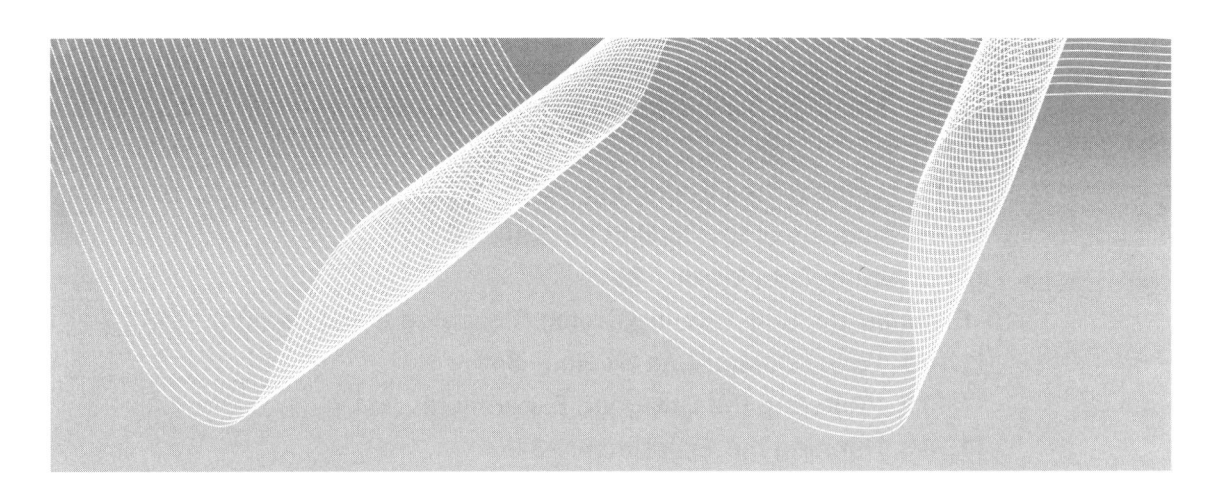

Chapter 11

The Concept of Optimal Designs

11.1 Introduction 308
11.2 Hotelling's Example 308
11.3 Weighing and Experimental Design 311
    11.3.1 Standard Method 312
    11.3.2 Hotelling's Method 313
11.4 Optimality 314
    11.4.1 Maximum Determinant (*D*-Optimal) Criterion 315
    11.4.2 Computing Optimal Designs 315
11.5 Optimal Designs with a Linear Model 319
11.6 When to Use Optimal Designs 322
11.7 Adaptability of Optimal Designs 323
11.8 Example 16: Developing a Fissure Detector 326
    11.8.1 Preparing the Designed Experiment 326
    11.8.2 Using a 2^3 Factorial with Center Points 327
    11.8.3 Using a *D*-Optimal Design with Repetitions 330

  11.9 Example 17: Pharmaceutical Tablets 333
    11.9.1 Preparing the Designed Experiment 333
    11.9.2 The Design 335
    11.9.3 Running the Experiment 336
    11.9.4 Analysis of the 28-Run Design 337
    11.9.5 Study Conclusion 340
  11.10 Example 18: Self-Tanning Cream (Rescuing a Bad Design) 343
    11.10.1 Why a Design Can Be Bad 343
    11.10.2 Preparing the Designed Experiment 344
    11.10.3 Running the Experiment 345
    11.10.4 Interpreting the Results 345
    11.10.5 Study Conclusion 349

11.1 Introduction

In the previous chapters of the book, we examined specific design types. Each design type dictated a certain number of runs. After some experience with designed experiments, many experimenters ask themselves: "How many runs do I really need to do?" When considering cost, this question often becomes "What is the *least* number of runs that I must to do?" This chapter, which introduces *optimal designs,* (also known as *custom designs*) answers this question.

11.2 Hotelling's Example

To illustrate the difficulty in picking a strategy for performing measurements, we show a problem of measuring mass as our experiment. In essence, our problem is to determine the mass of two small lead weights using an old two-pan balance scale. As an historical note, the first person to study this question was Hotelling. It is surprising that the study did not occur until 1944, even though people had been measuring mass for centuries.

Let's assume that an experimenter has an old two-pan balance like the one shown here (Figure 11.1).

Figure 11.1 Two-pan balance

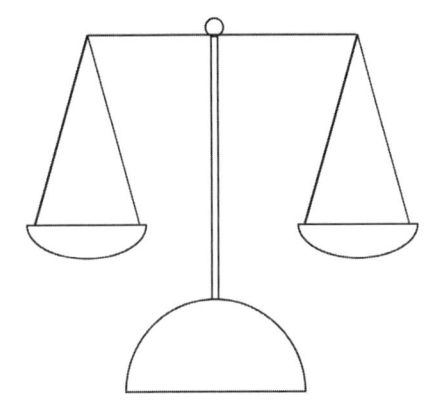

He has two objects A and B, and he wants to find their masses m_a and m_b. He also has a small bag of pellets of known masses to use as counterweights during his measurement.

He takes the obvious measurement strategy: Place object A on one pan, and then fill the other pan with pellets until the two pans return to equilibrium (Figure 11.2).

Figure 11.2 Classical weighing of object A

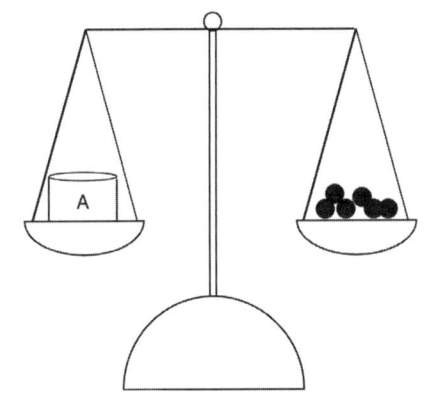

The number of pellets (say, p_1) gives the weight of object A, but with the unavoidable experimental error. Therefore, the experimenter writes:

$$m_a = p_1 + \sigma$$

For the second object, he does the same thing and finds that he needs p_2 pellets for the scale to return to equilibrium, so he writes:

$$m_b = p_2 + \sigma$$

If p_1 and p_2 had the values of 10 and 25 grams, respectively, and if σ is estimated to be 0.1 gram, then the experimenter can report the following results:

$$m_a = 10 \pm 0.1 \text{ g}$$

$$m_b = 25 \pm 0.1 \text{ g}$$

Therefore, the experimenter made two measurements and obtained two results with an error of $\pm\sigma$. This is how most people would make the two measurements. It seems straightforward, and appears to be as accurate as the scale allows, given the constraints on the pellet size. However, Hotelling noticed that for the same effort, greater precision could be obtained if both objects are included in each weighing.

Hotelling conducted the experiment by first putting A and B in the same pan, i.e., computed the sum of their masses (p_1). Then, he put A on one pan and B on the other to obtain the difference of their masses (p_2). He could therefore write the following system of equations, which allowed him to deduce the masses m_a and m_b with a simple calculation.

$$m_a + m_b = p_1$$

$$m_a - m_b = p_2$$

So,

$$m_a = \frac{1}{2}(p_1 + p_2)$$

$$m_b = \frac{1}{2}(p_1 - p_2)$$

Applying the theorem of variance addition (see Chapter 5, section 5.2.4.6 "Error Transmission") gives

$$V(m_a) = \frac{1}{4}[V(p_1) + V(p_2)]$$
$$= \frac{1}{4}[\sigma^2 + \sigma^2]$$
$$= \frac{1}{2}\sigma^2$$

The error on the mass measurements is only $\sigma/\sqrt{2}$ instead of σ (that is, it has been reduced by about 30%), so

$m_a = 10 \pm 0.07$ g

$m_b = 25 \pm 0.07$ g

Using the naïve method, getting the same precision would require weighing A twice and B twice, i.e., four measurements instead of two. This emphasizes one of the reasons for including all variables in an experimental run. When we do, the same number of runs, or, more bluntly, the same cost, gives better precision.

11.3 Weighing and Experimental Design

Let's try to put Hotelling's example in the context of a design matrix, introduced in Chapter 2. The factors are the two objects A and B, and the responses are the masses that return the scales to equilibrium each time an object is weighed. We will eventually need to distinguish the right pan from the left pan, so for convenience, consider the mass of an object placed in the left pan to be positive and the mass of an object placed in the right pan to be negative (Figure 11.3).

Figure 11.3 Sign convention for scale pans

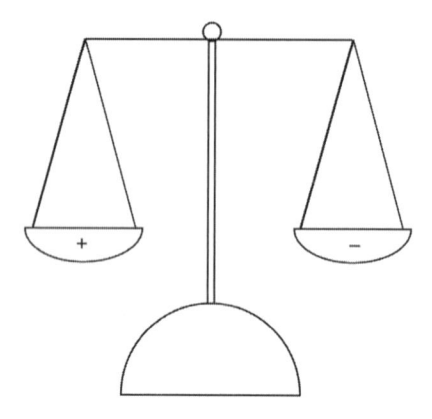

With this convention, we can say that the mass of object A is $-p_a$ or $+p_a$, depending on whether it is on the left or right pan. Figure 1 shows A to have mass $+p_a$. We can further simplify the notation by using coded variables, with $-p_a$ as -1 and $+p_a$ as $+1$. With no object on the pan, use the coded variable zero.

$+p_a$ _____ 0 _____ $-p_a$

$+1$ _____ 0 _____ -1

The same convention can be adopted for the object B.

$+p_b$ _____ 0 _____ $-p_b$

$+1$ _____ 0 _____ -1

The two methods of finding the masses, the standard method and Hotelling's method, can therefore be presented as experimental matrices. The calculations are performed as for an experimental design and the effects are the masses of each object.

11.3.1 Standard Method

- Trial 1: A on left pan, B is not used.
  Response: 10 g

- Trial 2: B is on the left pan, A is not used.
  Response: 25 g

Since there is no interaction between A and B, the experimental table worksheet is identical to the experimental matrix (Table 11.1).

Table 11.1 Experimental matrix: Standard method of finding the mass of two objects

Trial	A	B	Mass (g)
	Factor 1	*Factor 2*	*Response*
1	+ 1	0	10 g
2	0	+ 1	25 g
Effect	10 g	25 g	

The effects matrix **X** for the standard method is

$$\mathbf{X} = \begin{bmatrix} 1 & 0 \\ 0 & 1 \end{bmatrix} \quad (11.1)$$

It is therefore not surprising to see that the effects are the same as the responses, since the effects matrix is an identity matrix.

11.3.2 Hotelling's Method

- Trial 1: A and B on the left pan.
  Response: 35 g

- Trial 2: B on the left pan, A on the right pan.
  Response: 15 g

The effects matrix is

$$X = \begin{bmatrix} 1 & 1 \\ -1 & 1 \end{bmatrix}$$

This matrix, which contains no zeros, is characteristic of Hotelling's method (Table 11.2), where all the objects are included in all the tests.

The effects (weights of the two objects) are, of course, the same as in the standard method, but there is a noticeable difference in the precision.

Table 11.2 Experimental matrix: Hotelling's method of finding the mass of two objects

Trial	A	B	Mass (g)
	Factor 1	Factor 2	Response
1	+1	+1	35 g
2	−1	+1	15 g
Effect	10 g	25 g	

11.4 Optimality

We have seen that Hotelling's method gives more precise results than the standard method. The natural next question is, Can we do better? Could we, with two trials, get even more precise calculations of the effects? In statistical terms, is Hotelling's method *optimal*?

One definition of an optimal design (there are others that are beyond the scope of this book) is a design that gives the most precise estimate of the effects. Our challenge is to determine this design (in other words, determine the **X** matrix in the above examples) that is optimal.

Fortunately, it can be shown that this precision is directly correlated with the **X'X** matrix. Calculating the values of this matrix is quite tedious for all but the smallest designs. For this reason, in practice all designs are generated by software. However, we present some simple examples here to illustrate a common method.

11.4.1 Maximum Determinant (*D*-Optimal) Criterion

First, we state mathematically our optimality criterion. If $|\mathbf{A}|$ represents the *determinant* of $\mathbf{A}$, then a *D*-optimal design is one which maximizes the value of $|\mathbf{X'X}|$.

Because this optimality criterion involves the determinant of a matrix, it is called *D-optimality*.

Determinants can be calculated only for square matrices, which is not a problem since $\mathbf{X'X}$ is always square. If we use the example of the standard method and the Hotelling method, we can demonstrate that the Hotelling method is more optimal.

For the standard strategy, $\mathbf{X} = \begin{bmatrix} 1 & 0 \\ 0 & 1 \end{bmatrix}$, and $|\mathbf{X'X}| = 1$.

For Hotelling's strategy, $\mathbf{X} = \begin{bmatrix} 1 & 1 \\ -1 & 1 \end{bmatrix}$, and $|\mathbf{X'X}| = 4$.

Clearly, Hotelling's strategy is better. In fact, it is the best that we can do.

11.4.2 Computing Optimal Designs

Suppose we want to extend Hotelling's example above to find the masses of four objects (A, B, C, and D). How could you arrange the rows? The naïve strategy is to weigh them one at a time, which (hopefully) is clearly not the optimum strategy. However, it would be represented with

$$\mathbf{X} = \begin{bmatrix} 1 & 0 & 0 & 0 \\ 0 & 1 & 0 & 0 \\ 0 & 0 & 1 & 0 \\ 0 & 0 & 0 & 1 \end{bmatrix}$$

$|\mathbf{X'X}| = 1$

We could use the same approach as for weighing two objects, but repeating it for A and B, and then for C and D:

- Trial 1: A and B on the left pan
- Trial 2: A on the right, B on left
- Trial 3: C and D on the left pan
- Trial 4: C on the right, D on the left

This strategy yields the following matrices and determinant.

$$\mathbf{X} = \begin{bmatrix} 1 & 1 & 0 & 0 \\ -1 & 1 & 0 & 0 \\ 0 & 0 & 1 & 1 \\ 0 & 0 & -1 & 1 \end{bmatrix}$$

$$|\mathbf{X'X}| = 16$$

Clearly, this is better than the first. But is it the best?

For designs whose levels are only –1 or 1, the matrix $\mathbf{X'X}$ of rank n with the highest D-optimality has a determinant equal to $|\mathbf{X'X}| = n^n$.

For our example with four trials, $4^4 = 256$, so our second guess at an optimum strategy is not the most optimal. As stated earlier, optimal designs are normally computed with software. We illustrate a popular method for finding optimal designs called the *coordinate exchange* algorithm, the method used in JMP. We first describe the method, and then give an example.

The coordinate exchange algorithm goes as follows:

In preparation for using the algorithm,

- Create an $n \times n$ design matrix (named $\mathbf{X}$) filled with numbers from a uniform random distribution from the range (0, 1). This is called a *random start*.
- Create a set of values that you will use to substitute into each element of the matrix. This set of values partitions the range [–1, 1] by using the number of levels that each factor can have in your experiment. For example, two-level factors, like the ones we have here, partition the range by taking its two endpoints. So, the set of values we substitute into $\mathbf{X}$ is 1 or –1. If our factor

had three levels (e.g., high, medium, low), we would partition the space using the endpoints and the midpoint, i.e., −1, 0, and 1.

Now, begin the iterative portion of the algorithm.

1. Replace the number in the first row, first column with each of your substitution values. That is, replace it with 1 (or −1 for a two-level factor) and compute $|X'X|$ for each substitution.

2. If the determinant has increased by using one of the substitutions, leave the substituted number in place of the random number that originally held the spot. Note that this means it is possible to leave the random number in place.

3. Now, move to the first row, second column, and repeat steps 1 and 2.

4. Complete steps 1 and 2 for all of the elements of the first row, and then move to the second row. When you are finished with the second, move to the third, and so on, until you reach the end of the matrix.

5. If you have reached the maximum possible value of the determinant (i.e., $|X'X| = n^n$), then stop.

6. If you haven't reached the maximum possible determinant value, repeat the substitution process for the whole matrix. Repeat the substitution process until you reach the maximum determinant value, or until you come to the point where you have gone through the matrix without making any substitutions.

We illustrate this process with an example, answering the question posed at the beginning of this section. What is the most efficient design for finding the mass of four objects?

We use the following random start, a 4×4 matrix populated with random numbers.

$$X = \begin{bmatrix} 0.556 & 0.696 & 0.346 & 0.787 \\ 0.607 & 0.039 & 0.499 & 0.017 \\ 0.267 & 0.975 & 0.770 & 0.638 \\ 0.409 & 0.368 & 0.061 & 0.421 \end{bmatrix}$$

In this case

$$|X'X| = 0.0016$$

Since all of our factors have two levels, we use 1 and −1 as candidate values to be replaced in this matrix.

Table 11.3 Details of the exchange algorithm (weighing of four objects)

Iteration	X Matrix	|X'X| When −1 Is Used	|X'X| When +1 Is Used	Replace Number With	New X Matrix
1	$X = \begin{bmatrix} 0.556 & 0.696 & 0.346 & 0.787 \\ 0.607 & 0.039 & 0.499 & 0.017 \\ 0.267 & 0.975 & 0.770 & 0.638 \\ 0.409 & 0.368 & 0.061 & 0.421 \end{bmatrix}$	0.027	2.10^{-5}	−1	$X = \begin{bmatrix} -1 & 0.696 & 0.346 & 0.787 \\ 0.607 & 0.039 & 0.499 & 0.017 \\ 0.267 & 0.975 & 0.770 & 0.638 \\ 0.409 & 0.368 & 0.061 & 0.421 \end{bmatrix}$
2	$X = \begin{bmatrix} -1 & 0.696 & 0.346 & 0.787 \\ 0.607 & 0.039 & 0.499 & 0.017 \\ 0.267 & 0.975 & 0.770 & 0.638 \\ 0.409 & 0.368 & 0.061 & 0.421 \end{bmatrix}$	0.332	0.008	−1	$X = \begin{bmatrix} -1 & -1 & 0.346 & 0.787 \\ 0.607 & 0.039 & 0.499 & 0.017 \\ 0.267 & 0.975 & 0.770 & 0.638 \\ 0.409 & 0.368 & 0.061 & 0.421 \end{bmatrix}$
3	$X = \begin{bmatrix} -1 & -1 & 0.346 & 0.787 \\ 0.607 & 0.039 & 0.499 & 0.017 \\ 0.267 & 0.975 & 0.770 & 0.638 \\ 0.409 & 0.368 & 0.061 & 0.421 \end{bmatrix}$	0.187	0.418	1	$X = \begin{bmatrix} -1 & -1 & 1 & 0.787 \\ 0.607 & 0.039 & 0.499 & 0.017 \\ 0.267 & 0.975 & 0.770 & 0.638 \\ 0.409 & 0.368 & 0.061 & 0.421 \end{bmatrix}$
4	$X = \begin{bmatrix} -1 & -1 & 1 & 0.787 \\ 0.607 & 0.039 & 0.499 & 0.017 \\ 0.267 & 0.975 & 0.770 & 0.638 \\ 0.409 & 0.368 & 0.061 & 0.421 \end{bmatrix}$	0.024	0.497	1	$X = \begin{bmatrix} -1 & -1 & 1 & 1 \\ 0.607 & 0.039 & 0.499 & 0.017 \\ 0.267 & 0.975 & 0.770 & 0.638 \\ 0.409 & 0.368 & 0.061 & 0.421 \end{bmatrix}$
	…and so on to the two last lines:				
15	$X = \begin{bmatrix} -1 & -1 & 1 & 1 \\ 1 & -1 & 1 & -1 \\ -1 & 1 & 1 & -1 \\ 1 & 1 & 0.061 & 0.421 \end{bmatrix}$	32	187	1	$X = \begin{bmatrix} -1 & -1 & 1 & 1 \\ 1 & -1 & 1 & -1 \\ -1 & 1 & 1 & -1 \\ 1 & 1 & 1 & 0.421 \end{bmatrix}$
16	$X = \begin{bmatrix} -1 & -1 & 1 & 1 \\ 1 & -1 & 1 & -1 \\ -1 & 1 & 1 & -1 \\ 1 & 1 & 1 & 0.421 \end{bmatrix}$	64	256	1	$X = \begin{bmatrix} -1 & -1 & 1 & 1 \\ 1 & -1 & 1 & -1 \\ -1 & 1 & 1 & -1 \\ 1 & 1 & 1 & 1 \end{bmatrix}$

Since $4^4 = 256$, we know we have reached a global optimum. Therefore, our design matrix is

$$\mathbf{X} = \begin{bmatrix} -1 & -1 & 1 & 1 \\ 1 & -1 & 1 & -1 \\ -1 & 1 & 1 & -1 \\ 1 & 1 & 1 & 1 \end{bmatrix}$$

All of the objects are involved in each weighing, as expected. The value of $|\mathbf{X'X}| = 256$ was our indication that we should stop iterating on the algorithm. If, after completing all 16 elements, we had not reached 256, we would start from the first element and go through this iterative process again.

In reality, software that uses the coordinate exchange algorithm repeats it many times with many random start matrices. For example, JMP uses a default of 20 random start matrices. The algorithm repeats because some designs are so complex that the algorithm does not converge at the absolute optimal design, but rather with a local optimum. By repeating the algorithm, you become more sure that you have the optimum result. However, the cost of repeating the algorithm is computing time. Complex designs take more time.

In summary, we saw three approaches to weighing four elements. Their results are as follows:

- Standard strategy, with $|\mathbf{X'X}| = 1$.
- Intermediate strategy, with $|\mathbf{X'X}| = 16$.
- Optimum strategy, with $|\mathbf{X'X}| = 256$—the most efficient design possible.

11.5 Optimal Designs with a Linear Model

As you have seen in (other section of the book), we do not normally deal with simple problems such as weights. In general, we have a model with a response (y), several factors ($x_1, x_2, \ldots x_n$), and their interactions ($x_1 x_2$, and so on). How are optimal designs computed when a linear model is involved?

Let's examine this with an example. Suppose we have a simple linear model

$$y = a_0 + a_1 x_1 + a_2 x_2 + a_{12} x_1 x_2$$

That is, we start with a two-factor model with the single two-factor interaction. To use the coordinate exchange algorithm above, we would start by building a factor matrix. This factor matrix would then be used to give us our **X** matrix. In this example, we have two factors and four parameters, so we would build a 4×2 factor matrix of random uniform numbers.

$$\mathbf{F} = \begin{bmatrix} r_1 & r_2 \\ r_3 & r_4 \\ r_5 & r_6 \\ r_7 & r_8 \end{bmatrix}$$

We use this **F** design matrix to build the model matrix, **X**, which has a column of 1's for the intercept, columns for each factor, and a column representing the interaction term.

$$\mathbf{X} = \begin{bmatrix} 1 & r_1 & r_2 & r_1 r_2 \\ 1 & r_3 & r_4 & r_3 r_4 \\ 1 & r_5 & r_6 & r_5 r_6 \\ 1 & r_7 & r_8 & r_7 r_8 \end{bmatrix}$$

The process for the coordinate exchange algorithm is similar to what we learned above, except that the exchanges are done on the **F** design matrix. When the **F** matrix changes, corresponding changes trickle into the **X** model matrix. For example, when we replace r_1 with a 1 or –1, that change affects the **X** matrix in the second column (the r_1 entry) but also the fourth column (the $r_1 \times r_2$ entry). You still use **X** to compute $|\mathbf{X'X}|$ and determine whether the new entry should stay or not.

As before, an example may make the concept clear. We begin with an **F** design matrix whose levels are randomly chosen between 0 and 1.

$$\mathbf{F} = \begin{bmatrix} 0.736 & 0.414 \\ 0.239 & 0.124 \\ 0.328 & 0.770 \\ 0.318 & 0.723 \end{bmatrix}$$

This **F** matrix determines the **X** model matrix:

$$\mathbf{X} = \begin{bmatrix} 1 & 0.736 & 0.414 & 0.305 \\ 1 & 0.239 & 0.124 & 0.030 \\ 1 & 0.328 & 0.770 & 0.252 \\ 1 & 0.318 & 0.723 & 0.230 \end{bmatrix}$$

The difference between the **X** model matrix and the **F** design are a column for the intercept and a column for the interactions. The interaction column is the product of the two factor levels ($0.736 \times 0.414 = 0.305$).

Table 11.4 Details of the exchange algorithm (two-factor design)

Iteration	F	|X'X| When −1 Is Used	|X'X| When +1 Is Used	Replace Number with	New X Matrix
1	$\mathbf{F} = \begin{bmatrix} 0.736 & 0.414 \\ 0.239 & 0.124 \\ 0.328 & 0.770 \\ 0.318 & 0.723 \end{bmatrix}$	1.6×10^{-5}	5.5×10^{-6}	−1	$\mathbf{X} = \begin{bmatrix} 1 & -1 & 0.414 & -0.414 \\ 1 & 0.239 & 0.124 & 0.030 \\ 1 & 0.328 & 0.770 & 0.252 \\ 1 & 0.318 & 0.723 & 0.230 \end{bmatrix}$
2	$\mathbf{F} = \begin{bmatrix} -1 & 0.414 \\ 0.239 & 0.124 \\ 0.328 & 0.770 \\ 0.318 & 0.723 \end{bmatrix}$	5.6×10^{-4}	6.6×10^{-6}	−1	$\mathbf{X} = \begin{bmatrix} 1 & -1 & -1 & 1 \\ 1 & 0.239 & 0.124 & 0.030 \\ 1 & 0.328 & 0.770 & 0.252 \\ 1 & 0.318 & 0.723 & 0.230 \end{bmatrix}$

…and so on to the two last lines:

Iteration	F	|X'X| When −1 Is Used	|X'X| When +1 Is Used	Replace Number with	New X Matrix
7	$\mathbf{F} = \begin{bmatrix} -1 & -1 \\ -1 & 1 \\ 1 & -1 \\ 0.318 & 0.723 \end{bmatrix}$	0	190	1	$\mathbf{X} = \begin{bmatrix} 1 & -1 & -1 & 1 \\ 1 & -1 & 1 & -1 \\ 1 & 1 & -1 & -1 \\ 1 & 1 & 0.723 & 0.723 \end{bmatrix}$
8	$\mathbf{F} = \begin{bmatrix} -1 & -1 \\ -1 & 1 \\ 1 & -1 \\ 1 & 0.723 \end{bmatrix}$	0	256	1	$\mathbf{X} = \begin{bmatrix} 1 & -1 & -1 & 1 \\ 1 & -1 & 1 & -1 \\ 1 & 1 & -1 & -1 \\ 1 & 1 & 1 & 1 \end{bmatrix}$

So, the final **X** matrix is

$$\mathbf{X} = \begin{bmatrix} 1 & -1 & -1 & 1 \\ 1 & -1 & 1 & -1 \\ 1 & 1 & -1 & -1 \\ 1 & 1 & 1 & 1 \end{bmatrix}$$

Look at this matrix closely. You should recognize the two central columns as the classical 2^2 full-factorial design that you first saw in Chapter 2.

Generally, the coordinate exchange algorithm enables to find the classical experimental designs. It is a powerful means to rapidly build a design by focusing on the problem, even in simple cases.

11.6 When to Use Optimal Designs

Because of their statistical properties, optimal designs are always good choices, since they ensure properties desirable for screening and modeling. They also allow the experimenter to have a design tailored to the problem at hand. Optimal designs can overcome difficult situations and sometimes they are the only choice. They are useful in the following situations when you want:

- To reduce the number of runs of a standard factorial design to respect a budget or a deadline.
- To adapt the design to objectives and to resources of the company.
- To manage a study which includes mixture and regular process factors.
- To obtain a response surface in the presence of categorical variables.
- To take into account constraints imposed on the design. Constraints might include an experimental region that is irregularly shaped or the realization that not all combinations of the factors are feasible.
- To apply a blocking structure that ensures the quality of the result when the model does not fit the standard blocking designs.
- To find the supplementary runs to repair a poorly designed experiment.

11.7 Adaptability of Optimal Designs

Suppose you are an experimenter who has to investigate the effect of three factors on a response. Based on your budget, you can use up to 12 runs to analyze the factors. Since there are three factors, a natural design choice is a 2^3 design (using eight runs) and placing the four additional runs as center points to investigate curvature and to provide an estimate of pure error (Table 11.5).

Table 11.5 Classical factorial experimental design

Factor 1	Factor 2	Factor 3
−1	−1	−1
1	−1	−1
−1	1	−1
1	1	−1
−1	−1	1
1	−1	1
−1	1	1
1	1	1
0	0	0
0	0	0
0	0	0
0	0	0

If the standard deviation on the response is 1, the standard deviation on the coefficients is 0.125 (see Chapter 5, Equation (5.1)).

If you don't need to verify the model validity or obtain an estimate of the pure error, you can build a 12-run optimal design (Table 11.6).

Table 11.6 Optimal design for 12 runs

Factor 1	Factor 2	Factor 3
−1	−1	−1
1	−1	−1
−1	1	−1
1	1	−1
−1	−1	1
−1	−1	1
1	−1	1
1	−1	1
−1	1	1
−1	1	1
1	1	1
1	1	1

If the standard deviation on the response is 1, the standard deviation on the coefficients is 0.094 (see Chapter 5, Equation (5.1)). The variance is 75% of the variance of the classic design, so the standard errors of the coefficient estimates will be about 14% smaller than those of the classic design.

The purpose of screening designs is to determine which factors are important. Statistically, this means determining whether the coefficients are different from 0. By having smaller standard errors, we can be more confident in our conclusions. This increased confidence does not cost us anything—no extra runs are necessary to get the better estimates.

If you want to resolve a second-degree problem, use an optimal designer like the JMP Custom Design platform to build a 12-run second-degree design (Table 11.7). You just have to choose an *a priori* model:

$$y = a_0 + a_1 x_1 + a_2 x_2 + a_3 x_3 + a_{12} x_1 x_2 + a_{13} x_1 x_3 + a_{23} x_2 x_3 + a_{11} x_1^2 + a_{22} x_2^2 + a_{33} x_3^2 + e$$

Table 11.7 Second-degree design

Factor 1	Factor 2	Factor 3
1	−1	−1
−1	−1	1
−1	1	−1
0	1	0
1	1	1
−1	0	1
1	−1	1
−1	1	1
1	0	0
1	1	−1
−1	−1	−1
0	0	−1

Since we are using a second-degree model, the variance varies from one parameter to the other (Table 11.8).

Table 11.8 Variance of the coefficients (second-degree design)

Coefficient	Variance	Coefficient	Variance
a_0	0.819	a_{13}	0.119
a_1	0.111	a_{23}	0.125
a_2	0.123	a_{11}	0.836
a_3	0.111	a_{22}	0.523
a_{12}	0.125	a_{33}	0.836

The second-degree optimal design gave us all the parameters with a small variance.

With the same number of runs, three different situations are resolved:

- A classical factorial design with the validity test of the model
- A design with the smallest parameter variance possible

- A response surface design

We will now look at three different example applications of the optimal designs:

- Example 16: "Developing a Fissure Detector" showing the adaptive properties of *D*-optimal designs
- Example 17: "Pharmaceutical Tablets" which underlines the reduction of the trial number for a study with mixture and process factors
- Example 18: "Self-Tanning Cream" which shows the power of *D*-optimal designs to repair a poorly designed experiment

11.8 Example 16: Developing a Fissure Detector

11.8.1 Preparing the Designed Experiment

11.8.1.1 Description of the Study

This example is based on a report issued by the U.S. National Institute of Standards and Technology.

A researcher's goal is to develop a nondestructive, portable device for detecting cracks and fractures in metals (like airplane wings, building materials, and so on). The detector works by detecting changes in an internal magnetic field, which causes a change in the impedance level of the detector. This change in impedance is the response of study, called *sensitivity*.

11.8.1.2 Factors and Domain

The three factors for the detector wiring components under consideration were (Table 11.9):

- Factor 1: Number of wire turns
- Factor 2: Wire winding distance
- Factor 3: Gauge of the wire

Table 11.9 Factors and study domain

Factor	−1 Level	Level 0	+1 Level
Number of wire turns (1)	90	135	180
Wire winding distance (2)	0.38	0.76	1.14
Gauge of the wire (3)	40	44	48

11.8.1.3 Defining the Study Objective

The budget for this study is 12 runs. Since there are only three factors, eight runs constitute a full-factorial design. Here we describe two designs, each with a specific objective, so the designs are not the same. This shows how important it is to accurately specify the objective of the study before beginning any experiments.

The first experimenter wants to model the phenomenon. He chooses a classical full-factorial design, placing four additional runs as center points to investigate curvature and to provide an estimate of pure error. They are not used in estimating the coefficients. If needed, he will continue by using a composite design.

The second experimenter wants to detect influential factors, especially those that are only slightly influential. With this objective, he uses all the runs to estimate the coefficients, which decreases parameter variance.

11.8.2 Using a 2^3 Factorial with Center Points

11.8.2.1 Running the Experiment

First, the experimenter places the extra four runs at the center of the design in order to test for curvature. His experimental design and results are shown in Table 11.10.

Table 11.10 Experimental matrix

Trial	Number of Wire Turns	Wire Winding Distance	Wire Gauge	Sensitivity
	Factor 1	Factor 2	Factor 3	(mg/min)
1	−1	−1	−1	1.7
2	+1	−1	−1	4.57
3	−1	+1	−1	0.55
4	+1	+1	−1	3.39
5	−1	−1	+1	1.51
6	+1	−1	+1	4.59
7	−1	+1	+1	0.67
8	+1	+1	+1	4.29
9	0	0	0	2.7
10	0	0	0	2.76
11	0	0	0	3.21
12	0	0	0	1.97
Level −1	90	0.38	40	
Level +1	180	1.14	48	

11.8.2.2 Interpretation

The eight coefficients are calculated using model A without using the four center control points.

$$\text{Model A}: y = a_0 + a_1 x_1 + a_2 x_2 + a_3 x_3 + a_{12} x_1 x_2 + a_{13} x_1 x_3 + a_{23} x_2 x_3 + a_{123} x_1 x_2 x_3$$

The intercept is equal to 2.659, but there is no information available to estimate precision because the design is saturated. The response mean at the central point is 2.66 with a standard deviation of 0.51. The intercept (calculated at the central point with model A) and the measured responses at the same point are not statistically different. Therefore, the first-degree model with interactions is valid, and it is not necessary to carry out a composite design.

We can use the results at the central point to calculate the model coefficients. Calculations are done with all 12 experimental results (Table 11.11). The intercept is equal to 2.659, and this time there is information available to estimate precision. Factor 1 (number of wire turns) is influential. Factor 2 (wire winding distance) is perhaps influential, but the conclusion is not immediately clear because its *p*-value is slightly more than 0.05. It is close enough to consider including it in the study.

Table 11.11 Values of model A coefficients (coded units)

Coefficient	Estimate	Standard Deviation	t Ratio	p-Value
Intercept	2.659	0.128	20.7	<0.0001
Number of wire turns (1)	1.551	0.157	9.87	0.0006
Wire winding distance (2)	−0.434	0.1587	−2.76	0.0508
Wire gauge (3)	0.106	0.157	0.68	0.5360
a_{12}	0.064	0.157	0.41	0.7057
a_{13}	0.124	0.157	0.79	0.4750
a_{23}	0.149	0.157	0.95	0.3974
a_{123}	0.071	0.157	0.45	0.6738

We can also see that interactions are negligible. Therefore, a simplified model without interactions can be adopted (Model B). The degrees of freedom that were formerly used to estimate the interaction terms can be pooled into the error term of this new model.

Model B : $y = a_0 + a_1 x_1 + a_2 x_2 + a_3 x_3$

With more degrees of freedom, the parameter variance is reduced. The parameter estimate of factor 2 (wire winding distance) now has a *p*-value of 0.0123 (Table 11.12). This factor is influential.

Table 11.12 Values of model B coefficients (coded units)

Coefficient	Estimate	Standard Error	t Ratio	p-Value
Intercept	2.659	0.110	24.16	< 0.0001
Number of wire turns (1)	1.551	0.135	11.51	< 0.0001
Wire winding distance (2)	−0.434	0.135	−3.22	0.0123
Wire gauge (3)	0.106	0.135	0.79	0.4533

The conclusion is that the first-degree model without interaction correctly represents the phenomenon and that there are two influential factors: number of wire turns (factor 1) and wire winding distance (factor 2). Wire gauge (factor 3) is not influential.

We therefore have a model for the phenomenon.

$$y = 2.66 + 1.55\, x_1 - 0.43\, x_2$$

11.8.3 Using a *D*-Optimal Design with Repetitions

In this case, the objective is to detect influential factors and especially those that are slightly influential. The second experimenter builds a *D*-optimal screening design using a first-degree model with interactions and no runs at the center point. This results in a full-factorial design with repetitions of some points, located at the vertices of the study domain.

11.8.3.1 Experimentation

The design is calculated using software. A *D*-optimal design for this problem is shown in Table 11.13, with the results from the experimental trials.

Table 11.13 Experimental matrix

Trial	Number of Wire Turns	Wire Winding Distance	Wire Gauge	Sensitivity
	Factor 1	Factor 2	Factor 3	(mg/min)
1	−1	−1	−1	1.190
2	−1	−1	−1	2.21
3	−1	−1	1	1.51
4	−1	1	−1	0.823
5	−1	1	−1	0.277
6	−1	1	1	0.670
7	1	−1	−1	4.822
8	1	−1	−1	4.318
9	1	−1	1	4.590
10	1	1	−1	3.402
11	1	1	−1	3.378
12	1	1	1	4.290
Level −	90	0.38	40	
Level +	180	1.14	48	

11.8.3.2 Interpretation

The parameter estimates for this study are given in the following table (Table 11.14).

Table 11.14 Values of model A coefficients (coded units)

Coefficient	Estimate	Standard Deviation	t Ratio	p-value
Intercept	2.659	0.137	19.46	<0.0001
Number of wire turns (1)	1.551	0.137	11.35	0.0003
Wire winding distance (2)	−0.434	0.137	−3.17	0.0337
Wire gauge (3)	0.106	0.137	0.78	0.4802
a_{12}	0.064	0.137	0.47	0.6651
a_{13}	0.124	0.137	0.91	0.4163
a_{23}	0.149	0.137	1.09	0.3375
a_{123}	0.071	0.137	0.52	0.6296

Factor 1 (number of wire turns) and factor 2 (wire winding distance) are influential. As we have seen previously, interactions are negligible and it is possible to use the simplified linear model. Calculated coefficients for this linear model are shown in Table 11.15 and confirm the influence of wire winding distance (2), which now has a *p*-value of 0.003.

Table 11.15 Values of linear model coefficients (coded units)

Coefficient	Estimate	Standard Deviation	t Ratio	p-value
Intercept	2.659	0.122	21.80	<0.0001
Number of wire turns (1)	1.51	0.115	13.13	<0.0001
Wire winding distance (2)	−0.483	0.115	−4.20	0.0030
Wire gauge (3)	0.106	0.122	0.87	0.4090

All the runs are used to estimate the model and reduce the parameters' standard deviation. Using optimal designs gives increased precision for the same number of runs. This clearly shows the advantage of optimal designs, which can be adapted to different situations.

11.9 Example 17: Pharmaceutical Tablets

11.9.1 Preparing the Designed Experiment

1.9.1.1 Describing the Study

This study concerns the manufacture of pharmaceutical tablets. The experimenters wanted to attain certain specifications by studying the pills' contents and the manner in which they were made. The pill is prepared from a powder containing starch, lactose (sugar), and cellulose. This powder is then placed under strong pressure for a predetermined amount of time and becomes a pill. The word *pill* will be, in the rest of this example, synonymous with *tablet*. The pill (tablet) must have certain characteristics to be usable. It must hold together when gripped by the fingers, without disintegrating; it must not crumble in the box during transportation and storage; it must be porous enough to dissolve easily and quickly, and so on. The study of several starch-sugar-cellulose mixtures depending on the pressure and the duration of compression has, as its objective, finding the conditions that produce tablets that conform to these specifications.

This study was conducted using 11 mixture points located as shown in Figure 11.4. The process factors were studied, of each mixture point, using a full-factorial design with a central point. Therefore, the total number of runs was 11 x 5 = 55. Using optimal design lets us drastically reduce the number of runs while still achieving a good model of the results. We now describe how to reduce the 55-run design.

11.9.1.2 Problem Data

Responses

Many responses define the quality of a tablet. We consider only two in this example.

Cohesion

This response corresponds to the resistance to rupture or break. It is measured by exerting traction on the tablet and measuring the force necessary to break it. This force must not be too weak because the tablet's seals would break under the smallest force and probably wouldn't survive the shipping process. It should also not be too strong, since patients may have to break the tablet in half. Prior research shows that the cohesion should be between 3×10^6 and 5×10^6 Pascal.

Porosity

This response measures the volume of empty space in the tablet. It is obtained by comparing the initial volume of the powder with that of the compressed tablet. The porosity is given by the relative reduction in volume when the powder becomes compressed.

Water must easily penetrate into the interior of the tablet in order for it to rapidly dissolve. Consequently, the porosity must not be too small. So that the pill does not break apart, the porosity must not be too high. A good compromise has the porosity between 17% and 22%.

Mixture factors

The mixture to be considered has three constituent parts:

- Starch, whose content is x_1

The amount of starch is under a constraint: no more than 50% of the tablet's contents can be composed of starch, that is

$$x_1 \leq 0.5$$

- Lactose, whose amount is x_2
- Mineral cellulose, whose amount is x_3

There are no constraints on the lactose or cellulose amounts.

$$0 \leq x_2 \leq 1$$

$$0 \leq x_3 \leq 1$$

Process factors

Fabrication speed

This is the time that passes between the formation of one tablet and the next. This time is in direct relation with the duration of the pressure placed on the tablet. Note, too, that this factor has a strong effect on production. In other words, the faster the production speed, the more pills are produced. We designate this factor as z_1.

Pressure

This is the pressure applied to the powder at the moment of the creation of the pill. We call this factor z_2.

Study domain
The constraint must be taken into account when defining the study domain. The constraint allows only the lower part of the equilateral triangle to take part in the study (Figure 11.4).

Figure 11.4 Mixture study domain for powders used in making tablets

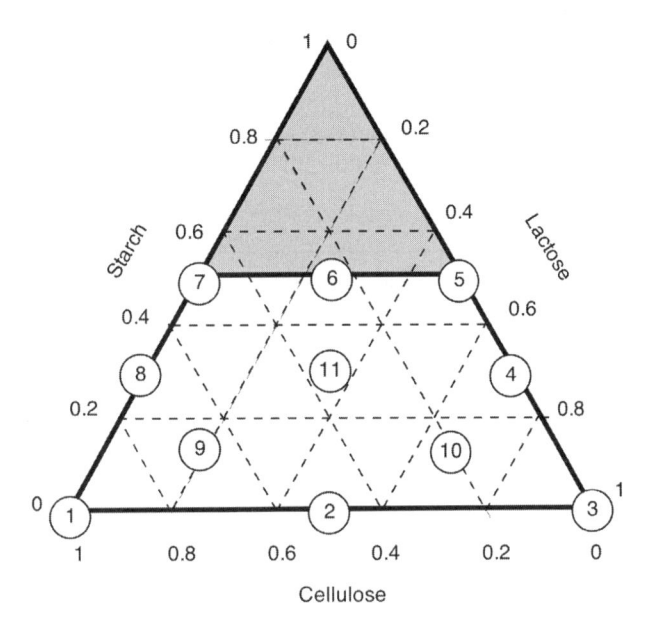

11.9.2 The Design
A design can be built from the basic mixture design:

$$y = b_1 x_1 + b_2 x_2 + b_3 x_3 + b_{12} x_1 x_2 + b_{13} x_1 x_3 + b_{23} x_2 x_3$$

As with all mixture models, there are neither intercept nor squared terms because of the mixture constraint $\sum x_i = 0$. (See Chapter 10 for details.)

From this basic design, let's modify the model parameters to depend on the levels of the process factors (the z_i's). So, for each $b_1, b_2, ..., b_i$ coefficient above, we use

$$b_i = a_{0,i} + a_{1,i} z_1 + a_{2,i} z_2$$

In other words, each coefficient in the mixture equation is replaced by a unique function of the form $a_0 + a_1 z_1 + a_2 z_2$.

$$y = (a_{0,1} + a_{1,1}z_1 + a_{2,1}z_2)x_1 + (a_{0,2} + a_{1,2}z_1 + a_{2,2}z_2)x_2 + (a_{0,3} + a_{1,3}z_1 + a_{2,3}z_2)x_3$$
$$+ (a_{0,12} + a_{1,12}z_1 + a_{2,12}z_2)x_1x_2 + (a_{0,13} + a_{1,13}z_1 + a_{2,13}z_2)x_1x_3 + (a_{0,23} + a_{1,23}z_1 + a_{2,23}z_2)x_2x_3$$

This model has 18 parameters, so at least 18 runs are needed to estimate all the coefficients. In order to have a good estimate of this model, we plan to carry out ten additional runs. Therefore, we plan to carry out 28 trials. This is almost half the number of runs of the 55-run design. However, this 28-run design cannot be built by hand like the 55-run design. Software is necessary to construct such a complicated optimal design. In general, there are several optimal designs calculated and the experimenter can choose the most convenient one. Table 11.16 shows our chosen experimental design and the results.

11.9.3 Running the Experiment

Table 11.16 28-Run experimental design

Trial	Starch x_1	Lactose x_2	Cellulose x_3	Speed z_1	Pressure z_2	Cohesion	Porosity
1	0.5	0	0.5	1	1	1.12	19.43
2	0.5	0.25	0.25	0	0	0.47	21.60
3	0	0	1	-1	-1	2.52	25.45
4	0	1	0	1	1	3.46	10.60
5	0.5	0.5	0	-1	1	0.49	15.88
6	0.5	0.5	0	1	-1	0.42	26.28
7	0	0	1	1	-1	2.27	27.96
8	0.25	0.35	0.4	-1	-1	0.51	26.19
9	0.25	0.375	0.375	1	1	1.80	14.56
10	0	1	0	1	-1	0.42	26.05
11	0.25	0	0.75	1	-1	0.31	28.10
12	0.25	0	0.75	0	1	2.87	14.94
13	0	0.5	0.5	-1	1	5.25	12.66

(continued)

Table 11.16 (*continued*)

Trial	Starch	Lactose	Cellulose	Speed	Pressure	Cohesion	Porosity
14	0.25	0.75	0	0	-1	0.19	24.83
15	0.5	0.5	0	1	1	0.38	18.20
16	0	1	0	-1	-1	0.91	21.62
17	0.5	0.5	0	-1	-1	0.53	21.82
18	0	1	0	-1	1	3.12	9.01
19	0.5	0	0.5	1	-1	0.41	27.81
20	0	0.5	0.5	-1	-1	1.49	24.37
21	0.5	0	0.5	-1	-1	0.07	25.83
22	0.5	0	0.5	-1	1	1.16	16.93
23	0	0.5	0.5	1	1	5.35	9.59
24	0	0	1	-1	1	7.09	8.32
25	0	0	1	1	1	7.39	10.65
26	0.25	0.75	0	-1	0	0.34	18.49
27	0	0.5	0.5	1	-1	1.49	23.29
28	0.25	0.75	0	1	0	0.72	20.55

11.9.4 Analysis of the 28-Run Design

Calculations are done as usual, and the parameters of models for cohesion and porosity are easily obtained. These parameters can be compared to those obtained with the 55-run design. For the two responses, parameter estimates are essentially the same (Table 11.17).

Standard deviations (RMSE) on individual responses are: 0.223 for cohesion and 0.654 for porosity. They were 0.256 for cohesion and 0.441 for porosity with the 55-run design. Therefore, the standard deviations are similar with the two designs.

Table 11.17 Parameter comparison for Cohesion and Porosity models established with 55 or 28 runs (coded units)

Coefficient	Cohesion 55	Cohesion 28	Porosity 55	Porosity 28
a_{01}	4.84	4.81	18.04	18.35
a_{02}	1.99	1.99	16.84	16.84
a_{03}	4.80	4.80	18.10	18.09
$a_{0,12}$	-11.80	-11.71	12.57	11.93
$a_{0,13}$	-16.69	-16.61	17.66	17.05
$a_{0,23}$	-0.01	0.03	0.11	-0.03
a_{11}	0.05	0.12	7.34	7.15
a_{12}	0.04	0.00	1.54	1.52
a_{13}	0.00	0.00	1.20	1.20
$a_{1,12}$	-0.10	-0.24	-10.90	-10.47
$a_{1,13}$	-0.03	-0.18	-12.61	-12.30
$a_{1,23}$	-0.01	-0.01	-9.66	-9.61
a_{21}	0.94	0.89	-0.16	0.07
a_{22}	1.31	1.31	-7.04	-7.02
a_{23}	2.45	2.45	-8.60	-8.60
$a_{2,12}$	-4.67	-4.58	0.34	-0.20
$a_{2,13}$	-4.86	-4.78	0.217	-0.14
$a_{2,23}$	0.01	-0.02	5.87	5.80

Bar charts of Figure 11.5 and Figure 11.6 show the agreement of the two designs. The conclusions of the 28-run study are identical to those of the 55-run study.

Figure 11.5 Bar chart showing cohesion model coefficients obtained with 55 runs (white) and 28 runs (gray)

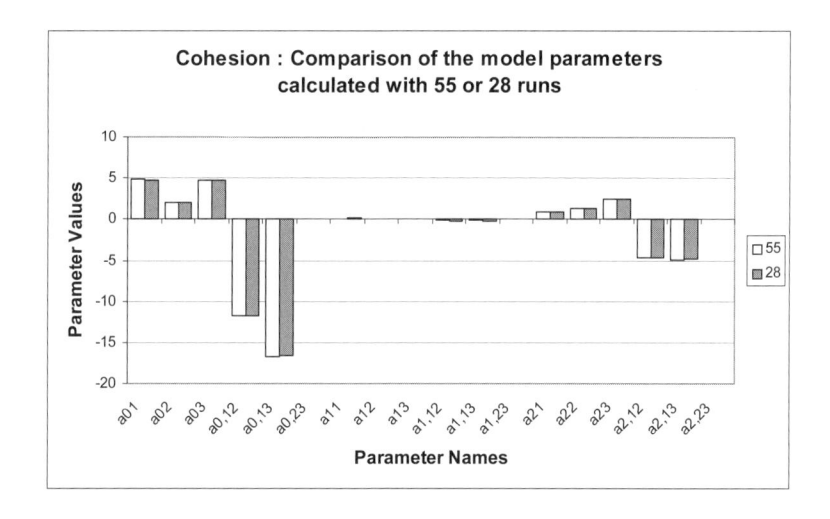

Figure 11.6 Bar chart showing porosity model coefficients obtained with 55 runs (white) and 28 runs (gray)

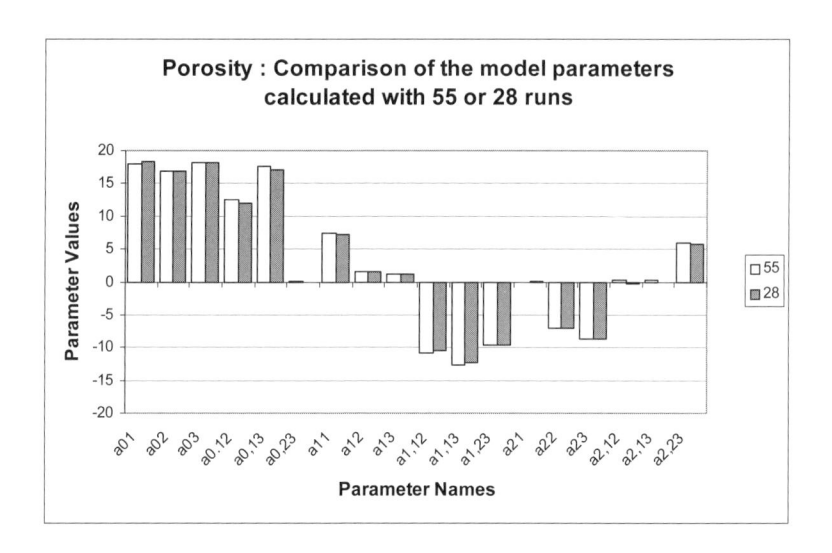

Although either design gives us a set of manufacturing rules that are within our specifications, using an optimal design has two distinct advantages:

- Instead of 55 runs, we can gather all needed information in 28 runs, an almost 50% savings in time and cost.
- Rather than have only five choices for manufacturing rules, we can completely characterize the response surface of the process and search for the best choices for our factor settings without the constraints of the pre-picked process variable values.

To design this experiment, it is necessary that the design software accommodate both mixture and process factors. JMP software does so using its Custom Design feature (**DOE → Custom Design**).

Note that even though we only used half the number of runs, we got nearly identical information.

- All effects that were declared significant in the first study were also declared significant in the second.
- The RMSE for both experiments were identical
- The parameter estimates for the two studies match exactly.

In addition, the profiles and maximum desirabilities are virtually identical.

11.9.5 Study Conclusion

Using our models, diagrams for speed × pressure can be drawn for different mixture compositions. We see that it is possible to obtain a porosity between 17 and 22 for any composition, provided that speed and pressure are correctly set (Figure 11.7).

Figure 11.7 The objective of porosity (white part of the speed x pressure diagrams) can be obtained for all mixture compositions.

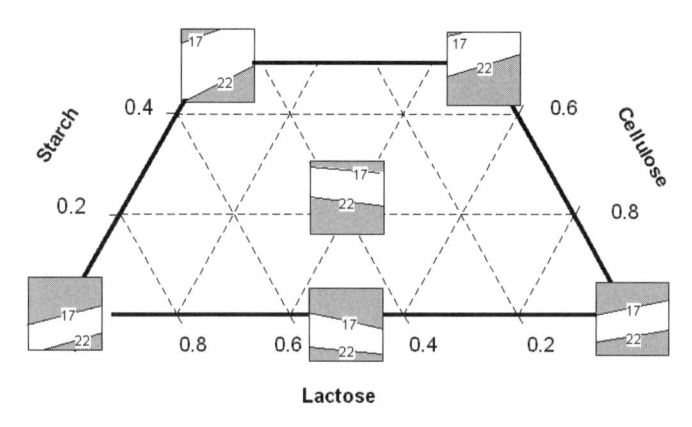

Porosity

We also can see that it is possible to obtain a cohesion between 3 and 5 if the mixture composition has a small content of starch (Figure 11.8).

Figure 11.8 The objective of cohesion (white part of the speed x pressure diagrams) can be obtained for mixture compositions with a low content of starch.

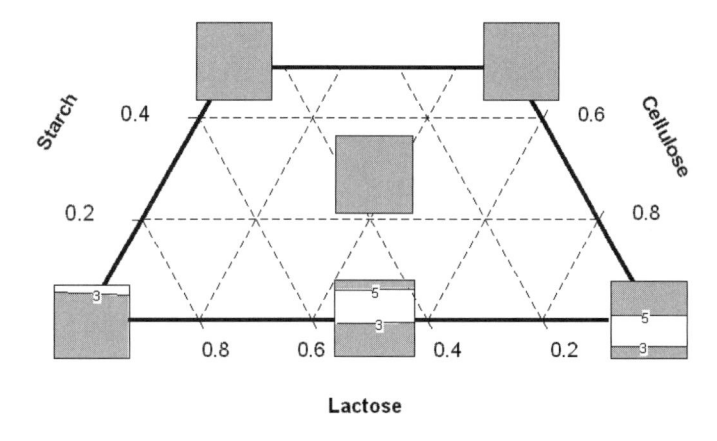

Cohesion

Several solutions are possible for the experimenter to select. An example could be the solution that minimizes the manufacturing cost while allowing work at high speed. Several mixtures characterized by a high content in cellulose are possible for maximizing the production. For example, a mixture of 94% cellulose, 4% lactose, and 2% starch suits the objectives. A mixture of 80% cellulose, 12% lactose, and 8 % starch also suits the objectives.

The experimenter decides to verify the interpretation and conclusions with a mixture of 85% cellulose, 10% lactose, and 5% starch (Figure 11.9).

Figure 11.9 With the mixture 85% cellulose, 10% lactose, and 5% starch, objectives are met if the pressure stays between +0.15 and −0.40 in coded units.

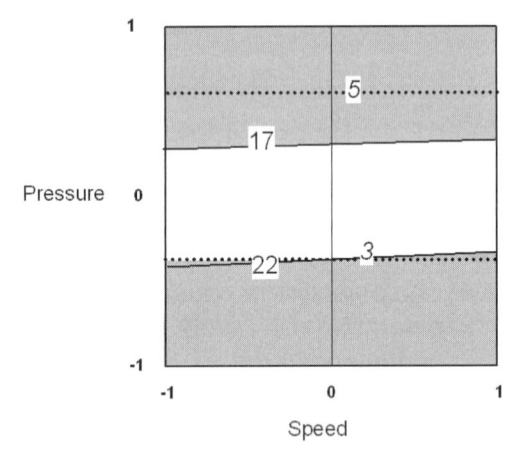

The conclusion was confirmed by the results of the control runs, and the experimenter was able to give his recommendation and the best production settings: a mixture of 85% cellulose, 10% lactose and 5% starch, a high speed to reduce cost, and a pressure between +0.15 and −0.40 (in coded units).

11.10 Example 18: Self-Tanning Cream (Rescuing a Bad Design)

11.10.1 Why a Design Can Be Bad

Optimal designs are also useful for rescuing a poorly constructed design. This situation arises when an experimenter conducts trials without organizing them in an optimal manner. The points are most likely dispersed in a random way throughout the experimental space, where there is a great risk of obtaining a poor-quality prediction model that should not be trusted. As a very pathological (and non-random) case, consider the following design for two variables as shown in Figure 11.10. The ill-conditioning problem is immediately apparent in this drawing: the points are completely collinear, so the experiment is measuring only one parameter.

Figure 11.10 Location of experimental points

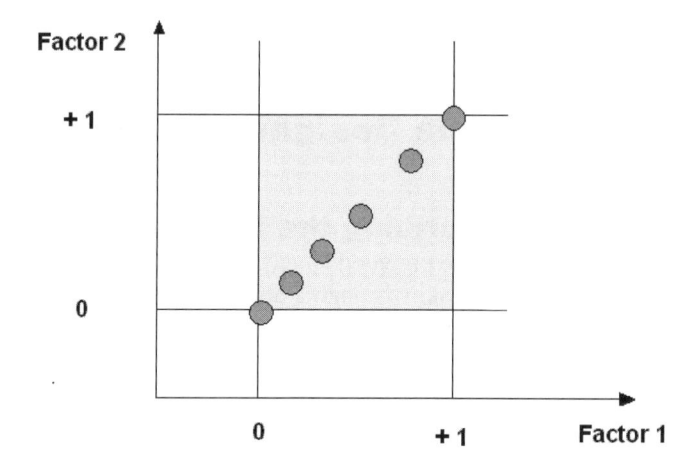

The model that the experimenter is most likely interested in

$$y = a_0 + a_1 x_1 + a_2 x_2$$

is deceiving, since in this case we have exactly:

$$\frac{x_1}{x_2} = 1$$

so

$$x_1 = x_2$$

Then, the real model is:

$$y = a_0 + (a_1 + a_2)x_1$$

This drastic example shows the effect of correlation on the factor levels. The parameters a_1 and a_2 cannot be estimated separately. We can estimate only their sum.

If the points in the experiment were not completely collinear, but were instead highly correlated, they would produce estimates with large confidence intervals. Their collinearity essentially means that the experimenter did not measure two distinct parameters. However, all is not lost. Using an optimal designer, you can add a few points to this study and obtain good estimates for the coefficients of a complex model.

As a real example, consider the following case involving self-tanning cream.

11.10.2 Preparing the Designed Experiment

11.10.2.1 Describing the Study

Self-tanning creams are prepared by extracting an active ingredient that causes a change in the pigmentation of skin through a natural sugar. The active ingredient is dihydroacetone (DHA), prepared industrially by a crystallization process. Raw DHA is dissolved in a mixture of water and an organic solvent. This mixture is cooled from 40°C (104°F) to 10°C (50°F) under agitation. While cooling, crystals form and are harvested by filtration. The engineer in charge of fabrication has specified that the process yield (currently 40% to 48%) needs to be increased. It's possible to change the water-to-solvent ratio, and also to change the agitation speed. Under normal working conditions, these are 70% and 200 rpm, respectively.

For the experiment, he decided to conduct some trials by modifying the water-to-solvent ratio between 60% and 80% and the agitation speed between 160 and 240 rpm. He carried out four different trials, taking the precaution of taking two measurements for each trial.

11.10.2.2 Factors and Domain of the Study
The experimenter therefore had the following factors and domains:

- Factor 1: water-to-solvent ratio   between 60% and 80%.
- Factor 2: agitation speed   between 160 rpm and 240 rpm.

He carried out the trials and measured the resulting yield. To be sure to have a complete experiment, he added two trials carried out in closely watched normal operating conditions.

11.10.3 Running the Experiment
The results of the experiment are shown in Table 11.18.

Table 11.18 Experimental matrix (classical units) and experimental results

Trial	Water-to-Solvent Ratio	Agitation Speed	Yield %	
	% Water	tours/min		
0	70	200	45.5	43
1	80	240	44	39.5
2	75	224	41	40
3	61	160	46	49
4	60	160	45	49.5

11.10.4 Interpreting the Results
The experimenter started by examining the coefficients of a polynomial model and their standard errors in coded units (Table 11.19).

Table 11.19 Experimental matrix (coded units) and experimental results

Coefficient	Estimate	Standard Deviation	t Ratio	p-Value
Intercept	41.875	3.72	11.27	0.0004
Water-to-solvent (1)	5.125	21.86	0.23	0.8261
Agitation speed (2)	−7.875	21.99	−0.37	0.7291
a_{12}	2.625	4.48	0.59	0.5898

To his great disappointment, he found that no coefficients were significant. What happened here, and why did the experiment not answer the experimental questions? Is the yield always about the same, regardless of operating conditions?

Close examination of the table shows a problem. The standard deviations of the coefficients of the model are all greater than the coefficients themselves. In other words, there is no way to distinguish the experimenter's model from the intercept.

Trying to understand, the experimenter writes the following model:

$$y = 41.9 + 5.1\, x_1 - 7.9\, x_2 + 2.6\, x_1 x_2 \quad \text{(model 1)}$$

Then, he calculates the expected responses and their confidence intervals. These confidence intervals are very large, and it is statistically impossible to distinguish one response from the others (Table 11.20).

Table 11.20 Confidence intervals of the expected responses (model 1)

Trial	Water-to-Solvent Ratio	Agitation Speed	Expected Yield	Confidence Interval (95 %)
	% Water	rpm		
1	80	240	41.75	From 33.2 to 50.3
2	75	224	40.50	From 31.9 to 49
3	61	160	47.50	From 38.9 to 56.0
4	60	160	47.25	From 38.7 to 55.8

11.10.4.1 A Closer Look
Rather than simply looking at tables, looking at a graphical representation of the study's domain reveals the problem (Figure 11.11).

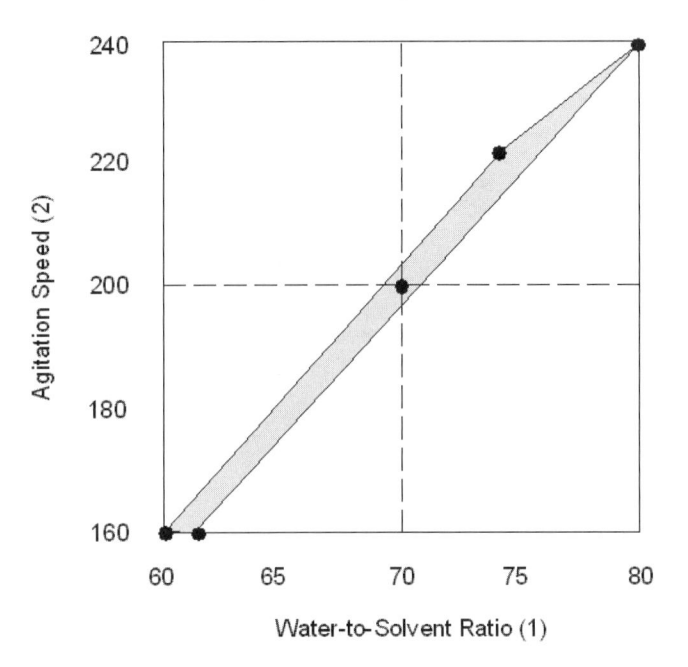

Figure 11.11 Location of the experimental points

By chance, the experimenter picked points that are almost collinear, and the study domain is quite small. As we saw earlier, this causes significant problems in parameter estimation. However, the situation is not lost, and is in fact easy to correct. Using software, we can add points to this design that greatly improve the estimates.

11.10.4.2 Repair Runs and New Interpretation
Using the D-optimality criterion, we can save this design by only adding two additional runs: a point at water-to-solvent ratio at 60% and agitation speed at 240 rpm, and another point at 80% and 160 rpm. The addition of two points greatly expands the study domain (Figure 11.12).

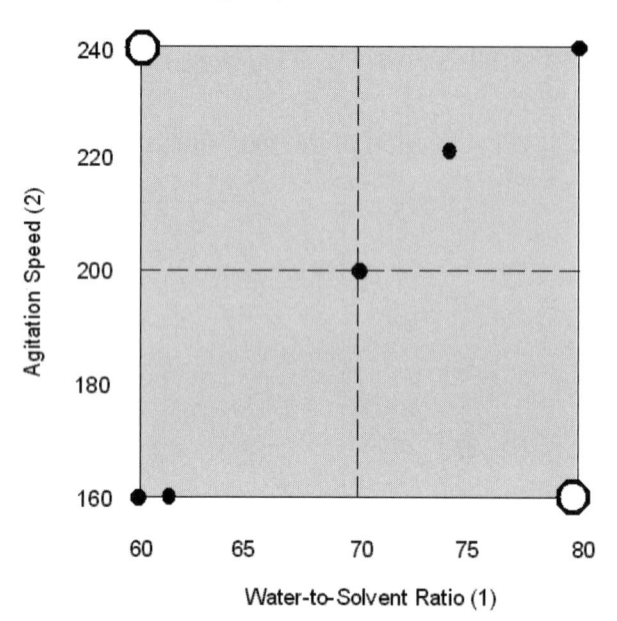

Figure 11.12 Location of the repair points

After running the experiment with these two extra points, the experimenter got the following results (Table 11.21).

Table 11.21 Repair points and experimental results

Trial	Water-to-Solvent Ratio	Agitation Speed	Yield	
	% Water	rpm		
5	60	240	59.5	60
6	80	160	24	21

The experimenter calculates the coefficients and their statistical properties. Standard deviations and p-values were greatly improved (Table 11.22):

Table 11.22 Confidence intervals of the expected responses (coded units)

Coefficient	Estimate	Standard Deviation	t Ratio	p-Value
Intercept	42.62	0.659	64.69	< 0.0001
Water-to-solvent ratio (1)	-11.07	0.722	-15.33	< 0.0001
Agitation speed (2)	7.49	0.702	10.66	< 0.0001
a_{12}	1.75	0.737	2.38	0.0447

These coefficients let the experimenter write a prediction model (model 2):

$$y = 42.6 - 11.1\, x_1 + 7.5\, x_2 + 1.7\, x_1 x_2 \quad \text{(model 2)}$$

With this model, he calculates the expected responses and their confidence intervals (95%). These confidence intervals are much smaller than before. The experimenter is now confident that he can improve the yield of DHA crystals by lowering the water-to-solvent ratio (1) and increasing the agitation speed (2). He can obtain a yield of about 60% plus or minus 6% (Table 11.23).

Table 11.23 Confidence Intervals of the expected responses (model 2)

Trial	Water-to-Solvent Ratio % Water	Agitation Speed rpm	Expected Yield	Confidence Interval (95 %)
1	80	240	40.78	From 34.8 to 46.8
2	75	224	42.10	From 36.6 to 47.6
3	61	160	46.7	From 41 to 52.4
4	60	160	47.9	From 42.2 to 53.7
5	60	240	59.4	From 53.2 to 65.7
6	60	160	22.3	From 16 to 28.5

11.10.5 Study Conclusion

The conclusion is very simple: the experimenter can easily and significantly improve the yield of the DHA production using a water-to-solvent ratio (1) of 60% and agitation speed (2) of 240 rpm (Figure 11.13).

Figure 11.13 The best yield is obtained when the water-to-solvent ratio is at level −1 (60 %) and the agitation speed is at level +1 (240 rpm).

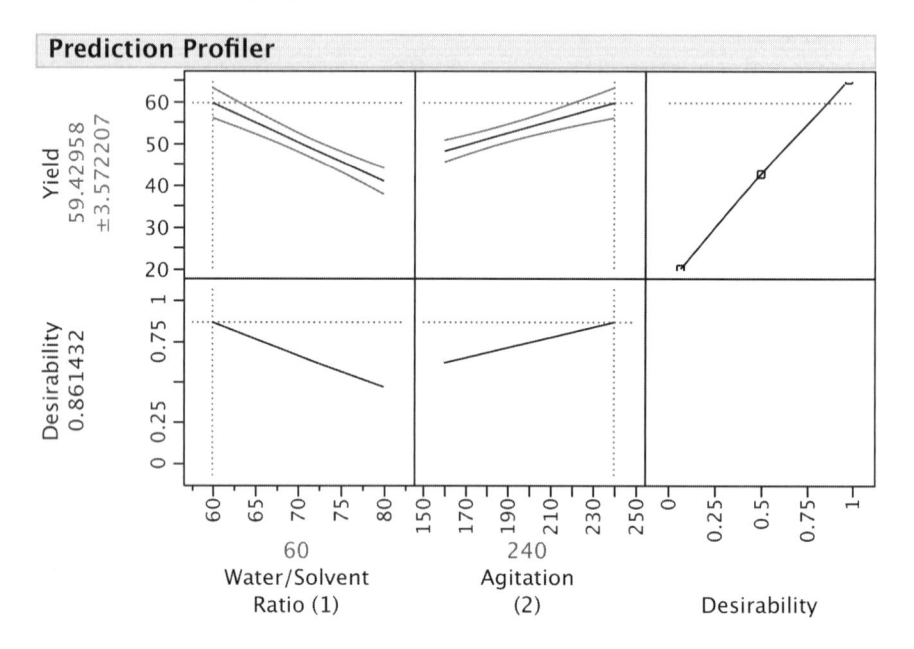

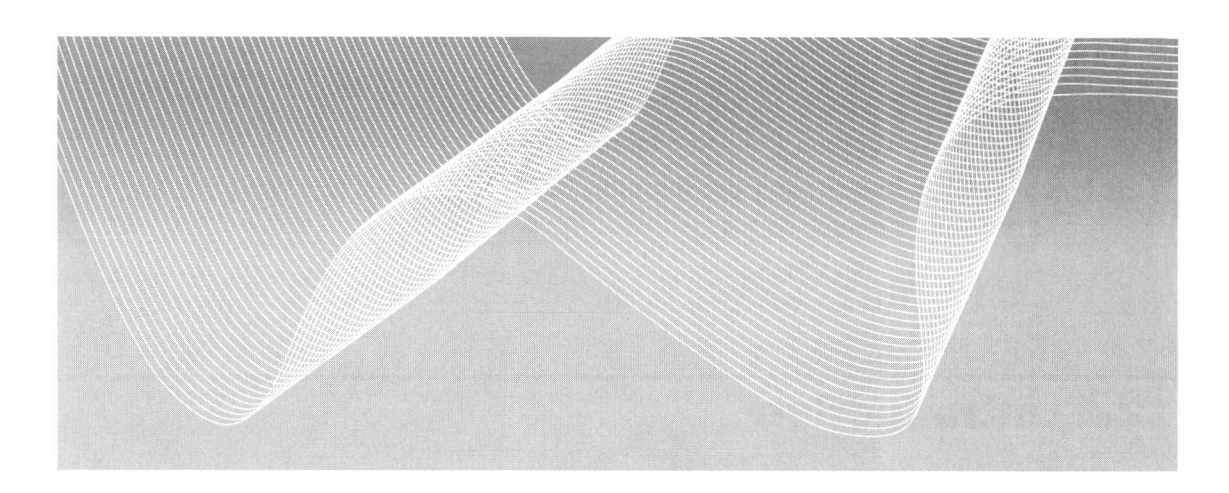

Chapter 12

Latin Squares and Similar Designs

12.1 Introduction 352
12.2 Example 19: Salaries and One Categorical Factor 353
    12.2.1 Mathematical Model 353
    12.2.2 Global Effect of a Factor 355
12.3 Example 19: Salaries and Two Categorical Factors 356
    12.3.1 Preparing the Designed Experiment 356
    12.3.2 Mathematical Model 357
    12.3.3 Effect of the Factors 359
    12.3.4 Analysis of Sums of Squares 361
    12.3.5 Analysis of Variance 365
12.4 Latin Squares 365
12.5 Greco-Latin Squares 367
12.6 Youden Squares 368

12.7 **Example 20: Penetrometry Study** 370
    12.7.1 Preparing the Designed Experiment 370
    12.7.2 Running the Experiment 370
    12.7.3 Interpreting the Results 371
12.7 **Study Conclusion** 373

12.1 Introduction

Latin squares were among the earliest experimental designs used in practice, and are particularly useful for categorical variables. A simple Latin square lets us study three factors with three levels using nine runs instead of $3^3=27$. If we extend the notation of fractional design to Latin squares, this is a 3^{3-1} design. Designs with three factors, but four or five levels per factor, are also known as Latin squares.

We can further envision designs with four factors with four levels per factor. In this case, they are called *Greco-Latin squares*, or 4^{4-2} designs, and have 16 runs rather than the 256 of the 4^4 full design.

The name Latin square comes from the original representation of these designs, which used Latin letters to designate the third factor. Greco-Latin comes from the Latin letter used to name the third factor (Figure 12.5) and the Greek letter naming the fourth (Figure 12.8).

If there are more than five levels, these designs are called *Youden designs,* named after the chemist who introduced them. They include, for example, designs with two seven-level factors or three eight-level factors. The same approach can be extended to any number of levels and any number of factors.

The modeling of categorical variables that we demonstrate in this chapter is different from continuous variables, as is the interpretation of these models. In fact, the experimental space is not continuous, so the notion of distance disappears. This difference makes it necessary to define the mathematical models used to study Latin squares, to specify the notion of effect, and to study the interpretation tools.

12.2 Example 19: Salaries and One Categorical Factor

We use Example 19, "Salaries," to begin this study of categorical designs.

12.2.1 Mathematical Model

Categorical designs have an important distinction from factorial designs. The following example examines the independence of the effects.

Three people earned different salaries. Jack earned $90, Lee $120, and Simon $180. Salaries can be modeled using the equation

$$y_i = \bar{y} + a_i + e_i \tag{12.1}$$

- y_i is the salary of person i. It is the response.
- $\bar{y}$ is the mean of the three salaries.
- a_i is the effect of person i.
- e_i is an error term composed of experimental error and lack of fit.

Therefore, Jack's effect is a_J, Lee's effect is a_L, and Simon's is a_S (Figure 12.1). Here, an effect is defined as a deviation from the mean. They are identical to the responses corrected from the mean that we encountered in Chapter 5, "Statistical Concepts for Designed Experiments." As deviations from the mean, these effects are not independent and there is a relationship among them:

$$a_J + a_L + a_S = 0$$

When any two effects are known, the third can be calculated. To see why, rewrite Equation (12.1) as:

$$y_i - \bar{y} = a_i + e_i$$

From this equation, we can write

$$\sum(y_i - \bar{y})^2 = \sum a_i^2 + \sum e_i^2$$

which shows that the sum of squares of the corrected responses is equal to the sum of squares of the effects plus the sum of squares of the deviation ($\sum a_i e_i$ terms are equal to zero).

Figure 12.1 Definition of the categorical variable effects

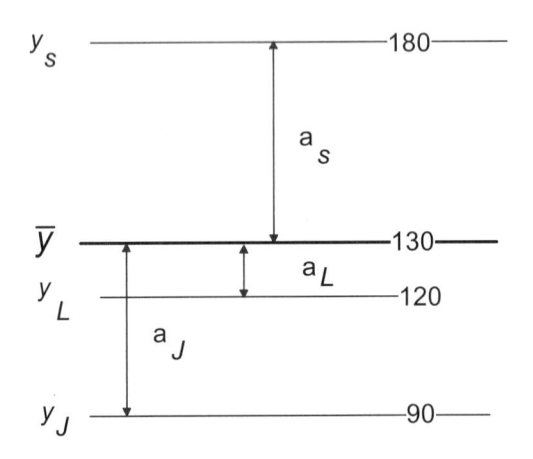

Returning to our example, we can calculate the mean salary:

$$\bar{y} = \frac{1}{3}(90 + 120 + 180) = 130$$

- Jack's effect is $a_J = y_J - \bar{y} = 90 - 130 = -40$
- Lee's effect is $a_L = y_L - \bar{y} = 120 - 130 = -10$
- Simon's effect is $a_S = y_S - \bar{y} = 180 - 130 = 50$

As expected, $a_J + a_L + a_S = -40 - 10 + 50 = 0$

In this example, there are three equations, so three unknowns can be calculated. These three unknowns are the mean and two effects. The third effect can be deduced from the two other effects because the sum of the three effects is equal to zero.

The sum of squares of the corrected responses is equal to:

$$(y_J - \bar{y})^2 + (y_L - \bar{y})^2 + (y_S - \bar{y})^2 = (-40)^2 + (-10)^2 + (50)^2 = 4200$$

12.2.2 Global Effect of a Factor

Since the sum of the effects is always zero, the mean is not useful to estimate the global effect. The quadratic mean is used instead. So, the global effect, a, is defined by the equation:

$$a^2 = \frac{1}{3}\left[a_J^2 + a_L^2 + a_S^2\right]$$

Generally, if a factor has n levels, the *global effect* is defined by:

$$a^2 = \frac{1}{n}\sum_{i=1}^{n} a_i^2$$

Be careful not to confuse this equation with the mean square. The quadratic mean has a denominator equal to n, whereas the mean square has a denominator of $n - 1$.

In our example, the global effect is

$$a^2 = \frac{1}{3}(a_J^2 + a_L^2 + a_S^2) = \frac{1}{3}\left[(-40)^2 + (-10)^2 + (50)^2\right]$$

$$a^2 = \frac{1}{3}(4200) = 1400$$

$$a = 37.41$$

12.3 Example 19: Salaries and Two Categorical Factors

12.3.1 Preparing the Designed Experiment

Let's extend this same example so that the response depends on two categorical factors, each having three levels: the effect of each person (Jack has an effect a_J; Lee, an effect a_L; Simon, an effect a_S) and the effect of the person's company (Company A has an effect b_A; Company B, an effect b_B; Company C, an effect b_C). Jack worked with A, then with B, and finally with C. The same sequence is true for Lee and for Simon. The nine experimental points are located as shown in Figure 12.2, a 3^2 design.

Figure 12.2 Complete design for two three-level categorical factors

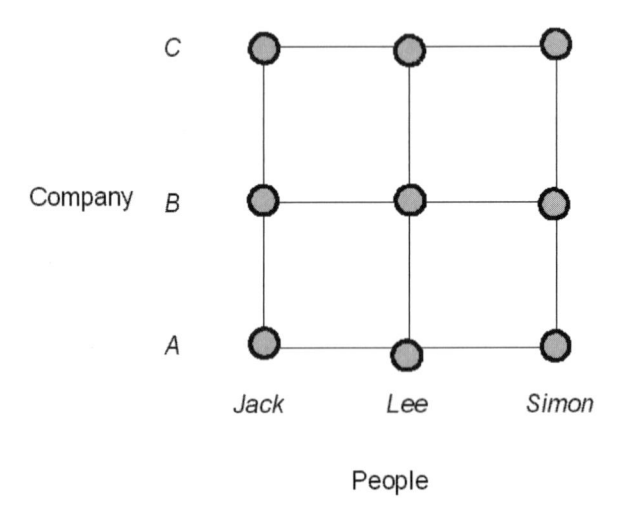

The salary earned by each person from each of the three companies is shown in Table 12.1 and represented graphically in Figure 12.3.

Table 12.1 Experimental matrix

Trial	People (1)	Company (2)	Salary ($)
1	Jack	A	85
2	Jack	B	93
3	Jack	C	92
4	Lee	A	116
5	Lee	B	121
6	Lee	C	123
7	Simon	A	174
8	Simon	B	182
9	Simon	C	184

Figure 12.3 Location of the responses around the means

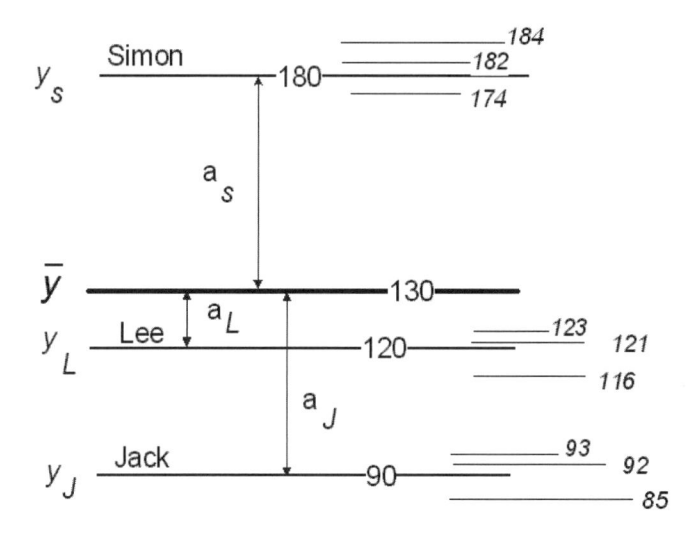

12.3.2 Mathematical Model

These salaries can be modeled by the relationship:

$$y_{i,j} = \bar{y} + a_i + b_j + e_{i,j} \tag{12.2}$$

where

- $y_{i,j}$ is the salary of person i who worked for Company j.
- $\bar{y}$ is the mean of the nine salaries.
- a_i is the effect of person i.
- b_j is the effect of company j.
- $e_{i,j}$ is a deviation term which depends on the people and the company.

Since the effects are defined in terms of the mean, they are not independent and have the following relationships:

$$a_J + a_L + a_S = 0$$

$$b_J + b_L + b_S = 0$$

We can calculate the mean earnings of each person. For example, Jack's mean earning, $\bar{y}_J$, is equal to

$$\bar{y}_J = \frac{1}{3}\left[y_{J,A} + y_{J,B} + y_{J,C}\right] \qquad (12.3)$$

with the constraint

$$(y_{J,A} - \bar{y}_J) + (y_{J,B} - \bar{y}_J) + (y_{J,C} - \bar{y}_J) = 0$$

The same constraints are true for Lee and Simon

$$(y_{L,A} - \bar{y}_L) + (y_{L,B} - \bar{y}_L) + (y_{L,C} - \bar{y}_L) = 0$$

$$(y_{S,A} - \bar{y}_S) + (y_{S,B} - \bar{y}_S) + (y_{S,C} - \bar{y}_S) = 0$$

and for companies

$$(y_{J,A} - \bar{y}_A) + (y_{L,A} - \bar{y}_A) + (y_{S,A} - \bar{y}_A) = 0$$

$$(y_{J,B} - \bar{y}_B) + (y_{L,B} - \bar{y}_B) + (y_{S,B} - \bar{y}_B) = 0$$

$$(y_{J,C} - \bar{y}_C) + (y_{L,C} - \bar{y}_C) + (y_{S,C} - \bar{y}_C) = 0$$

Interpretation is based partly on the effects of each factor and partly on the analysis of the squares of responses corrected for the mean.

12.3.3 Effect of the Factors

Effects are estimated from the mean of all the responses $\bar{y}$:

$$\bar{y} = \frac{1}{9}[85 + 93 + 92 + 116 + 121 + 123 + 174 + 182 + 184] = 130$$

Jack's effect is the mean of his three salaries, $\bar{y}_J$, compared to the mean $\bar{y}$:

$$a_J = \bar{y}_J - \bar{y} = \left[\frac{1}{3}(85 + 92 + 93)\right] - 130 = -40$$

The effects for Lee and Simon are calculated in the same manner, giving $a_L = -10$ and $a_S = 50$.

The effect of Company A is the mean of the salaries it has paid, calculated as a comparison to the mean $\bar{y}$:

$$b_A = \bar{y}_A - \bar{y} = \left[\frac{1}{3}(85 + 116 + 174)\right] - 130 = -5$$

The effects of Companies B and C are calculated in the same manner giving $b_B = 2$ and $b_C = 3$.

Effects of the two factors can be found in Table 12.2 and Figure 12.4.

Table 12.2 Factor effects

Term	Estimate	Std Error	t Ratio	Prob>|t|
Intercept	130	0.408248	318.43	<.0001*
Person[Jack]	−40	0.57735	−69.28	<.0001*
Person[Lee]	−10	0.57735	−17.32	<.0001*
Person[Simon]	50	0.57735	86.60	<.0001*
Company[A]	−5	0.57735	−8.66	0.0010*
Company[B]	2	0.57735	3.46	0.0257*
Company[C]	3	0.57735	5.20	0.0065*

Expanded Estimates — Nominal factors expanded to all levels

Figure 12.4 Bar graph of the factor effects: people and companies

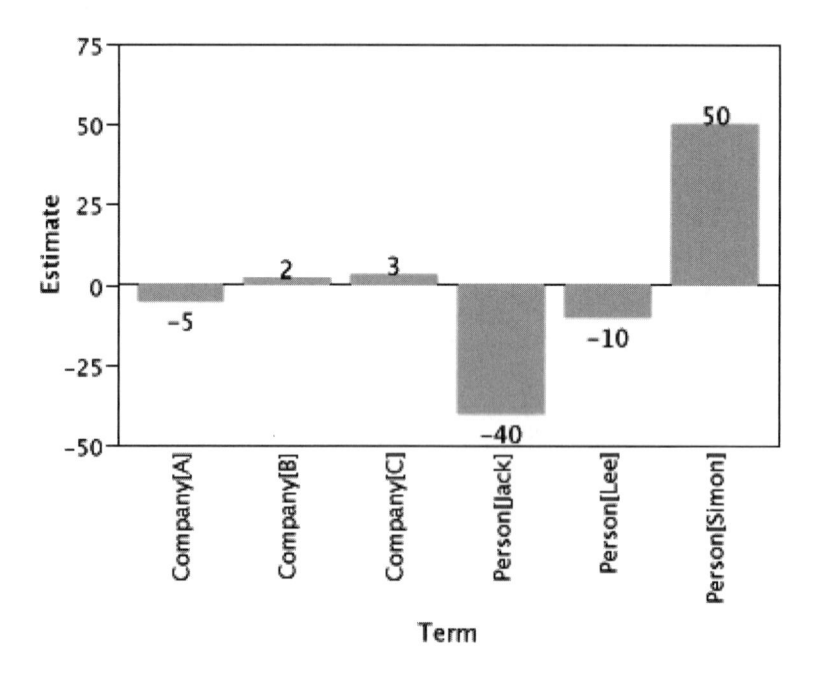

12.3.4 Analysis of Sums of Squares

Relationship (Equation 12.2) is squared and these squares are summed:

$$\sum (y_{i,j} - \bar{y})^2 = \sum a_i^2 + \sum b_j^2 + \sum e_{i,j}^2$$

The sum of the corrected (for the mean) response squares ($\sum (y_{i,j} - \bar{y})^2$) is equal to the sum of the effect squares ($\sum a_i^2$ and $\sum b_j^2$) plus the sum of the deviation square ($\sum e_{i,j}^2$). For our example,

1. Calculation of $\sum (y_{i,j} - \bar{y})^2$

   Let's calculate the measured response corrected for the mean and their squares (Table 12.3).

   Table 12.3 Calculation of the corrected response squares

Trial	Initial Responses	Mean	Responses Corrected for the Mean	Squares of Responses Corrected for the Mean
1	85	130	−45	2025
2	93	130	−37	1369
3	92	130	−38	1444
4	116	130	−14	196
5	121	130	−9	81
6	123	130	−7	49
7	174	130	44	1936
8	182	130	52	2704
9	184	130	54	2916

   Now, sum these squares. The sum of the corrected response squares is 12,720.

2. Calculation of $\sum a_i^2$

We now calculate the effects of each person and the corresponding square for the trials (Table 12.4).

Table 12.4 Calculation of the squares of people effects

Trial	Mean of the Received Salaries	Mean	Individual Effects	Squares of People Effects
1	90	130	−40	1600
2	90	130	−40	1600
3	90	130	−40	1600
4	120	130	−10	100
5	120	130	−10	100
6	120	130	−10	100
7	180	130	50	2500
8	180	130	50	2500
9	180	130	50	2500

Now, sum these squares to find the sum of the squares of people effects is 12,600.

3. Calculation of $\sum b_j^2$

Company A paid $85 to Jack, $166 to Lee, and $174 to Simon, that is, an average of $125. The effect of Company A is therefore $125−$130 = −$5. Likewise, the effect of Company B is $132−$130 = $2, and effect of Company C is $133−$130 = $3.

Now calculate the effect of each company and the corresponding squares for all the trials (Table 12.5).

Table 12.5 Calculation of the squares of company effects

Trial	Mean of the Given Salaries	Mean	Company Effects	Squares of Company Effects
1	125	130	−5	25
2	132	130	2	4
3	133	130	3	9
4	125	130	−5	25
5	132	130	2	4
6	133	130	3	9
7	125	130	−5	25
8	132	130	2	4
9	133	130	3	9

Sum these squares to find the sum of the squares of company effects is 114.

4. Calculation of $\sum e_{i,j}^2$

Finally, we calculate the difference between each measured and calculated response.

$$e_{J,A} = y_{J,A} - (\bar{y} + a_J + b_A) = 85 - (130 - 40 - 5) = 0$$

$$e_{J,B} = y_{J,B} - (\bar{y} + a_J + b_B) = 93 - (130 - 40 + 2) = 1$$

$$e_{J,C} = y_{J,C} - (\bar{y} + a_J + b_C) = 92 - (130 - 40 + 3) = -1$$

$$e_{L,A} = y_{L,A} - (\bar{y} + a_L + b_A) = 116 - (130 - 10 - 5) = 1$$

$$e_{L,B} = y_{L,B} - (\bar{y} + a_L + b_B) = 121 - (130 - 10 + 2) = 1$$

$$e_{L,C} = y_{L,C} - (\bar{y} + a_L + b_C) = 123 - (130 - 10 + 3) = 0$$

$$e_{S,A} = y_{S,A} - (\bar{y} + a_S + b_A) = 174 - (130 + 50 - 5) = -1$$

$$e_{S,B} = y_{S,B} - (\bar{y} + a_S + b_B) = 182 - (130 + 50 + 2) = 0$$

$$e_{S,C} = y_{S,C} - (\bar{y} + a_S + b_C) = 184 - (130 + 50 + 3) = -1$$

which gives us a residual sum of squares of

$$\sum e_{i,j}^2 = e_{JA}^2 + e_{JB}^2 + e_{JC}^2 + e_{LA}^2 + e_{LB}^2 + e_{LC}^2 + e_{SA}^2 + e_{SB}^2 + e_{SC}^2$$

$$\sum e_{i,j}^2 = 0^2 + 1^2 + (-1)^2 + 1^2 + 1^2 + 0^2 + 1^2 + 0^2 + (-1)^2 = 6$$

All the squares that we have calculated so far are gathered in a table for easy comparison: the sum of squares table (Table 12.6). The sum of squares of the measured responses is split into three sums of squares: one for person, one for company, and one for residual. The factor with the highest sum of squares has the greatest influence. In this example, results show that person is the most influential factor on salaries. The model explains 12714 of the total 12720, which gives an R^2 of 0.9995. The model is therefore satisfactory.

Table 12.6 Analysis of the sum of squares

Variation Source	Sum of Squares
Person	12600
Companies	114
Residual	6
Total (measured responses)	12720

The sums of squares are summed to obtain the model sum of squares. Here, the model sum of squares is equal to the people sum of squares added to the companies sum of squares, that is

$$\text{Model sum of squares} = 12600 + 114 = 12714$$

12.3.5 Analysis of Variance

Once degrees of freedom are taken into account, it is possible to transform Table 12.6 into an ANOVA table. Variances are sums of squares of the corrected responses divided by the corresponding number of degrees of freedom.

There are nine measured responses, all mathematically independent. Responses corrected for the mean are not independent since the ninth response can be calculated from the first eight and the mean. Therefore, the sum of squares of the corrected responses have eight degrees of freedom. The people effects have two degrees of freedom since they also involve the mean, as do the company effects. The sum of squares of the model therefore has four degrees of freedom. Once the constraints between the responses and the mean used to calculate the residual are taken into effect, there are four degrees of freedom for the residual.

These facts give us the ANOVA table (Table 12.7).

Table 12.7 ANOVA table

Analysis of Variance

Source	DF	Sum of Squares	Mean Square	F Ratio
Model	4	12714.000	3178.50	2119.000
Error	4	6.000	1.50	Prob > F
C. Total	8	12720.000		<.0001*

Parameter Estimates

Effect Tests

Source	Nparm	DF	Sum of Squares	F Ratio	Prob > F
Person	2	2	12600.000	4200.000	<.0001*
Company	2	2	114.000	38.0000	0.0025*

The F-Ratio is very high. We can conclude that the model explains the measured responses quite well.

12.4 Latin Squares

In order to study three categorical factors that each have three levels, $3^3 = 27$ trials are necessary (in the case of a full-factorial design). This high number of runs is impractical and expensive, so we want to reduce it. Fractional designs have been discussed earlier in the book. By using one, it is possible to construct a nine-run design. Written in our notation, we have to carry out a 3^{3-1} design. To successfully construct such a design, experimental points must be carefully chosen. Start with a 3^2 design and assign Latin letters A, B, and C to the experimental points so that they fall on each row and each column without repetition (Figure 12.5). There are 12 possible arrangements with this constraint. We can randomize the trials by randomly choosing one of these arrangements.

Figure 12.5 Latin square for three three-level factors

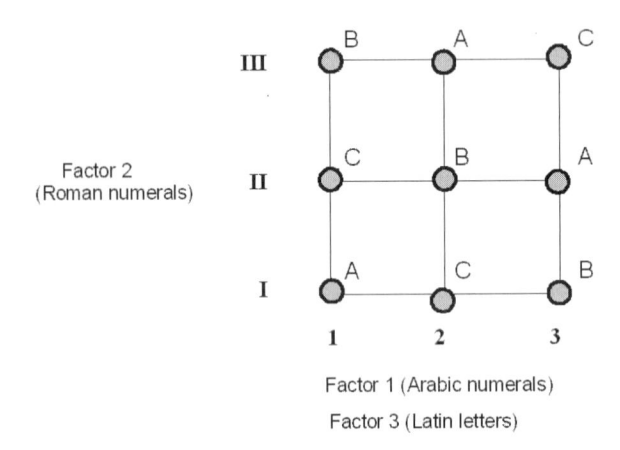

Latin squares can be shown in three dimensions (Figure 12.6).

Figure 12.6 Three-dimensional view of a Latin square

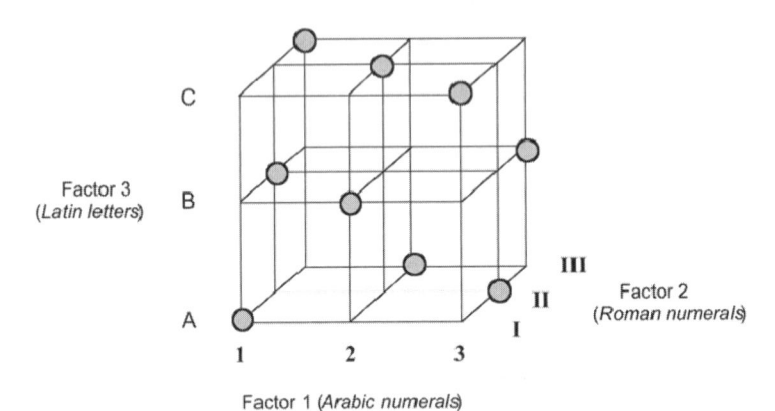

If there are three factors, each with four levels, $4^3=64$ trials are needed to conduct a full design. The corresponding Latin square has 16 trials with the experimental points carefully placed, like our previous example, to avoid row or column repetitions (Figure 12.7).

Figure 12.7 Latin square for studying three four-level factors

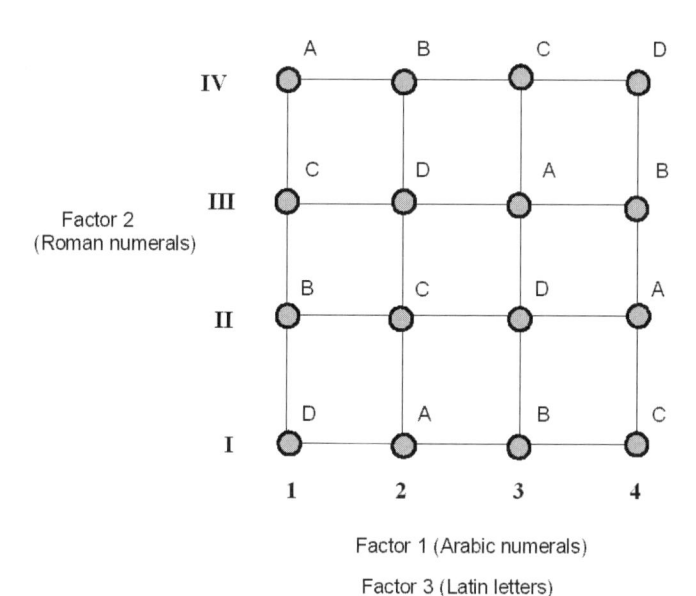

These designs are principally used for categorical variables. The mathematical model is

$$y_{i,j,k} = \overline{y} + a_i + b_j + c_k + e_{i,j,k}$$

12.5 Greco-Latin Squares

Greco-Latin squares are 16-run designs that allow the study of four four-level factors. They are 4^{4-2} designs (Figure 12.8). The locations of the experimental points are dictated by the following rule: Each letter, Greek or Latin, appears once on each line and once on each column without repetition.

Figure 12.8 Greco-Latin square for four four-level factors

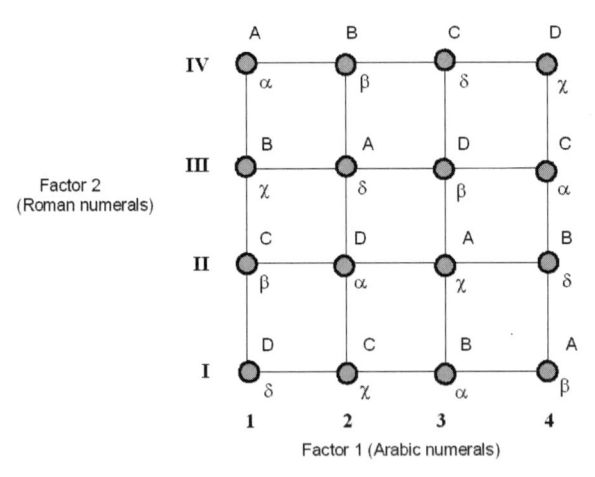

```
Factor 2 (Roman numerals)

IV   A α    B β    C δ    D χ
III  B χ    A δ    D β    C α
II   C β    D α    A χ    B δ
I    D δ    C χ    B α    A β
      1      2      3      4
         Factor 1 (Arabic numerals)

Factor 3 : Latin letters        Factor 4 : Greek letters
```

These designs are principally used for categorical variables and the mathematical model is:

$$y_{i,j,k,l} = \bar{y} + a_i + b_j + c_k + d_l + e_{i,j,k,l}$$

12.6 Youden Squares

W. J. Youden proposed these designs in 1951 for two or more categorical variables that have more than four levels (Figure 12.9).

The principle is the same as for Latin squares. The number of trials is reduced by removing experimental points from a full design. The location of experimental points follows the same rule as the Greco-Latin and Latin Squares.

Chapter 12: Latin Squares and Similar Designs

Figure 12.9 Youden squares for two factors, each with seven levels

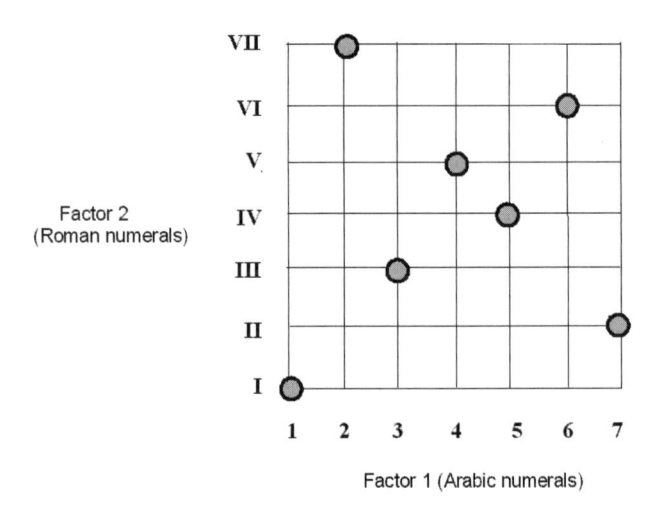

Instead of one trial per level, we can imagine two or more trials (Figure 12.10).

Figure 12.10 Youden square for two factors with two runs for each of the seven levels

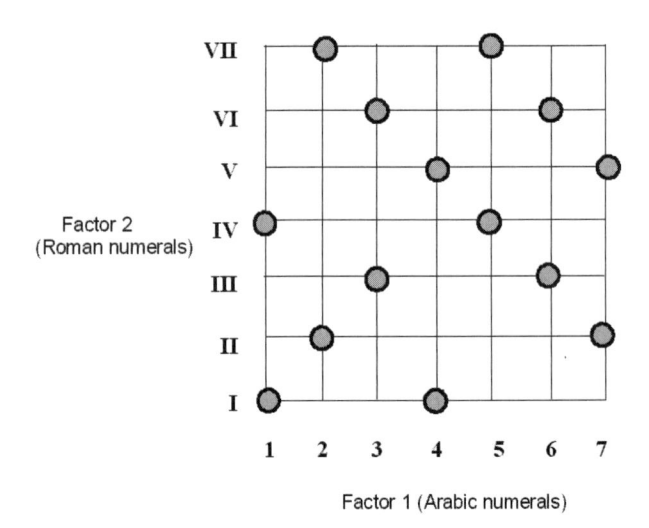

12.7 Example 20: Penetrometry Study

12.7.1 Preparing the Designed Experiment

An experimenter wants to select a method for measuring a gel's consistency. He plunges a stylus into the gel at a specified speed and a depth and measures the resistance opposed by the gel. He studies three kinds of styluses (cylinder, cone, and disk) at three speeds (slow, intermediate, and fast) for three depths (low, intermediate, and high) (Table 12.8).

He runs a 9-run Latin square design instead of the 27-run 3^3 full factorial design. The objective is to find out the shape of the stylus and the operating conditions that maximize the resistance against the motion.

Table 12.8 Factors and study domain

Factor	Low Level	Intermediate Level	High Level
Shape (1)	Cylinder	Cone	Disk
Speed (2)	Slow	Intermediate	Fast
Depth (3)	Low	Intermediate	High

12.7.2 Running the Experiment

Results of the experimental trials are shown in Table 12.9.

Table 12.9 Latin square design experimental matrix

Trial	Shape (1)	Speed (2)	Depth (3)	Resistance
1	−	−	−	17.1
2	−	0	0	20.2
3	−	+	+	27.0
4	0	−	0	8.7
5	0	0	+	10.6
6	0	+	−	7.4
7	+	−	+	62.3
8	+	0	−	70.8
9	+	+	0	86.1
−	Cylinder	Slow	Low	
0	Cone	Intermediate	Intermediate	
+	Disk	Fast	High	

12.7.3 Interpreting the Results

The interpretation is based on the individual effects of the factors (Table 12.10) and on the analysis of variance (ANOVA) (Table 12.11). Shape is the most important factor. Among the three shapes, the highest resistance disk is the best choice.

Table 12.10 Factor effects

Expanded Estimates				
Nominal factors expanded to all levels				
Term	Estimate	Std Error	t Ratio	Prob>|t|
Intercept	34.466667	2.357101	14.62	0.0046*
Shape[Cone]	−25.56667	3.333444	−7.67	0.0166*
Shape[Cylinder]	−13.03333	3.333444	−3.91	0.0596
Shape[Disk]	38.6	3.333444	11.58	0.0074*
Speed[Fast]	5.7	3.333444	1.71	0.2294
Speed[Intermediate]	−0.6	3.333444	−0.18	0.8737
Speed[Slow]	−5.1	3.333444	−1.53	0.2657
Depth[High]	−1.166667	3.333444	−0.35	0.7598
Depth[Intermediate]	3.8666667	3.333444	1.16	0.3658
Depth[Low]	−2.7	3.333444	−0.81	0.5030

This table can be represented in the JMP profiler (Figure 12.11).

Figure 12.11 The highest resistance is obtained by using a disk at a fast speed and an intermediate depth.

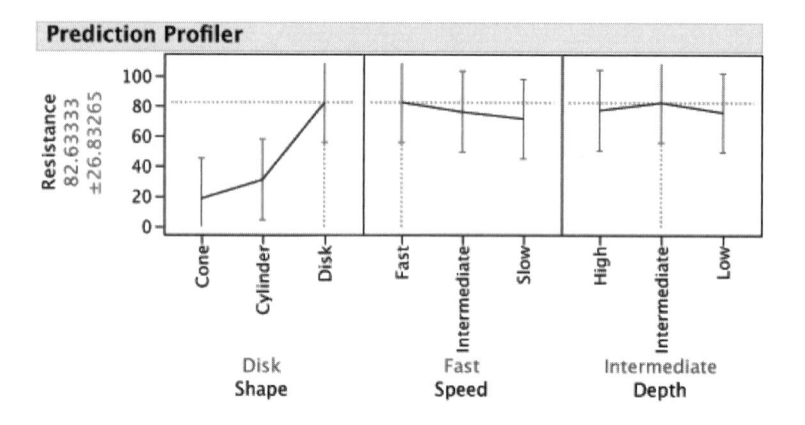

Table 12.11 Analysis of Variance

Source	Nparm	DF	Sum of Squares	F Ratio	Prob > F
Shape	2	2	6940.4467	69.3998	0.0142*
Speed	2	2	176.5800	1.7657	0.3616
Depth	2	2	70.8067	0.7080	0.5855

12.7 Study Conclusion

Shape is the factor that contributes most to the response, with the disk shape giving the greatest resistance to moves of the stylus. The other two factors, Speed and Depth, have only a slight influence on the response. Control runs strengthened this conclusion and showed that a fast rotating disk at intermediate depth gives satisfactory results.

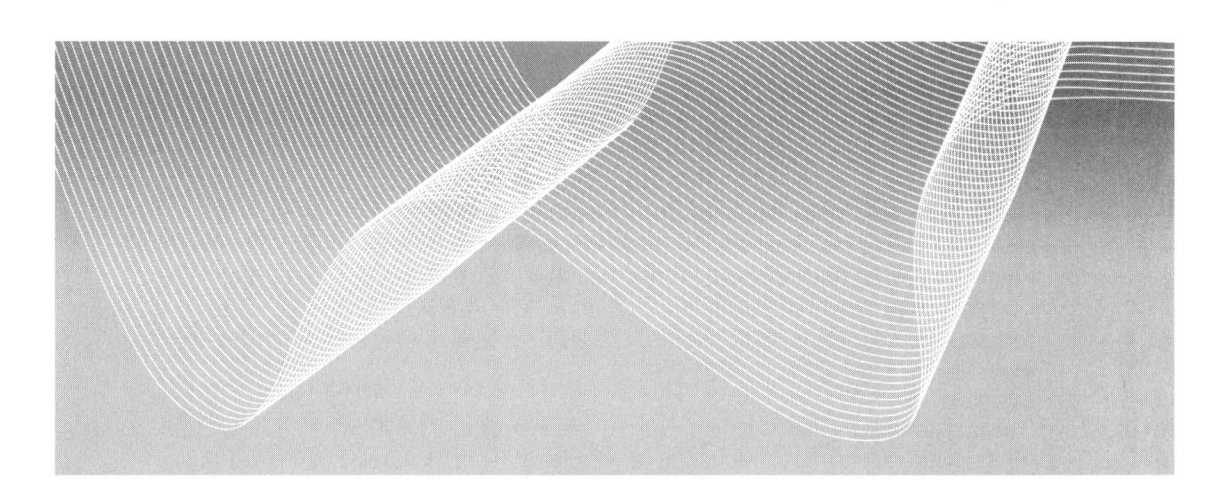

Chapter 13

Summary and Advice

13.1 Introduction   376
13.2 Choosing the Experimental Method   376
    13.2.1 Posing the Problem Well   376
    13.2.2 Preliminary Questions   378
    13.2.3 Choosing a Design   381
13.3 Running the Experiment   382
13.4 Interpreting the Results   382
    13.4.1 Critical Examination   382
    13.4.2 What to Do Next   384
13.5 Progressively Acquiring Knowledge   385
13.6 Recommendations   386
13.7 What Experiments Cannot Do   386

13.1 Introduction

The methodology described in this book, which shows how to carry out research and how to organize tests, brings flexibility, precision, safety, and savings in time and money to any series of experiments. Does this method have only good points, or are there also limitations? That is, what are the method's limits and field of validity? In this final chapter we want to synthesize all that you have learned so far: we examine what designed experimentation can and cannot do. We also take advantage of this discussion to give some advice and show some further activities to continue exploring designed experiments.

The steps used to carry out successful experiments can be shown in a flow chart (Figure 13.1), which we discuss in detail and which contains the three schemes of the overarching experimental method, sometimes called *experimentology*:

- Choosing the experimental method
- Analyzing the results
- Acquiring knowledge progressively

13.2 Choosing the Experimental Method

The choice of method should be made after posing a series of questions that focus the problem, express the problem well, and make sure that no factors are left out. All this should be done before the first trial is carried out.

13.2.1 Posing the Problem Well

This phase of the study should never be omitted. On the contrary, devoting time to it, or calling any specialists who may be helpful, is money well spent. All existing knowledge about the question should be gathered, analyzed, criticized, and evaluated. Frequently, the problem is changed after an in-depth analysis of this review. The most important thing is to start the study under the best possible conditions by integrating all the available information. This speeds up the research and makes correct solutions more likely. Neglecting this phase virtually ensures unpleasant surprises or even major setbacks.

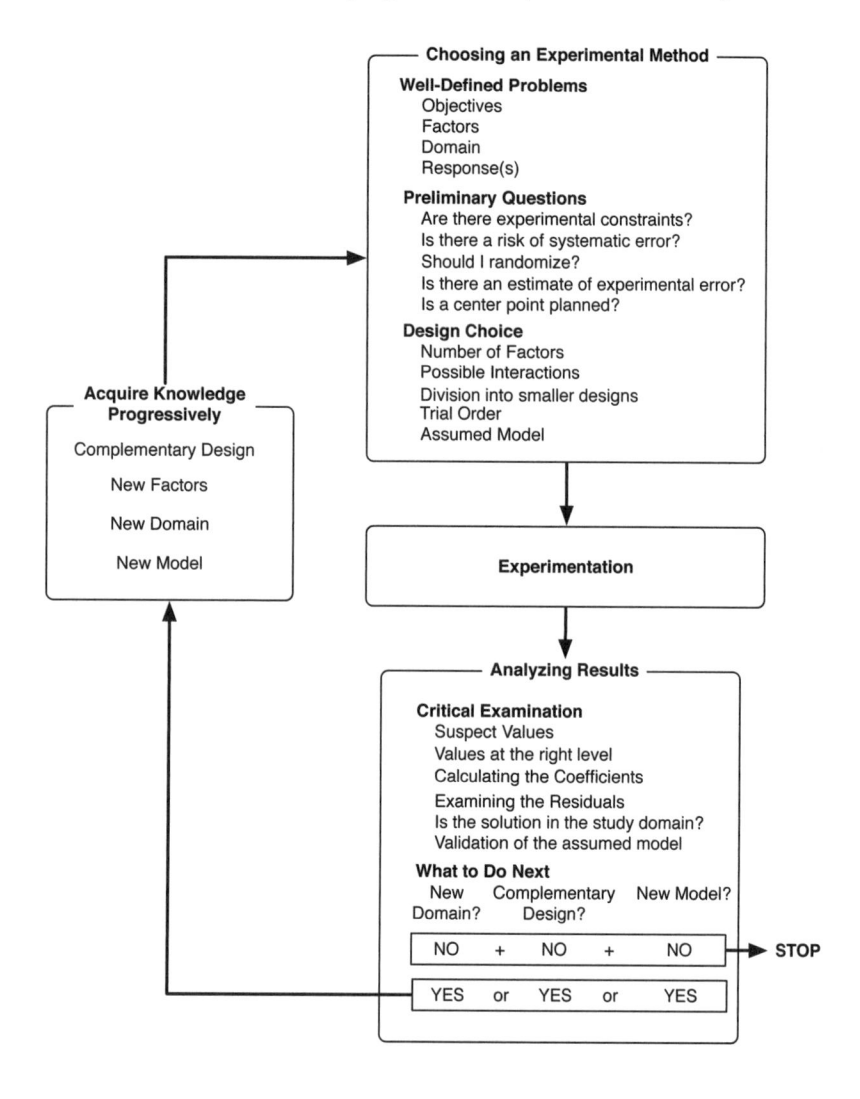

Figure 13.1 Flow chart for carrying out an experimental study

```
                                  ┌─ Choosing an Experimental Method ─┐
                                  │ Well-Defined Problems              │
                                  │    Objectives                      │
                                  │    Factors                         │
                                  │    Domain                          │
                                  │    Response(s)                     │
                                  │ Preliminary Questions              │
                                  │    Are there experimental constraints? │
                                  │    Is there a risk of systematic error? │
                                  │    Should I randomize?             │
                                  │    Is there an estimate of experimental error? │
                                  │    Is a center point planned?      │
        ┌─ Acquire Knowledge ─┐   │ Design Choice                      │
        │   Progressively     │   │    Number of Factors               │
        │                     │   │    Possible Interactions           │
        │ Complementary Design│   │    Division into smaller designs   │
        │                     │   │    Trial Order                     │
        │ New Factors         │   │    Assumed Model                   │
        │                     │   └────────────────────────────────────┘
        │ New Domain          │                  │
        │                     │                  ▼
        │ New Model           │          ┌─ Experimentation ─┐
        └─────────────────────┘          └───────────────────┘
                  ▲                              │
                  │                              ▼
                  │                   ┌─ Analyzing Results ─┐
                  │                   │ Critical Examination │
                  │                   │    Suspect Values    │
                  │                   │    Values at the right level │
                  │                   │    Calculating the Coefficients │
                  │                   │    Examining the Residuals │
                  │                   │    Is the solution in the study domain? │
                  │                   │    Validation of the assumed model │
                  │                   │ What to Do Next      │
                  │                   │   New    Complementary  New Model? │
                  │                   │   Domain?   Design?                │
                  │                   │   NO   +   NO   +   NO   → STOP    │
                  └───────────────────│   YES  or  YES  or  YES            │
                                      └─────────────────────────────────────┘
```

13.2.1.1 Study Objective

It is essential to specify the objectives of the study precisely. Are you conducting a general study to gain knowledge, a study where a precise goal should be achieved, or an optimization study in search of one or several responses? Depending on this objective, different trials or designs are carried out.

You must always define the study objective in a *quantifiable* way. Never say, for example, "to obtain a good yield," but rather "to obtain a yield of at least 80%." At the end of the study, you should be able to say whether the objective has been reached or not. If not, you should be able to say whether the results are close to or far from the goal.

13.2.1.2 Factors

Make a list of any factor that may possibly have influence on the results. This list should be a brainstorming list, where there are "no bad answers." Completeness is the goal. Don't worry about generating a large number of factors, since we have designs like fractional factorials that allow the number of trials to be reduced.

It's necessary to overcome the bad habits of the traditional "one-factor-at-a-time" method. Don't hesitate to study all the factors that might have influence. Give up restrictive hypotheses and dead ends. One method for remembering the various aspects of a study is the mnemonic technique of Ishikawa:

Methods, Machines, Manpower, Milieu, Materials, Measures.

13.2.1.3 Domain

Also, pay attention when assigning levels to the chosen factors. The domain should not be so small that the conclusions lose their generality. Neither should it be too large, because the mathematical models are then likely to be inappropriate. A compromise is hard to find without sufficient knowledge of the phenomenon in question. In these cases, we advise making a preliminary study to direct the choice of the high and low levels of each factor.

13.2.1.4 Responses

The selection of response(s) is vitally important. The whole analysis and therefore all the conclusions depend on this choice. A response that does not reflect the problem's objective makes the experiment unusable and arrives at incorrect conclusions. The selected response must allow an unambiguous answer to the posed question. The choice is not as simple as it seems, and is sometimes the most difficult question of the entire process. For example, we have spent hours of thought and imagination deciding how to measure the sparkle of tonic water or the stress on air traffic controllers.

13.2.2 Preliminary Questions

Before beginning trials, pose a certain number of questions as needed to direct the choice of the initial design and any possible complementary designs or trials. Here is an incomplete (yet hopefully helpful) list of questions to get you started:

Are there any experimental constraints?

If something is difficult to regulate—for example, if a temperature setting takes a long time to reach—trials may need to be carried out in sequential order. Consider an experiment that may start with a series of tests on the low setting (low temperature), followed by a series of tests at the high setting (high temperature). Only one factor can be studied in this way. Or consider the case of a 2^3 design, in which the third column (when the design is in the traditional arrangement) is chosen to study this hard to change factor. With Hadamard matrices, there is always exactly one column that consists of a series of minus signs followed by a series of plus signs (or vice versa). The position of this column depends on the order in which the tests were selected.

Is there a risk of systematic errors?

We have seen the repercussions of systematic errors (Chapter 8) on the evaluation of effects and interactions. It is therefore important to guard against these errors and to minimize their consequences by choosing a suitable order of trials.

If the systematic error is likely to affect the parameter estimates, a blocking model should be used. This is the case, for example, in a design carried out at two time periods separated by a long interval or in a design carried out in two different physical locations. Blocking makes it possible to estimate the effects as if there were no average change between the two levels.

If there is a risk of drift, you must then do one of the following:

- Choose a trial order so that the main effects are not skewed by the error.

- Control the drift by placing measurements at the center point (or another control point) and adjust the responses accordingly. This second solution is more precise, but more expensive in terms of the number of trials.

Should you randomize?

The goal of randomization is to distribute any small systematic errors, allowing experimental error to be treated as if it were composed of only random error. Randomization therefore allows us to apply the usual statistical tests. However, it has the disadvantage of inflating experimental error. The best method is to account for all the constraints and to carry out the arbitrations in three steps:

Step one   Account for experimental constraints by grouping the sequence of low and high levels for one factor. Inside this grouping, the other factors can still be randomized. Any other arrangements allowing us to simplify the experiment are still possible and can be considered by the experimenter.

Step two   Account for systematic errors by dividing the design into blocks.

Step three   Randomize what is left. For example,

- Randomize trials within each block if the design is blocked.
- If there are no experimental constraints and if there is no reason to choose a particular order (drift) or to block, randomize all the trials of the design.

Is there an estimate of experimental error?

It is important to know the value of the experimental error in order to determine if an effect is significant or not. The ideal is to have an estimate of this error based on a large number of measurements. Unfortunately, this is not often the case and we have to make assumptions to get an approximation of this error.

Comparing an effect to its standard deviation is not as simple a task as many textbooks present. Don't forget the many assumptions (frequently unstated) that are needed to make this comparison valid. Indeed, to the assumptions used to calculate and experimental error, it is necessary to add those assumptions used when calculating effects, such as

- The deviations do not depend on the response. This hypothesis is seldom checked.
- The distribution of the deviations is normal. There are tests to check this normality assumption.
- The deviations are not autocorrelated—that is, correlated with themselves. The Durbin-Watson test addresses this assumption.
- There is no systematic error. This assumption is seldom checked.
- The standard deviation is the same throughout the study domain (homoscedasticity). This assumption is seldom verified.
- The variables are independent. It can happen that two variables appear to be independent, but that there is actually a correlation between them. This hidden correlation can be introduced by a commonality in the studied population.
- The postulated mathematical model is only one approximation of the real natural phenomenon.
- The mathematical model associated with factorial designs is additive.

This list is certainly not complete, but it shows how careful you have to be when using this line of reasoning. In the majority of studies, these assumptions are not all respected. Therefore, you have to carefully examine the validity of error calculations and be wary of automatic methods. Decreasing the number of trials often gives useful information, but also requires additional simplifying assumptions. These assumptions can be useful and even essential, but, if forgotten, can cause a blunder or (worse) a catastrophe.

If there is no chance of getting a good estimate of experimental error but there is the possibility of carrying out some additional runs, the best solution is to add some center points (or other point of interest if the center is not available). We can't overemphasize the utility of these measurements.

Can I study all the factors at once?

Sometimes, the list of factors is long and the time and budget do not allow as many trials as we'd like. In this case, start by selecting the factors that are likely to be the most influential. Other possible influential factors are given a fixed level during the experiments. For example, if ten factors seem likely, but only eight tests are available, use a 2^{7-4} design to study seven factors and assign a constant level to the three others during the trials. This reserves the possibility of reintroducing the unstudied variables without losing the first eight tests. They are assigned different levels from their original constant levels, and a new design is made similar to the original. This operation is the reverse of fractionation: start from a 2^k design and add $1, 2, 3,\ldots, p$ additional factors to carry out a 2^{k+p} design.

Is a center point planned?

The domain's central point is special. It is the point where the calculated responses generally have their best precision. It's also the point where the experimental response is equal to the intercept of the model. If you carry out several measurements at the central point, you can also get an idea of the experimental error.

For these reasons, we strongly advise doing measurements at the central point if at all possible (or at another control point if the central point isn't accessible). This is a wise precaution which validates assumptions or gives good direction to future experimentation, a second-degree model in many cases.

13.2.3 Choosing a Design

The design choice is guided by:

- The number of factors
- The interactions that might be significantly different from zero
- Using a full-factorial, a fractional-factorial or a optimal (custom) design depending on the experimental constraints
- The defined order of the trials
- The inclusion of a control point with or without repetition

This design may be cut into sub-designs (blocking, fractional designs) so that the entire budget isn't used up in a single round of research. This approach respects the principle of progressive acquisition of knowledge.

If a factor is not studied in an initial study but might be influential, it should be fixed at a constant level. This sets up any necessary continuation of the study. It's sufficient, as we already said, to give this factor another level in follow-up experiments to generate a design with one (or more) additional factors.

Follow the approach that we implemented in our examples. This gathers all the information (factors, domain, and responses) in an organized way. It also facilitates any follow-up experiments and analysis of the results.

13.3 Running the Experiment

This is of course an important phase of the study since it is the data gathering. Practice the greatest care in carrying out the experiments. The quality of both the work and the recommendations depends on the quality of the collected data. Not even the best designs can make up for poorly executed experiments. In fact, just the opposite is true. Designed experiments are a powerful tool. The more powerful the tool, the more risk in using it.

13.4 Interpreting the Results

Before carrying our any calculations, examine the experimental conditions and the results of the trials before deciding what to do next.

13.4.1 Critical Examination

Are the results coherent? Are there any suspect values?

A single bad data point has repercussions on all the coefficients. It is therefore advisable to ensure the quality of the results before beginning calculations and interpretation. A suspect result can come from a transcription error, a wrongly set dial, a defective measuring apparatus, or other sources.

Were the levels of the factors set at the proper values?

It's entirely possible that a factor's prescribed low (or high) level was respected for some trials and not for others. For example, the high level of a factor may be set at 1.2 rather than 1 during trials 2 and 5. The experiment is not lost, since we need only to enter the observed level into the software so that the results are correct.

When the critical examination of the experiment is finished and when you're sure that all is well, proceed to the calculations and principal statistics like the standard deviation, p-values and R^2. Graphs and deep analysis of the results follows.

Calculating the coefficients

This step is carried out in several steps. Never forget that fractional factorial designs give contrasts, not effects, although the two terms are often used interchangeably. Preliminary calculations and the examination of aliases prevents any hasty conclusions. Analysis is a long and delicate phase during which the experimenter devotes himself to a thorough examination of the results, answering questions like

What are the influential factors?

What are the significant interactions?

Are there confoundings in the calculated contrasts?

Does the mathematical model associated with the design give us information on future work?

Does the comparison of the intercept to the center points validate the linear model?

Is it realistic to assume additive effects?

Does the solution to the problem lie within the experimental domain?

Was there an analysis of the residuals to make sure that all possible information was extracted?

These questions, in addition to those particular to specific studies, lead you to carry out calculations, make graphs, review results, and carry out comparisons. That is, they lead you to make a critical and in-depth examination of the whole experiment. The phenomenon under study may have already delivered most of its secrets, perhaps sufficiently so that the study is finished after a single design. However, additional experiments may be necessary to get enough information to answer the question under scrutiny. Several paths are possible.

13.4.2 What to Do Next

Depending on the conclusions from the first design, you could ask yourself the following questions:

- Should the domain be changed?
- Should I consider a complementary design or complementary trials?
- Should I consider a different mathematical model?

Domain of interest

An extension of the original domain should be considered if initial results show that the desired solution is not inside the original study domain. The initial results should give you a good idea of where the solution lies.

Complementary (augmented) designs and trials

This kind of design is considered when there are main effects aliased with interactions that cannot be neglected. It's also possible to consider a complementary design when the postulated linear model does not do a good job in explaining the results of the design. We then consider a second-degree model.

Is the postulated model valid?

If there are very strong interactions, or if the intercept of the model differs from the response measured at the center, the mathematical model (linear in most initial experiments) is not valid. This leads us to a second-degree model. Alternatively, we can build an optimal design adapted to the mathematical model that best represents the studied phenomena.

Ending the experimental cycle

Depending on the answers to the previous questions, the experimenter will be able either to stop the trials (when there is enough information to make recommendations about the study questions) or to use this study to progressively acquire knowledge.

In the chart from Figure 13.1:

- Three NOs are needed to stop.
- If there is a single YES, the loop is repeated. Of course, each loop can be repeated several times.

13.5 Progressively Acquiring Knowledge

If additional information is needed, we have several tools and methods that can be used. The analysis of the initial results defines the strategy for new experimentation.

- Complementary designs or trials
  These trials are necessary to de-alias the main effects from certain interactions. They are also necessary to move from a linear model to a second-degree model (star points). It is also necessary to plan additional trials to extend the study domain.

- New factors
  If you have taken the precaution to keep factors "on hold," at a fixed level, then use these factors in a new design by assigning them new levels.

- Optimization
  The study domain may be appropriate, but the fitted model may be insufficient to answer the question under scrutiny. In this case, enrich the original design with new trials. The sites of the new experimental points in the domain must be carefully selected.

The great flexibility of experimental design allows us (without the loss of any trials)

- to enrich existing results with new trials. The designs or the complementary tests refine information from the initial designs.

- to add new factors that are kept at a constant level throughout the original design.

The preceding remarks may lead you to think that it is better to start with a design having few trials. That makes it possible to quickly obtain invaluable information for the continuation of the study. Then, we carry out the directed experimentation: complementary trials or additional factors based on initial results. The principle of progressive acquisition of knowledge is the source of these remarks. It fits in well with the first two parts of the experimental method: choosing the experimental method and analyzing the results.

13.6 Recommendations

The experimenter is solely responsible for conclusions and recommendations. Take all possible precautions to be sure of any conclusions. The adjustment of the factors to obtain or approach the aims of the study as well as possible is initially determined by simple calculation. It is therefore a subject of caution. We must remove doubt and carry out control experiments. These validation trials are indispensable and are part of the best practices of designed experiments.

13.7 What Experiments Cannot Do

A designed experiment is a methodical way to conduct a series of trials by optimizing the means at the disposal of the researcher: time and money. But this method is not a substitute for actual experiments, and especially cannot replace human intelligence and ingenuity. It is the experimenter that has to

Define the objective
It is essential to precisely quantify the objective of the study.

Pose the problem well
A poorly posed problem cannot be saved by a designed experiment.

Be imaginative and creative
Conducting a designed experiment is not only a technique. It helps with the interpretation of the results, but it is the experimenter who is responsible for the hypotheses and conclusions.

Choose the factors
If the experimenter forgets an important factor in the study, it is he who is responsible for anomalies and erroneous conclusions.

Define limits on the study domain
This is one of the big difficulties encountered by the experimenter. If the domain is too small, the hoped-for responses may not be inside the domain, which means additional trials. If the domain is too large, the postulated model will not serve well in interpretation of the results.

Carefully conduct the experiments
Badly conceived experiments, uncontrolled factors, vague measurements, errors in notation, location, or transcription cannot be repaired by an experimental design. On the

contrary: they require a great deal of care in the experiments themselves to pull out all the information.

Choose the responses

This is an equally vital point for the quality of interpretation. All responses are not equal. Some are not precise enough; others do not provide effects that are sufficiently clear-cut to draw conclusions from. Finally, it's necessary that the chosen responses allow us to answer the question of the study.

In summary, the designed experiment is a useful and strong technique, but both control of the experiment and the responsibility for the conclusions drawn remains firmly in the hands of the experimenter.

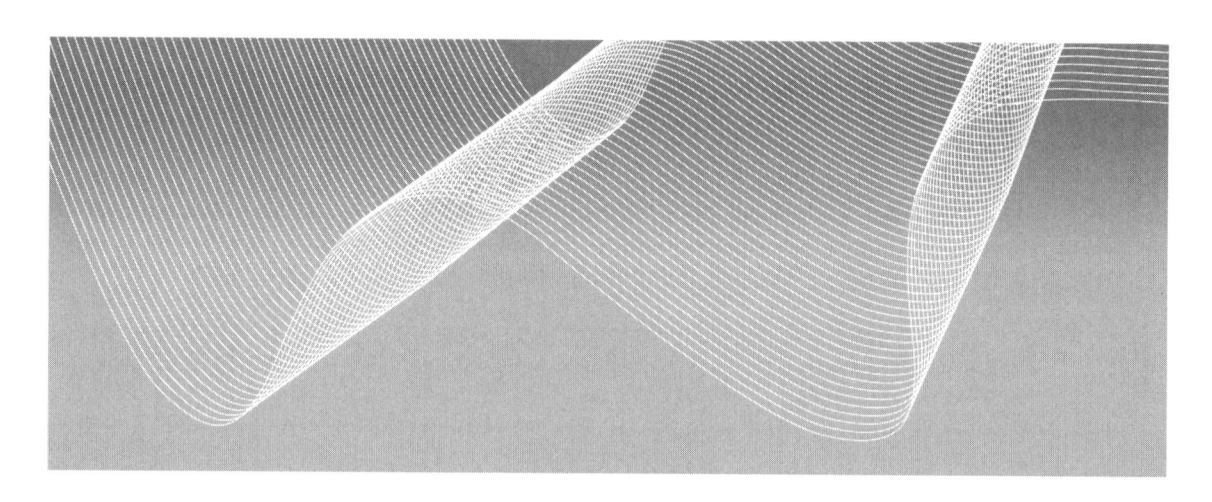

Chapter 14

Using JMP to Design Experiments

14.1 Introduction 390
14.2 Designing an Experiment 390
    14.2.1 Screening Designer (Classical Designs Only) 391
    14.2.2 Custom Designer (Classical and Other Optimal Designs) 393
14.3 The JMP Data Table 396
14.4 Choosing and Fitting a Model 398
    14.4.1 The Screening Designer 401
14.5 Examining and Analyzing Results 402
14.6 Principal Graphics and Analysis Reports 404
14.7 Transferring and Saving Analysis Results 406

14.1 Introduction

JMP is a statistical software package from SAS that is particularly well adapted for the construction and analysis of designed experiments. It is designed for desktop computers, with Windows, Macintosh, and Linux versions available. It is point-and-click software that has a complete set of tools for the design, exploration, and analysis of experimental data. This chapter is a short introduction to JMP. Here are resources for more information.

- Follow the directions on the inside cover of this book to download the sample code and data sets from the companion Web site for this book at support.sas.com/goupycreighton.
- If you did not install the JMP documentation (in PDF format) when you installed JMP, go to the JMP Web site at www.jmp.com/support/books.shtml, where you can download PDF versions of the JMP manuals. In particular, the *Design of Experiments* and *Statistics and Graphics Guide* give many details on the resources and use of JMP. The *Introductory Guide* from the same site provides 10 hands-on lessons on the use of JMP that are useful for the beginner.

This chapter describes the key actions that you can do with JMP: construct a designed experiment, fit a mathematical model, interpret the experimental results, and save JMP results for use in other software such as presentation and document preparation.

14.2 Designing an Experiment

In many real-world situations, custom designs are the most appropriate tool. The JMP Custom Designer generates an optimal design adapted to your problem and to your means, as described in Chapter 7. However, in many other situations, classical designs (like the majority of those described in this book) are sufficient. In these cases, other means of construction may be used (the JMP Screening Designer, Full Factorial Designer, or Response Surface Designer). We are going to see how to construct a design using both the Screening Designer and the Custom Designer. We use Example 1, "Control Your Car's Gas Consumption," which has gas consumption as the response, and speed and additional weight as the factors.

14.2.1 Screening Designer (Classical Designs Only)

1. Enter the responses.

    Select **DOE → Screening Design**. When the dialog box appears, double-click the name of the response and enter **Gas Consumption**.

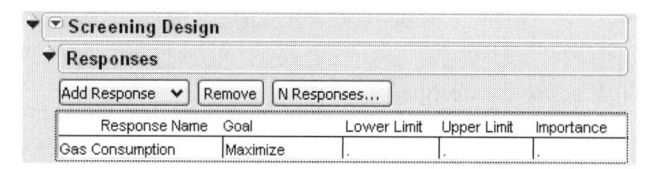

2. Enter the factors.

    In the **Factors** list, enter the number 2 in the **Continuous** box and click **Add** to add two factors.

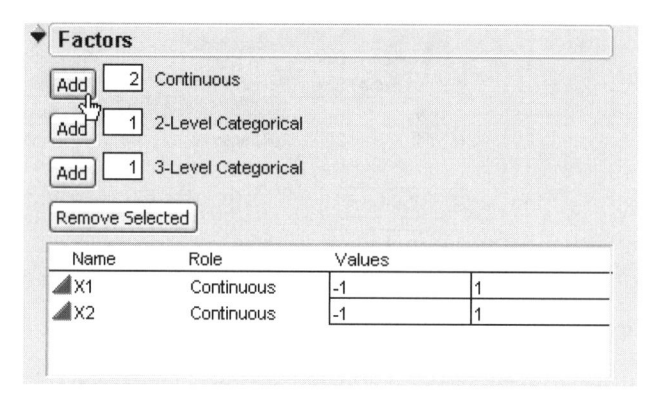

3. Change the factor names.

    Change **X1** to **Speed**. Use the Tab key to move from one editable field to the next. Enter the low level (45) and the high level (70) for **Speed**. Repeat these operations for **Additional Weight** (with levels 0 and 300). Click **Continue** to move to the next section.

Name	Role	Values	
Speed	Continuous	45	70
Additional Weight	Continuous	0	300

Screening Design
Specify Factors
Add a Continuous or Categorical factor by clicking its button. Double click on a factor name or level to edit it.
[Continue]

4. Choose the design.

   JMP proposes several classical designs, from which you can choose the one that you find most appropriate. In addition, you have the option of choosing a plan divided into blocks. For this example, choose the first plan in the list. It has four trials and no blocks. Then, click **Continue**.

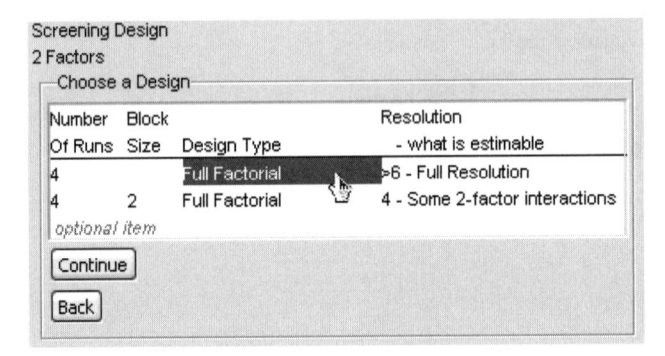

   Screening Design
   2 Factors
   Choose a Design

Number Of Runs	Block Size	Design Type	Resolution - what is estimable
4		Full Factorial	6 - Full Resolution
4	2	Full Factorial	4 - Some 2-factor interactions

   optional item
   [Continue]
   [Back]

5. Choose the aliasing and the order of the factors.

   You now see the control panel that lets you modify your design. For example, to change the aliasing structure, open the list **Aliasing of Effects** and use the check boxes to define your own aliasing.

   You can now select the order of the trials. **Randomize** is the default, but here select **Sort Right to Left** to get Yates order.

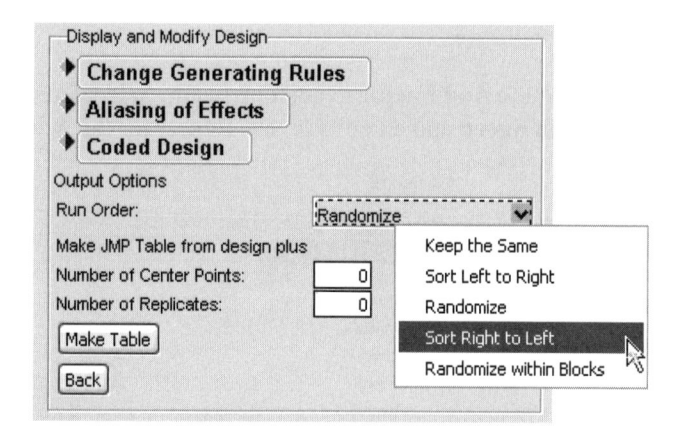

6. Construct the design.

   Click **Make Table** to generate the design as a data table. The factors are the columns and the trials are the rows. The column of responses will be filled in after the experiment is run, and the experiment will be analyzed.

14.2.2 Custom Designer (Classical and Other Optimal Designs)

1. Enter the response.

   Select **DOE → Custom Design**. When the dialog box appears, double-click the name of the response and enter **Gas Consumption**.

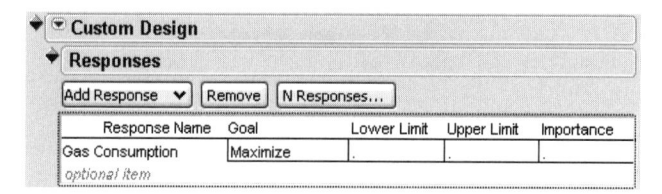

2. Enter the factors.

   Then, click **Add Factor** to add one factor. Select **Continuous**. Change the factor name to **Speed** and enter its levels. Repeat for the **Additional Weight** factor.

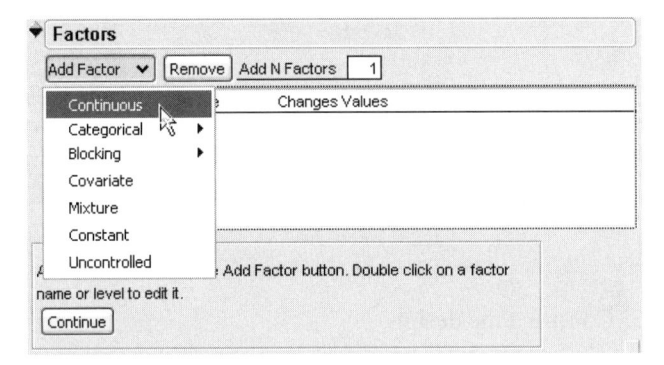

3. Enter the interactions.

   Next, specify the model. JMP automatically enters in all main effects.

   To enter an interaction, highlight the first factor of the interaction in the **Factors** list, the second in the **Models** list, and click **Cross**. To list all the interactions of a certain order involving one factor, select the factor, then click **Interactions** and select the order from the resulting menu. If you select an Interactions order but select no names, all interactions of that order, involving all factors, are entered.

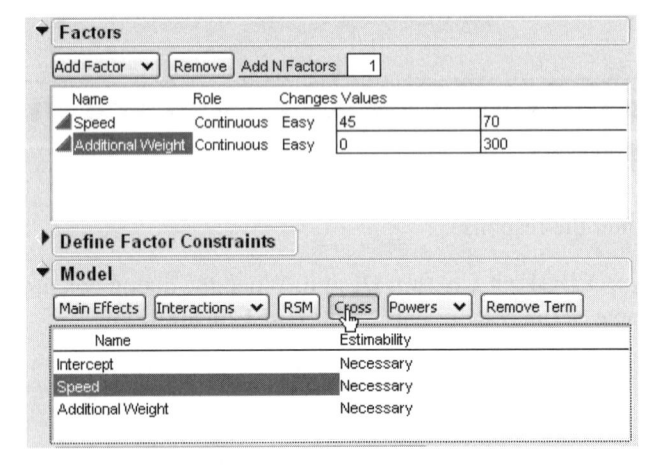

4. Choose the number of trials.

   Now that you have specified the model, JMP asks you to choose the number of trials. Select the appropriate one using the dialog box, or enter your own in the **Number of Runs** edit field. Here, we need four runs, so click **Minimum**. Click **Make Design** to generate the design.

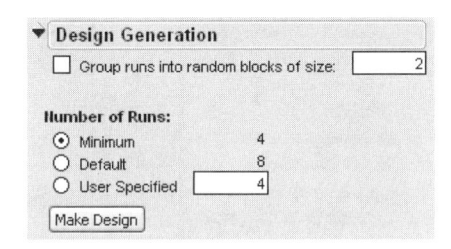

5. Examine and set the design's run order.

   You now see the design and four closed outlines that contain information about the design. Two of these, **Prediction Variance Profile** and **Relative Variance of Coefficients**, are shown here.

   You now select the order for the runs to appear. Randomize is the default choice, but change this to **Sort Right to Left** to obtain the Yates order. Click **Make Table** to generate the design.

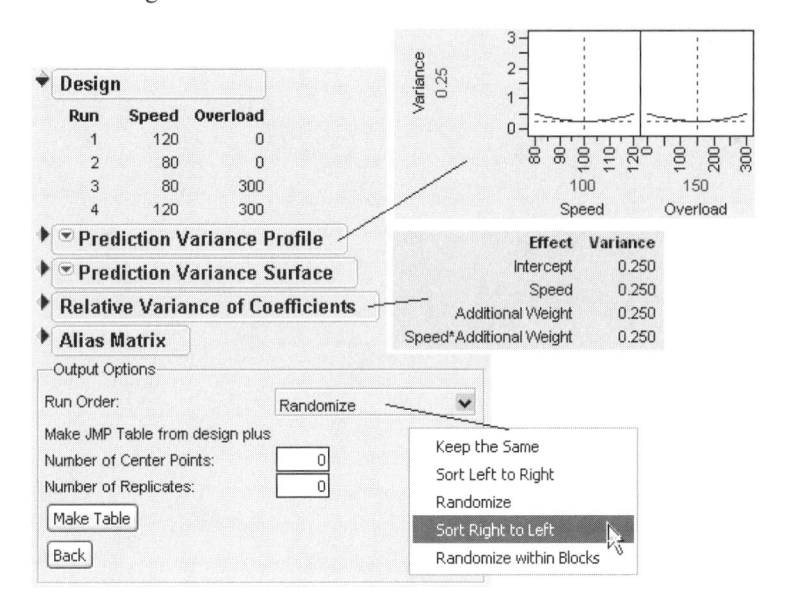

6. Review the design.

   The design appears as a data table. The factors are the columns, and the rows are the trials. The column of responses is filled in after the experiment is run, and the experiment will be analyzed.

	Speed	Additional Weight	Gas Consumption
1	45	0	·
2	70	0	·
3	45	300	·
4	70	300	·

14.3 The JMP Data Table

When you click **Make Table**, JMP generates a data table (Figure 14.1). It is divided into two parts: On the left, there is an information zone, and on the right, the data table itself.

Figure 14.1 Example JMP data table

[Annotated screenshot of a JMP data table with the following elements labeled: "Deselection Zone" pointing to the top area; "Factor Names" pointing to the column headers (popcorn, oil amt, batch, yield, trial); "Nominal Variables" pointing to popcorn, oil amt, batch; "Continuous Variables" pointing to yield; "Ordinal Variables" pointing to trial; "Trial Number" pointing to the row numbers.]

The information zone includes:
- Popcorn
- Notes Artificial data ins[...]
- Fit Model
- Columns (5/0): popcorn, oil amt, batch, yield, trial
- Rows: All rows 16, Selected 0, Excluded 0, Hidden 0, Labelled 0

	popcorn	oil amt	batch	yield	trial
1	plain	little	large	8.2	1
2	gourmet	little	large	8.6	1
3	plain	lots	large	10.4	1
4	gourmet	lots	large	9.2	1
5	plain	little	small	9.9	1
6	gourmet	little	small	12.1	1
7	plain	lots	small	10.6	1
8	gourmet	lots	small	18.0	1
9	plain	little	large	8.8	2
10	gourmet	little	large	8.2	2
11	plain	lots	large	8.8	2
12	gourmet	lots	large	9.8	2
13	plain	little	small	10.1	2
14	gourmet	little	small	15.9	2
15	plain	lots	small	7.4	2
16	gourmet	lots	small	16.0	2

The information zone

The information zone is divided into several sections.

- The top section, called ***Tables***, shows the name of the data file (***Popcorn*** in this example), one or more scripts (here, a script entitled **Fit Model**), and other information about the table (here, Notes that discuss the data's origin).

- The second section, called **Columns**, shows a list of the table's columns and identifies the modeling type of each variable. **Designating the correct modeling type is important, since JMP uses this information in producing its graphs and reports.** To change the modeling type, click the icon in the **Columns** section beside the variable and select the appropriate type from the menu that appears. There are three options for modeling type: continuous (a continuous variable is designated by a blue triangle icon), ordinal (a discrete yet orderable variable, designated by a green set of increasing stair steps), and nominal (an unordered discrete variable, designated by a red set of discrete unordered steps). Graphs and statistics appropriate for continuous variables are only shown when the modeling type is set to continuous. Similarly, statistics appropriate for ordinal and nominal variables only appear when the corresponding modeling type is chosen.

- The next section, called ***Rows***, shows information about the rows in the table. It is important to remember, especially when entering data by hand, that each row in the table represents one experimental run.

The data grid

This is the design itself, represented in spreadsheet form. The factors are laid out in columns, and the experimental trials are laid out in rows.

Rows and columns can be selected with the mouse. To deselect rows or columns, click in the deselection zone, to the left of the column names (Figure 14.1). Click above the diagonal to clear column selection, or below the diagonal line to clear the row selection.

14.4 Choosing and Fitting a Model

If you construct your design by hand, or if you want to keep total control over your analysis, you must fill out the Fit Model dialog box yourself (Figure 14.2).

Figure 14.2 Fit Model dialog box

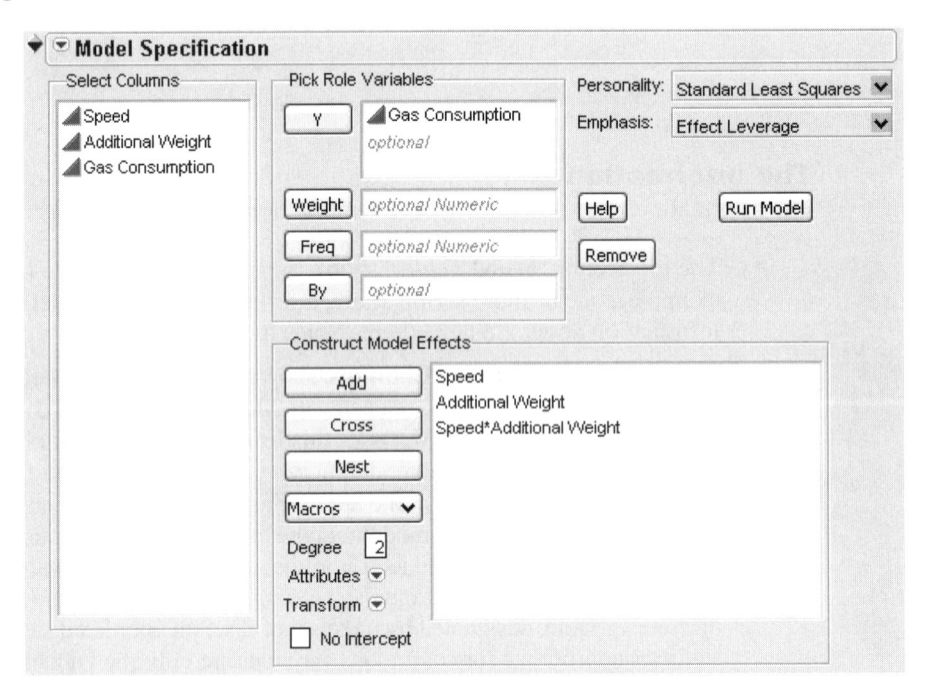

1. Select the response(s) in the **Select Columns** list and click **Y** to move the variable into the **Pick Role Variables** list. You could also use drag-and-drop, dragging the variable(s) to their appropriate destinations on the dialog box.

2. Select the factor(s) in the **Select Columns** list and click **Add** to move the variable into the **Construct Model Effects** list.

3. If you want to add interactions to the model, select the variables involved in the interaction in the **Select Columns** list and click **Cross**. To select several variables at once, hold down the CTRL key (Windows and Linux) or the ⌘ key (Macintosh) while clicking on the variable name.

Figure 14.3 Fit Model dialog box: variable selection

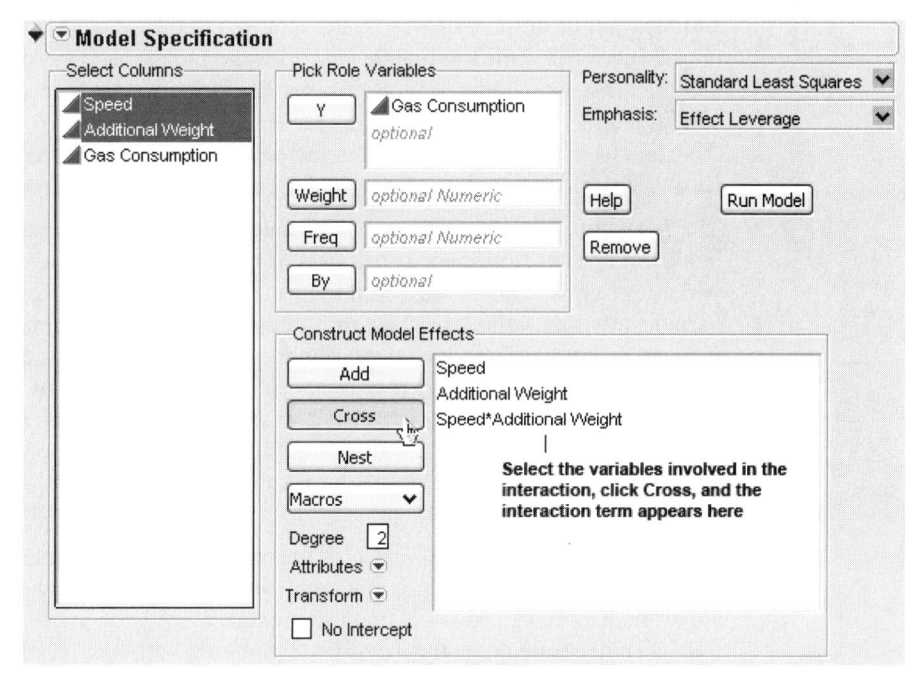

4. After adding the factors and the responses, defining the model, and choosing the statistical analysis, click **Run Model** to launch the statistical analysis calculations.

There are a few things to note about using the Fit Model dialog box.

- To remove a variable from its current role, double-click the variable. Alternatively, select the variable and click **Remove** or simply drag the variable back to the **Select Columns** list.

- Unlike most dialog boxes in JMP, the Fit Model dialog box does not disappear when you click **Run Model**. This is so that you can look at several models successively, using the results of one model to guide your analysis of the next. For example, you may note that a full-factorial model has interaction terms that are insignificant. Data analysts commonly remove these interaction terms from the model and re-run it. Use one of the previously mentioned techniques to remove the interaction; click **Run Model** and you quickly generate a new analysis.

- Certain models are frequently used. For example, you may have three variables A, B, and C, and you want to examine a full-factorial analysis of these variables. Entering all the effects would be tedious, involving many column selections and many button clicks. To simplify these common tasks, the Fit Model dialog box has a **Macros** list that lists these common combinations. For example, to enter a full factorial of three variables, select all three in the **Select Columns** list and click **Macros → Full Factorial**. This adds the factors, all two-way interactions, and the three-way interaction. Similarly, **Factorial To Degree** adds all factors and all interactions up to the value specified in the **Degree** box (located below the **Macros** list). By default (and in the picture on the previous page), the degree is two. Therefore, all main effects and second order interactions are added.

- The **Attributes** list allows you to designate the purpose of some variables. In this book, we discuss two special attributes of variables: those that are **Mixture** variables (whose values must sum to one) and those that are **Response Surface** variables (whose values are used in finding maxima and minima of the response). See the JMP documentation for a more complete discussion of these attributes. The simplest way to use them is through the **Macros** list. If you have variables that need to be analyzed as a response surface model, select them and then select **Response Surface** from the **Macros** menu. All appropriate attributes, interactions, and power terms are automatically added. This is also true for mixture designs.

- By default, JMP centers all variables that are involved in interaction or power terms. This results in p-values that are more interpretable. However, some experimenters have protocols that use the uncentered version of these crossed terms. To generate an analysis with non-centered variables, click the red triangle in the upper left corner of the dialog box (to the right of **Model Selection**) and clear **Center Polynomials**. To tell JMP to *never* center variables, you must change a global preference. For Windows and Linux, select **File → Preference**. On the Macintosh, select **JMP → Preferences**. Regardless of the operating system, continue by selecting **Preferences → Platforms → Model Dialog**, and among those options, clear **Center Polynomials [default on]**.

- In the upper right of the Fit Model dialog box, there are two drop-down lists for **Personality** and **Emphasis**. If you get an unexpected report when you click **Run Model**, review the settings of these drop-down lists.

- The selected **Personality** tells JMP what type of analysis to run. There are default selections that appear, based on the modeling type of the response variables. In this book, all response variables are continuous and therefore result in the **Standard Least Squares** personality. Other options, such as **Stepwise** or **Manova**, are also appropriate for continuous responses, and can be chosen with this drop-down list. **Nominal Logistic** and **Ordinal Logistic** are the default choices for other response modeling types, but are not discussed here.

- The selected **Emphasis** tells JMP which analysis displays to show. The choice of emphasis does not affect the calculations, but instead pre-selects some output that is likely to be helpful in the three given situations. **Effect Leverage** gives plots and reports appropriate for examining model coefficients and how each factor influences the model. **Effect Screening** is more appropriate for designs with large numbers of factors, where the interest lies in discovering which factors are active. **Minimal Report** is used when only numerical output (no graphs) is needed. In any case, all of the JMP output options are available (but perhaps hidden), regardless of which personality is selected.

14.4.1 The Screening Designer

JMP has a special modeling platform for screening designs. To use it, select **Analyze → Modeling → Screening** and specify responses and effects. Unlike the Fit Model platform, the screening platform automatically adds interactions and crossed effects as long as there are enough observations to estimate them.

Figure 14.4 Screening platform launch dialog box

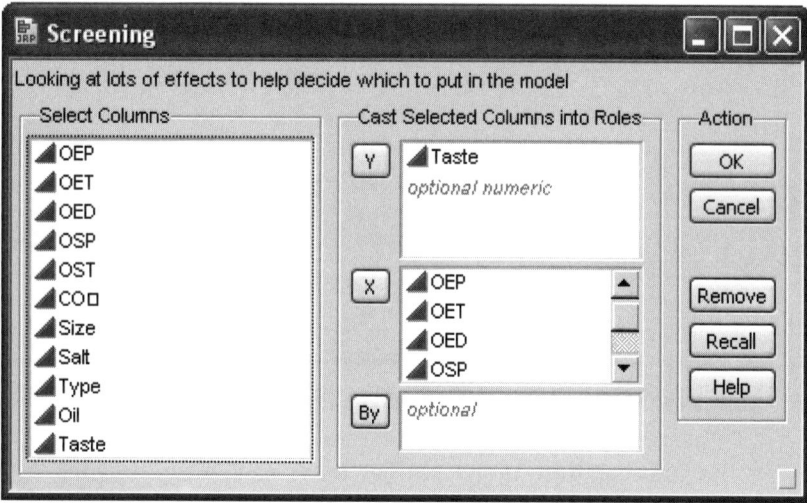

The Screening report shows a list of coefficients with their contrasts and *p*-values. Significant terms (with a *p*-value less than 0.1) are highlighted. Below the text report is a half-normal plot, as well as buttons that let you make or run the model in the Fit Model platform. See Section 14.5, "Examining and Analyzing Results," for an explanation of these items.

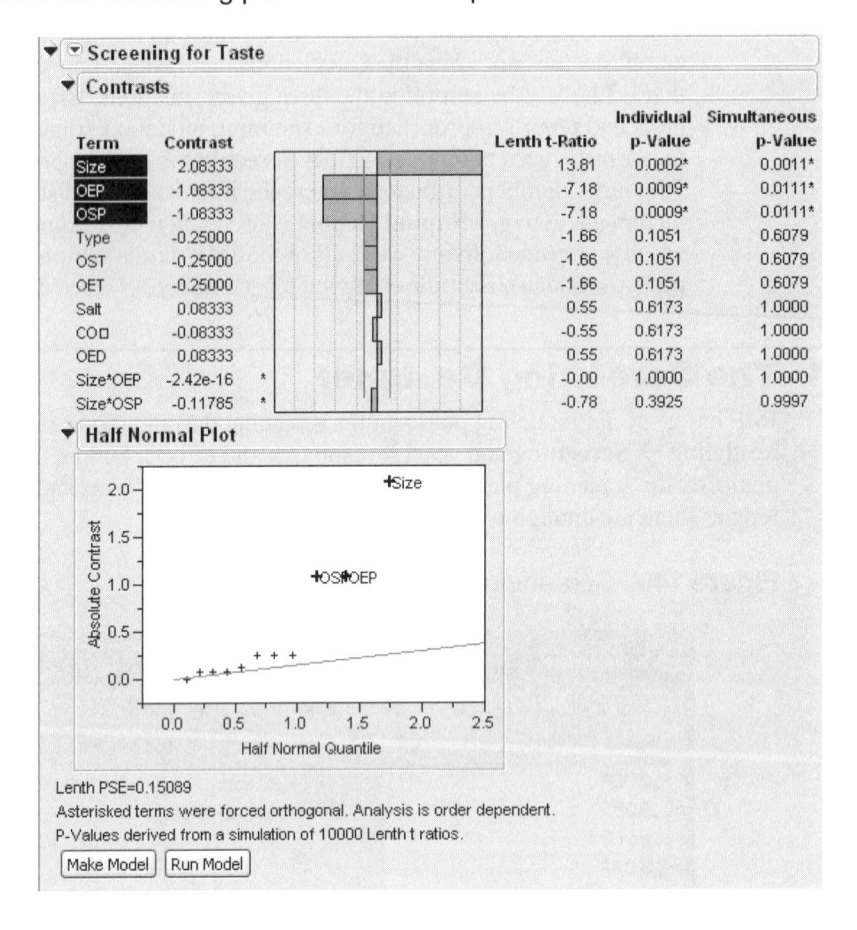

Figure 14.5 Screening platform results report

Term	Contrast		Lenth t-Ratio	Individual p-Value	Simultaneous p-Value
Size	2.08333		13.81	0.0002*	0.0011*
OEP	-1.08333		-7.18	0.0009*	0.0111*
OSP	-1.08333		-7.18	0.0009*	0.0111*
Type	-0.25000		-1.66	0.1051	0.6079
OST	-0.25000		-1.66	0.1051	0.6079
OET	-0.25000		-1.66	0.1051	0.6079
Salt	0.08333		0.55	0.6173	1.0000
COD	-0.08333		-0.55	0.6173	1.0000
OED	0.08333		0.55	0.6173	1.0000
Size*OEP	-2.42e-16	*	-0.00	1.0000	1.0000
Size*OSP	-0.11785	*	-0.78	0.3925	0.9997

Lenth PSE=0.15089
Asterisked terms were forced orthogonal. Analysis is order dependent.
P-Values derived from a simulation of 10000 Lenth t ratios.

14.5 Examining and Analyzing Results

After you click **Run Model**, JMP produces a report showing the results of the analysis. Some of the textual output is shown here (Figure 14.6).

Some important areas to examine are the **Analysis of Variance** outline node, which shows the overall *F*-value and the associated *p*-value (denoted as **Prob → F**) for the entire model. A small *p*-value indicates a model with at least one significant effect. The **Parameter Estimates** area shows the coefficients of the model terms. **Effect Tests** shows an *F*-value and a *p*-value for each effect in the model.

To the left of the **Response Y** title, there is a small blue triangle that allows opening and closing of the outline node.

Figure 14.6 Example statistical analysis

Response Y

Summary of Fit

RSquare	0.98288
RSquare Adj	0.97004
Root Mean Square Error	1.927884
Mean of Response	20.85875
Observations (or Sum Wgts)	8

Analysis of Variance

Source	DF	Sum of Squares	Mean Square	F Ratio
Model	3	853.53954	284.513	76.5492
Error	4	14.86695	3.717	Prob > F
C. Total	7	868.40649		0.0005*

Parameter Estimates

Term	Estimate	Std Error	t Ratio	Prob>|t|
Intercept	20.85875	0.68161	30.60	<.0001*
X1	-7.52625	0.68161	-11.04	0.0004*
X2	6.86375	0.68161	10.07	0.0005*
X1*X2	1.71375	0.68161	2.51	0.0658

Effect Tests

Source	Nparm	DF	Sum of Squares	F Ratio	Prob > F
X1	1	1	453.15551	121.9229	0.0004*
X2	1	1	376.88851	101.4030	0.0005*
X1*X2	1	1	23.49551	6.3215	0.0658

In addition to the blue icons, note the red icon to the left of **Response Y** at the top of the report. These red triangle icons are vital for using JMP, since they show where you can click to get more analysis graphs and options. Among many other things, this is the place to turn on reports for each effect, to get a graphical report of parameter estimates, or to see reports on the correlation of estimates, and so on.

14.6 Principal Graphics and Analysis Reports

For designed experiments, the most important information is found in the **Effect Screening** and the **Factor Profiling** menus. Pay particular attention to the following:

- The Normal Plot (Figure 14.7), also known as the Daniel plot, shows the most significant effects.

Figure 14.7 The Normal Plot and drop-down menus associated with the analysis red triangle

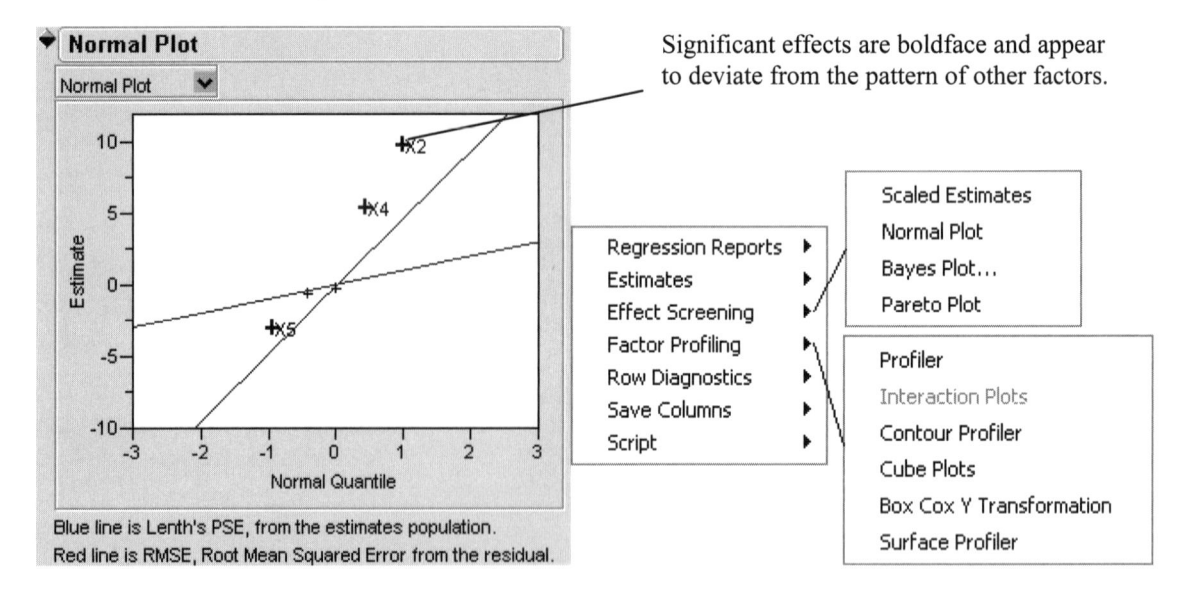

- The Half Normal Plot, which uses absolute values instead of algebraic values, is also available by changing the **Normal Plot** drop-down list to **Half-Normal Plot**. In addition, the half-normal plot appears in the JMP screening platform.

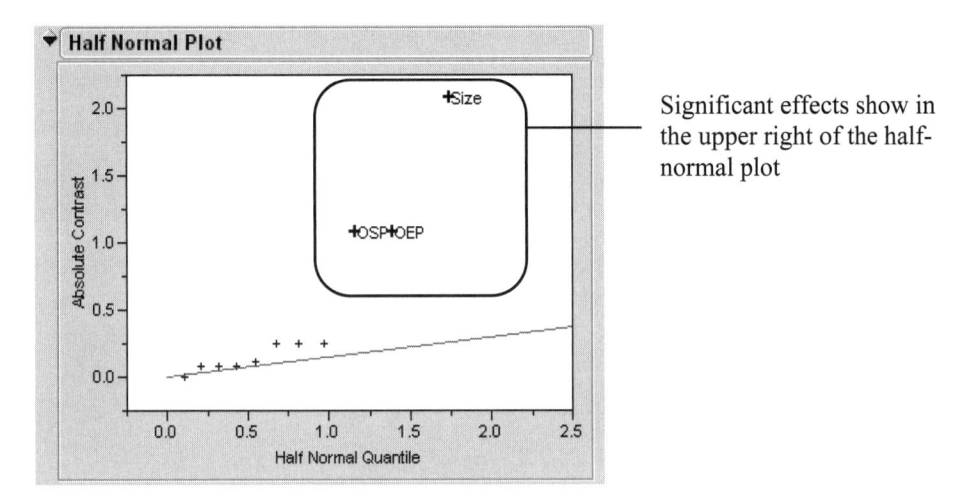

Figure 14.8 The Half-Normal Plot

Significant effects show in the upper right of the half-normal plot

- The Prediction Profiler is an interactive graphic that allows you to see the influence of variations of the levels of the factors on the responses (Figure 14.9). Click or drag the red vertical lines to see how changes of the factor levels modify the response.
- The red triangle to the left of the Prediction Profiler outline node lists the desirability functions. You use these functions to optimize several responses with the **Maximize Desirability** command. See Chapter 4.

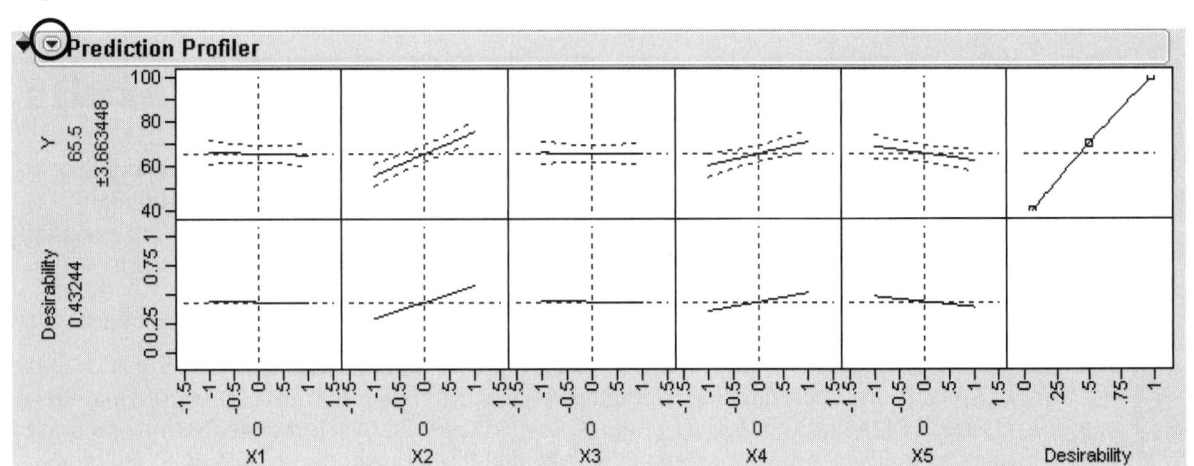

Figure 14.9 The Prediction Profiler

- The Contour Profiler command brings up an interactive graph that lets you study isoresponse curves (level curves) of a response surface (Figure 14.10). Also available is the Surface Profiler, a graph that lets you study the response surface in three dimensions.

Figure 14.10 The Contour Profiler (left) and the Surface Profiler (right)

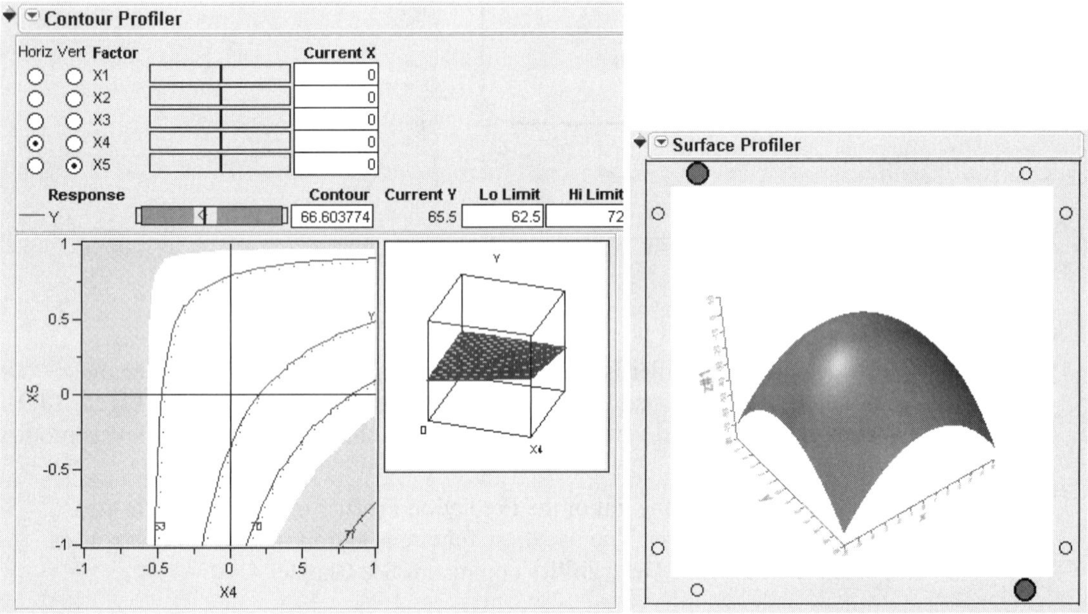

14.7 Transferring and Saving Analysis Results

After you complete an analysis, it is often necessary to transfer JMP tables and graphs to another application, such as a word processor or presentation software. Additionally, results may need to be posted on a Web site for widespread viewing. There are essentially two ways of transferring these results.

First, you can cut and paste any part of a JMP report into another application by using the *selection tool* (⊕ or ⊕). After clicking this tool, which is found on the toolbar or in the **Tools** menu, click and drag over the parts of a JMP report that are of interest. Hold down the CTRL key (PC or Linux) or the ⌘ key (Macintosh) to select more than one section of a report. Then, use your computer's Copy and Paste functions (commonly found on the

Edit menu) to move the sections to the other application. In general, text should be transferred as text and pictures should be transferred as pictures.

If you want to place an analysis report on a Web server or convert it to HTML format, follow these steps:

1. Select **Edit → Journal**. This action copies the report into the JMP journal facility. Journals are commonly used to concatenate several disparate reports into a single window. In our case, they are a necessary step toward saving the report in another format.

2. With the journal as the front-most window, select **File → Save As** or **File → Export** (Macintosh). You are then presented with a standard saving window that lets you select what format the report should be saved in (Figure 14.11). Use RTF if you plan to continue to edit the report in an editor. Choose HTML to generate a browser-readable page with graphics stored in a separate folder.

Figure 14.11 Save Journal As window

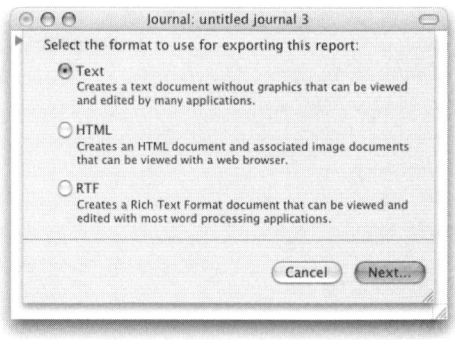

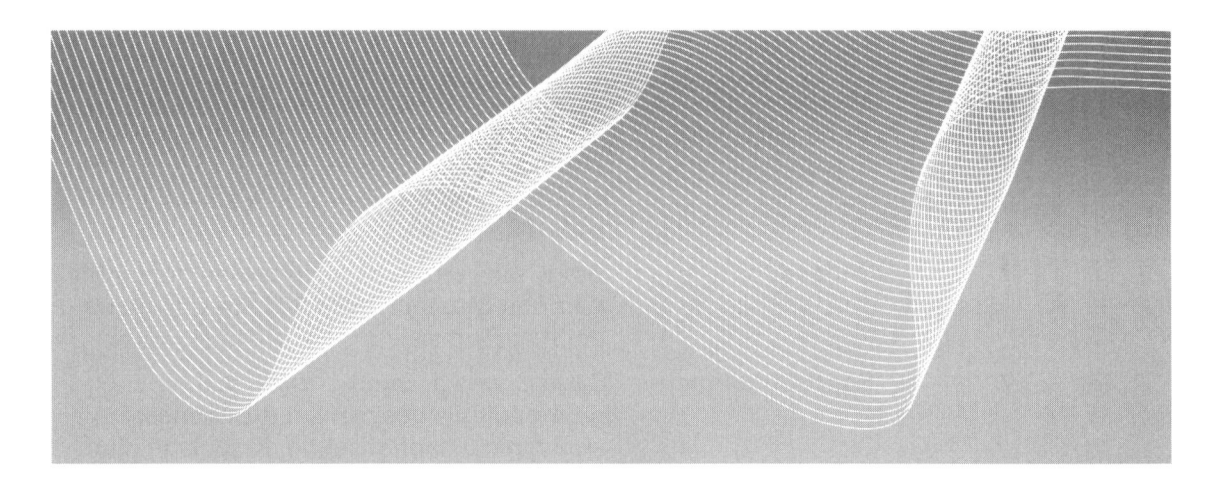

Appendix A

Example Data Sources

Example	Chapter	Title	Source
1	2	Control Your Car's Gas Consumption	Goupy, J.
2	3	Gold Jewelry	Chalumeau, L., et al. 2004. "Application of a Doehlert experimental design to the optimization of an Au-Co plating electrolyte." *Journal of Applied Electrochemistry*. 34. 1177–1184.
3	4	The Galette des Rois	Study proposed by an industrial manufacturer. The data has been slightly modified to ensure the confidentiality of the manufacturing process.
4	5	Lifespan of Disposable Cutting Tools	Data graciously provided by la Société MINITAB France, manufacturers and importers of industrial materials. The units of measurement have been suppressed to protect confidential information.

(continued)

Example	Chapter	Title	Source
5	6	Measuring Tellurium Concentration	Grotti, M., E. Magi, and R. Leadri. 1996. "Study of interferences in graphite furnace atomic absorption spectrometry by means of experimental design." *Analytica Chimica Acta.* 327. 47–51.
6	7	Sulfonation	Study taken from a thesis carried out by Ms. Kamoun-Messedi in 2000 at the Université de Sfax (Tunisia).
7	7	Spectrofluorimetry	Sado G. and J. Goupy. 1986. "La méthodologie des plans d'expériences appliquée à l'optimisation du réglage d'un spectrofluorimètre." *Analysis.* 14. 389–400.
8	7	Potato Chips	Data graciously provided by la Société MINITAB France, manufacturers and importers of industrial materials.
9	8	Penicillium Chrysogenum (Blocking Example)	Davies, O. 1971. *The Design and Analysis of Industrial Experiments.* Edinburgh: Oliver and Boyd.
			Daniel, C. 1976. *Applications of Statistics to Industrial Experimentation.* New York: John Wiley and Sons.
10	8	Yates's Beans	Yates, F. 1937. *The Design and Analysis of Factorial Experiments.* Bulletin 35. Harpenden, England: Imperial Bureau of Soil Science.
11	8	"The Crusher" (Example of an Anti-Draft Design)	Goupy, J. 2001. *Introduction aux Plans d'Expériences,* 2nd ed. Paris: Dunod.
12	9	The Foreman's Rectification (Example of a Composite Plan)	Goupy, J. 1999. *Plans d'expériences pour surfaces de réponse.* Paris: Dunod. Design kindly communicated by Professor P. Lantéri.
13	9	Soft Yogurt (Box-Behnken Design Example)	Goupy, J. 1999. *Plans d'expériences pour surfaces de réponse.* Paris: Dunod.

(continued)

Example	Chapter	Title	Source
14	9	Insecticide (Example of a Doehlert Design)	Goupy, J. 1999. *Plans d'expériences pour surfaces de réponse.* Paris: Dunod. Design kindly communicated by Dr. Tralongo.
15	10	Three Polymers	Goupy, J. 2001. *Plans d'expériences: les mélanges.* Paris: Dunod.
16	11	Developing a Fissure Detector	Capobianco, T. E., J.D. Splett, and H.K. Iyer. 1990. "Eddy Current Probe Sensitivity as a Function of Coil Construction Parameters." *Research in Nondestructive Evaluation.* 2. 169–186.
17	11	Pharmaceutical Tablets	Goupy, J. 2001. *Plans d'expériences: les mélanges.* Paris: Dunod.
18	11	Self-Tanning Cream (Rescuing a Bad Design)	Delacroix A, C. Porte, and D. Youssef. 1999. "Application d'une méthode chimiométrique dans l'étude de la cristallisation de la dihydrocétone (DHA)." Paris: Congrès Chimométie.
19	12	Salaries	Goupy, J.
20	12	Penetrometry Study	Goupy, J.

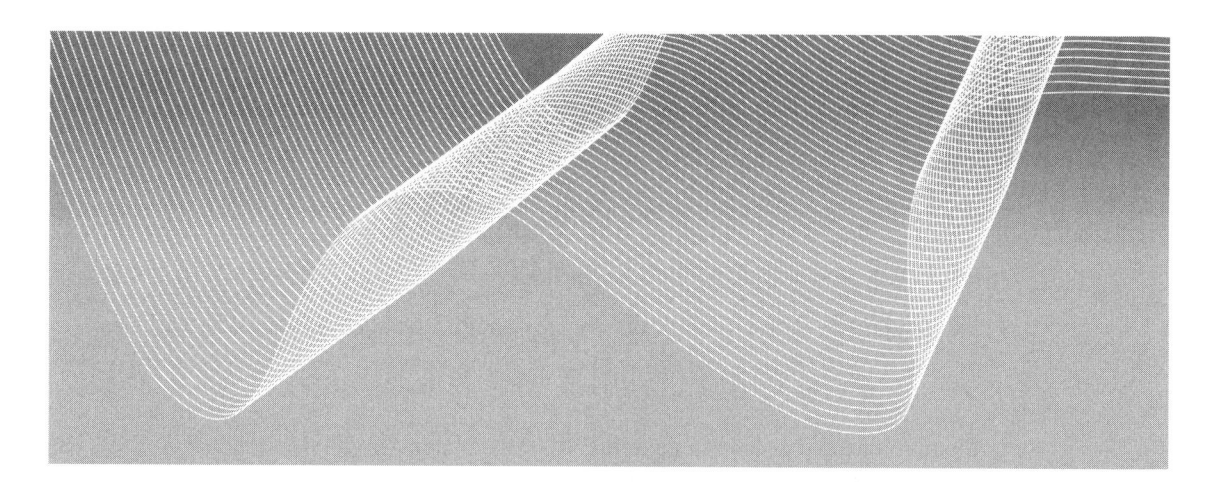

Appendix B

Comparing Two Independent Means

We would like to compare the means of two series of measurements.

First mean

We carry out n_1 repetitions at the same experimental point. This gives us the first series of measurements $y_{1,i}$ where the mean is $\bar{y}_1$, calculated as

$$\bar{y}_1 = \frac{1}{n_1}\sum_{i=1}^{n_1} y_{1,i}$$

The variance of the $y_{1,i}$ measurements is

$$V(y_{1,i}) = \frac{1}{n_1 - 1}\sum_{i=1}^{n_1}(y_{1,i} - \bar{y}_1)^2$$

Second mean

We carry out n_2 repetitions at the same experimental point. This gives us a second series of measures $y_{2,i}$ whose mean is $\bar{y}_2$. The variance of the $y_{2,i}$ measures is

$$V(\bar{y}_{2,j}) = \frac{1}{n_2 - 1} \sum_{j=1}^{n_2} (y_{2,j} - \bar{y}_2)^2$$

To compare $\bar{y}_1$ and $\bar{y}_2$, calculate

1. the absolute value of their difference $\Delta = |\bar{y}_1 - \bar{y}_2|$
2. the variance of their difference $V(\Delta) = V(\bar{y}_2) + V(\bar{y}_1)$
3. the standard deviation of their difference—that is, the square root of the variance

$$\sigma_\Delta = \sqrt{V(\Delta)} = \sqrt{V(\bar{y}_2) + V(\bar{y}_1)}$$

4. the ratio of the absolute value of the difference (step 1) with the standard deviation of the difference (step 3)

$$\frac{\Delta}{\sigma_\Delta} = \frac{|\bar{y}_1 - \bar{y}_2|}{\sqrt{V(\bar{y}_1 - \bar{y}_2)}}$$

This ratio follows a Student's t-distribution with $v = (n_1 - 1) + (n_2 - 1)$ degrees of freedom.

Assumptions
1. The two series are drawn from the same population. They therefore have the same theoretical mean and standard deviation.
2. The responses are drawn from a population having a normal distribution.

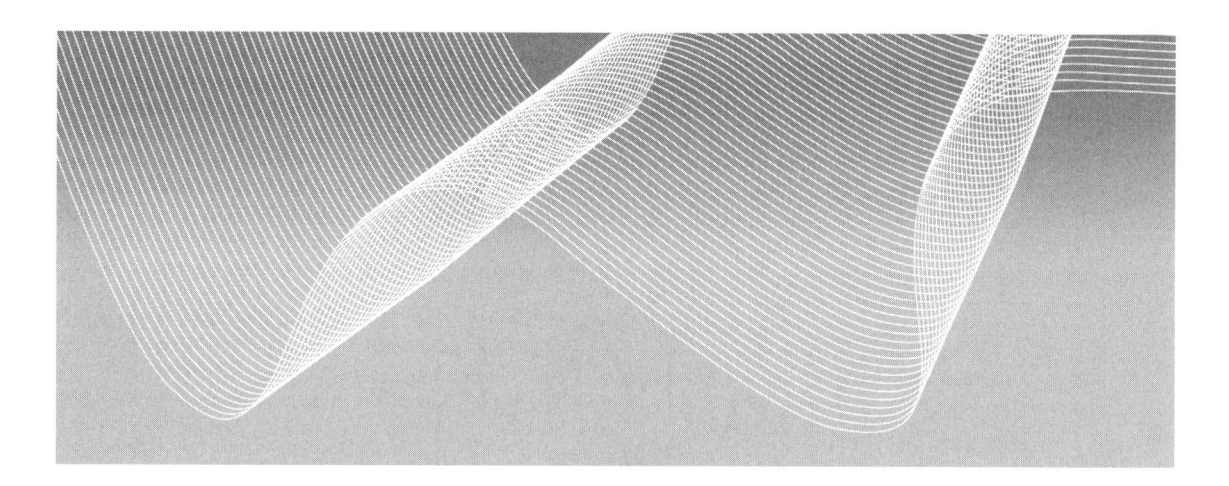

Appendix C

Introduction to Matrix Calculations

C1.1 Definitions 416
C2.1 Definitions for Square Matrices 418
C3.1 Matrix Operations 421
C4.1 Matrix Algebra 426
C5.1 Special Matrices 427

Matrices are tables that simplify very complex calculations. Although their creation and (especially) their manipulation are carried out by computers and calculators, it is advisable for experimenters to be able to understand the significance of the operations and the interpretation of the results.

C1.1 Definitions

Matrix
A matrix is an array made up of elements laid out in lines and columns.

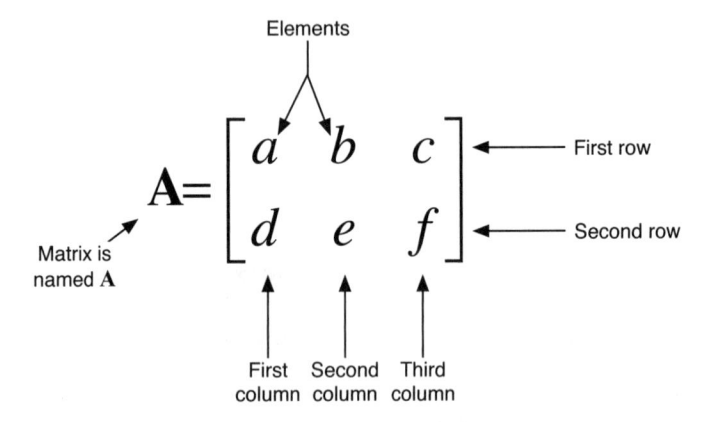

$$\mathbf{A} = \begin{bmatrix} a & b & c \\ d & e & f \end{bmatrix}$$

The array itself is inside square brackets.

Size of a matrix
An *m*×*n* matrix is a matrix having *m* rows and *n* columns. The matrix above is a 2×3 matrix. By convention, the number of rows is listed first, then the number of columns. The variable representing the matrix (A in our example) is written in boldface, without italics (**A**), compared to the six elements inside the matrix, which are written in lowercase, with italics (*a*, *b*, etc.)

Sometimes the size of a matrix is written as a subscript to the matrix name. With matrix A above, we could write $\mathbf{A}_{3\times 2}$.

Square matrix
A square matrix has the same number of rows and columns. For example,

$$\mathbf{I} = \begin{bmatrix} 1 & 0 & 0 \\ 0 & 1 & 0 \\ 0 & 0 & 1 \end{bmatrix}$$

is a square matrix, since it is 3×3.

Column matrix, or vector

An $m \times n$ matrix where $n = 1$ is sometimes called an $m \times 1$ vector or column vector. For example,

$$\mathbf{B} = \begin{bmatrix} -1 \\ 0 \\ 1 \\ 2 \end{bmatrix}$$

is a 4×1 column vector.

Element notation

The elements from the lines and columns of the matrix are designated by an index. For example, matrix **A** above could be written

$$\mathbf{A} = \begin{bmatrix} a_{11} & a_{12} & a_{13} \\ a_{21} & a_{22} & a_{23} \end{bmatrix}$$

As before, the row is listed first in the index, the column second. Therefore a_{13} is the element in the first row, third column. The element a_{22} is the element in the second row, second column. When referring to all the elements of a matrix, we often write $[a_{ij}]$.

Corresponding elements

Corresponding elements occupy the same place in two matrices of the same order.

What are elements?

Matrix elements can be any of a variety of things: real numbers, complex numbers, polynomials, functions, operators, or even other matrices.

Entering matrices into JMP

To do manual matrix calculations in JMP, the matrices and operations should be entered into a JMP script window. The results are displayed in the JMP log window.

To show the log, select **View → Log** from the main menu. To begin a new script, select **File → New → New Script** from the main menu.

Matrices are entered row-wise in JMP. That is, enter the first row of the matrix, then the second, and so on. Each row is separated by commas. As an example, enter the following script into a script window to store a 3×3 identity matrix into a variable called I.

```
I = [1 0 0, 0 1 0, 0 0 1];
```

To run the script, select **Edit → Run**. The output in the log shows that the matrix has been assigned.

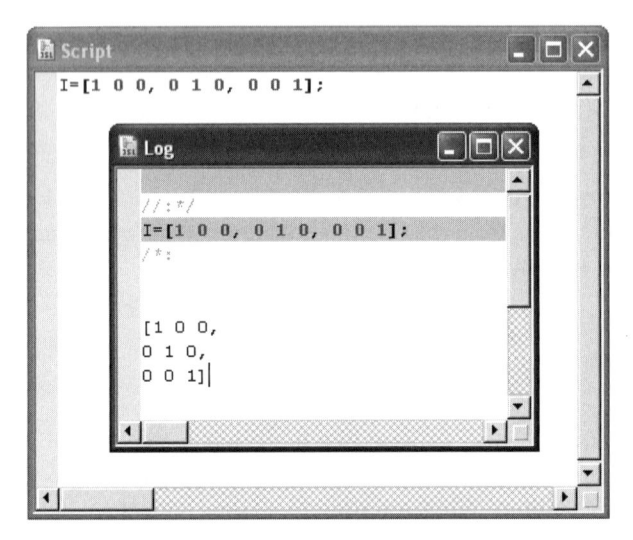

C2.1 Definitions for Square Matrices

Main diagonal
The diagonal of a square matrix is formed by all the elements a_{ii}, where the row number and column number are the same. This main diagonal is shown in the following matrix.

$$\mathbf{A} = \begin{bmatrix} a_{11} & a_{12} & a_{13} \\ a_{21} & a_{22} & a_{23} \\ a_{31} & a_{32} & a_{33} \end{bmatrix}$$

Symmetric matrix

A symmetric matrix has a symmetry around the main diagonal. The elements a_{ij} are equal to the elements a_{ji}. That is, $a_{ij} = a_{ji}$. For example,

$$S = \begin{bmatrix} 1 & 2 & 3 \\ 2 & 1 & 4 \\ 3 & 4 & 1 \end{bmatrix}$$

is a symmetric matrix.

Antisymmetric matrix

An antisymmetric matrix is symmetric along the diagonal, where corresponding elements are opposite in sign. That is, $a_{ij} = -a_{ji}$. Antisymmetric matrices are commonly called *skew symmetric*.

For example,

$$T = \begin{bmatrix} 0 & 2 & 3 \\ -2 & 0 & 4 \\ -3 & -4 & 0 \end{bmatrix}$$

is an antisymmetric matrix. Note that this example has zeros on its main diagonal. This is true for all cases of antisymmetric matrices. Since one of the conditions is that $a_{ij} = -a_{ji}$, it must be true that $a_{ii} = -a_{ii}$. This means that all diagonal elements must be their own negative, and zero is the only number that fills this requirement.

Identity matrix

An identity matrix is a square matrix whose elements are zeros except for the main diagonal, whose elements are ones.

$$I = \begin{bmatrix} 1 & 0 & 0 \\ 0 & 1 & 0 \\ 0 & 0 & 1 \end{bmatrix}$$

Zero matrix

The zero matrix has all elements equal to zero, i.e., $[a_{ij}] = 0$

Determinant of a matrix

The determinant of a matrix is a number (when we refer to matrices, regular numbers are often called *scalars*). Be careful not to confuse a matrix and its determinant, because they look similar. A matrix is represented in square brackets, but the determinant of a matrix is represented with simple lines. For example, on the left we define an identity matrix. On the right, we ask for its determinant.

$$\begin{bmatrix} 1 & 0 & 0 \\ 0 & 1 & 0 \\ 0 & 0 & 1 \end{bmatrix} \quad \begin{vmatrix} 1 & 0 & 0 \\ 0 & 1 & 0 \\ 0 & 0 & 1 \end{vmatrix}$$

A matrix is an array made up of elements. A determinant may present itself as an array, but it evaluates to a number using well-defined calculation rules. With designed experiments, we use determinants to calculate inverse matrices and to construct *D*-optimal designs.

Trace of a matrix

The trace of a matrix is the sum of its diagonal elements. For the identity matrix above, Tr(**I**) = 3.

To compute the determinant or trace of a matrix in JMP, use the Det() or Trace() functions. For example, to compute the determinant and trace of the matrices **S** and **T** above, submit the following script:

```
S=[1 2 3, 2 1 4, 3 4 1];
T=[0 2 3, -2 0 4, -3 -4 0];
Show(Det(S), Det(T));
Show(Trace(S), Trace(R));
```

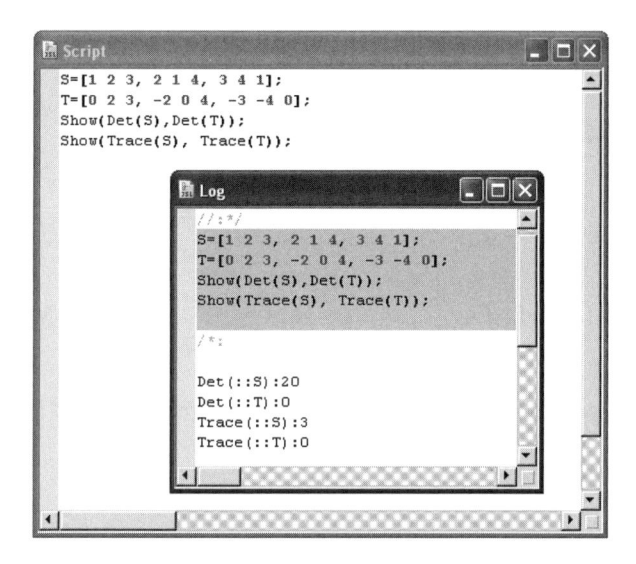

```
S=[1 2 3, 2 1 4, 3 4 1];
T=[0 2 3, -2 0 4, -3 -4 0];
Show(Det(S),Det(T));
Show(Trace(S), Trace(T));
```

```
//:*/
S=[1 2 3, 2 1 4, 3 4 1];
T=[0 2 3, -2 0 4, -3 -4 0];
Show(Det(S),Det(T));
Show(Trace(S), Trace(T));

/*:

Det(::S):20
Det(::T):0
Trace(::S):3
Trace(::T):0
```

Diagonal matrix
A diagonal matrix has all its elements equal to zero except those on the main diagonal.

C3.1 Matrix Operations

Equality of two matrices
Two matrices of the same order are equal when their corresponding elements are equal.

$\mathbf{A} = \mathbf{B}$ if and only if $[a_{ij}]=[b_{ij}]$.

Addition of two matrices
Only matrices of the same order can be added together. The result is another matrix of the same order.

The elements of the matrix sum are the sums of the corresponding elements of the matrices being added.

For example, suppose we have two matrices

$$\mathbf{M}_1 = \begin{bmatrix} a_{11} & a_{12} & a_{13} \\ a_{21} & a_{22} & a_{23} \end{bmatrix} \quad \text{and} \quad \mathbf{M}_2 = \begin{bmatrix} b_{11} & b_{12} & b_{13} \\ b_{21} & b_{22} & b_{23} \end{bmatrix}$$

Their sum is

$$\mathbf{M}_1 + \mathbf{M}_2 = \begin{bmatrix} a_{11}+b_{11} & a_{12}+b_{12} & a_{13}+b_{13} \\ a_{21}+b_{21} & a_{22}+b_{22} & a_{23}+b_{23} \end{bmatrix} = \mathbf{M}_3$$

That is, the matrix $\mathbf{M}_3$ is the sum of the matrices $\mathbf{M}_1$ and $\mathbf{M}_2$.

$$\mathbf{M}_1 + \mathbf{M}_2 = \mathbf{M}_3$$

Subtraction
As with addition, only matrices of the same order can be subtracted. The result is another matrix of the same order. The elements of the difference matrix are the differences of the corresponding elements of the matrices being subtracted.

$$\mathbf{M}_1 - \mathbf{M}_2 = \begin{bmatrix} a_{11}-b_{11} & a_{12}-b_{12} & a_{13}-b_{13} \\ a_{21}-b_{21} & a_{22}-b_{22} & a_{23}-b_{23} \end{bmatrix}$$

$$\mathbf{M}_1 - \mathbf{M}_2 = \mathbf{M}_3$$

Multiplication of a matrix by a scalar
To multiply a matrix by a scalar, multiply all matrix elements by the scalar.

$$c \times \mathbf{M}_1 = \begin{bmatrix} c\,a_{11} & c\,a_{12} & c\,a_{13} \\ c\,a_{21} & c\,a_{22} & c\,a_{23} \end{bmatrix}$$

Multiplication of two matrices
This is an important operation. The multiplication of two matrices results in a third matrix. This multiplication is possible only if the number of columns of $\mathbf{A}$ is equal to the number of columns of $\mathbf{B}$. That is, $\mathbf{A}_{m \times p}$ can be multiplied by $\mathbf{B}_{p \times n}$ with the result having size $m \times n$.

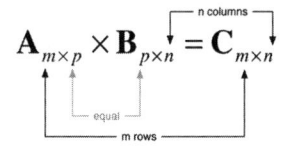

$$\mathbf{A}_{m \times p} \times \mathbf{B}_{p \times n} = \mathbf{C}_{m \times n}$$

(n columns; equal; m rows)

Matrix multiplication is done **line by column** in such a way that the element in the product matrix c_{ij} is equal to

$$c_{ij} = a_{i1}b_{1j} + a_{i2}b_{2j} + \ldots + a_{ip}b_{pj}$$

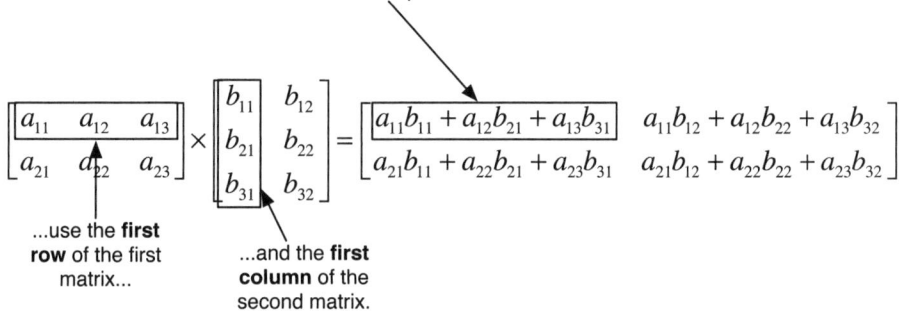

To calculate the element in the **first row, first column** of the product matrix...

$$\begin{bmatrix} a_{11} & a_{12} & a_{13} \\ a_{21} & a_{22} & a_{23} \end{bmatrix} \times \begin{bmatrix} b_{11} & b_{12} \\ b_{21} & b_{22} \\ b_{31} & b_{32} \end{bmatrix} = \begin{bmatrix} a_{11}b_{11} + a_{12}b_{21} + a_{13}b_{31} & a_{11}b_{12} + a_{12}b_{22} + a_{13}b_{32} \\ a_{21}b_{11} + a_{22}b_{21} + a_{23}b_{31} & a_{21}b_{12} + a_{22}b_{22} + a_{23}b_{32} \end{bmatrix}$$

...use the **first row** of the first matrix...

...and the **first column** of the second matrix.

Note that matrix multiplication is not commutative in general.

AB ≠ BA

As an example, given

$$\mathbf{A} = \begin{bmatrix} 3 & 2 & 1 \\ 3 & 1 & 1 \\ 1 & 0 & 2 \end{bmatrix} \text{ and } \mathbf{B} = \begin{bmatrix} 2 & 3 & 1 \\ 3 & 1 & 1 \\ 1 & 0 & 3 \end{bmatrix}$$

find **AB** and **BA**.

This is easy using JMP.

```
A=[3 2 1, 3 1 1, 1 0 2];
B=[2 3 1, 3 1 1, 1 0 3];
show(A*B);
show(B*A);
```

```
A=[3 2 1, 3 1 1, 1 0 2];
B=[2 3 1, 3 1 1, 1 0 3];
show(A*B);
show(B*A);

::A * ::B:
[   13 11  8,
    10 10  7,
     4  3  7]
::B * ::A:
[   16  7  7,
    13  7  6,
     6  2  7]
```

Inverse matrix
Only square matrices have inverses. The inverse of A is denoted $\mathbf{A}^{-1}$.

The matrix $\mathbf{A}^{-1}$ is the inverse of $\mathbf{A}$ if their product is the identity matrix.

$$\mathbf{A}^{-1}\mathbf{A} = \mathbf{I}$$

The inverse matrix $\mathbf{A}^{-1}$ exists if the determinant of $\mathbf{A}$ is non-zero.

$$|\mathbf{A}| \neq 0$$

If $|\mathbf{A}| = 0$, the matrix $\mathbf{A}$ is said to be *singular* and *non-invertible*.

Transpose of a matrix
The transpose of a matrix $\mathbf{A}$ is denoted as $\mathbf{A}'$ and is obtained by inverting the rows and columns of $\mathbf{A}$. That is, the first row of $\mathbf{A}$ becomes the first column of $\mathbf{A}'$. The second row of $\mathbf{A}$ becomes the first column of $\mathbf{A}'$, and so on. For example, if

$$\mathbf{A} = \begin{bmatrix} a_{11} & a_{12} & a_{13} \\ a_{21} & a_{22} & a_{23} \end{bmatrix}$$

then

$$\mathbf{A'} = \begin{bmatrix} a_{11} & a_{21} \\ a_{12} & a_{22} \\ a_{13} & a_{23} \end{bmatrix}$$

Suppose we want to use both operations to compute $(\mathbf{A'A})^{-1}$ on a matrix

$$\mathbf{A} = \begin{bmatrix} 1 & 1 & 1 \\ 1 & -1 & 1 \\ -1 & 1 & 1 \end{bmatrix}$$

That is, we want to compute the product of **A** with its transpose, then find the inverse of the result. Again, JMP does the calculations. Note that the JMP symbol for transpose is the single open quote, found under the ~ key on American keyboards.

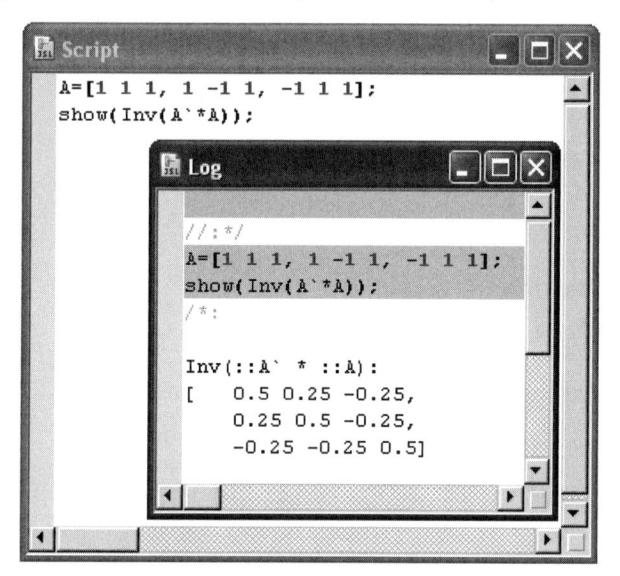

```
A=[1 1 1, 1 -1 1, -1 1 1];
show(Inv(A`*A));
```

```
A=[1 1 1, 1 -1 1, -1 1 1];
show(Inv(A`*A));

Inv(::A` * ::A):
[  0.5  0.25 -0.25,
   0.25  0.5 -0.25,
  -0.25 -0.25  0.5]
```

$$(\mathbf{A'A})^{-1} = \begin{bmatrix} \frac{1}{2} & \frac{1}{4} & -\frac{1}{2} \\ \frac{1}{4} & \frac{1}{2} & -\frac{1}{2} \\ -\frac{1}{2} & -\frac{1}{2} & \frac{1}{2} \end{bmatrix}$$

C4.1 Matrix Algebra

Starting from the definitions and the operations that we have just seen, it is possible to construct matrix algebra (often referred to as *linear algebra*). We encourage the reader to verify any of the following using JMP.

Transpose of a product
$$(\mathbf{X}_1\mathbf{X}_2)' = \mathbf{X}_2'\mathbf{X}_1'$$

$$(\mathbf{X}_1\mathbf{X}_2\mathbf{X}_3)' = \mathbf{X}_3'\mathbf{X}_2'\mathbf{X}_1'$$

Inverse of a product
$$(\mathbf{X}_1\mathbf{X}_2)^{-1} = \mathbf{X}_2^{-1}\mathbf{X}_1^{-1}$$

$$(\mathbf{X}_1\mathbf{X}_2\mathbf{X}_3)^{-1} = \mathbf{X}_3^{-1}\mathbf{X}_2^{-1}\mathbf{X}_1^{-1}$$

Transpose of a transpose
$$(\mathbf{X}')' = \mathbf{X}$$

Inverse of an inverse
$$(\mathbf{X}^{-1})^{-1} = \mathbf{X}$$

We illustrate the first of these equalities using two matrices

$$\mathbf{X}_1 = \begin{bmatrix} 1 & 2 \\ 3 & 4 \end{bmatrix} \text{ and } \mathbf{X}_2 = \begin{bmatrix} -1 & 3 \\ -5 & 7 \end{bmatrix}$$

and showing $(\mathbf{X}_1\mathbf{X}_2)' = \mathbf{X}_2'\mathbf{X}_1'$ and also showing the counter-example $(\mathbf{X}_1\mathbf{X}_2)' \neq \mathbf{X}_1'\mathbf{X}_2'$.

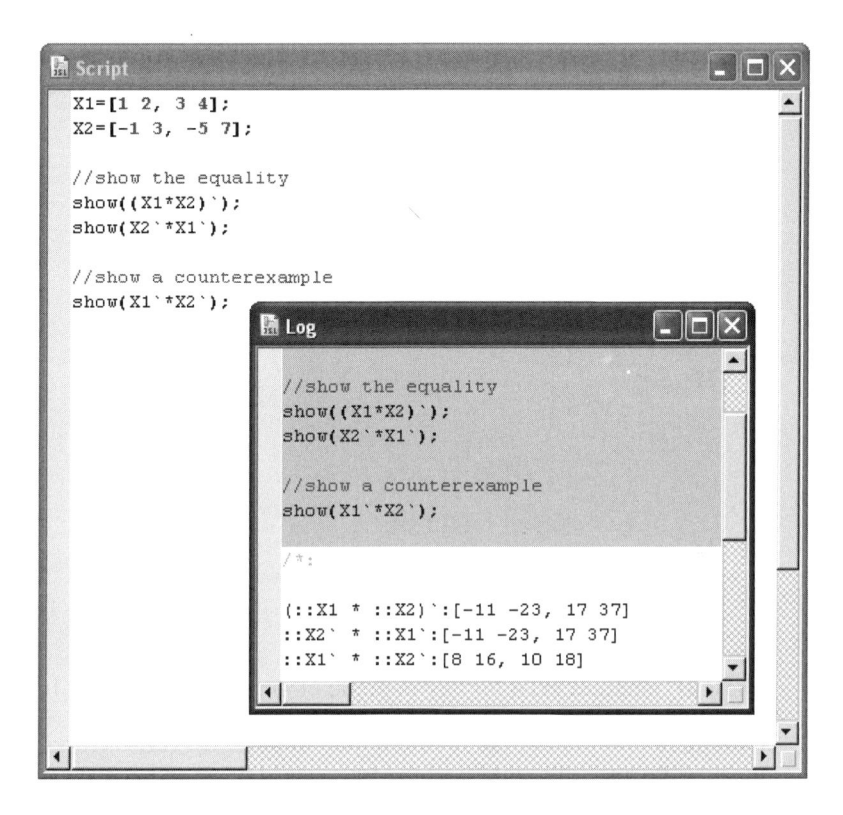

```
Script
X1=[1 2, 3 4];
X2=[-1 3, -5 7];

//show the equality
show((X1*X2)`);
show(X2`*X1`);

//show a counterexample
show(X1`*X2`);
```

```
Log
//show the equality
show((X1*X2)`);
show(X2`*X1`);

//show a counterexample
show(X1`*X2`);

/*:

(::X1 * ::X2)`:[-11 -23, 17 37]
::X2` * ::X1`:[-11 -23, 17 37]
::X1` * ::X2`:[8 16, 10 18]
```

C5.1 Special Matrices

Orthogonal matrices
A matrix is orthogonal if the scalar product of its columns are all zero. The transpose of an orthogonal matrix is equal to its inverse.

$$\mathbf{X}' = \mathbf{X}^{-1}$$

Hadamard matrices
There are some square matrices where the elements are either +1 or –1 such that
$\mathbf{X}'\mathbf{X} = n\mathbf{I}$

These matrices satisfy the following relationships.

$$X'X = XX'$$

$$X' = nX^{-1}$$

$$X^{-1} = \frac{1}{n}X'$$

Here are some examples.

$$H_2 = \begin{bmatrix} 1 & 1 \\ -1 & 1 \end{bmatrix}$$

$$H_4 = \begin{bmatrix} 1 & -1 & -1 & 1 \\ 1 & 1 & -1 & -1 \\ 1 & -1 & 1 & -1 \\ 1 & 1 & 1 & 1 \end{bmatrix}$$

These H_n matrices exist for any multiple of $4n$, that is, for 8, 12, 16, 20, and so on.

Hadamard matrices are the matrices used to construct full-factorial, fractional-factorial, Plackett-Burman, Taguchi, and the fractional part of composite (augmented) designs.

Computing linear models with matrices

These matrix calculations are used by software to do many of the calculations showing the results from designed experiments. One of the most important calculations is that of the coefficients of a linear model.

As an example, let's reexamine the results from our experiment in Chapter 2 where we modeled the gas consumption of a car. The results are in the following table.

Speed	Additional Weight	Consumption
Factor 1	*Factor 2*	mpg
−1	−1	30
+1	−1	25
−1	+1	27
+1	+1	21

Let's arrange the data into two matrices: one representing the coefficients (**X**), one representing the response (**Y**).

$$\mathbf{X} = \begin{bmatrix} 1 & -1 & -1 & 1 \\ 1 & 1 & -1 & -1 \\ 1 & -1 & 1 & -1 \\ 1 & 1 & 1 & 1 \end{bmatrix}$$

Intercept | Speed (x1) | Additional Weight (x2) | Interaction (x1x2)

$$\mathbf{Y} = \begin{bmatrix} 30 \\ 25 \\ 27 \\ 21 \end{bmatrix}$$

With this setup, the regression coefficients are calculated as $(\mathbf{X'X})^{-1}(\mathbf{X'Y})$. Using JMP to do these calculations reveals

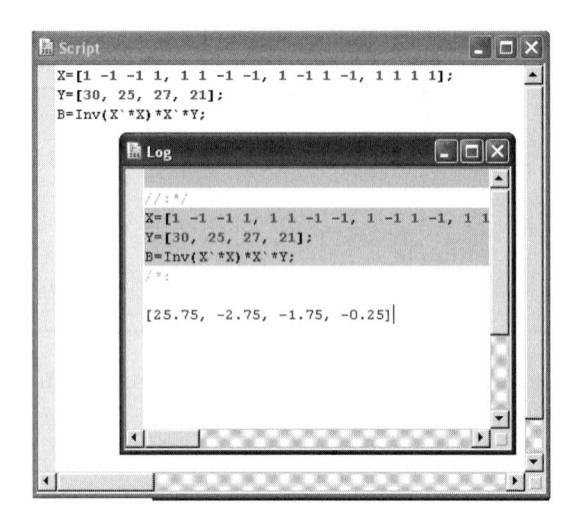

```
Script
X=[1 -1 -1 1, 1 1 -1 -1, 1 -1 1 -1, 1 1 1 1];
Y=[30, 25, 27, 21];
B=Inv(X`*X)*X`*Y;
```

```
Log
//:*/
X=[1 -1 -1 1, 1 1 -1 -1, 1 -1 1 -1, 1 1
Y=[30, 25, 27, 21];
B=Inv(X`*X)*X`*Y;
/*:

[25.75, -2.75, -1.75, -0.25]
```

$$b = \begin{bmatrix} 25.75 \\ -2.75 \\ -1.75 \\ -0.25 \end{bmatrix}$$

In Chapter 2, we found the relationship

$$y = 25.75 - 2.75x_1 - 1.75 x_2 - 0.25x_1x_2$$

which demonstrates the relationship between the matrix calculations and the regression model.

Bibliography

Recommended Readings

Box, George E.P. and D.W. Behnken. 1960. "Some new three level designs for the study of quantitative variables." *Technometrics* 2:455 - 475.

Box, George E. P., William G. Hunter, and J. Stuart Hunter. 2005. *Statistics for Experimenters: Design, innovation, and discovery.*. 2nd ed. Hoboken, NJ: John Wiley & Sons.

Capobianco, T. E., J.D. Splett, and H.K. Iyer. 1990. "Eddy Current Probe Sensitivity as a Function of Coil Construction Parameters." *Research in Nondestructive Evaluation.* 2. 169-186.

Chalumeau, L., et al. 2004. "Application of a Doehlert experimental design to the optimization of an Au-Co plating electrolyte." *Journal of Applied Electrochemistry.* 34. 1177- 1184.

Cornell, John A. 1981. *Experiments with Mixtures: Designs, models, and the analysis of mixture data.* New York: John Wiley & Sons.

Daniel, C. 1959."Use of half-normal plots in interpreting factorial two-level experiments." *Technometrics* 1:311-341.

Daniel, C. 1976. *Applications of Statistics to Industrial Experimentation.* New York: John Wiley & Sons.

Davies, O. 1971. *The Design and Analysis of Industrial Experiments.* Edinburgh: Oliver and Boyd.

Delacroix, A., C. Porte, and D. Youssef. 1999. *Application d'une méthode chimiométrique dans l'étude de la cristallisation de la dihydrocétone (DHA).* Paris: Congrès Chimométie.

Derringer, George, and Ronald Suich. 1980. "Simultaneous optimization of several response variables." *Journal of Quality Technology.* 12. 214 – 219.

Doehlert, David H. 1970. "Uniform Shell Designs." *Applied Statatistics.* 19. 231-239.

Draper, Norman R., and H. Smith. 1981. *Applied Regression Analysis.* New York: John Wiley & Sons.

Draper, Norman R., and J.A. John. 1988. "Response-surfaces Designs for Quantitative and Qualitative Variables." *Technometrics* 30:423-428.

Fisher, Ronald A. 1935. *The Design of Experiments.* Edinburgh: Oliver and Boyd.

Fisher, Ronald A. 1970. *Statistical Methods for Research Workers*. 14th ed. Edinburgh: Oliver and Boyd.

Freund, Rudolf, Ramon Littell, and Lee Creighton. 2003. *Regression Using JMP*. Cary, NC: SAS Institute.

Goupy, Jacques. 1993. *Methods for Experimental Design: Principles and Applications for Physicists and Chemists*. Elsevier: Amsterdam.

Goupy, Jacques. 1999. *Plans d'expériences pour surfaces de réponse*. Paris: Dunod.

Goupy, Jacques. 2000. *Plans d'expériences: les mélanges*. Paris: Dunod.

Goupy, Jacques. 2001. *Introduction aux Plans d'Expériences*, 2nd ed. Paris: Dunod.

Grotti, M., E. Magi, and R. Leadri. 1996. "Study of interferences in graphite furnace atomic absorption spectrometry by means of experimental design." *Analytica Chimica Acta*. 327. 47-51.

Hotelling, Harold. 1944. "Some improvements in weighing and other experimental techniques." *The Annals of Mathematical Statistics*. 15. 297-306.

Mitchell, Toby J. 1974. "An algorithm for the Construction of D-Optimal Experimental Designs." *Technometrics* 16:203-210.

Plackett, R.L., and J.P. Burman. 1946. "The design of optimum multifactorial experiments." *Biometrika*. 33. 305-325.

Sado, G., and J. Goupy. 1986. "La méthodologie des plans d'expériences appliquée à l'optimisation du réglage d'un spectrofluorimètre." *Analysis*. 14. 389-400.

Sall, John, Lee Creighton, and Ann Lehman. 2005. *JMP Start Statistics*. 3rd ed. Cary, NC: SAS Institute Inc.

Yates, Frank. 1937.The Design and Analysis of Factorial Experiments. Bulletin 35. Harpenden, England: Imperial Bureau of Soil Science.

Yates, Frank. 1970. "Experimental Design. Selected papers of Frank Yates." Darien, Conn: Hafner.

Youden, W.J. 1951. "Statistical Methods for Chemists." New York: John Wiley & Sons.

Works and General Articles

AFNOR. 1982. X. 02-110 de juin 1982. "Symboles et vocabulaire du calcul matriciel."

AFNOR. 1987. ISO 9001. "Systèmes qualité - Modèle pour l'assurance de la qualité en conception/développement, production, installation et soutien après la vente."

AFNOR. 1987. "Systèmes qualité - Modèle pour l'assurance de la qualité en production et installation."

AFNOR. 1987. ISO 9003 "Systèmes qualité - Modèle pour l'assurance de la qualité en contrôle et essais finals."

AFNOR. 1989. X 06-080 de novembre 1989. "Application de la statistique. Plan d'Expériences. Vocabulaire et indications générales."

AFNOR. 1994. ISO 5725-2. "Accuracy (trueness and precision) of measurement methods and results. Part 2: Basic method for the determination of repeatability and reproducibility of a standard measurement method."

AFNOR. 1994. ISO 5725-3. "Accuracy (trueness and precision) of measurement methods and results. Part 3: Intermediate measures of the precision of a standard measurement method."

Alexis, Jacques. 1995. "Pratique industrielle de la Méthode Taguchi." AFNOR.

Atkinson, A. C. 1996. "The Usefulness of Optimum Experimental Designs." *Journal of the Royal Statistical Society, Series B.* 58. 59-76.

Baleo, J.N., et al. 2003. "Méthodologie expérimentale." Paris: *TEC & DOC*.

Benoist. Daniel, Yves Tourbier, and Sandrine Germain-Tourbier. 1994. *Plans d'expériences: construction et analyse.* Paris: Lavoisier. Technique et Documentation.

Blaquiere, Austin. 1960. *Calcul matriciel. Volume 1: Application a la physique.* Paris: Hachette.

Box, George E.P., and Norman R. Draper. 1987. *Empirical Model-Building and Response Surface.* New York: John Wiley & Sons.

Box, George E.P., and Norman R. Draper. 1969. *Evolutionary Operation. A Statistical Method for Process Improvement.* New York: John Wiley & Sons.

Box, George E.P., and S. Jones. 1992. "Split-plot designs for robust product experimentation." *Journal of Applied Statistics.* 19. 3-26.

Brereton, R.G. 1997. "Multilevel multifactor designs for multivariate calibration." *Analyst.* 122. 1521-1529.

Carlson, Rolf. 1992. "Preludes to a screening experiment. A tutorial." *Chemometrics and Intelligent Laboratory Systems.* 14. 103-114.

Carlson, Rolf. 1992. "Design and Optimisation in organic synthesis." Amsterdam: Elsevier.

Cornell, John A., and J.C. Deng. 1982. "Combining Process Variables and Ingredient Components in Mixing Experiments." *Journal of Food Science.* 47. 836 - 843; 848.

Cornell, John A. 1988. "Analysing Data from Mixture Experiments containing Process Variables: A split-Plot Approach." *Journal of Quality Technology.* 20. 2 - 23.

Cornell, John A. 1990. "Embedding Mixture Experiments Inside Factorial Experiments." *Journal of Quality Technology.* 23. 265-276.

Czitrom, Veronica. 1988. "Mixture Experiments with Process Variables: D-Optimal Orthogonal Experimental Designs." *Communications in Statistics, Theory and Methods.* 17. 105–121.

Dagnelie, Pierre. 2003. *Principes d'expérimentation.* Presses agronomiques de Gembloux.

Daniel, Cuthbert. 1976. *Applications of Statistics to Industrial Experimentation.* New York: John Wiley & Sons.

Draper, Norman R. and Agnes M. Herzberg. 1971. "On lack of fit." *Technometrics* 13: 231-241.

Draper, Norman R. 1985. "Small composite Designs." *Technometrics* 27:173-180. (1985).

Droesbeke, Jean-Jacques, Jeanne Fine, and Gilbert Saporta. 1997. *Plans d'expériences. Applications à l'entreprise.* Paris: Editions Technip.

Duineveld, C.A.A., A.K. Smilde, and D.A. Doornbos. 1993. "Comparison of Experimental designs combining Process and Mixture variables. Part 1 Design construction and theorical evaluation." *Chem. Intel. Lab. Syst.* 19. 295-308. Part II Design and evaluation on mesured data." *Chem. Intel. Lab. Syst.* 19. 309-318.

Federov, V.V. 1972. *Theory of Optimal Experiments.* New York: Academic Press.

Genetay, Michel. 2000. *La coloration des matériaux.* Paris: Hermes.

Gorman, J.W., and J.E. Hinman. 1962. "Simplex-Lattice Designs for multicomponent systems." *Technometrics* 4:463-488.

Goupy, Jacques. 1989. "Erreur de dérive et choix de l'ordre des essais d'un plan d'expériences factoriel." *Revue de statistique appliqué.* 37. 5-22.

Goupy, Jacques. 1992. "Plans d'expériences." *Techniques de l'ingénieur. Traité Analyse Chimique et Caractérisation.* 230. 1-20.

Goupy, Jacques. 1995. "Chemometrics: Experimental Designs." In: *Encyclopedia of Analytical Sciences.* 659-666. London: Academic Press.

Goupy, Jacques. 1995. "Plans d'Expériences non conventionnels. Théorie et applications (ou comment sauver un plan raté). *Analusis.* 23. 152-158.

Goupy, Jacques. 1996. "Outliers and Experimental Designs." *Chem. Intel. Lab. Syst.* 35. 145-156.

Goupy, Jacques L. 1996. "Unconventional experimental designs. Theory and Application." *Chem. Intel. Lab. Syst.* 33. 3-16.

Goupy, Jacques. 2000. "Boolean Experimental Designs." *Analusis.* 28. 563-570.

Goupy, Jacques. 2000. "Modélisation par les plans d'expériences." *Techniques de l'ingénieur. Traité Mesures et Contrôle.* 275. 1-23.

ISO 3534-3. 1999. " Statistics – Vocabulary and symbols—Part 3: Design of Experiments," 46 pages.

Khuri, A.I., and J.A. Cornell. 1996. *Response surfaces. Design and Analyses*. New York: Marcel Dekker.

Lenth, Russel V. 1989. "Quick and Easy Analysis of unreplicated Fractional Factorials." *Technometrics* 31:469-473.

Liang, Yi-zeng, K.T. Fang, and Q.S. Xu. 2001. "Uniform design and its applications in chemistry and chemical engineering." *Chemometrics and Intelligent Laboratory Systems*. 58. 43-57.

Lundstedt, T, et al. 1998. "Experimental design and optimization." *Chemometrics and Intelligent Laboratory Systems*. 42. 3-40.

McLean, R. A., and V.L. Anderson. 1966. "Extreme vertices design of mixture experiments." *Technometrics* 8.:447-454.

Mead, Roger. 1988. *Design of Experiments: Statistical Principles for Practical applications*. Cambridge: Cambridge University Press.

Mee, R.W., and R.L. BATES. 1998. "Split-lot designs: Experiments for multistage batch processes." *Technometrics* 40:127-140.

Montgomery, Douglas C. 1984. *Design and Analysis of Experiments*. New York: John Wiley & Sons.

Morgan, Ed. 1995. *Chemometrics: Experimental Design*. New York: John Wiley & Sons.

Myers, Raymond H., Andre I. Khuri, and Walter H. Carter. 1989. "Response Surface Methodology: 1966-1988." *Technometrics* 31:137-157.

Piepel, Gregory F. and John A. Cornell. 1994. "Mixture Experiment Approaches: Examples, Discussion, and Recommendations." *Journal of Quality Technology*. 26. 177 - 195.

Pillet, Maurice. 1992. *Introduction aux Plans d'expériences par la méthode Taguchi*. Paris: Les Editions d'organisation.

Rechtschaffner, R. L. 1967. "Saturated Fractions of 2n and 3n Factorial Designs." *Technometrics* 9:569-575.

Roquemore, K.G. 1976. "Hybrid Designs for Quadratic Response Surfaces.". *Technometrics* 18:419-423.

Sado, Gilles, and Marie-Christine Sado. 2000. "Les plans d'expériences. De l'expérimentation à l'assurance de qualité." AFNOR technique.

Sall, J.P. 1990. "Leverage Plots for General Linear Hypotheses." *The American Statistician*. 44. 308 - 315.

Scheffe, Henri. 1958. "Experiments with mixtures." *Journal of the Royal Statistical Society. Series B.* 20. 344-360.

Scheffe, Henri. 1963. "The simplex-centroid design for Experiments with mixtures." *Journal of the Royal Statistical Society. Series B.* 25. 235-263.

Schimmerling, Paul, Jean-Claude Sisson, and Ali Zaidi. 1998. *Pratique des plans d'expériences.* Paris: Lavoisier.

Scibilia, B. et al. 2000. "Plans complémentaires et plans imbriqués."*Revue de Statistique appliquée.* 48. 27-44.

Shelton, J.T., A.I. Khuri, and John A. Cornell. 1983. "Selecting check points for testing lack of fit in response surface models." *Technometrics* 25:357-365.

Silvey, Samuel David. 1980. *Optimal Design: An introduction to the theory for parameter estimation.* London: Chapman and Hall.

Smith, A.T. 1998. "Comparison of information-yield from different experimental designs used in algal toxicity testing of chemical mixtures." *Environmental Pollution.* 102. 205-212.

Snee, Ronald D. 1979. "Experimenting with mixtures." *Chemtech.* 9. 702-710.

Snee, Ronald D. 1981. "Developing Blending Models for Gasoline and Other Mixtures." *Technometrics* 23:119 - 130.

Stansbury, W.F. 1997. "Development of experimental designs for organic synthetic reactions."*Chemometrics and Intelligent Laboratory Systems.* 36. 199-206.

Student. 1908. "The probable error of a mean." *Biometrika.* 6.1-25.

Sundberg, Rolf. 1994. "Interpretation of unreplicated two-level factorial experiments by examples." *Chem. Intel. Lab. Syst.* 24. 1-17.

Tomassone, Richard, et al. 1992. *La régression, nouveaux regards sur une ancienne méthode statistique.* Paris: Masson.

Vander Heyden, Y., et al. 1995. "Ruggedness tests on the High Performance Liquid Chromatography assay of the United States Pharmacopeia XXII for tetracycline hydrochloride. A comparison of experimental designs and statistical interpretations."*Analytica Chimica Acta.* 312. 245-262.

Vander Heyden, Y., A. Bourgeois, and D.L. Massart. 1997. "Influence of the sequence of experiments in a ruggedness test when drift occurs." *Analytica Chimica Acta.* 347. 369-384.

Vander Heyden, Y., F. Questier, and D.L. Massart. 1998. "A ruggedness test strategy for procedure related factors: experimental set-up and interpretation." *Journal of Pharmaceutical and Biomedical Analysis.* 17.153-168.

Vander Heyden, Y., F. Questier, and D.L. Massart. 1998. "Ruggedness testing of chromatographic methods: selection of factors and levels." *Journal of Pharmaceutical and Biomedical Analysis.* 18. 43-56.

Wolters, R., and G. Kateman. 1990. "The construction of simultaneous optimal experimental designs for several polynomials in the calibration of analytical methods." *Journal of Chemometrics.* 4. 171-185.

Youden, W.J. 1951. *Statistical Methods for Chemists.* New York: John Wiley & Sons.

Yuzhu, Hu. 1989. "Program for Doehlert matrix design of Experiments." *Tr. Anal. Chem.* 8. 126-128.

Application of Designed Experiments

Azubel, M. et al. 1999. "Novel application and comparison of multivariate calibration for the simultaneous determination of Cu, Zn and Mn at trace levels using flow injection diode array spectrophotometry." *Analytica Chimica Acta.* 398. 93-102.

Dorthe, A.M., J.L. Ramberti, and A. Thienpont. 2000. "Experimental design optimization of chromatographic separation for polycyclic aromatic hydrocarbons in vegetable oils." *Analusis.* 28. 587-591.

Fournier, J.L. et al. 1998. "Application des plans d'expériences à l'analyse de pesticides dans l'eau par chromatographie en phase gazeuse couplée à la spectrométrie de masse." *Analusis.* 26. M44-M52.

Guervenou, J. et al. 2002. "Experimental design methodology and data analysis technique applied to optimise an organic synthesis." *Chem. Intel. Lab. Syst.* 63. 81-89.

Gunduz, U. 2000. "Partitioning of bovine serum albumin in an aqueous two-phase system: optimisation of partition coefficient." *J. Chromatogr. B: Biomed.Applied.* 743. 259-262.

Heck, G., C. Mileham, and G.J. Martin. 1997. "Hydrogen exchange in aromatic compounds: substituent effects studied by experimental designs." *Analusis.* 25. 202-206.

Massumi, A., N.M. Najafi, and H. Barzegari. 2002. "Speciation of Cr(VI) / Cr(III) in environmental waters by fluorimetric method using central composite, full and fractional factorial design." *Microchemical Journal.* 72. 93 – 101.

Mathia, T. et al. 1996. "Optimal design in abrasive resistance of refractory concretes." *International Journal of Applied Mechanics and Engineering.* 1. 367-380.

Morand, P., et al. 1998. "Explosive formulation by experimental design." *Analusis.* 26. 291-294.

Morita, K., K. Kubota, and T. Aishima. 2001. "Sensory characteristics and volatile components in aromas of boiled prawns prepared according to experimental designs." *Food Research International.* 34. 473-481.

Morita, K, K. Kubota, and T. Aishima. 2002. "Investigating influence of pH and parts on sensory characteristics and volatile components in boiled squid using experimental designs." *J. of Food Science*. 67. 848-854.

Motamed, B., et al. 2000. "Development of an HPLC method for the determination of phenolic by-products: optimisation of the separation by means of the experimental designs methodology." *Analusis*. 28. 592-599).

Rogowski, I., et al. 2000. "Les plans d'expériences pour étudier l'usure du matériel sportif : application à l'étude de la perte de tension de cordage de raquettes de tennis." *Chimiométrie 2000*, Dec 6-7. Paris.

Rudaz, S. et al. 2001."Experimental designs to investigate capillary electrophoresis-electrospray ionization-mass spectrometry enantioseparation with the partial-filling technique." *Electrophoresis*. 22. 3316-3326.

Veuthey, J-L. et al. 1997. "Central composite design in the chiral analysis of amphetamines by capillary electrophoresis." *Electrophoresis*. 18. 931 - 937.

Xu, Q.S., Y.Z. Liang, and K.T. Fang. 2000. "The effects of different experimental designs on parameter estimation in the kinetics of a reversible chemical reaction." *Chemometrics and Intelligent Laboratory Systems*. 52. 155-166.

Index

A

a priori model
    for galette des rois example 76
    of response surface 18–20
acquiring knowledge
    See knowledge acquisition process
addition of matrices 421–422
AGF (alias generating function) 147–149, 155
alias theory
    alias generating function 147–149
    Box calculations 141–144
    contrasts in 138–140, 147
    equivalence relation 144–147
    in fractional factorial design 136–138
    interpretation hypotheses in 140–141
    tellurium example 157–160
analysis of variance
    See ANOVA
analysis reports 404–406
analyzing results
    See result analysis
ANOVA (analysis of variance)
    application 119–126
    degrees of freedom and 110
    presentation of 118–119
    principles of 115–118
    salaries example 365
anti-drift designs
    "Crusher" example 233–241
    nature of errors in 209–210
    randomization and 243–244
antisymmetric matrix 419
augmented simplex-centroid designs
    overview 298–299
    three polymers example 302–306

B

base design 144
base matrix 144–145
bell curve 104
binary mixture plot 291–292
blocking
    defined 207–208
    in experimental design 207–209
    penicillium chrysogenum example 212–224
    uncontrolled factors 208–209
    Yates's beans example 225–233
blocking factor 213
Boolean factors 7
Box-Behnken designs
    overview 249–250
    soft yogurt example 269–276
Box calculations
    Box notation 141–142, 146
    defined 141
    operations on column of signs 142–144
Box notation 141–142, 146
Box's method 132

C

candidate set 15–17
categorical designs
    Greco-Latin squares 352, 367–368
    Latin squares 352, 365–367
    penetrometry example 370–373
    salaries with one categorical factor 353–355
    salaries with two categorical factors 356–365
    Youden squares 352, 368–369
center, measure of
    See measure of center

center points
    fissure detector example 327–330
    preliminary questions 381
centered and scaled variables (csv) 11–13
CI (confidence interval) 112–113
coded units 11–13
coded variables 11–13
coefficient matrix 20
coefficient of determination 118–119
coefficients
    calculating 383
    factors and influential interactions 113–114
    in screening designs 133
    interpreting 28–39
    standard deviation of 123–125
column matrix 417
commutative property 144
complete cubic model 301
composite designs
    foreman's rectification example 255–268
    overview 247–249
composition point 290
confidence interval (CI) 112–113
constant term 29
constraints
    examining in experimental designs 24
    experimental design with 15–17
    experimental design without 14–15
    in mixture designs 289–290
    preliminary questions 379
continuous factors 6–7
contrasts in alias theory 138–140, 147
controlled factors 49, 207–208
coordinate exchange algorithm 316–319, 321–322
corresponding elements 417
"Crusher" example
    design selection 237
    interpreting results 238–241
    linear drifts 233–236
    preparing designed experiment 236–237
    running trials 237–238
    study conclusion 241
csv (centered and scaled variables) 11–13
Custom Designer (JMP) 393–396
cutting tools example
    See lifespan of disposable cutting tools example

D

D-optimal design with repetitions 330–332
D-optimality criterion 12, 315
data grid (JMP) 398
data sources 409–411
Data Table (JMP) 396–398
defining equation 147–149, 155
degrees of freedom 103–104, 110
deposition speed 54–60, 64–65
design matrix 20
design of experiments software
    See DOE software
designing experiments
    See experimental design
desirability functions
    applied to responses 83–90
    curved piece-wise 85
    linear piece-wise 85
    maximum desired values 84–85, 90, 128
    minimum desired values 85–86
    target range 87–88
    target values 86–87
determinant 315, 420
diagonal matrix 421
discrete factors 6–7
dispersion matrix 20
dispersion measure
    See standard deviation
disposable cutting tools example
    See lifespan of disposable cutting tools example
distribution 104–105
DOE (design of experiments) software
    alias theory support 149
    centered and scaled variables 12
    desirability function support 83

modeling phenomenon 16–17
response surface 18
statistical concepts in 99–113
Doehlert, David H. 250
Doehlert designs
   insecticide example 277–286
   overview 250–254
domain of variation 9
drift
   defined 206, 209
   linear 233–236
   randomization and 243–244
   uncontrolled factor 209–210

E

effect diagram (prediction profiler)
   defined 57
   galette des rois example 80–83
   in gold jewelry example 57–58
effect of speed
   See speed effect
element notation 417
elements 417
engineering units 11
equality of matrices 421
equilateral triangle
   for simplex-centroid designs 297, 299
   for simplex-lattice designs 295
   for ternary mixture plot 293
equivalence relation in alias theory 144–147
error
   See experimental error
error matrix 20
error transmission 109–112, 311
experiment examples
   "Crusher" 233–241
   data sources 409–411
   fissure detector 326–332
   foreman's rectification 255–268
   galette des rois 69–91
   gas consumption 22–44
   gold jewelry 45–68
   insecticide 277–286

lifespan of disposable cutting tools 95–129
penetrometry example 370–373
penicillium chrysogenum 212–224
pharmaceutical tablets 333–342
potato chips 198–204
salaries and one categorical factor 353–355
salaries and two categorical factors 356–365
self-tanning cream 343–350
soft yogurt 269–276
spectrofluorimetry 174–197
sulfonation 163–173
tellurium concentration 133–137, 157–160
three polymers 302–306
Yates's beans 225–233
experimental design
   blocking in 207–209
   centered and scaled variables 11–13
   choosing 381–382
   examining constraints in 24
   experimental points 13–14
   knowledge acquisition process 2–5
   limitations 386–387
   principal stages 21–22
   response surface in study domain 17–18
   statistical concepts 93–95
   studying phenomenons 5–6
   terminology 6–11
   three-factor 45–46
   trial order in 206–207
   with constraints 15–17
   with JMP software 390–407
   without constraints 14–15
experimental error
   in total error 94, 114
   mean 99
   nature of 207–208
   preliminary questions 380–381
   standard deviation 99–101
   uncontrolled factors and 49

experimental matrix   25–26
experimental methods
    acquiring knowledge via   385
    choosing   5, 376–382
    factors and   378
experimental modeling   19, 398–402
experimental points   13–17
experimental space   7–8, 13–14
experimental subjects   22
experimental table worksheet   25–26
experimentology
    See experimental methods
experiments, running   27–28, 382

F

F-ratio   118
factor domain   8–11
factorial designs
    See also fractional factorial designs
    factors in   288
    foreman's rectification example   258–262
factors
    See also uncontrolled factors
    blocking   213
    Boolean   7
    choosing the design   24–26
    continuous   6–7
    controlled   49, 207–208
    discrete   6–7
    domain of variation   8–11
    experimental methods and   378
    four-factor full-factorial experiments   69–70
    global effects of   355
    in factorial designs   288
    in response surface models   288
    influencing responses   23, 48
    interaction effect   37–39
    maximum number of   157
    ordinal   7
    preliminary questions   381
    three-factor experimental design   45–46

first-degree mathematical models   29, 299–300
fissure detector example
    D-optimal design with repetitions   330–332
    experimentation   327–328, 330–331
    factorial with center points   327–330
    interpreting   328–332
    preparing designed experiment   326–327
Fit Model dialog box   398–399
foreman's rectification example
    complementary design   262–263
    design selection   257
    experimentation   258
    factorial design   258–262
    interpreting results   263–268
    preparing designed experiment   255–257
    study conclusion   268
four-component mixture   294–295
four-factor designs
    See galette des rois example
fractional factorial designs
    alias theory   136–138
    assumptions in   140–141
    Box calculations   141–144
    definition of contrasts   138–140
    equivalence relation   144–147
    in composite designs   247
    levels in   132–133
    maximum number of factors   157
    potato chips example   198–204
    practical construction of   149–156
    spectrofluorimetry example   174–197
    sulfonation example   163–173
    tellurium concentration example   133–137, 157–160
full-factorial experiments   69–70, 247
fundamental mixture constraint   289–290

G

galette des rois example
    a priori model for   76
    design selection   73–74

desirability function 83–90
effect diagram 80–83
factors 69–70
interpreting results 76–83
preparing designed experiment 70–73
running experiment 74–75
study conclusion 91
gas consumption example
design selection 24–26
interpreting coefficients 28–39
interpreting results 40–44
preparing designed experiment 22–24
running experiment 27–28
Gaussian distribution 104
gold jewelry example
design selection 50–53
effect diagram 57–58
factors 45–46
interpreting results 54–67
preparing designed experiment 46–50
running experiment 53–54
study conclusion 67–68
graphics 404–406
Greco-Latin squares 352, 367–368

H

Hadamard matrices 261, 427–428
high level (factor)
defined 8
defining in experiments 23–24
fractional factorials 132
histogram 102–103
homoscedasticity 111, 125–126
Hotelling's method 308–314

I

identity matrix 419
information matrix 20
information zone (JMP) 397
insecticide example
experimentation 278–279
interpreting results 279–285
preparing designed experiment 277–278
study conclusion 286
interaction 29
interaction diagram (interaction profiler) 57–60
interaction effect 37–39
interaction profiler (interaction diagram) 57–60
intercept (model) 29–30
interpretation hypotheses in alias theory 140–141
inverse matrix 424
Ishikawa diagram 48

J

JMP software
alias theory support 149
analysis reports 404–406
choosing models 398–402
Custom Designer 393–396
designing experiments 390–396
desirability function support 85
entering matrices 417–418
interaction profiler 57–60
JMP data table 396–398
Maximize Desirability command 90, 128
overview 390
prediction profiler 57–58, 80–83
principal graphics 404–406
result analysis 402–407
Screening Designer 391–393, 401–402

K

knowledge acquisition process
centered and scaled variables 11–13
experimental points 13–14
overview 2–5
result analysis in 5
studying phenomenons 5–6
terminology 6–11
via experimental methods 385

L

lack of fit
   defined   19
   in total error   94, 114
Laplace-Gaussian distribution   104
Latin squares   352, 365–367
least squares method   115
level (factor)
   centered and scaled variables   11
   defined   8
   defining in experiments   23–24
   experimental design constraints and   14–17
   in fractional factorials   132–133
   random variation   210–211
lifespan of disposable cutting tools example
   analysis of variance   115–119
   application   119–124
   experimentation   97–98
   factors and influential interactions   113–114
   interpreting results   98–99
   preparing designed experiment   95–96
   residual analysis   125–126
   statistical concepts   99–113
   study conclusion   126–129
linear drifts   233–236
linear models
   computing with matrices   428–430
   optimal designs with   319–322
low level (factor)
   defined   8
   defining in experiments   23–24
   fractional factorials   132

M

main diagonal (square matrix)   418
mass measurement
   Hotelling's method   308–314
   standard method   312–313
mathematical models
   a priori model   18–20
   first-degree   29, 299–300
   for mixture designs   299–301
   salaries example   353–355, 357–359
   screening designs   132–133
   second-degree   300–301, 325
   sources of error   94
   third-degree   301
matrices
   addition of   421–422
   antisymmetric   419
   base   144–145
   coefficient   20
   column   417
   computing with linear models   428–430
   defined   14, 415–416
   design   20
   determinant of   420
   diagonal   421
   dispersion   20
   entering into JMP   417–418
   equality of   421
   error   20
   experimental   25–26
   Hadamard   261, 427–428
   identity   419
   information   20
   inverse   424
   model   20
   multiplication of   422–424
   orthogonal   427
   size of   416
   square   416, 418–421
   subtraction of   422
   symmetric   419
   trace of   420
   transpose of   424–425
   zero   419
matrix notation   19–20, 417
matrix operations   421–425
Maximize Desirability command (JMP)   90, 128
maximum desired values
   in desirability function   84–85, 90, 128

Maximize Desirability command (JMP)
    90, 128
maximum determinant criterion 315
mean
    as measure of center 99
    comparing 413–414
    defined 99
    population 101, 103–105
    sample 102–105
    sum of squares corrected for 120–121
mean square
    model variance and 121
    of the errors 122–123
    of the residuals 117, 122–123
measure of center
    centered and scaled variables and 11
    mean as 99
    population mean as 101
    sample mean 102
minimum desired values in desirability
        function 85–86
mixture designs
    appropriate use of 288
    augmented simplex-centroid designs
        298–299
    binary mixture plot 291–292
    constraints in 289
    four-component mixture 294–295
    mathematical models 299–301
    simplex-centroid designs 297–298
    simplex-lattice designs 295–297
    ternary mixture plot 293–294
    three polymers example 302–306
    two-component mixtures 289–291
mixture point 290, 295
model matrix 20
modeling, experimental 19, 398–402
modeling phenomenon 16–17
models, choosing 398–402
multiplication
    Box calculations 142–144
    of matrices 422–424

N

near-orthogonality criterion 249, 261–262
negative signs in Box calculations 143–144
non-controlled factors
    See uncontrolled factors
normal distribution
    defined 104–105
    principal properties 105–109

O

optimal designs
    acquiring knowledge via 385
    adaptability of 323–326
    computing 315–319
    fissure detector example 326–332
    Hotelling's method 308–314
    maximum determinant criterion 315
    pharmaceutical tablets example 333–342
    self-tanning cream example 343–350
    usage considerations 322
    with linear models 319–322
ordinal factors 7
orthogonal matrix 427

P

p-value 114, 123–125
peaks per unit length 256, 266–267
penetrometry example
    interpreting results 371–373
    preparing designed experiment 370
    running experiment 370–371
    study conclusion 373
penicillium chrysogenum example
    design selection 214
    interpreting results 218–224
    plan construction 214–217
    preparing designed experiment 212–214
    running trials 217–218
    study conclusion 224
pharmaceutical tablets example
    analyzing design 337–340
    design selection 335–336
    preparing designed experiment 333–335

pharmaceutical tablets example (*continued*)
  running experiment   336–337
  study conclusion   340–342
Placket-Burman design   200, 261
plus signs in Box calculations   143
polymers example
  See three polymers example
population mean   101, 103–105
population standard deviation   101, 103–105
postulated model
  See a priori model
potato chip example
  design selection   200
  interpreting results   201–203
  preparing designed experiment   198–200
  running experiment   201
  study conclusion   204
prediction profiler (effect diagram)
  defined   57
  galette des rois example   80–83
  in gold jewelry example   57–58
pure error   19, 114

R

random error   19
random start   316
random variation   210–211
randomization   211–212, 242–244, 379–380
rectification   255
  See also foreman's rectification example
replicates   112–113
residual analysis
  foreman's rectification example   264–265
  lifespan of disposable cutting tools example   125–126
  soft yogurt example   273–274
residual variance   117, 122–123
residuals   115, 117
response surface   17–18
response surface models
  Box-Behnken designs   249–250, 269–276
  composite designs   247–249, 255–268

defined   247
Doehlert designs   250–254, 277–286
factors in   288
foreman's rectification example   255–268
insecticide example   277–286
soft yogurt example   269–276
response vector in matrix notation   20
responses
  choosing   22, 47, 71, 378
  confidence interval of   112–113
  desirability function support   83–90
  error transmission   109–112
  factors influencing   23, 48
  in a priori model   18–20
result analysis
  in knowledge acquisition process   5
  overview   382–384
  transcription error and   76
  with JMP software   402–407
RMSE (root mean square error)   117, 125
roughness, measuring   256, 265–267
running experiments   27–28, 382

S

salaries example
  with one categorical factor   353–355
  with two categorical factors   356–365
sample   102–103
sample mean   102–105
sample standard deviation   102–105
Screening Designer (JMP)   391–393, 401–402
screening designs   132–133
second-degree mathematical models   300–301, 325
self-tanning cream example
  analyzing design   337–340
  design selection   343–344
  interpreting results   345–349
  preparing designed experiment   344–345
  running experiment   345
  study conclusion   349–350

sequentiality, property of   249
simplex-centroid designs
    augmented   298–299, 302–306
    equilateral triangle for   297, 299
    overview   297–298
simplex-lattice designs   295–297
size of matrices   416
soft yogurt example
    design selection   271
    experimentation   271–272
    interpreting design   272–274
    interpreting results   274–276
    preparing designed experiment   269–271
    study conclusion   276
spectrofluorimetry example
    building complementary design   190–196
    design selection   177–179
    influential factors   170–172
    interpreting results   180–190
    preparing designed experiment   174–179
    running experiment   180
    study conclusion   196–197
speed effect
    depicted   34–35
    interpreting   30–32
    representing   32–33
square matrix   416, 418–421
standard deviation
    defined   99–101
    of the coefficients   123–125
    of the residuals   117
    population   101, 103–105
    sample   102–105
star points   247, 260–262
statistical concepts
    error transmission   109–112
    experimental design   93–95
    experimental error   49, 94, 99–101
    lifespan of disposable cutting tools
        example   99–113
    population   101
    sample   102–103

step   11
Student's t-ratio   114
study domain
    choosing the design   25, 378
    defined   9–11
    experimental design constraints in   14–17
    in two-dimensional space   13–14
    response surface in   17–18
study objectives in experiments   22, 377–378
subtraction of matrices   422
sulfonation example
    design selection   164
    influential factors   170–172
    interpreting results   166–172
    preparing designed experiment   163–165
    running experiment   165–166
    study conclusion   173
sum of squares
    coefficient of determination and
        118–119
    corrected for the mean   120–121
    of the residuals   115–116
    salaries example   361–364
symmetric matrix   419
system of equations   19
systematic error
    blocking   207
    preliminary questions   379
    randomization   211–212, 242–244

T

t-ratio   114, 123
target range in desirability function   87–88
target values in desirability function   86–87
tellurium concentration example
    alias theory with   157–160
    design selection   135
    interpreting results   136–137
    preparing designed experiment   133–135
    running experiment   135–136
ternary mixture plot   293–294
tetrahedron   294–295

third-degree mathematical models   301
three-factor experiments
    See gold jewelry example
three polymers example
    design selection   302–303
    interpreting results   304–305
    preparing designed experiment   302–303
    running experiment   303
    study conclusion   306
trace of matrix   420
transcription error   76
transpose of matrix   424–425
trial order
    in experimental design   206–207
    penicillium chrysogenum example   212–224
    randomization   212, 242–244
    Yates's beans example   225–233
two-component mixtures   289–291
two-factor designs
    Doehlert designs   250–254
    gas consumption example   22–44
    linear models   319–322

U

uncontrolled factors
    anti-drift designs   209–210
    blocking   208–209
    defined   49, 207–208
    experimental error and   49
    random variation   210–211
    randomization   211–212

V

variables
    centered and scaled   11–13
    coded   11–13
    experimental space of   7–8
    factor types for   6–7
variance
    defined   100, 110
    residual   117, 122–123
variance addition theorem   110–111, 311

variation, domain of   9
vectors   417

Y

Yates order   74
Yates's beans example
    design selection   226–227
    interpreting results   230–232
    preparing designed experiment   225–228
    running experiment   228–230
    study conclusion   232–233
Youden, W. J.   368
Youden squares   352, 368–369

Z

zero matrix   419

Books Available from SAS Press

Advanced Log-Linear Models Using SAS®
by **Daniel Zelterman**

Analysis of Clinical Trials Using SAS®: A Practical Guide
by **Alex Dmitrienko, Geert Molenberghs, Walter Offen, and Christy Chuang-Stein**

Analyzing Receiver Operating Characteristic Curves with SAS®
by **Mithat Gönen**

Annotate: Simply the Basics
by **Art Carpenter**

Applied Multivariate Statistics with SAS® Software, Second Edition
by **Ravindra Khattree**
and **Dayanand N. Naik**

Applied Statistics and the SAS® Programming Language, Fifth Edition
by **Ronald P. Cody**
and **Jeffrey K. Smith**

An Array of Challenges — Test Your SAS® Skills
by **Robert Virgile**

Basic Statistics Using SAS® Enterprise Guide®: A Primer
by **Geoff Der**
and **Brian S. Everitt**

Building Web Applications with SAS/IntrNet®: A Guide to the Application Dispatcher
by **Don Henderson**

Carpenter's Complete Guide to the SAS® Macro Language, Second Edition
by **Art Carpenter**

Carpenter's Complete Guide to the SAS® REPORT Procedure
by **Art Carpenter**

The Cartoon Guide to Statistics
by **Larry Gonick**
and **Woollcott Smith**

Categorical Data Analysis Using the SAS® System, Second Edition
by **Maura E. Stokes, Charles S. Davis,**
and **Gary G. Koch**

Cody's Data Cleaning Techniques Using SAS® Software
by **Ron Cody**

Common Statistical Methods for Clinical Research with SAS® Examples, Second Edition
by **Glenn A. Walker**

The Complete Guide to SAS® Indexes
by **Michael A. Raithel**

CRM Segmemtation and Clustering Using SAS® Enterprise Miner™
by **Randall S. Collica**

Data Management and Reporting Made Easy with SAS® Learning Edition 2.0
by **Sunil K. Gupta**

Data Preparation for Analytics Using SAS®
by **Gerhard Svolba**

Debugging SAS® Programs: A Handbook of Tools and Techniques
by **Michele M. Burlew**

support.sas.com/publishing

Decision Trees for Business Intelligence and Data Mining: Using SAS® Enterprise Miner™
by **Barry de Ville**

Efficiency: Improving the Performance of Your SAS® Applications
by **Robert Virgile**

The Essential Guide to SAS® Dates and Times
by **Derek P. Morgan**

Fixed Effects Regression Methods for Longitudinal Data Using SAS®
by **Paul D. Allison**

Genetic Analysis of Complex Traits Using SAS®
by **Arnold M. Saxton**

A Handbook of Statistical Analyses Using SAS®, Second Edition
by **B.S. Everitt**
and **G. Der**

Health Care Data and SAS®
by **Marge Scerbo, Craig Dickstein,**
and **Alan Wilson**

The How-To Book for SAS/GRAPH® Software
by **Thomas Miron**

In the Know... SAS® Tips and Techniques From Around the Globe, Second Edition
by **Phil Mason**

Instant ODS: Style Templates for the Output Delivery System
by **Bernadette Johnson**

Integrating Results through Meta-Analytic Review Using SAS® Software
by **Morgan C. Wang**
and **Brad J. Bushman**

Introduction to Data Mining Using SAS® Enterprise Miner™
by **Patricia B. Cerrito**

Introduction to Design of Experiments with JMP® Examples, Third Edition
by **Jacques Goupy**
and **Lee Creighton**

Learning SAS® by Example: A Programmer's Guide
by **Ron Cody**

Learning SAS® in the Computer Lab, Second Edition
by **Rebecca J. Elliott**

The Little SAS® Book: A Primer
by **Lora D. Delwiche**
and **Susan J. Slaughter**

The Little SAS® Book: A Primer, Second Edition
by **Lora D. Delwiche**
and **Susan J. Slaughter**
(updated to include SAS 7 features)

The Little SAS® Book: A Primer, Third Edition
by **Lora D. Delwiche**
and **Susan J. Slaughter**
(updated to include SAS 9.1 features)

The Little SAS® Book for Enterprise Guide® 3.0
by **Susan J. Slaughter**
and **Lora D. Delwiche**

The Little SAS® Book for Enterprise Guide® 4.1
by **Susan J. Slaughter**
and **Lora D. Delwiche**

Logistic Regression Using the SAS® System: Theory and Application
by **Paul D. Allison**

Longitudinal Data and SAS®: A Programmer's Guide
by **Ron Cody**

Maps Made Easy Using SAS®
by **Mike Zdeb**

Measurement, Analysis, and Control Using JMP®: Quality Techniques for Manufacturing
by **Jack E. Reece**

Models for Discrete Date
by **Daniel Zelterman**

support.sas.com/publishing

Multiple Comparisons and Multiple Tests Using SAS® Text and Workbook Set
(books in this set also sold separately)
by **Peter H. Westfall, Randall D. Tobias, Dror Rom, Russell D. Wolfinger,** and **Yosef Hochberg**

Multiple-Plot Displays: Simplified with Macros
by **Perry Watts**

Multivariate Data Reduction and Discrimination with SAS® Software
by **Ravindra Khattree**
and **Dayanand N. Naik**

Output Delivery System: The Basics
by **Lauren E. Haworth**

Painless Windows: A Handbook for SAS® Users, Third Edition
by **Jodie Gilmore**
(updated to include SAS 8 and SAS 9.1 features)

Pharmaceutical Statistics Using SAS®: A Practical Guide
Edited by **Alex Dmitrienko, Christy Chuang-Stein,** and **Ralph D'Agostino**

The Power of PROC FORMAT
by **Jonas V. Bilenas**

Predictive Modeling with SAS® Enterprise Miner™: Practical Solutions for Business Applications
by **Kattamuri S. Sarma**

PROC SQL: Beyond the Basics Using SAS®
by **Kirk Paul Lafler**

PROC TABULATE by Example
by **Lauren E. Haworth**

Professional SAS® Programmer's Pocket Reference, Fifth Edition
by **Rick Aster**

Professional SAS® Programming Shortcuts, Second Edition
by **Rick Aster**

Quick Results with SAS/GRAPH® Software
by **Arthur L. Carpenter**
and **Charles E. Shipp**

Quick Results with the Output Delivery System
by **Sunil Gupta**

Reading External Data Files Using SAS®: Examples Handbook
by **Michele M. Burlew**

Regression and ANOVA: An Integrated Approach Using SAS® Software
by **Keith E. Muller**
and **Bethel A. Fetterman**

SAS® For Dummies®
by **Stephen McDaniel**
and **Chris Hemedinger**

SAS® for Forecasting Time Series, Second Edition
by **John C. Brocklebank**
and **David A. Dickey**

SAS® for Linear Models, Fourth Edition
by **Ramon C. Littell, Walter W. Stroup,**
and **Rudolf Freund**

SAS® for Mixed Models, Second Edition
by **Ramon C. Littell, George A. Milliken, Walter W. Stroup, Russell D. Wolfinger,** and **Oliver Schabenberger**

SAS® for Monte Carlo Studies: A Guide for Quantitative Researchers
by **Xitao Fan, Ákos Felsővályi, Stephen A. Sivo,**
and **Sean C. Keenan**

SAS® Functions by Example
by **Ron Cody**

SAS® Graphics for Java: Examples Using SAS® AppDev Studio™ and the Output Delivery System
by **Wendy Bohnenkamp**
and **Jackie Iverson**

SAS® Guide to Report Writing, Second Edition
by **Michele M. Burlew**

support.sas.com/publishing

*SAS® Macro Programming Made Easy,
Second Edition*
by **Michele M. Burlew**

SAS® Programming by Example
by **Ron Cody**
and **Ray Pass**

SAS® Programming for Enterprise Guide® Users
by **Neil Constable**

*SAS® Programming for Researchers and
Social Scientists, Second Edition*
by **Paul E. Spector**

SAS® Programming in the Pharmaceutical Industry
by **Jack Shostak**

*SAS® Survival Analysis Techniques for Medical Research,
Second Edition*
by **Alan B. Cantor**

*SAS® System for Elementary Statistical Analysis,
Second Edition*
by **Sandra D. Schlotzhauer**
and **Ramon C. Littell**

SAS® System for Regression, Third Edition
by **Rudolf J. Freund**
and **Ramon C. Littell**

SAS® System for Statistical Graphics, First Edition
by **Michael Friendly**

The SAS® Workbook and *Solutions* Set
(books in this set also sold separately)
by **Ron Cody**

Saving Time and Money Using SAS®
by **Philip R. Holland**

*Selecting Statistical Techniques for Social Science Data:
A Guide for SAS® Users*
by **Frank M. Andrews, Laura Klem, Patrick M. O'Malley,
Willard L. Rodgers, Kathleen B. Welch,**
and **Terrence N. Davidson**

Statistical Quality Control Using the SAS® System
by **Dennis W. King**

*A Step-by-Step Approach to Using SAS®
for Univariate and Multivariate Statistics,
Second Edition*
by **Norm O'Rourke, Larry Hatcher,**
and **Edward J. Stepanski**

*Step-by-Step Basic Statistics Using SAS®: Student
Guide* and *Exercises*
(books in this set also sold separately)
by **Larry Hatcher**

*Survival Analysis Using SAS®:
A Practical Guide*
by **Paul D. Allison**

*Tuning SAS® Applications in the OS/390 and z/OS
Environments, Second Edition*
by **Michael A. Raithel**

*Univariate and Multivariate General Linear Models:
Theory and Applications Using SAS® Software*
by **Neil H. Timm**
and **Tammy A. Mieczkowski**

Using SAS® in Financial Research
by **Ekkehart Boehmer, John Paul Broussard,**
and **Juha-Pekka Kallunki**

*Using the SAS® Windowing Environment:
A Quick Tutorial*
by **Larry Hatcher**

Visualizing Categorical Data
by **Michael Friendly**

*Web Development with SAS® by Example, Second
Edition*
by **Frederick E. Pratter**

*Your Guide to Survey Research Using the
SAS® System*
by **Archer Gravely**

support.sas.com/publishing

JMP® Books

Elementary Statistics Using JMP®
by **Sandra D. Schlotzhauer**

*JMP® for Basic Univariate and Multivariate Statistics:
A Step-by-Step Guide*
by **Ann Lehman, Norm O'Rourke, Larry Hatcher,**
and **Edward J. Stepanski**

*JMP® Start Statistics: A Guide to Statistics and Data
Analysis Using JMP®, Fourth Edition*
by **John Sall, Lee Creighton,**
and **Ann Lehman**

Regression Using JMP®
by **Rudolf J. Freund, Ramon C. Littell,**
and **Lee Creighton**

support.sas.com/publishing